Malware Analysis and Intrusion Detection in Cyber–Physical Systems

S.L. Shiva Darshan
Department of Information and Communication Technology, Manipal Institute of Technology, India

M.V. Manoj Kumar
Department of Information Science and Engineering, Nitte Meenakshi Institute of Technology, India

B.S. Prashanth
Department of Information Science and Engineering, Nitte Meenakshi Institute of Technology, India

Y. Vishnu Srinivasa Murthy
Department of Computational Intelligence, Vellore Institute of Technology, India

A volume in the Advances in Information Security, Privacy, and Ethics (AISPE) Book Series

Published in the United States of America by
    IGI Global
    Information Science Reference (an imprint of IGI Global)
    701 E. Chocolate Avenue
    Hershey PA, USA 17033
    Tel: 717-533-8845
    Fax: 717-533-8661
    E-mail: cust@igi-global.com
    Web site: http://www.igi-global.com

Library of Congress Cataloging-in-Publication Data

Names: Darshan, S.L. Shiva, 1990- editor. | Manoj Kumar, M. V., editor. |
    Prashanth, B.S., 1989- editor. | Srinivasa, Y. Vishnu, 1985- editor.
Title: Malware analysis and intrusion detection in cyber-physical systems /
    edited by S.L. Shiva Darshan, M.V. Manoj Kumar, B.S. Prashanth, Y.
    Vishnu Srinivasa.
Description: Hershey, PA : Information Science Reference, [2023] | Includes
    bibliographical references and index. | Summary: "Malware Analysis and
    Intrusion Detection in Cyber-Physical Systems focuses on dynamic malware
    analysis and its time sequence output of observed activity, including
    advanced machine learning and AI-based malware detection and
    categorization tasks in real time. Covering topics such as intrusion
    detection systems, low-cost manufacturing, and surveillance robots, this
    premier reference source is essential for cyber security professionals,
    computer scientists, students and educators of higher education,
    researchers, and academicians"-- Provided by publisher.
Identifiers: LCCN 2023008193 (print) | LCCN 2023008194 (ebook) | ISBN
    9781668486665 (h/c) | ISBN 9781668486672 (s/c) | ISBN 9781668486689
    (eISBN)
Subjects: LCSH: Malware (Computer software)--Prevention. | Intrusion
    detection systems (Computer security)
Classification: LCC QA76.76.C68 .M323 2023 (print) | LCC QA76.76.C68
    (ebook) | DDC 005.8/8--dc23/eng/20230317
LC record available at https://lccn.loc.gov/2023008193
LC ebook record available at https://lccn.loc.gov/2023008194

This book is published in the IGI Global book series Advances in Information Security, Privacy, and Ethics (AISPE) (ISSN: 1948-9730; eISSN: 1948-9749)

British Cataloguing in Publication Data
A Cataloguing in Publication record for this book is available from the British Library.

For electronic access to this publication, please contact: eresources@igi-global.com.

Advances in Information Security, Privacy, and Ethics (AISPE) Book Series

ISSN:1948-9730
EISSN:1948-9749

Editor-in-Chief: Manish Gupta, State University of New York, USA

MISSION

As digital technologies become more pervasive in everyday life and the Internet is utilized in ever increasing ways by both private and public entities, concern over digital threats becomes more prevalent.

The **Advances in Information Security, Privacy, & Ethics (AISPE) Book Series** provides cutting-edge research on the protection and misuse of information and technology across various industries and settings. Comprised of scholarly research on topics such as identity management, cryptography, system security, authentication, and data protection, this book series is ideal for reference by IT professionals, academicians, and upper-level students.

COVERAGE

- Privacy Issues of Social Networking
- Cookies
- Computer ethics
- IT Risk
- Information Security Standards
- Internet Governance
- Data Storage of Minors
- Network Security Services
- Technoethics
- CIA Triad of Information Security

IGI Global is currently accepting manuscripts for publication within this series. To submit a proposal for a volume in this series, please contact our Acquisition Editors at Acquisitions@igi-global.com or visit: http://www.igi-global.com/publish/.

Titles in this Series

701 East Chocolate Avenue, Hershey, PA 17033, USA
Tel: 717-533-8845 x100 ● Fax: 717-533-8661
E-Mail: cust@igi-global.com ● www.igi-global.com

Table of Contents

Manoj Kumar M. V., Department of Information Science and Engineering, NITTE Meenakshi Institute of Technology, Bengaluru, India

S. L. Shiva Darshan, Department of Information Technology, Manipal Institute of Technology Bengaluru, Manipal Academy of Higher Education, Manipal, India

Prashanth B. S, Department of Information Science and Engineering, NITTE Meenakshi Institute of Technology, Bengaluru, India

Vishnu Yarlagadda, Department of Information Technology, Manipal Institute of Technology Bengaluru, Manipal Academy of Higher Education, Manipal, India

Manoj Kumar M. V., Department of Information Science and Engineering, NITTE Meenakshi Institute of Technology, Bengaluru, India

S. L. Shiva Darshan, Department of Information Technology, Manipal Institute of Technology Bengaluru, Manipal Academy of Higher Education, Manipal, India

Prashanth B. S., Department of Information Science and Engineering, NITTE Meenakshi Institute of Technology, Bengaluru, India

Vishnu Yarlagadda, Department of Information Technology, Manipal Institute of Technology Bengaluru, Manipal Academy of Higher Education, Manipal, India

Detailed Table of Contents

Chapter 1

    Manoj Kumar M. V., Department of Information Science and
        Engineering, NITTE Meenakshi Institute of Technology, Bengaluru,
        India
    S. L. Shiva Darshan, Department of Information Technology, Manipal
        Institute of Technology Bengaluru, Manipal Academy of Higher
        Education, Manipal, India
    Prashanth B. S, Department of Information Science and Engineering,
        NITTE Meenakshi Institute of Technology, Bengaluru, India
    Vishnu Yarlagadda, Department of Information Technology, Manipal
        Institute of Technology Bengaluru, Manipal Academy of Higher
        Education, Manipal, India

The importance of cybersecurity in the contemporary digital age is profound. In this chapter, the authors will traverse through the complex and evolving landscape of cybersecurity, exploring its progression, the driving forces behind it, the key challenges it faces, and its future trajectory. With an in-depth analysis of various threat actors and types of cyber threats, the authors will delve into the tools and technologies developed to combat these threats. The authors also explore and compare different cybersecurity approaches, studying their effectiveness and their implications. Through real-world case studies of major cyber-attacks, the chapter will provide insightful lessons learned and the impact they had on the cybersecurity landscape. We will also discuss the often-overlooked human factor in cybersecurity, focusing on the significance of cybersecurity training and the psychology of social engineering attacks. By providing a comprehensive overview of the field, this chapter aims to equip the reader with a well-rounded understanding of cybersecurity.

Manoj Kumar M. V., Department of Information Science and
Engineering, NITTE Meenakshi Institute of Technology, Bengaluru,
India
S. L. Shiva Darshan, Department of Information Technology, Manipal
Institute of Technology Bengaluru, Manipal Academy of Higher
Education, Manipal, India
Prashanth B. S., Department of Information Science and Engineering,
NITTE Meenakshi Institute of Technology, Bengaluru, India
Vishnu Yarlagadda, Department of Information Technology, Manipal
Institute of Technology Bengaluru, Manipal Academy of Higher
Education, Manipal, India

In today's interconnected digital world, the threat of malware looms large, posing significant risks to individuals, businesses, and governments. This chapter serves as a comprehensive introduction to the critical field of malware analysis and detection. The chapter begins with a definition of malware, exploring its various forms and the historical perspective of its evolution. The authors delve into the different types of malware, including viruses, worms, Trojans, ransomware, and more, understanding their unique behaviors and propagation methods. Building upon this foundation, they introduce the fundamental concepts of malware analysis methodologies, including static and dynamic analysis, reverse engineering, virtualization, and sandboxing. These techniques enable cybersecurity professionals to gain insights into malware behavior and functionality. To address this challenge, the chapter introduces advanced malware analysis techniques, such as memory forensics, behavioral analysis, kernel-level rootkit detection, and machine learning-based analysis.

Jairaj Singh, Birla Institute of Technology, India
Kishore Kumar Kumar Senapati, Birla Institute of Technology, India

Malicious applications can be a security threat to Cyber-physical systems as these systems are composed of heterogeneous distributed systems and mostly depends on the internet, ICT services and products. The usage of ICT products and services gives the opportunity of less expensive data collection, intelligent control and decision systems using automated data mining tools. Cyber-physical systems become exposed to the internet and the public networks as they have integrated to the ICT networks for easy automated options. Cyber-attacks can lead to functional failure, blackouts, energy theft, data theft etc. and this will be a critical security concern for Cyber-physical systems. There have been many instances of cyber-attacks on CPS systems earlier, the most popular being the Stuxnet virus attack. In total there have been 7 instances of such attacks on CPS systems that have the potential to totally cripple critical infrastructures causing huge business impacts including loss of life in some cases. Earlier these CPS or process level systems used to work in an isolated manner with very less intelligence, but as the convergence between CPS and IT is increasing their cyber-attack surface is increasing for threat actors to exploit. Therefore, in this chapter, the authors shall be seeing the technical threats in the form of malware which can exploit the CPS systems and how it can be protected from cyber-attacks.

Chapter 4

    *M. Gaayathri, Avinashilingam Institute for Home Science and Higher
        Education for Women, India*
    *Padmavathi Ganapathi, Avinashilingam Institute for Home Science and
        Higher Education for Women, India*
    *A. Roshni, Avinashilingam Institute for Home Science and Higher
        Education for Women, India*
    *D. Shanmugapriya, Avinashilingam Institute for Home Science and
        Higher Education for Women, India*

Phishing is one of the most serious issues now-a-days, and many internet users are falling prey to it. Website phishing is a major threat that focuses on developing spoofed sites as a legal ones. Phishers develop cloned websites and distribute the uniform resource locator (URLs) to a large number of people in the form of e-mail, short message service, or through social media. In the current scenario, phishing is the topmost cyber threat/cyber-attack that intrudes into the system to steal or capture sensitive information from the target. Machine learning methods, an important branch of artificial intelligence, are used to detect many critical problems. This chapter investigates the lexical features of website URLs to detect the phishing URL using wrapper-based feature selection on ensemble learning technique. To evaluate the model developed, the dataset from Mendeley repository is taken. The highest level of accuracy for the phishing websites was reached using bagging classifier with 95% accuracy compared with boosting algorithm.

Chapter 5

Sri Danalaksmi, Avinashilingam Institute for Home Science and Higher
Education for Women, India
Geethalakshmi, Avinashilingam Institute for Home Science and Higher
Education for Women, India
A. Roshni, Avinashilingam Institute for Home Science and Higher
Education for Women, India
Padmavathi Ganapathi, Avinashilingam Institute for Home Science and
Higher Education for Women, India

A firewall prevents traffic entering and departing the domain it was supposed to protect. The logging feature keeps track of how the firewall handles different sorts of traffic. Monitoring and analyzing log files can assist IT businesses in improving the end-user reliability of their systems. This book chapter investigates and classifies the firewall log files using supervised machine learning algorithms. The main objective of this chapter is to examine firewall security by analyzing the firewall log files. Supervised machine learning classifiers such as support vector machine (SVM), Naïve Bayes, logistic regression and k-nearest neighbor (KNN) models are developed to classify the firewall log files. Feature selection using Ranker and Info_Gain_Attribute_Eval methods within the Weka tool is applied to derive the robust features from the data. Finally, a comparative analysis is performed to evaluate the efficiency of the supervised machine learning models. Results that, the Naïve Bayes Classifier attains the highest accuracy of 99.26% for the classification of firewall log files.

Chapter 6

Guneet Kaur, Dr. B.R. Ambedkar National Institute of Technology, India
Urvashi Bansal, Dr. B.R. Ambedkar National Institute of Technology,
India
Harsh K. Verma, Dr. B.R. Ambedkar National Institute of Technology,
India
Geeta Sikka, National Institute of Technology, Delhi, India
Lalit K. Awasthi, National Institute of Technology, Srinagar, India

The examination of vulnerabilities is vital to network security, and finding the route to the flaw's source is essential for the analysis and mitigation of software vulnerabilities that attackers can exploit. The automation of secure software development can be easily achieved by using vulnerability ID. Prior to this, manually tagged communications with vulnerability ID was a laborious process that had scalability problems and room for human mistakes. To facilitate code examination, several vulnerability detection techniques have been developed and to support code inspection, several vulnerability detection techniques have been developed. A series of research that uses machine learning approaches and provide encouraging outcomes are among these strategies. This chapter discusses recent research trend that uses deep learning to identify vulnerabilities and demonstrates how cutting-edge neural approaches are used to identify potentially problematic code patterns. It also highlights a few publications from research that have analyzed vulnerability identification using deep learning.

Chapter 7

Kunal Sinha, Artificial Computing Machines, India
Kishore Kumar Senapati, Birla Institute of Technology, India

Cyber-attacks are serious problems for the IT sector. According to a survey, 66 percent of businesses have experienced these attacks. It's difficult and tiresome to fend against these attacks. Cyber analysts are now studying hacker intentions and purposes for incidents in addition to analysing cyber occurrences as a result of the rise in cyberattacks. DBMS may also establish itself as a key technology in the field of computer security and addressing cyber threats among the several technologies being designed and developed to avoid cybercrime. Research on cybercrime and hacker's interpretation can be honed with the use of DBMS. Through its logical and physical models and query processing, it aids in supplying sufficient knowledge to understand upcoming cyber-attacks.

Chapter 8

Kishore Kumar Senapati, Birla Institute of Technology, India
Abhishek Kumar, Birla Institute of Technology, India
Kunal Sinha, Artificial Computing Machines, India

The rise of globally integrated technology with a pace in technical intervention in diversified fields of social, financial, governmental, and defense services the world today is transforming into data age. This scientific development of storing and processing tasks within software territory had invaded the privacy of the users and individuals through technical attacks of existing and innovated technical solutions to discover and mine related information that may use for illegal and legal activities as per demand. Such a data, if extracted from a secured system, may harm a user or an individual in various ways depending on culprit's intention. It therefore becomes important to learn and understand the technical art of safeguarding their data while going digital. Privacy conserved data publishing should be an essential precondition for all data driven technologies. Keeping data safe and legal is another aspect. Existing protection mechanisms may not help in privacy mechanism due to unbalanced research in legal and illegal related technical innovations.

Chapter 9

C. M. Nalayini, Velammal Engineering College, India
Jeevaa Katiravan, Velammal Engineering College, India
V. Sathya, Panimalar Engineering College, India

Distributed denial of service attack is a kind of cyber smack. Though this attack is known by everyone, its severity is increasing day by day. It denies the services of the network or online services by flooding with unwanted data and makes things unavailable. The impact of DDoS is very high, always. Recently, Twitter, Spotify, Amazon, and Paypal were severely affected by this DDoS. This made the services unavailable to their customers. Blockchain is one of the trending technology can be used to find the misbehaving nodes alias bots from the peer to peer networks. Due to lack of interoperability in blockchain, Multichain is proposed in this chapter to detect DDoS attacks along with cross chain technology. It is designed to communicate with multiple networks and the cross chain technology is built to have the flow between the different chains using smart contract. Deep learning models such as CNN and LSTM are trained and tested with CICDDOS2019 dataset and selected LSTM as the best model and installed at Multichain for detecting the malicious activity and blacklisting it immediately.

Chapter 10

Ravi Singh, National Institute of Technology, Patna, India
Piyush Kumar, National Institute of Technology, Patna, India

Malware attacks are growing years after years because of increasing android, IOT along with traditional computing devices. To protect all these devices malware analysis is necessary so that interest of the organizations and individuals can be protected. There are different approaches of malware analysis like static, dynamic and heuristic. As the technology is advancing malware authors also use the advanced malware attacking techniques like obfuscation and packing techniques, which cannot be detect by signature based on static approaches. To overcome all these problems behavior of malware must be analyzed using dynamic approaches. Now a days malware author using some more advanced evasion techniques in which malware suspends its malicious behavior after detecting virtual environment. So, evasion techniques give a new challenge to malware analysis because even dynamic approach some time fails to detect and analyze the malwares.

Chapter 11

T. Sarath, Vellore Institute of Technology, India
K. Brindha, Vellore Institute of Technology, India
Sudha Senthilkumar, Vellore Institute of Technology, India

In day to day life, the internet is becoming an essential part for making use of services like online banking or advertising. On the internet, just as in the real world, there are those who wish to harm others by taking advantage of trustworthy individuals anytime whenever money is exchanged. For accomplishing their goals, people intent with malicious software to harm the internet and this attack is named as Malware. The malware denotes as malevolent software which is installed in computer or mobile without awareness of owner or user. As a result, by looking into this malicious software, the IT team is better able to assess a security incident and help stop more infections from spreading to the victim's computer or server. For this kind of performance, IT responders typically look for solutions known technically as malware forensics. The importance of malware forensics has grown as the cybercrime community targets financial institutions, technological companies, and retail businesses with malicious software. This virus can be broken down into two categories: static malware and dynamic malware. While dynamic malware analysis offers various tools and code, static malware analysis has several limitations. As a result, dynamic malware analysis is often preferred in most contexts. This chapter deals with the study of malware types, how it is affecting the users, static malware limitations, and dynamic malware tools that are used for analyzing malicious software. Further focuses on issues, challenges that are facing in malware analysis and available online malware analysis tools that work on cloud along with feature research prospects.

Chapter 12

D. R. Janardhana, Nitte Meenakshi Institute of Technology, Bengaluru.
India & Visvesvaraya Technological University, Belagavi, India
A. P. Manu, PES Institute of Technology and Management, Shivamogga,
India & Visvesvaraya Technological University, Belagavi, India
K. Shivanna, Malnad College of Engineering, India
K. C. Suhas, Channabasaveshwara Institute of Technology, India

In the present digital era, most of our communication and personal sensitive information are transmitted through smart devices and stored on them. Therefore, it becomes imperative to secure both the device and the data from various security and privacy threats. These threats aim to gain unauthorized access to the data, or worse, destroy it. This chapter presents an overview of malware analysis and its mitigation tools. Malware has become a serious threat to computer systems and networks, and it is important to understand how to analyze and mitigate the risks associated with it. Here, the authors discuss malware and its classification, as well as various techniques used in malware analysis, including static and dynamic analysis. The chapter also presents an overview of the mitigation tools available to prevent and detect malware, including antivirus software, firewalls, intrusion detection systems, and sandboxes. Furthermore, the chapter highlights some of the limitations of these tools and provides insights into the future direction of malware analysis and mitigation.

Chapter 13
    C. V. Suresh Babu, Hindustan Institute of Technolgy and Science, India
    G. Suruthi, Hindustan Institute of Technology and Science, India
    C. Indhumathi, Hindustan Institute of Technology and Science, India

Malware continues to plague all organizations causing data loss and reputational damage. Malware forensics helps protect companies from such attacks. The data is going to be organized in a manner that covers the multiple malware attacks, the methods for detecting them, and then makes a suggestion for a tool that is comparable but also equivalent to reach the attacker. Considering that the concept signifies that malware forensics will be performed using a variety of tools and techniques, a procedure will be followed in order to get the desired outcome. This chapter discusses these issues in detail with an intensive literature review and feasible recommendations and suggestions.

Chapter 14
    Priyam Subhash Patel, Rashtriya Raksha University, India
    Rakesh Singh Kunwar, Rashtriya Raksha University, India
    Akash Thakar, Rashtriya Raksha University, India

In this cyber world, working from the office to the home, security has never been more challenging. To detect attacks on the host computers and prevent further malicious activities, host intrusion detection systems (HIDS) are often used. Use of open-source SEIM tool Wazuh for monitoring and combines with YARA for file analysis. YARA rules are like those of a programming language that operates by specifying variables that indicate patterns identified in malware, depending on the rule. If any or all the conditions are satisfied, it can be used to effectively identify at least a portion of malware that defines variable parameters. YARA rules help SIEM operators analyse the file tag for malware detection before using it to its full potential. In this chapter, we are going to learn and implement malware analysis using Wazuh, and YARA rules before infecting the system fully. A flexible and effective method for detecting malware in system logs, network traffic, and other data sources is produced by combining WAZUH and YARA rules. By utilising the advantages of YARA rules and the sophisticated features of WAZUH, security teams can quickly identify malware attacks and respond to them. This lessens the effect on their business. A modern cybersecurity strategy must contain WAZUH SIEM and YARA rules. With YARA rules, security teams may spot malware attacks in WAZUH and take appropriate action to maintain the security and integrity of their organization's data and systems.

Chapter 15

J. Jeyshri, SRM Institute of Science and Technology, India
R. Sasirekha, SRM Institute of Science and Technology, India

Over time, malware attacks have become more frequent and sophisticated, causing substantial harm to organisations and individuals. In response, malware mitigation technologies have been created by cybersecurity specialists in order to identify, stop, and correct such assaults. Network traffic is monitored by intrusion detection and prevention systems, which also notify security professionals of possible threats. By preventing unwanted access to a network, firewalls give an extra degree of security. Untrusted software is isolated and run in a secure environment using sandboxing technologies to look for suspected malware activities. Instead of relying on malware's signature, behavioural analysis techniques identify malware by its activity. Despite the availability of these technologies, malware assaults continue to pose a serious danger, necessitating ongoing improvement and updating of mitigation strategies. Future developments in malware mitigation solutions, such as the use of artificial intelligence and machine learning, will also be covered in this chapter.

Chapter 16

C. V. Suresh Babu, Hindustan Institute of Technolgy and Science, India
P. Andrew Simon, Hindustan Institute of Technology and Science, India
S. Barath Kumar, Hindustan Institute of Technology and Science, India

This study dives into the field of cybersecurity, analyzing current trends and laying out a conceptual framework for spotting new issues with societal bearing that call for more study in the area. The research eventually seeks to better society's general cybersecurity posture by effectively spotting trends and new risks by using text mining to examine cybersecurity material distributed between 2008 and 2018 in both scholarly and media sources. There is a significant time-based connection between the resources, as shown by the study's discovery of both convergences and divergences between the two cybersecurity corpora. Overall, the study's methodology shows how well automatic methods can be used to offer insightful information on socially significant and new cybersecurity subjects. The framework directs future academic study in this area with the intention of strengthening society's overall cybersecurity stance.

Preface

As the editors of *Malware Analysis and Intrusion Detection in Cyber-Physical Systems*, we are delighted to present this comprehensive reference book that delves into the critical domain of cybersecurity. The volume and sophistication of cyber-attacks continue to rise, posing significant threats to businesses, organizations, and individuals alike. In the face of this evolving landscape, the need for effective malware detection and intrusion prevention has become paramount.

This edited reference book brings together the expertise and insights of distinguished authors, including students, academicians, researchers, and industry specialists, who share their knowledge on various aspects of cyber-threat detection and mitigation. Our primary focus is on dynamic malware analysis, which involves understanding the time sequence output of observed behavior to identify and categorize malicious activities. We explore cutting-edge machine-learning and AI-based solutions that empower real-time detection and categorization of malware, contributing to the field's advancement.

The book addresses a wide array of cybersecurity concerns, covering protection against worms, viruses, hackers, unauthorized access, data leaks, and more. It delves into the intricacies of safeguarding digital assets, software, hardware, and IT infrastructures while maintaining privacy, integrity, and business continuity. Additionally, we examine the vital aspect of building trust with stakeholders and customers by ensuring robust information security practices.

This book is designed to be an indispensable guide for anyone seeking to comprehend the intricacies of cybersecurity and its applications. Whether you are a student, researcher, or industry professional, the diverse range of topics covered herein will provide valuable insights into identifying, assessing, and mitigating cyber-security dangers.

The chapters in this book cover a broad spectrum of subjects, including malware analysis and categorization, static malware analysis, sandboxing and behavior analysis, code obfuscation trends, and malware forensics. The exploration of machine learning and AI-based detection methods provides critical context on the ever-evolving threat landscape. Additionally, we delve into the significance of risk analysis, vulnerability assessment, and the emerging future challenges in cybersecurity.

As editors, we believe this book will serve as a comprehensive reference and a valuable resource for academia, researchers, and professionals working in the field of cybersecurity. It encapsulates the current state of cyber-threat research, while also shedding light on the potential future directions of the domain.

We extend our heartfelt appreciation to all the authors for their contributions, as well as the readers who have chosen to embark on this enlightening journey through the pages of *Malware Analysis and Intrusion Detection in Cyber-Physical Systems*. May this book foster a deeper understanding of cybersecurity and aid in fortifying our digital world against the ever-persistent threats that surround us.

CHAPTER OVERVIEW

Chapter 1: Introduction to Cyber-Security Landscape

In the opening chapter of our edited reference book, *Malware Analysis and Intrusion Detection in Cyber-Physical Systems*, Manoj Kumar M V, Shiva Darshan S.L, Prashanth B S, and Vishnu Yarlagadda present a compelling exploration of the crucial domain of cybersecurity. The chapter begins by emphasizing the profound importance of cybersecurity in the contemporary digital age, setting the stage for an in-depth journey through its complex and ever-evolving landscape.

The authors provide a comprehensive analysis of the progression of cybersecurity, shedding light on the driving forces that have shaped its development over time. They also address the key challenges that the field faces, acknowledging the growing sophistication of cyber threats and the need for robust defenses. To this end, the chapter delves into the tools and technologies that have been developed to combat these threats, ensuring that readers gain insights into the latest approaches for safeguarding systems and data.

One of the primary focal points of this chapter is a thorough exploration of various threat actors and types of cyber threats. By studying these adversaries and their tactics, readers will gain a deeper understanding of the ever-changing threat landscape and the importance of staying ahead of potential risks.

The authors not only discuss technical solutions but also compare different cybersecurity approaches, highlighting their respective strengths, weaknesses, and implications. Real-world case studies of major cyber-attacks are presented, drawing insightful lessons from historical events and their impact on the overall cybersecurity landscape.

A notable aspect of this chapter is the attention given to the human factor in cybersecurity. The authors emphasize the significance of cybersecurity training and awareness to empower individuals to play a proactive role in safeguarding digital assets. They also delve into the psychology of social engineering attacks, underlining the need for a multi-layered defense that includes addressing human vulnerabilities.

In summary, this opening chapter serves as an essential foundation for the entire book, equipping readers with a well-rounded understanding of cybersecurity. By addressing the past, present, and future of the field, the authors ensure that readers are prepared to explore the subsequent chapters with a comprehensive perspective on the challenges and opportunities that lie ahead.

Chapter 2: Foundation of Malware Analysis and Detection

In Chapter 2 of *Malware Analysis and Intrusion Detection in Cyber-Physical Systems*, authored by Manoj Kumar M V, Shiva Darshan S.L, Prashanth B S, and Vishnu Yarlagadda, readers are introduced to the critical field of malware analysis and detection. In today's interconnected digital world, the threat of malware poses significant risks to individuals, businesses, and governments, making it imperative to have a strong foundation in understanding and combating these malicious entities.

The chapter begins by providing a comprehensive definition of malware, encompassing its various forms and exploring the historical perspective of its evolution. By understanding the roots and progression of malware, readers gain valuable context on the ever-changing landscape of cyber-threats.

Next, the authors delve into the different types of malware, including viruses, worms, Trojans, ransomware, and more. Each type is examined in detail, highlighting their unique behaviors and methods of propagation. This exploration of malware characteristics lays the groundwork for building effective strategies to detect and combat these threats.

The chapter proceeds to introduce readers to fundamental concepts in malware analysis methodologies. Static and dynamic analysis techniques are explained, equipping cybersecurity professionals with essential tools to dissect and understand the inner workings of malicious code. Reverse engineering, virtualization, and sandboxing are also explored as effective approaches to gain insights into malware behavior and functionality.

Recognizing that advanced malware presents increasingly sophisticated challenges, the authors introduce readers to cutting-edge malware analysis techniques. Memory forensics is covered, providing a deeper understanding of how to extract crucial information from a system's memory to uncover hidden threats. Behavioral analysis is explored as another powerful method to identify malware based on its activities and patterns of behavior. Kernel-level rootkit detection, a critical aspect of modern malware analysis, is also discussed.

The chapter culminates in an examination of machine learning-based analysis. This approach leverages the power of artificial intelligence and data-driven insights to enhance malware detection and classification. By employing machine learning algorithms, cybersecurity professionals can stay ahead of new and emerging threats with greater accuracy and efficiency.

In summary, Chapter 2 serves as a comprehensive introduction to the foundation of malware analysis and detection. By covering a broad range of topics, from malware types and behaviors to advanced analysis methodologies, the authors equip readers with the essential knowledge to effectively combat malware in the dynamic and ever-evolving cybersecurity landscape.

Chapter 3: Malware Analysis and Classification

In Chapter 3 of our edited reference book, *Malware Analysis and Intrusion Detection in Cyber-Physical Systems*, Jairaj Singh and Kishore Kumar Senapati shed light on the significant security threat posed by malicious applications to Cyber-Physical Systems (CPS). These systems, characterized by their composition of heterogeneous distributed systems, heavily rely on the internet, ICT services, and products, making them susceptible to cyber-attacks.

The authors emphasize that the utilization of ICT products and services offers several advantages, such as cost-effective data collection and intelligent control through automated data mining tools. However, this integration with ICT networks also exposes CPS to the internet and public networks, creating vulnerabilities that malicious actors can exploit.

Cyber-attacks targeting CPS can have severe consequences, including functional failures, blackouts, energy theft, and data theft. The potential impact of such attacks on CPS underscores the critical security concern that must be addressed to safeguard these systems from harm.

In this chapter, Singh and Senapati delve into the intricacies of malware analysis and classification within the context of CPS security. By understanding the various forms of malware that threaten CPS, cybersecurity professionals can better prepare to detect, analyze, and mitigate these threats effectively.

Through their insightful analysis, the authors underscore the significance of proactively addressing cyber-physical security challenges. As CPS becomes increasingly interconnected and dependent on ICT networks, the need for robust malware analysis and classification becomes paramount to protect these systems from potential devastating consequences.

With a focus on CPS-specific threats and vulnerabilities, this chapter serves as a valuable resource for readers seeking a deeper understanding of malware's implications on cyber-physical security. By arming professionals with knowledge and insights on malware analysis and classification in CPS environments, Singh and Senapati contribute to strengthening the overall cybersecurity posture of these critical systems.

Chapter 4: Wrapper Based Feature Selection for Detecting the Lexical Phishing Websites Using Ensemble Learning Algorithms

Authored by Gaayathri M, Roshni A, Padmavathi Ganapathi, and Shanmugapriya D, Chapter 4 delves into the pressing issue of phishing, which has become one of the most serious threats in the digital landscape. With an increasing number of internet users falling prey to phishing attacks, the development of spoofed websites poses a major challenge to cybersecurity.

The chapter specifically focuses on phishing websites that attempt to mimic legitimate ones to deceive unsuspecting users. Phishers create cloned websites and disseminate their URLs through various means, such as email, short message service, and social media. Once users access these fraudulent URLs, sensitive information becomes vulnerable to theft and misuse.

To combat this ever-evolving cyber threat, the authors turn to machine learning methods, a crucial branch of artificial intelligence, to detect and prevent phishing attacks. Their investigation revolves around the lexical features of website URLs, which play a crucial role in distinguishing phishing URLs from legitimate ones. Using wrapper-based feature selection on ensemble learning techniques, the authors propose a novel approach to enhance phishing URL detection.

To evaluate the efficacy of their model, the authors leverage a dataset from the Mendeley repository, which serves as a representative sample of real-world data. Through rigorous experimentation, the authors demonstrate the effectiveness of their approach in accurately identifying phishing websites. The chapter highlights that the highest level of accuracy achieved for phishing website detection was through the Bagging Classifier, which achieved an impressive 95% accuracy compared to the Boosting algorithm.

By presenting their findings and insights, the authors contribute valuable knowledge to the field of cybersecurity. Their work not only emphasizes the significance of machine learning techniques in detecting critical cyber threats like phishing but also underscores the importance of feature selection for improving detection accuracy. The chapter offers practical implications for cybersecurity practitioners and researchers alike, providing a potential solution to combat the pervasive and damaging effects of phishing attacks on unsuspecting internet users.

Chapter 5: Classification of Firewall Log Files using Supervised Machine Learning Techniques

In Chapter 5 of our edited reference book, *Malware Analysis and Intrusion Detection in Cyber-Physical Systems*, Sri Danalaksmi P, Geethalakshmi S.N, Roshni A, and Padmavathi Ganapathi delve into the crucial realm of firewall log file analysis and classification. Firewalls play a vital role in protecting domains by monitoring and controlling incoming and outgoing network traffic. The logging feature of firewalls keeps a record of how different types of traffic are handled, providing valuable insights into network activity.

The main objective of this chapter is to enhance firewall security by utilizing supervised machine learning algorithms to analyze and classify firewall log files. By analyzing these log files, IT businesses can improve the reliability and security of their systems, ensuring robust protection against potential cyber threats.

The authors employ well-known supervised machine learning classifiers, including Support Vector Machine (SVM), Naïve Bayes, Logistic Regression, and K-Nearest Neighbor (KNN) models, to perform the classification task. These algorithms enable accurate categorization of firewall log entries based on their characteristics, providing valuable context for network administrators and security professionals.

To optimize the classification process, the authors employ feature selection methods, specifically Ranker and Info_Gain_Attribute_Eval, within the Weka tool. These methods help identify the most relevant and robust features from the data, enhancing the accuracy and efficiency of the machine learning models.

The chapter culminates in a comparative analysis to evaluate the performance of the supervised machine learning models. By comparing the results of each classifier, readers gain insights into the strengths and weaknesses of different approaches for classifying firewall log files.

The authors' findings reveal that the Naïve Bayes Classifier achieves the highest accuracy, reaching an impressive 99.26% for the classification of firewall log files. This insight can guide cybersecurity professionals in selecting appropriate machine learning models to optimize their firewall log analysis processes.

By presenting this comprehensive analysis of firewall log file classification using supervised machine learning techniques, the authors contribute valuable knowledge to the field of cybersecurity. Their work equips readers with practical tools and methods to enhance firewall security and strengthen overall network protection against potential threats and attacks.

Chapter 6: Discernment and Perusal of Software Vulnerability

Authored by Guneet Kaur, Urvashi Bansal, Harsh Verma, Geeta Sikka, and Lalit Awasthi, Chapter 6 delves into the critical examination of software vulnerabilities and their significance in ensuring network security. Identifying the source of flaws within software is essential for effective analysis and mitigation, as attackers often exploit these vulnerabilities to compromise systems.

In the past, manually tagging communications with vulnerability IDs was a laborious process, prone to scalability issues and human errors. To automate and streamline secure software development, the authors propose the use of vulnerability IDs. This identification process serves as a foundation for vulnerability analysis and enables efficient software vulnerability mitigation.

To support code examination and enhance vulnerability detection, various techniques have been developed. The chapter explores existing vulnerability detection methods, with a particular focus on those employing machine learning approaches. These techniques, including deep learning, have shown promising outcomes in identifying vulnerabilities and detecting potentially problematic code patterns.

The authors highlight the increasing trend of research that employs deep learning for vulnerability identification. Deep learning, a cutting-edge neural approach, has emerged as a powerful tool in detecting complex patterns and vulnerabilities within software code. By utilizing neural networks, cybersecurity professionals can uncover hidden vulnerabilities that may not be easily discernible through traditional methods.

Throughout the chapter, the authors present recent research findings that demonstrate the effectiveness of deep learning in vulnerability identification. These studies serve as examples of successful applications of deep learning techniques and showcase their potential in bolstering software security.

By discussing the use of deep learning in identifying software vulnerabilities, this chapter sheds light on the ever-evolving landscape of cybersecurity research. The exploration of cutting-edge neural approaches provides valuable insights for readers seeking to understand and implement advanced methods for vulnerability detection and mitigation.

In summary, Chapter 6 serves as a comprehensive overview of the importance of identifying and addressing software vulnerabilities in ensuring network security. By showcasing the potential of deep learning in vulnerability identification, the authors contribute to the ongoing efforts to enhance the resilience of software systems against potential threats and attacks.

Chapter 7: Knowledge Repository on Cyber Security

In Chapter 7 of our edited reference book, *Malware Analysis and Intrusion Detection in Cyber-Physical Systems*, Kunal Sinha and Kishore Senapati address the critical issue of cyber-attacks that continue to plague the IT industry. As per surveys, approximately 66 percent of industries have faced these relentless attacks, highlighting the severity of the problem. Defending against cyber-attacks is no easy task and is often perceived as a challenging and time-consuming endeavor.

The escalating frequency of cyber-attacks has led cyber analysts to not only analyze individual cyber incidents but also to adopt a long-term perspective in studying hackers' intentions and purposes behind such incidents. In this context, various technologies are being designed and developed for preventing cyber-crimes. Among these technologies, Database Management Systems (DBMS) emerge as a significant player in the field of computer security, cyber-crime prevention, and cyber threat handling.

DBMS has the potential to provide invaluable support to researchers in the study of cyber-crimes and hackers' modus operandi. By utilizing logical and physical models and employing query processing techniques, DBMS assists in understanding future cyber-attacks. It facilitates the organization and analysis of vast amounts of data related to cyber incidents, enabling researchers to gain insights into patterns, trends, and potential threats.

A key advantage of using DBMS is its ability to efficiently manage databases, enabling seamless sharing of information among users and applications. This feature makes databases an excellent tool for the analysis and prevention of cyber-crimes. By centralizing data and facilitating information sharing, DBMS contributes to a comprehensive knowledge repository on cyber security, empowering cybersecurity professionals in their efforts to safeguard critical systems and data.

This chapter emphasizes the significance of adopting a proactive and knowledge-based approach to combat cyber threats. The use of DBMS as a key technology in the prevention and handling of cyber-crimes offers promising opportunities for cyber analysts to stay one step ahead of adversaries.

In conclusion, Chapter 7 serves as a testament to the importance of creating and maintaining a knowledge repository on cyber security. By harnessing the capabilities of DBMS, cybersecurity professionals can build a robust foundation for analysis, prevention, and response to cyber-attacks. The chapter highlights the potential of databases as powerful tools in the ongoing fight against cyber-crime, providing valuable insights for researchers and practitioners in the field of cybersecurity.

Chapter 8: Impact of Information Leakage and Conserving Digital Privacy

In Chapter 8 of our edited reference book, *Malware Analysis and Intrusion Detection in Cyber-Physical Systems*, Dr. Kishore Senapati, Abhishek Kumar, and Kunal Sinha explore the profound impact of information leakage and the critical importance of conserving digital privacy in today's data-driven world.

The rapid advancements in globally integrated technology have led to widespread technical interventions across various fields, including social, financial, governmental, and defense services. This transformation into the data age has brought forth scientific developments in storing and processing tasks within software realms. However, it has also resulted in a significant invasion of user and individual privacy through various technical attacks and innovative solutions that aim to discover and mine sensitive information for both legal and illegal purposes.

The chapter highlights the potential dangers associated with data extraction from supposedly secure systems, which can lead to severe consequences for users and individuals, depending on the malicious intentions of the culprits. Such extracted data may be exploited for both legitimate and illicit activities, posing serious risks to personal security and confidentiality.

Given this scenario, the authors emphasize the utmost importance of learning and understanding the technical art of safeguarding data while embracing the digital world. Conserving digital privacy and ensuring data safety become imperative preconditions for the successful implementation of data-driven technologies.

To address these challenges, privacy-conserved data publishing is advocated as an essential practice. Protecting data and ensuring its legal usage is also emphasized as a critical aspect of digital privacy preservation. However, the chapter also points out that existing protection mechanisms may not be sufficient to address the privacy challenges due to unbalanced research in both legal and illegal technical innovations.

By shedding light on the impact of information leakage and the significance of conserving digital privacy, this chapter raises awareness about the potential risks posed by data breaches and unauthorized access. It highlights the need for a comprehensive approach to safeguarding sensitive data and encourages further research and advancements in privacy-preserving technologies.

In summary, Chapter 8 serves as a wake-up call for the protection of digital privacy in the data-driven age. The authors' insights on privacy-conserved data publishing and the limitations of existing protection mechanisms provide valuable guidance for researchers, policymakers, and practitioners in the ongoing efforts to ensure data security and confidentiality in an increasingly interconnected world.

Chapter 9: Intrusion Detection in Cyber Physical Systems Using Multichain

Authored by Nalayini CM, Jeevaa Katiravan, and Sathya V, Chapter 9 delves into the critical issue of Distributed Denial of Service (DDoS) attacks in cyber-physical systems. DDoS attacks have become increasingly severe, denying network and online services by flooding them with unwanted data, rendering them unavailable to legitimate users. The impact of these attacks is substantial and can have far-reaching consequences for businesses and organizations.

The severity of DDoS attacks is exemplified by recent incidents affecting well-known platforms such as Twitter, Spotify, Amazon, and Paypal, causing significant disruptions to their services and inconveniencing their customers.

In response to the growing threat of DDoS attacks, blockchain technology is proposed as a potential solution. Blockchain's decentralized and immutable nature can be leveraged to identify misbehaving nodes or bots within peer-to-peer networks. However, due to the lack of interoperability in traditional blockchain networks, the authors introduce Multichain as an alternative. Multichain is designed to communicate with multiple networks and incorporates cross-chain technology, enabling the flow of data and transactions between different chains using smart contracts.

The chapter focuses on the utilization of deep learning models, specifically Convolutional Neural Networks (CNN) and Long Short-Term Memory (LSTM), to detect DDoS attacks. These models are trained and tested using the CICDDOS2019 dataset, with LSTM emerging as the most effective model for detecting malicious activities. The chosen LSTM model is then integrated into the Multichain system, enabling real-time detection of DDoS attacks and immediate blacklisting of malicious activities.

By incorporating Multichain and LSTM-based intrusion detection, this chapter proposes an innovative approach to combatting DDoS attacks in cyber-physical systems. The integration of blockchain and deep learning technologies offers enhanced security and resiliency, ensuring swift identification and mitigation of cyber threats.

In summary, Chapter 9 presents a novel perspective on using Multichain with deep learning models for intrusion detection in cyber-physical systems. By harnessing the capabilities of blockchain and LSTM, the authors provide valuable insights into a potential solution for tackling the ever-evolving threat landscape of DDoS attacks. The proposed approach contributes to the ongoing efforts to fortify cyber-physical systems against malicious activities and safeguard critical infrastructures and services.

Chapter 10: Malware Analysis With Machine Learning Methods, Challenges, and Future Directions

Authored by Ravi Singh and Piyush Kumar, Chapter 10 delves into the critical domain of malware analysis, considering the increasing threat posed by malware attacks across various computing devices, including Android, Internet of Things (IoT), and traditional systems. As the technology landscape evolves, malware authors continuously adapt and employ advanced techniques such as obfuscation and packing to evade detection by static approaches based on signatures.

To effectively protect organizations and individuals from these evolving threats, malware analysis becomes a necessary practice. The chapter discusses different approaches to malware analysis, including static, dynamic, and heuristic techniques. While static approaches may have limitations in detecting advanced malware, dynamic analysis offers promise by observing the behavior of malware in a controlled environment.

As malware authors continue to develop sophisticated evasion techniques, even dynamic analysis faces challenges in detecting and analyzing certain types of malwares. One such technique involves malware suspending its malicious behavior upon detecting a virtual environment, making it harder to identify.

In this ever-changing landscape, machine learning methods have emerged as a valuable tool in malware analysis. By leveraging data-driven insights and pattern recognition, machine learning models can adapt and improve their ability to detect and analyze malware. These models offer potential solutions to the challenges posed by advanced evasion techniques and evolving malware behaviors.

The chapter also highlights the need for continued research and innovation in the field of malware analysis. As new evasion techniques emerge, researchers must stay ahead of the curve and develop advanced methodologies to identify and counter these threats. By exploring the challenges and future directions of malware analysis, the authors provide valuable guidance for researchers and practitioners in the ongoing efforts to combat malware and protect digital systems.

In summary, Chapter 10 serves as a comprehensive overview of malware analysis with a particular focus on the role of machine learning methods. By addressing the challenges posed by advanced evasion techniques and highlighting the importance of dynamic analysis, the authors contribute to the growing body of knowledge in the field of cybersecurity. The chapter also underscores the importance of continuous research and development to stay ahead in the battle against evolving malware threats.

Chapter 11: Malware Forensics Analysis and Detection in Cyber-Physical Systems

Authored by Brindha K, T Sarath, and Sudha Senthilkumar, Chapter 11 delves into the critical domain of malware forensics analysis and detection in the context of Cyber-Physical Systems (CPS). In today's world, the internet has become an essential part of daily life, with individuals relying on it for services such as online banking and advertising. Unfortunately, just like in the real world, there are malicious actors on the internet who seek to harm others and take advantage of unsuspecting individuals, especially during financial transactions.

Malware, a term used to describe malicious software, is one of the key tools employed by cybercriminals to achieve their nefarious goals. As cybercrime continues to target financial institutions, technology companies, and retail businesses, the importance of malware forensics has grown significantly. This chapter delves into the study of malware, its various types, and how it affects users across the digital landscape.

The authors explore both static and dynamic malware analysis techniques. Static analysis, while useful, has its limitations, especially in detecting advanced and sophisticated malware. Dynamic analysis, on the other hand, involves the use of tools and techniques to analyze malicious software behavior in a controlled environment. By studying malware in action, analysts can gain valuable insights into its behavior and intent.

The chapter also addresses the challenges and issues faced in malware analysis, emphasizing the ever-evolving nature of cyber threats and the need for continuous research and development to stay ahead. Additionally, the authors shed light on available online malware analysis tools that operate on the cloud, providing an efficient and scalable approach to analyzing and detecting malware.

With a focus on CPS environments, this chapter presents a comprehensive exploration of the importance of malware forensics in countering cyber threats. By examining different types of malware and their impact on users, the authors contribute to the growing body of knowledge in the field of cybersecurity. The chapter serves as a valuable resource for researchers, practitioners, and cybersecurity professionals seeking to enhance malware analysis and detection methodologies in Cyber-Physical Systems.

Chapter 12: Malware Analysis and its Mitigation Tools

Authored by Janardhana D R, Manu A P, Shivanna K, and Suhas K C, Chapter 12 addresses the critical need to secure smart devices and sensitive data in the present digital era. With our communication and personal information transmitted and stored on smart devices, the threat of security and privacy breaches has become ever more pressing. Malicious actors aim to gain unauthorized access to data or even destroy it, making malware a serious threat to computer systems and networks.

The chapter presents an insightful overview of malware analysis and its mitigation tools. Understanding how to analyze and mitigate malware risks is crucial in safeguarding digital assets and sensitive information. The authors begin by discussing malware and its classification, shedding light on the various forms it can take and the diverse range of threats it poses.

To combat these threats effectively, the chapter explores different techniques used in malware analysis, including static and dynamic analysis. Static analysis involves examining malware without executing it, while dynamic analysis entails observing malware behavior in a controlled environment. Both approaches offer valuable insights into malware's capabilities and intentions.

In addition to malware analysis, the chapter also presents an overview of the various mitigation tools available to prevent and detect malware. These tools encompass a wide range of solutions, such as antivirus software, firewalls, intrusion detection systems, and sandboxes. Each tool plays a crucial role in enhancing overall cybersecurity and defending against malware attacks.

However, the authors also acknowledge the limitations of these tools, recognizing that cyber threats continue to evolve rapidly. As such, the chapter provides insights into the future direction of malware analysis and mitigation, emphasizing the need for ongoing research and innovation to stay ahead of the ever-changing threat landscape.

In summary, Chapter 12 serves as a comprehensive guide to understanding malware analysis and its mitigation tools. By addressing the significance of protecting smart devices and sensitive data, the authors contribute to the broader conversation on enhancing cybersecurity measures in the digital age. The chapter's exploration of malware analysis techniques and mitigation tools provides valuable guidance for researchers, practitioners, and cybersecurity professionals seeking to fortify their systems against malware threats.

Chapter 13: Malware Forensics - An Application of Scientific Knowledge to Cyber Attacks

Authored by C.V. Suresh Babu, Suruthi G, and Indhumathi C, Chapter 13 focuses on the persistent challenge of malware and its detrimental impact on organizations, causing data loss and reputational damage. In response to these threats, malware forensics emerges as a crucial field that aids in protecting companies from cyber attacks.

The chapter presents a comprehensive organization of data, covering various aspects of malware attacks, their detection methods, and proposing a tool that can effectively confront and counteract attackers. To achieve this, malware forensics employs a range of tools and techniques, and a well-structured procedure is followed to obtain the desired outcomes.

The authors delve into the intricacies of malware forensics, emphasizing the importance of an intensive literature review to gain insights from existing research and real-world cases. By studying past incidents and responses, cybersecurity professionals can enhance their understanding of the evolving threat landscape and devise more effective countermeasures.

The chapter highlights the need for feasible recommendations and suggestions in the realm of malware forensics. In a rapidly changing cybersecurity landscape, adaptable and robust solutions are essential to confront sophisticated cyber attacks effectively.

By presenting in-depth discussions on these issues, Chapter 13 contributes to the broader understanding of malware forensics and its practical applications in mitigating cyber threats. The integration of scientific knowledge and practical approaches underscores the significance of continuous research and development in this critical area of cybersecurity.

In conclusion, Chapter 13 serves as a valuable resource for researchers, practitioners, and cybersecurity professionals seeking to strengthen their defenses against malware attacks. The emphasis on thorough literature review and feasible recommendations provides practical guidance for implementing malware forensics effectively. As the cybersecurity landscape evolves, the insights offered in this chapter will aid in maintaining a proactive stance against ever-evolving cyber threats.

Chapter 14: Malware Detection Using YARA Rules in SIEM

Authored by Priyam Patel, Rakesh Kunwar, and Akash Thakar, Chapter 14 addresses the increasing challenges of security in the ever-evolving cyber world, where remote work and diverse computing environments have made detecting and preventing attacks more complex. Host Intrusion Detection Systems (HIDS) play a crucial role in identifying attacks on host computers and thwarting further malicious activities.

The chapter introduces the use of the open-source SIEM (Security Information and Event Management) tool, Wazuh, for monitoring and combining it with YARA for file analysis. YARA rules are akin to those of a programming language, utilizing variables that represent patterns found in malware. These rules help identify specific characteristics and behaviors of malware, enabling effective detection based on predefined variable parameters.

The authors illustrate how YARA rules can be leveraged to analyze file tags for malware detection before the malware can fully infect the system. By utilizing

YARA's flexibility and power, SIEM operators can proactively identify potential threats and take appropriate measures to mitigate risks.

The chapter provides a practical approach to malware analysis using Wazuh and YARA rules, demonstrating how these tools can work in synergy to enhance malware detection capabilities. By incorporating YARA into the SIEM workflow, cybersecurity professionals gain valuable insights into potential malware activities and can respond promptly to protect their systems and data.

In summary, Chapter 14 offers valuable guidance for implementing malware analysis using YARA rules within a SIEM framework. The combination of Wazuh and YARA provides an efficient and effective solution for detecting malware and strengthening cybersecurity defenses. The chapter's emphasis on proactive detection and mitigation showcases the importance of staying ahead of cyber threats in the dynamic landscape of information security. This practical guide will be beneficial for researchers, practitioners, and cybersecurity specialists seeking to enhance their malware detection capabilities using YARA rules and SIEM technologies.

Chapter 15: Malware Mitigation Tools

Authored by Jeyshri J and Sasirekha R, Chapter 15 provides a comprehensive overview of the escalating threat posed by malware attacks and the corresponding development of malware mitigation technologies. As malware attacks have increased in frequency and sophistication, they have inflicted significant harm on both organizations and individuals, necessitating robust defenses against these threats.

In response, cybersecurity specialists have developed various malware mitigation technologies to identify, prevent, and remediate such attacks. Intrusion detection and prevention systems play a vital role by monitoring network traffic and alerting security professionals to potential threats, allowing for timely action to be taken.

Firewalls offer an additional layer of security by preventing unauthorized access to networks, effectively reducing the attack surface and mitigating potential damage caused by malware infiltration.

Sandboxing technologies provide a secure environment to isolate and execute untrusted software, allowing for the detection of suspected malware activities without endangering the overall system.

Behavioral analysis techniques are employed to identify malware based on its activity, moving away from reliance solely on malware signatures. This approach offers increased efficacy in detecting zero-day and polymorphic malware, which can evade traditional signature-based detection methods.

Despite the availability of these mitigation technologies, malware attacks continue to pose a serious threat, necessitating continuous improvement and updating of mitigation strategies. The chapter emphasizes the need for a dynamic and adaptive approach to counter evolving malware tactics.

Moreover, the authors shed light on future developments in malware mitigation solutions, including the integration of artificial intelligence and machine learning. These emerging technologies hold the potential to enhance malware detection and mitigation capabilities, enabling more proactive and efficient responses to cyber threats.

In conclusion, Chapter 15 serves as a comprehensive guide to understanding the landscape of malware mitigation tools. By exploring the various technologies employed to combat malware attacks, the authors provide valuable insights for researchers, practitioners, and cybersecurity professionals seeking to strengthen their defense against ever-evolving malware threats. The chapter's emphasis on future advancements showcases the importance of continuous innovation in the fight against cybercrime and reinforces the necessity of staying at the forefront of malware mitigation strategies.

Chapter 16: The Future of Cybersecurity Starts Today, Not Tomorrow

Authored by C.V. Suresh Babu, Andrew Simon P, and Barath Kumar S, Chapter 16 delves into the realm of cybersecurity, examining current trends and presenting a conceptual framework to identify emerging issues with societal implications that demand further exploration. The research aims to enhance society's overall cybersecurity posture by effectively recognizing trends and novel risks through text mining analysis of cybersecurity material disseminated between 2008 and 2018, encompassing both scholarly and media sources.

The study uncovers a significant time-based connection between the resources, revealing both convergences and divergences within the two cybersecurity corpora. By systematically analyzing the material from various sources, the research sheds light on emerging cybersecurity topics that are socially relevant and require attention.

Employing automatic methods such as text mining, the study demonstrates the effectiveness of these techniques in providing valuable insights into socially significant and emerging cybersecurity subjects. By leveraging automated analysis, the research paves the way for a deeper understanding of the evolving cybersecurity landscape and enables timely responses to potential threats.

The conceptual framework developed in this chapter lays the groundwork for future academic studies in the cybersecurity domain, with the ultimate aim of bolstering society's overall cybersecurity readiness. By identifying new risks and trends, researchers can proactively address potential vulnerabilities and design effective mitigation strategies.

In conclusion, Chapter 16 highlights the urgency of addressing cybersecurity challenges in the present rather than postponing action to the future. By employing innovative research methodologies and analyzing diverse sources of cybersecurity information, the authors emphasize the importance of staying ahead in the dynamic field of cybersecurity. The chapter's focus on proactively strengthening society's cybersecurity stance serves as a call to action for researchers and practitioners, reminding them of the imperative to be vigilant and responsive in the face of evolving cyber threats.

IN SUMMARY

In conclusion, the edited reference book *Malware Analysis and Intrusion Detection in Cyber-Physical Systems* serves as a comprehensive and invaluable resource for anyone seeking to delve into the complex and ever-evolving world of cybersecurity. The book, authored by esteemed experts in the field, addresses the critical need for robust cybersecurity solutions, particularly in the context of Cyber-Physical Systems (CPS).

Throughout the chapters, we have explored various aspects of malware analysis, detection, and mitigation, acknowledging the escalating threat posed by cyber-attacks. The book covers a wide array of topics, including dynamic malware analysis, intrusion detection, firewall log classification, software vulnerability discernment, and privacy preservation, among others. Each chapter offers valuable insights, presenting state-of-the-art research and practical methodologies to combat cyber threats effectively.

We have also emphasized the significance of machine learning and artificial intelligence in enhancing malware detection capabilities, further highlighting the future directions of cybersecurity research. As the cyber threat landscape continues to evolve, the adoption of cutting-edge technologies and innovative approaches remains crucial for staying ahead of adversaries.

This reference book serves as a platform for students, academicians, researchers, and industry experts to share their knowledge and insights, fostering collaboration and advancements in the field of cybersecurity. By exploring the challenges, limitations, and potential solutions, we hope to equip our readers with the tools and knowledge necessary to safeguard critical business and personal information in the face of increasing cyber-attacks.

We extend our heartfelt gratitude to all the contributing authors for their invaluable contributions, expertise, and dedication to this collaborative effort. Their diverse perspectives and scholarly work have enriched the content of this book, making it a comprehensive and well-rounded guide to malware analysis and intrusion detection in Cyber-Physical Systems.

As editors, we firmly believe that the knowledge shared in this book will empower our readers, inspire further research, and foster innovation in cybersecurity. The journey towards a more secure digital future starts with the insights gained from understanding the threats we face today. We encourage our readers to seize the opportunities presented in this book and embark on a collective mission to fortify our cyber defenses, for the future of cybersecurity starts today, not tomorrow.

S.L. Shiva Darshan
Department of Information and Communication Technology, Manipal Institute of Technology, India

M.V. Manoj Kumar
Department of Information Science and Engineering, Nitte Meenakshi Institute of Technology, India

B.S. Prashanth
Department of Information Science and Engineering, Nitte Meenakshi Institute of Technology, India

Y. Vishnu Srinivasa Murthy
Department of Computational Intelligence, Vellore Institute of Technology, India

Chapter 1
Introduction to the Cyber-Security Landscape

Manoj Kumar M. V.

(iD) https://orcid.org/0000-0002-9848-6234

Department of Information Science and Engineering, NITTE Meenakshi Institute of Technology, Bengaluru, India

S. L. Shiva Darshan

Department of Information Technology, Manipal Institute of Technology Bengaluru, Manipal Academy of Higher Education, Manipal, India

Prashanth B. S

(iD) https://orcid.org/0000-0003-4539-662X

Department of Information Science and Engineering, NITTE Meenakshi Institute of Technology, Bengaluru, India

Vishnu Yarlagadda

(iD) https://orcid.org/0000-0001-6146-5272

Department of Information Technology, Manipal Institute of Technology Bengaluru, Manipal Academy of Higher Education, Manipal, India

ABSTRACT

The importance of cybersecurity in the contemporary digital age is profound. In this chapter, the authors will traverse through the complex and evolving landscape of cybersecurity, exploring its progression, the driving forces behind it, the key challenges it faces, and its future trajectory. With an in-depth analysis of various threat actors and types of cyber threats, the authors will delve into the tools and technologies developed to combat these threats. The authors also explore and compare different cybersecurity approaches, studying their effectiveness and their implications. Through real-world case studies of major cyber-attacks, the chapter

DOI: 10.4018/978-1-6684-8666-5.ch001

will provide insightful lessons learned and the impact they had on the cybersecurity landscape. We will also discuss the often-overlooked human factor in cybersecurity, focusing on the significance of cybersecurity training and the psychology of social engineering attacks. By providing a comprehensive overview of the field, this chapter aims to equip the reader with a well-rounded understanding of cybersecurity.

1. INTRODUCTION

The role of cybersecurity has become more important than it has ever been in a world that is increasingly becoming more interconnected. It is essential to maintaining people's faith in digital systems, fostering economic growth, and protecting individual and national security interests, all of which it does very effectively.

The figure 1 shows the mind map diagram offers a comprehensive overview of the cybersecurity landscape, divided into four main categories: Threats, Defences, Challenges, and Opportunities. The Threats category outlines various types of cyber threats, including malware, phishing, man-in-the-middle attacks, denial-of-service attacks, and SQL injection. These represent different methods that attackers might use to compromise a system or network. The Defences category lists measures such as firewalls, antivirus software, intrusion detection systems, and secure coding practices, which are crucial components of a robust cybersecurity defense strategy. The Challenges category underscores the difficulties faced in cybersecurity, including rapidly evolving threats, increasingly sophisticated attackers, and the need for constant vigilance and updating. Despite these challenges, the Opportunities category highlights the growing demand for cybersecurity professionals, advances in AI and machine learning for defines, and increasing awareness and prioritization

Figure 1. Introduction to cybersecurity landscape

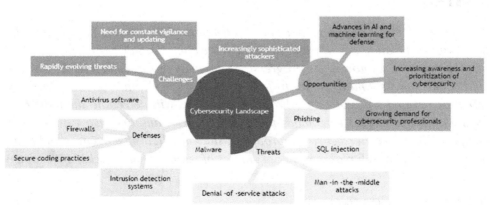

of cybersecurity. This diagram serves as a valuable starting point for understanding the complex and ever-changing field of cybersecurity.

1.1 Definition of Cybersecurity

Cybersecurity is not merely a technical issue. It also entails legal, policy, and societal aspects, extending to the realms of law enforcement, policymaking, and user awareness and behaviour. The term "cybersecurity" refers to a wide variety of processes, technologies, and systems that are all designed to protect digital and networked environments from a variety of different types of cyberattacks. The term was coined by the American National Standards Institute (ANSI). According to (Von Solms and Van Niekerk (2013)), the primary goal of the field is to guarantee that the availability, integrity, and confidentiality of data are preserved across all digital networks and systems. This is the primary objective of the field. The issue of ensuring the safety of information transmitted online is not solely one of a technical nature. In addition to this, it is very important to take into consideration the legal, societal, and policy implications, which extend into the realms of law enforcement, policymaking, as well as user awareness and behaviour.

1.2 Importance of Cybersecurity

In this day and age of information, when the global economy and social infrastructure are so heavily dependent on digital and networked systems, cybersecurity is an absolute necessity. Because of our ever-increasing reliance on technological systems, the role of cybersecurity in ensuring the continued operation and reliability of these systems has become an increasingly important one. Cybersecurity helps ensure that these systems will continue to function as intended. For comprehensive overview of importance of cyber security in various horizons, see figure 2.

The proliferation of digital technology has been accompanied by an increase in cybercrime, which can take on a variety of forms, ranging from espionage and attacks on essential infrastructure to financial fraud and the theft of personally identifying information. This rise in cybercrime has been accompanied by the proliferation of digital technology. Cybersecurity measures are an absolute requirement if one is to effectively combat the threats and protect not only individuals and businesses but also the security of the nation. In addition, a data breach can cause a significant amount of damage to an organization's reputation, in addition to significant financial losses, which further emphasises the requirement for robust cybersecurity measures (Romanosky, 2016).

Figure 2. Importance of cybersecurity

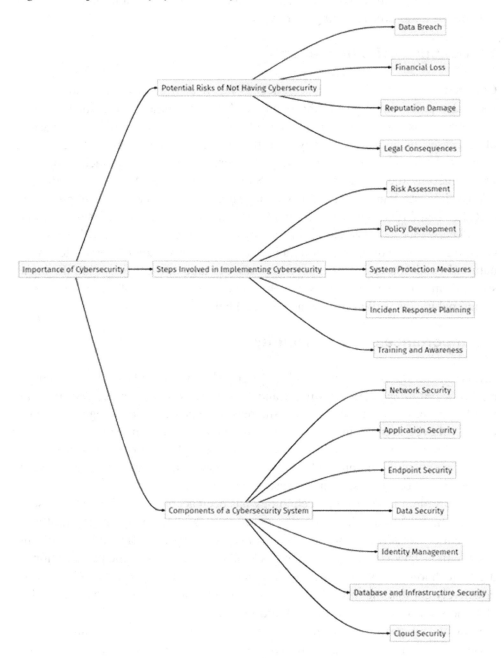

The chapter will offer an overview of the key elements of the cybersecurity landscape, shedding light on different threat actors and common types of cyber threats. We'll examine the tools and techniques used to prevent, detect, and respond to these threats, along with the policies and regulations designed to protect data and privacy. Subsequent sections will provide a comparative analysis of different cybersecurity approaches, case studies of major cyber-attacks, and a discussion on the role of human factors in cybersecurity. The chapter concludes with an outlook of the cybersecurity landscape, emphasizing the continuous evolution and adaptation required in the face of advancing cyber threats.

2. THE EVOLUTION OF CYBERSECURITY

Cybersecurity, like the technology it protects, has rapidly evolved over the years. Understanding its history helps us appreciate its current state and anticipate future trends. Table 1 and Figure 3 briefs the evolution of cybersecurity.

Table 1. Evolution of cyber security

Cybersecurity Aspects	Past	Present	Future
Threat Landscape	Less diverse, mostly physical threats	Multifaceted - individual hackers to state-sponsored attacks	Growing, with even more diverse sources and sophisticated techniques
Focus	Prevention of attacks	Detection and response, alongside prevention	Proactive threat hunting, automated responses
Influence of New Tech	Limited	Significant (Cloud Computing, IoT, AI)	More pronounced with emerging technologies like quantum computing
Use of AI and Machine Learning	Rare or non-existent	Common for predicting, identifying, and responding to threats	Advanced AI, like deep learning, for more accurate detection and prevention
Behavioural Analytics	Not prevalent	Key tool for identifying potential threats	Integration of user behavior with AI for enhanced threat prediction
Encryption	Simple methods	Advanced encryption standards	Quantum encryption, Homomorphic encryption for data privacy
Regulatory Framework	Limited	Robust with regulations like GDPR, CCPA	Global unified cybersecurity standards and regulations
Cybersecurity Training	Limited, mostly for IT professionals	Growing for all employees, awareness campaigns	Continuous training, simulated cyber-attack drills, widespread awareness

Figure 3. Evolution of cyber security

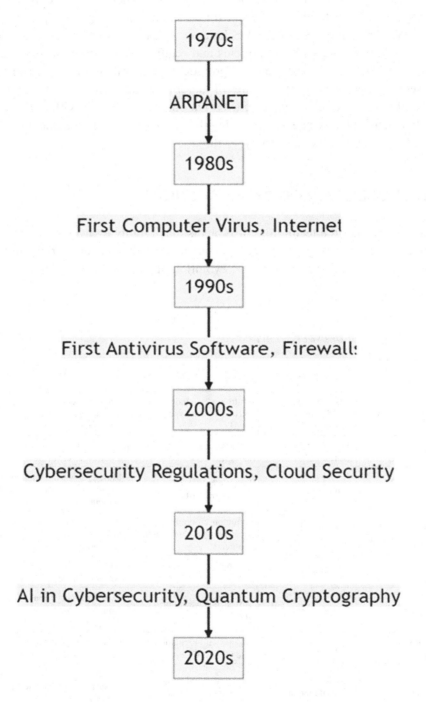

2. 1. Cybersecurity in the Past

During the early days of computing (1960s to late 1980s), cybersecurity wasn't a primary concern. Computers operated as standalone machines, used mainly by universities, governments, and corporations for specialized tasks, limiting public access. Existing threats were primarily physical - unauthorized access altering or stealing data (Yost, 2017). The overview of the cyber security in the past is detailed in the table 2.

Table 2. Cybersecurity in the past

Time Period	Cybersecurity Landscape	Key Threats	Protective Measures
1970s	- Emergence of early computer networks	- Limited security awareness	- Basic password protection
	- Minimal internet connectivity	- Insider threats	- Physical security measures
	- Lack of standardized security measures		
1980s	- Growth of interconnected systems	- Malware, including viruses and worms	- Antivirus software
	- First computer viruses appear	- Unauthorized access and data breaches	- Firewall implementations
	- Password-based authentication		- Data encryption
1990s	- Internet adoption expands rapidly	- Cyber espionage and data theft	- Intrusion Detection Systems (IDS)
	- Proliferation of e-commerce	- DDoS attacks	- Increased focus on cybersecurity awareness
	- Advancements in encryption	- Social engineering attacks	- Secure Socket Layer (SSL) for secure browsing
2000s	- Rise of social media and cloud computing	- Advanced persistent threats (APTs)	- Network Access Control (NAC)
	- Increase in cybercrime and data breaches	- Phishing attacks	- Cybersecurity certifications and training
	- Mobile device proliferation	- Exploitation of software vulnerabilities	- Two-factor authentication
2010s	- Sophistication of cyber threats	- Ransomware attacks	- Security Information and Event Management (SIEM)
	- Internet of Things (IoT) connectivity	- State-sponsored cyber attacks	- Advanced Endpoint Protection
	- Growing concern over data privacy		- Incident Response Planning and Testing

With the internet's emergence in the late 1980s and early 1990s, computers interconnected, enabling global information sharing and transforming work and communication. However, this connectivity brought new vulnerabilities and cyber threats. Initial cybersecurity was reactive, fixing issues as they arose due to the novelty of threats. Early efforts focused on securing network perimeters, employing firewalls to monitor and control traffic. Authentication relied on passwords, but they proved weak as cybercriminals found ways to guess or steal them. As technology advanced, cyber threats evolved, with hackers exploiting software vulnerabilities and creating sophisticated phishing attacks and malware. This era marked a transition to proactive cybersecurity, anticipating threats and implementing preventive measures. Modern cybersecurity practices emerged, shaping the field today.

2. 2. Cybersecurity Today

In today's era, cybersecurity holds paramount importance, propelled by the escalating complexity of threats, global business operations, and the ubiquity of technology. The threats now range from individual hackers exploiting systems to state-sponsored cyberattacks causing significant economic and political repercussions (Burton et al., 2020). The current overview of the cybersecurity today is detailed in the table 3.

While prevention remains integral, detection and response have emerged as key components in cybersecurity strategies. The advent of new technologies such as cloud computing and the Internet of Things (IoT) has introduced new vulnerabilities along with potential opportunities (Hashizume et al., 2013; Roman, Zhou, & Lopez, 2013).

Artificial Intelligence (AI) and machine learning are progressively utilized in enhancing threat prediction and detection. Similarly, behavioural analytics is employed to detect suspicious activities by analyzing user behaviour patterns (Buczak & Guven, 2016).

In a nutshell, the current cybersecurity landscape is intricate, with escalating threats on one side and technological advancements providing new protective tools on the other. Looking ahead, cybersecurity will continue its rapid evolution, responding to shifting threats and technological advancements.

2. 3. Predicted Trends in Cybersecurity and Their Implications

As the cybersecurity landscape continues to evolve, the integration of emerging technologies like quantum computing and artificial intelligence (AI) is anticipated to have profound impacts. These technological advancements offer both promise and challenge, transforming the way cybersecurity defences are strengthened and introducing novel threats that demand attention. The predicted trends in cybersecurity and their implication has been detailed in the table 4.

Table 3. Cybersecurity today

Topic	Current Challenges	Emerging Technologies	Best Practices
Cyber Threats	Sophisticated and targeted attacks	AI and Machine Learning	- Regular software updates
	Ransomware and extortion	Quantum Computing	- Strong password policies
	- Phishing and social engineering	- Internet of Things (IoT)	- Multi-factor authentication
		- Blockchain	- Employee cybersecurity training
		- Biometrics	
Security Solutions	- Endpoint protection	- Cloud Security	- Network segmentation and monitoring
	- Firewalls and intrusion detection	- Behavioural Analytics	- Encryption of sensitive data
	- Security Operations Center (SOC)	- Zero Trust Architecture	- Incident response planning and testing
	- Security Information and	- Next-generation antivirus	- Vendor risk assessment and management
	Event Management (SIEM)	- Secure Access Service Edge (SASE)	
Compliance &	- GDPR and data privacy regulations	- Homomorphic Encryption	- Regular security audits
Governance	- HIPAA, PCI DSS, and other standards	- Privacy-preserving technologies	- Data classification and access controls
	- Cybersecurity laws and policies	- Identity and Access Management	- Compliance with industry-specific regulations
	- Insider threats and data breaches		- Creating and enforcing cybersecurity policies and procedures

Table 4. Predicted trends in cybersecurity

Predicted Trends in Cybersecurity and Their Implications	Emerging Technologies	Roles	Implications
Quantum Computing	Unprecedented processing power	Enhancing cybersecurity defences	• Potential to break current encryption methods. • Necessitates the development of quantum-resistant encryption algorithms. • Urgent need for proactive response to safeguard data and information integrity
Artificial Intelligence (AI)	Real-time threat detection	Posing new threats	• Enables real-time threat detection and response. • Empowers proactive incident response. • Enhanced accuracy and speed in identifying potential attacks. • AI can be exploited for sophisticated cyber-attacks

Quantum computing, with its unprecedented processing power, presents an exciting opportunity for various industries, including cybersecurity. However, this power also raises concerns about potential vulnerabilities. Of particular concern is its capacity to disrupt current encryption methods, which form the bedrock of data protection. The sheer computational abilities of quantum computers, exemplified by algorithms like Shor's algorithm, have the potential to crack encryption keys that currently secure sensitive information. Consequently, there is a pressing need to develop quantum-resistant encryption algorithms that can withstand the computational prowess of quantum machines (Zhang, Jung, & Liu, 2019). This proactive response from the cybersecurity community is vital to safeguarding data and maintaining the confidentiality, integrity, and authenticity of information.

On the other hand, AI is proving to be a game-changer in the realm of cybersecurity. Its ability to process and analyse vast amounts of data in real-time equips cybersecurity professionals with powerful tools for threat detection and response. AI-driven security solutions excel at identifying anomalies and potential attacks with remarkable accuracy and speed, surpassing human capabilities alone. By swiftly identifying emerging threats, AI enhances incident response, allowing for a proactive defense posture in the face of cyber-attacks. However, this same potential that enables AI to protect digital ecosystems can also be exploited for malicious purposes. Adversaries can harness AI's automation and adaptability to launch sophisticated and targeted cyber-attacks with increased precision. These AI-driven attacks pose new challenges for defense mechanisms, as they can dynamically adjust their strategies in response to countermeasures, making them harder to detect and mitigate effectively.

To navigate the predicted trends in cybersecurity effectively, it is essential to strike a delicate balance between embracing the advantages of quantum computing and AI while acknowledging and mitigating their potential risks. Cybersecurity professionals and researchers must remain vigilant and agile, collaborating across disciplines to devise innovative strategies for securing digital infrastructures. Continuous research and development efforts are paramount in staying ahead of evolving threats and enhancing the resilience of cybersecurity defenses. Moreover, fostering international cooperation and coordinated efforts among governments, organizations, and industry stakeholders is crucial to address global cybersecurity challenges and ensure the protection of our increasingly interconnected digital world. By anticipating and adapting to these trends, the cybersecurity community can better prepare for the dynamic future of digital security and safeguard against emerging threats.

3. KEY ELEMENTS OF THE CYBERSECURITY LANDSCAPE

To better understand the current state of cybersecurity, it's important to grasp its core elements: threat actors, cyber threats, cybersecurity technologies and tools, and cybersecurity policies and regulations.

3. 1. Threat Actors

Threat actors are entities that carry out cyber-attacks. They have diverse motivations, including financial gain, political beliefs, or simply causing disruption. They range from individual hobbyists to organized crime groups, and state-sponsored actors.

- Hackers: Hackers are individuals skilled in exploiting weaknesses in computer systems and networks. They vary widely in their motivations and objectives. Some hackers, known as "black hat hackers," engage in malicious activities for personal or financial gain. In contrast, "white hat hackers," or ethical hackers, use their skills to find and fix security vulnerabilities (Soares, L. F., Fernandes, D. A., Gomes, 2014).
- Insiders: Insiders, such as employees or contractors, have legitimate access to an organization's information systems and pose a significant cybersecurity risk. Insider threats can be intentional (e.g., disgruntled employees) or unintentional (e.g., employees falling victim to phishing attacks or mistakenly disclosing sensitive information) (Probst, Hunker, Gollmann, & Bishop, 2009).
- State-Sponsored Actors: State-sponsored actors are backed by governments and engage in cyber warfare or cyber espionage. They are usually highly skilled and well-funded, making them capable of carrying out sophisticated attacks on a large scale (Shakarian, Shakarian, & Ruef, 2013).
- Non-State Groups: Non-state groups include terrorist organizations and hacktivist groups. They may use cyber-attacks to cause disruption, push political or ideological agendas, or carry out cyber-terrorism (Conway, 2007).

3. 2. Cyber Threats

Cyber threats are potential dangers to digital assets, including data, systems, and networks. Here, we discuss some of the most common types of cyber threats.

- Malware: Malware is any malicious software used to disrupt computer operations, gather sensitive information, or gain unauthorized access to systems. It includes viruses, worms, trojan horses, ransomware, spyware, adware, and botnets (Singh, 2023).

- Phishing: Phishing is a type of cyber-attack where attackers impersonate legitimate organizations in emails, messages, or other communication platforms to trick victims into revealing sensitive information, such as passwords or credit card numbers (Jagatic, Johnson, Jakobsson, & Menczer, 2007).
- Man-in-the-middle attacks: In man-in-the-middle attacks, the attacker secretly intercepts and potentially alters the communication between two parties who believe they are directly communicating with each other (De la Hoz et al. (2014)).
- Denial of Service (DoS) attacks: DoS attacks aim to make a machine or network resource. unavailable to its intended users by temporarily or indefinitely disrupting services. These attacks often involve overwhelming the target with a flood of internet traffic (Mirkovic & Reiher,2004).

Advanced Persistent Threats (APTs): APTs are long-term targeted attacks where attackers gain unauthorized access to a network and remain undetected for an extended period. They are typically carried out by state-sponsored actors aiming at stealing information rather than causing damage (Scarfone et al. 2007).

- In the following subsections, we will delve into the tools and technologies used to combat these threats, as well as the relevant policies and regulations governing cybersecurity.

3. 3. Cybersecurity Technologies and Tools

Cybersecurity technologies and tools are employed to protect systems and data from cyber threats. They are an integral part of an organization's cybersecurity strategy. The overview of the cyber security technologies and tools, and the purpose is detailed in the table 5, and figure 4.

- Firewalls: Firewalls are network security devices that monitor, and control incoming and outgoing network traffic based on predetermined security rules. They establish a barrier between secured and controlled internal networks and untrusted external networks, such as the internet (Kshirsagar et al., 2012).
- Intrusion Detection Systems (IDS) are designed to detect suspicious activity within a network. They monitor network traffic or system behaviour for malicious activities or policy violations and produce reports to a management station (Scarfone & Mell, 2007).

Table 5. Cybersecurity technologies and tools

Technology/Tool	Purpose
Firewalls	Protects the network by controlling internet traffic to and from a network or specific devices. They create a barrier between secured internal networks and untrusted external networks.
Intrusion Detection Systems (IDS)	Monitors a network or systems for malicious activities or policy violations and reports to a management station.
Antivirus software	Protects a computer system from malicious software, including viruses, worms, trojans, ransomware, and spyware. It works by comparing a database of known malware signatures with files on a computer or network to identify threats.
Encryption	Protects information by converting it into an unreadable code that can only be read with a key. Used to protect data in transit and at rest.
General Data Protection Regulation (GDPR)	A regulation in EU law on data protection and privacy for all individual citizens of the European Union and the European Economic Area.
California Consumer Privacy Act (CCPA)	A state statute intended to enhance privacy rights and consumer protection for residents of California, United States.
Payment Card Industry Data Security Standard (PCI DSS)	An information security standard for organizations that handle branded credit cards from the major card schemes. It is intended to decrease payment card fraud across the internet and increase cardholder data protection.
Virtual Private Network (VPN)	Provides a secure connection to a network over the internet, shielding your browsing activity from prying eyes on public Wi-Fi, and more.
Multi-Factor Authentication (MFA)	Adds an additional layer of security by requiring multiple methods of verification.
Security Information and Event Management (SIEM)	Provides real-time analysis of security alerts generated by applications and network hardware.
Email Security Solutions	Protect email accounts and content from cyber threats and attacks.
Network Segmentation	Separates a network into multiple segments, allowing each to be managed and controlled independently.
Data Loss Prevention (DLP)	Ensures that end users do not send sensitive or critical information outside the corporate network.
AI and Machine Learning	Automates the detection of threats and combats them, predicting new and emerging threats based on data analysis.

- Antivirus software: Antivirus software is used to prevent, detect, and remove malware, including viruses, trojans, worms, spyware, and more. It typically works by comparing a database of known malware signatures with files on a computer or network to identify threats (Hansman & Hunt, 2005).
- Encryption: Encryption is a process that transforms readable data (plaintext) into an unreadable format (ciphertext) to prevent unauthorized access. Only those who possess the decryption key can convert the data back into its original form. It is widely used to protect sensitive information in transit and at rest (Abd Elminaam et al., 2008).

Figure 4. Cybersecurity technologies and tools

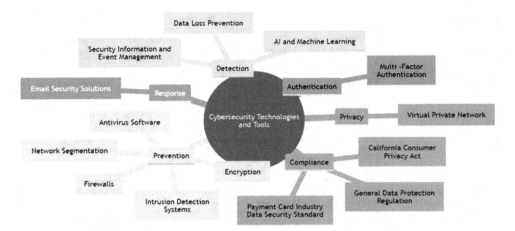

- Cybersecurity Policies and Regulations: Policies and regulations in cybersecurity provide guidelines and rules to protect personal and sensitive information. They are designed to prevent misuse, unauthorized access, and disruptions to computer networks.
- General Data Protection Regulation (GDPR): The General Data Protection Regulation (GDPR) is a regulation in EU law on data protection and privacy for all individual citizens of the European Union and the European Economic Area. It also addresses the transfer of personal data outside the EU and EEA areas (Voigt & Von dem Bussche, 2017).
- California Consumer Privacy Act (CCPA): The California Consumer Privacy Act (CCPA) is a state statute intended to enhance privacy rights and consumer protection for residents of California, United States. It has been described as the most comprehensive privacy legislation in the United States (Pollman & Barry, 2016).
- Payment Card Industry Data Security Standard (PCI DSS): The Payment Card Industry Data Security Standard (PCI DSS) is an information security standard for organizations that handle branded credit cards from the major card schemes. It is intended to decrease payment card fraud across the internet and increase cardholder data protection (Ali, Warren, & Mathiassen, 2017).

4. COMPARATIVE ANALYSIS OF DIFFERENT CYBERSECURITY APPROACHES

Understanding the effectiveness of different cybersecurity approaches is critical for developing a comprehensive cybersecurity strategy. This section provides a comparative analysis of the various cybersecurity technologies and strategies discussed earlier, along with a table illustrating their pros and cons.

Furthermore, the effectiveness of these technologies and strategies can vary based on the type of threat they are mitigating. For example, firewalls and IDS are effective tools for preventing DoS attacks, while encryption is vital for protecting data integrity during a man-in-the-middle attack. Antivirus software, on the other hand, is particularly effective against malware attacks but might struggle with APTs that use new or unrecognized malware.

Table 6. Pros and cons of different cybersecurity technologies and strategies

Approach	Pros	Cons
Firewalls	Able to filter network traffic and block unauthorized access	May not detect internal threats; unable to filter encrypted traffic
Intrusion Detection Systems (IDS)	Effective at detecting known threats; Provides real-time monitoring	Limited effectiveness against zero-day threats; can generate false positives
Antivirus Software	Good at identifying and removing known malware	Often ineffective against new, unknown malware variants
Encryption	Provides strong data protection; Ensures data integrity and confidentiality	Can be resource-intensive; encrypted traffic can still hide threats
VPN	Provides secure remote access; Can mask IP address	Can be slow; might not encrypt all traffic if not configured properly
Multi-Factor Authentication (MFA)	Adds an extra layer of security; Reduces risk of password breaches	Can be inconvenient for users; might not protect against phishing attacks
SIEM	Gives comprehensive view of security posture; Helps with regulatory compliance	Can be complex and costly to implement; Requires expertise to analyze data
Email Security Solutions	Protects against phishing, spam, and malware	May not catch all malicious emails; can occasionally filter out legitimate emails
Network Segmentation	Reduces attack surface; Can contain breaches within a segment	Can be complex to manage; Requires careful planning and implementation
Data Loss Prevention (DLP)	Protects sensitive data; Helps with regulatory compliance	Can produce false positives; requires regular updates of policies
AI and Machine Learning	Proactive threat detection; Can predict and identify threats	Depends on quality of training data; May not catch all types of threats

5. CASE STUDIES OF MAJOR CYBER ATTACKS

Real-world examples of cyber-attacks provide valuable insights into the tactics used by threat actors, the vulnerabilities they exploit, and the defensive measures that can be effective in mitigating these threats. Here are three case studies of major cyber-attacks.

- WannaCry Ransomware Attack: In May 2017, the world bore witness to one of the most widespread cyber-attacks in history: the WannaCry ransomware attack. This insidious attack paralyzed more than 200,000 computers in 150 countries, causing enormous economic and operational disruptions. The ransomware exploited a Windows vulnerability known as EternalBlue, which was leaked online by a hacker group dubbed The Shadow Brokers. Once the ransomware infiltrated a system, it encrypted all accessible files, effectively holding them hostage. Victims were greeted with a ransom note demanding payment in Bitcoin in exchange for the decryption key. High-profile victims included Britain's National Health Service, telecom companies, and major corporations, underlining the severity and global reach of this cyber threat. Despite a patch being available prior to the attack, its effectiveness was undermined by the tardiness or lack of its application by organizations, highlighting the importance of prompt patch management in cybersecurity (O'Kane, 2018).
- Equifax Data Breach: Equifax, one of the three largest consumer credit reporting agencies in the United States, fell victim to a massive data breach

Table 7.

Case Study	Year	Affected Entities	Impact	Cause
WannaCry Ransomware Attack	2017	200,000+ computers across 150 countries	Data encrypted; ransom demanded	Exploitation of Windows vulnerability 'EternalBlue'
Equifax Data Breach	2017	Approximately 147 million people	Sensitive information like social security numbers, birth dates, and addresses were accessed	Failure to patch a vulnerability in the Apache Struts web application framework
SolarWinds Hack	2020	Thousands of companies and government organizations worldwide, including several parts of the U.S. federal government	Access to networks gained; supply chain vulnerabilities exposed	Compromise of SolarWinds' Orion software

in September 2017. The breach had far-reaching consequences, affecting approximately 147 million people. Hackers exploited a vulnerability in the Apache Struts web application framework, which Equifax had not yet patched, to access sensitive information. The stolen data included social security numbers, birth dates, and addresses—information that could be used for a myriad of fraudulent activities, including identity theft. The breach resulted in a significant financial loss for Equifax and severely damaged its reputation. The aftermath of the breach demonstrated the importance of regularly updating and patching software, and the potentially catastrophic consequences of failing to do so (Biener et al., 2015).

- SolarWinds Hack: The SolarWinds hack, disclosed in December 2020, was a high-profile supply chain attack that struck at the heart of public and private organizations worldwide, including major parts of the U.S. federal government. The cyber threat actors orchestrated a sophisticated campaign in which they compromised SolarWinds' Orion software—a platform used by thousands of firms for IT resource monitoring and management. The attackers were then able to gain access to the networks of organizations using the compromised software. The SolarWinds hack emphasized the potential risks associated with supply chain vulnerabilities and laid bare the complexities in defending against state-sponsored cyber threats, thought to be backed by Russia. The attack had significant implications for cybersecurity, highlighting the need for a robust, coordinated response to defend against such high-level threats (Perlroth, 2021).

6. THE ROLE OF HUMAN FACTOR IN CYBERSECURITY

In addition to technological approaches, the human factor plays a significant role in the cybersecurity landscape. This section explores the importance of cybersecurity training and the psychology behind social engineering attacks.

The Importance of Cybersecurity Training: While having advanced cybersecurity technologies in place is critical, they can be undermined if users lack the awareness or knowledge to use them effectively or if they fall victim to social engineering attacks. Cybersecurity training is thus crucial for empowering users with the knowledge and skills to identify and react to cybersecurity threats. Training can help users understand the value of the data they interact with and the potential consequences if it is compromised. Additionally, it can teach users safe online behaviors, such as how to create and manage strong passwords, how to identify and avoid phishing emails, and when to apply security patches and updates (Parsons, McCormac, Butavicius, Pattinson, & Jerram, 2014).

Table 8.

Role/Aspect	Description	Impact
User Awareness	The degree to which users are aware of cybersecurity threats and best practices.	Higher awareness can reduce the likelihood of falling victim to cyber-attacks like phishing or social engineering.
Employee Training	The extent and quality of cybersecurity training provided to employees.	Proper training can empower employees to recognize and respond appropriately to cyber threats, reducing risk.
Password Practices	The habits of users in creating, storing, and updating passwords.	Strong password practices are a basic, yet critical line of defence against unauthorized access.
Compliance with Policies	Adherence to organization's cybersecurity policies and guidelines.	Non-compliance can result in vulnerabilities being introduced into systems and networks, increasing risk.
User Actions/ Behavior	The everyday actions taken by users that can either protect or expose networks and systems.	Careless or uninformed behaviors (e.g., clicking on suspicious links, using unsecured networks) can greatly increase cybersecurity risk.
Reporting	Willingness and ability of users to report suspicious activities.	Timely reporting can help in rapid identification and mitigation of cyber threats.

Psychology of Social Engineering Attacks: Social engineering attacks manipulate individuals into revealing sensitive information or performing actions that compromise cybersecurity. The psychology behind these attacks often involves exploiting individuals' natural tendencies and cognitive biases. For example, phishing emails often create a sense of urgency (e.g., warning of account suspension) to provoke immediate, less-considered actions. Similarly, pretexting involves creating a false scenario (e.g., posing as IT support) to gain the victim's trust and cooperation. Understanding these psychological tricks can aid in designing more effective cybersecurity training and policies (Hadnagy & Fincher, 2015).

7. CONCLUSION

As we have explored in this chapter, cybersecurity is an increasingly important concern in our digital society. From the evolution of cybersecurity practices to the broad landscape of threats, actors, technologies, and policies, cybersecurity is a complex and multi-faceted field.

The examples of major cyber-attacks we discussed underscore the severity and far-reaching impacts of these threats. These cases demonstrate that no organization is immune to cyber threats, and that both technological defences and human factors play critical roles in maintaining cybersecurity.

Looking towards the future, we can expect the cybersecurity landscape to continue evolving as new technologies emerge and threat actors devise new tactics. Several trends appear likely: the continued growth of state-sponsored cyber warfare, the increasing importance of AI and machine learning in both cyber-attacks and defences, and the ongoing struggle to balance privacy and security in the face of growing data collection and surveillance.

Ultimately, the field of cybersecurity will need to continually adapt and innovate to address these challenges. Through a combination of technological advancements, effective regulations and policies, comprehensive training programs, and international cooperation, it is possible to build a safer and more secure digital world.

REFERENCES

Abd Elminaam, D. S., Abdual-Kader, H. M., & Hadhoud, M. M. (2010). Evaluating The Performance of Symmetric Encryption Algorithms. *International Journal of Network Security*, *10*(3), 216–222.

Aitzhan, N. Z., & Svetinovic, D. (2016). Security and privacy in decentralized energy trading through multi-signatures, blockchain and anonymous messaging streams. *IEEE Transactions on Dependable and Secure Computing*, *15*(5), 840–852. doi:10.1109/TDSC.2016.2616861

Ali, A., Warren, D., & Mathiassen, L. (2017). Cloud-based business services innovation: A risk management model. *International Journal of Information Management*, *37*(6), 639–649. doi:10.1016/j.ijinfomgt.2017.05.008

Biener, C., Eling, M., & Wirfs, J. H. (2015). Insurability of cyber risk: An empirical analysis. *The Geneva Papers on Risk and Insurance. Issues and Practice*, *40*(1), 131–158. doi:10.1057/gpp.2014.19

Bodin, L., Gordon, L. A., & Loeb, M. P. (2008). Information security and risk management. *Communications of the ACM*, *51*(4), 64–68. doi:10.1145/1330311.1330325

Buczak, A. L., & Guven, E. (2015). A survey of data mining and machine learning methods for cyber security intrusion detection. *IEEE Communications Surveys and Tutorials*, *18*(2), 1153–1176. doi:10.1109/COMST.2015.2494502

Burton, J., & Christou, G. (2021). Bridging the gap between cyberwar and cyberpeace. *International Affairs*, *97*(6), 1727–1747. doi:10.1093/ia/iiab172

Conway, M. (2006). Terrorism and the Internet: New media—New threat? *Parliamentary Affairs*, *59*(2), 283–298. doi:10.1093/pa/gsl009

De la Hoz, E., Cochrane, G., Moreira-Lemus, J. M., Paez-Reyes, R., Marsa-Maestre, I., & Alarcos, B. (2014, June). Detecting and defeating advanced man-in-the-middle attacks against TLS. In *2014 6th International Conference On Cyber Conflict (CyCon 2014)* (pp. 209-221). IEEE. 10.1109/CYCON.2014.6916404

Hadnagy, C., & Fincher, M. (2015). *Phishing dark waters: The offensive and defensive sides of malicious Emails*. John Wiley & Sons. doi:10.1002/9781119183624

Hansman, S., & Hunt, R. (2005). A taxonomy of network and computer attacks. *Computers & Security*, *24*(1), 31–43. doi:10.1016/j.cose.2004.06.011

Hashizume, K., Rosado, D. G., Fernández-Medina, E., & Fernandez, E. B. (2013). An analysis of security issues for cloud computing. *Journal of Internet Services and Applications*, *4*(1), 1–13. doi:10.1186/1869-0238-4-5

Jagatic, T. N., Johnson, N. A., Jakobsson, M., & Menczer, F. (2007). Social phishing. *Communications of the ACM*, *50*(10), 94–100. doi:10.1145/1290958.1290968

Kshirsagar, V. K., Tidke, S. M., & Vishnu, S. (2012). Intrusion detection system using genetic algorithm and data mining: An overview. [PRINT]. *International Journal of Computer Science and Informatics ISSN*, *2231*(5292), 118–122. doi:10.47893/IJCSI.2012.1076

Mirkovic, J., & Reiher, P. (2004). A taxonomy of DDoS attack and DDoS defense mechanisms. *Computer Communication Review*, *34*(2), 39–53. doi:10.1145/997150.997156

O'Kane, P., Sezer, S., & Carlin, D. (2018). Evolution of ransomware. *IET Networks*, *7*(5), 321–327. doi:10.1049/iet-net.2017.0207

Parsons, K., McCormac, A., Butavicius, M., Pattinson, M., & Jerram, C. (2014). Determining employee awareness using the human aspects of information security questionnaire (HAIS-Q). *Computers & Security*, *42*, 165–176. doi:10.1016/j.cose.2013.12.003

Perlroth, N. (2021). *This is how they tell me the world ends: The cyberweapons arms race*. Bloomsbury Publishing USA.

Pollman, E., & Barry, J. M. (2016). Regulatory entrepreneurship. *S. Cal. L. Rev.*, *90*, 383.

Probst, C. W., Hunker, J., Bishop, M., & Gollmann, D. (Eds.). (2010). *Insider threats in cyber security* (Vol. 49). Springer Science & Business Media. doi:10.1007/978-1-4419-7133-3_1

Romanosky, S. (2016). Examining the costs and causes of cyber incidents. *Journal of Cybersecurity, 2*(2), 121-135.

Scarfone, K., & Mell, P. (2007). Guide to intrusion detection and prevention systems (idps). *NIST special publication, 800*(2007), 94.

Scarfone, K., & Mell, P. (2007). Guide to intrusion detection and prevention systems (idps). *NIST special publication, 800*(2007), 94.

Shakarian, P., Shakarian, J., & Ruef, A. (2013). *Introduction to cyber-warfare: A multidisciplinary approach*. Newnes.

Singh, A., & Patel, N. D. (2023). Security Issues, Attacks and Countermeasures in Layered IoT Ecosystem. *International Journal of Next-Generation Computing*.

Soares, L. F., Fernandes, D. A., Gomes, J. V., Freire, M. M., & Inácio, P. R. (2014). Cloud security: state of the art. *Security, Privacy and Trust in Cloud Systems*. Insiders.

Voigt, P., & Von dem Bussche, A. (2017). The eu general data protection regulation (gdpr). A Practical Guide, 1st Ed., Cham: Springer International Publishing, 10(3152676), 10-5555.

Von Solms, R., & Van Niekerk, J. (2013). From information security to cyber security. *Computers & Security, 38*, 97-102.

Yost, J. R. (2017). *Making IT Work: A History of the Computer Services Industry*. MIT Press. doi:10.7551/mitpress/9375.001.0001

Chapter 2
Foundation of Malware Analysis and Detection

Manoj Kumar M. V.
iD https://orcid.org/0000-0002-9848-6234
Department of Information Science and Engineering, NITTE Meenakshi Institute of Technology, Bengaluru, India

S. L. Shiva Darshan
Department of Information Technology, Manipal Institute of Technology Bengaluru, Manipal Academy of Higher Education, Manipal, India

Prashanth B. S.
iD https://orcid.org/0000-0003-4539-662X
Department of Information Science and Engineering, NITTE Meenakshi Institute of Technology, Bengaluru, India

Vishnu Yarlagadda
iD https://orcid.org/0000-0001-6146-5272
Department of Information Technology, Manipal Institute of Technology Bengaluru, Manipal Academy of Higher Education, Manipal, India

ABSTRACT

In today's interconnected digital world, the threat of malware looms large, posing significant risks to individuals, businesses, and governments. This chapter serves as a comprehensive introduction to the critical field of malware analysis and detection. The chapter begins with a definition of malware, exploring its various forms and the historical perspective of its evolution. The authors delve into the different types of malware, including viruses, worms, Trojans, ransomware, and more, understanding their unique behaviors and propagation methods. Building upon this foundation, they introduce the fundamental concepts of malware analysis methodologies, including static and dynamic analysis, reverse engineering, virtualization, and sandboxing.

DOI: 10.4018/978-1-6684-8666-5.ch002

These techniques enable cybersecurity professionals to gain insights into malware behavior and functionality. To address this challenge, the chapter introduces advanced malware analysis techniques, such as memory forensics, behavioral analysis, kernel-level rootkit detection, and machine learning-based analysis.

1. INTRODUCTION

In today's digital age, the rapid growth of technology has brought about immense benefits and conveniences. However, it has also given rise to a darker side of computing - the ever-present threat of malware. Malicious software, commonly known as malware, poses a significant risk to individuals, businesses, and governments alike, causing data breaches, financial losses, and disrupting critical infrastructure [1]. As cybercriminals continually evolve their techniques, understanding and effectively countering malware has become a paramount concern for cybersecurity professionals.

This chapter serves as an essential starting point for comprehending the complex world of malware analysis and detection. It lays the groundwork for exploring the techniques and strategies employed by cybersecurity experts to identify, analyze, and mitigate malware threats.

1.1 Definition of Malware

Before delving into the depths of malware analysis, it is essential to define precisely what constitutes malware. Malware, short for malicious software, refers to any program or code intentionally designed to compromise the integrity, confidentiality, or availability of computer systems, networks, and data [2]. Malware encompasses a wide range of harmful software, including viruses, worms, Trojans, ransomware, adware, spyware, and more. Understanding the various forms of malware is crucial for distinguishing their behaviors and characteristics during analysis.

1.2 The Evolving Landscape of Malware

Malware has a long and storied history, evolving alongside advancements in technology and computing. Early malware was often relatively simple, spreading through infected floppy disks and email attachments [3]. However, as the internet became ubiquitous, malware became more sophisticated and distributed, exploiting various attack vectors, such as social engineering, drive-by downloads, and malicious links. Figure 1 shows the evolution of malware over last five years. This section provides a historical perspective on malware, highlighting significant events and developments that shaped the modern threat landscape.

Figure 1. Evolution of different types of malwares in India over the last five years (2018-2022)

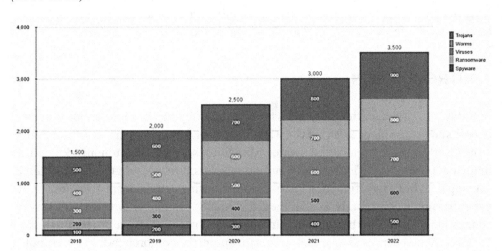

1.3 The Impact of Malware

The impact of malware attacks can be severe, both for individuals and organizations. From financial losses and identity theft to widespread data breaches and large-scale disruptions, the consequences of malware can be far-reaching. This section examines real-world examples of notable malware incidents and their aftermath to illustrate the urgency of implementing effective malware analysis and detection measures [4].

1.4 The Need for Malware Analysis and Detection

As the capabilities of malware continue to advance, traditional security measures alone are often insufficient to thwart these threats. This section emphasizes the critical need for malware analysis and detection methodologies as proactive approaches to identifying and combating malicious software. By gaining insights into how malware operates, security professionals can develop effective countermeasures and strengthen overall cybersecurity defenses.

2. TYPES OF MALWARE

Malware comes in various forms, each with its own distinctive characteristics and malicious objectives. Understanding the different types of malware is crucial for effective analysis and detection. In this chapter, we explore the most common categories of malware and their specific behaviors [5].

2.1 Viruses

Definition and Characteristics: Viruses are self-replicating programs that attach themselves to legitimate files or programs. They spread by infecting other files, and when these infected files are executed, the virus activates and continues its propagation. Viruses can cause damage by corrupting or destroying data, slowing down system performance, and disrupting operations.

Infection Methods: Viruses typically spread through infected email attachments, file-sharing networks, or compromised websites.

2.2 Worms

Definition and Characteristics: Worms are standalone malicious programs capable of self-replication and spreading across networks without requiring a host file. They exploit vulnerabilities in network services to propagate rapidly from one system to another. Worms can consume network bandwidth, overload systems, and create botnets for further malicious activities.

Infection Methods: Worms spread by exploiting network vulnerabilities, email attachments, and removable media.

2.3 Trojans (Trojan Horses)

Definition and Characteristics: Trojans are deceptive programs disguised as legitimate software, tricking users into installing them. Unlike viruses and worms, Trojans do not self-replicate. Instead, they provide a backdoor for attackers to gain unauthorized access to the victim's system, steal sensitive information, or carry out other malicious activities.

Infection Methods: Trojans are often distributed through deceptive social engineering techniques, such as fake software updates or cracked software downloads.

2.4 Ransomware

Definition and Characteristics: Ransomware is a type of malware that encrypts the victim's files or locks them out of their system, rendering the data inaccessible. The attackers demand a ransom from the victim in exchange for the decryption key, coercing victims to pay to regain access to their data.

Infection Methods: Ransomware commonly spreads through malicious email attachments, exploit kits, and compromised websites.

2.5 Spyware

Definition and Characteristics: Spyware is designed to stealthily monitor and collect information about the victim's activities without their knowledge or consent. It can track web browsing habits, capture keystrokes, and record sensitive data, which is then transmitted to the attacker.

Infection Methods: Spyware often piggybacks on seemingly benign software downloads or is distributed through malicious websites.

2.6 Adware

Definition and Characteristics: Adware is a type of malware that displays unwanted advertisements on the victim's computer. While not as malicious as other types of malware, adware can be intrusive and negatively impact the user experience.

Infection Methods: Adware is typically bundled with free software, and users unknowingly install it during the installation process.

2.7 Rootkits

Definition and Characteristics: Rootkits are designed to conceal the presence of other malware or unauthorized access on a system. They operate at the kernel level, making them extremely difficult to detect by traditional antivirus software.

Infection Methods: Rootkits are often installed through Trojans or exploit vulnerabilities to gain kernel-level access.

2.8 Botnets

Definition and Characteristics: Botnets are networks of compromised computers (often referred to as "bots" or "zombies") under the control of a malicious actor. These bots can be remotely controlled to carry out coordinated attacks, send spam emails, or engage in distributed denial-of-service (DDoS) attacks.

Infection Methods: Botnets are created by infecting computers with malware, such as worms or Trojans, that enable the attacker to control them remotely.

Understanding the characteristics and behaviors of these different types of malware is essential for implementing effective detection and mitigation strategies as illustrated in Table 1.

Table 1. Impact of different malware with examples of their effect in recent time

Malware Type	Hypothetical Impact	Example
Trojans	Trojans can provide a backdoor to your system, allowing an attacker to access and control your computer.	In 2022, a large corporation in the United States was compromised by a Trojan, leading to the theft of sensitive customer data.
Worms	Worms can replicate themselves and spread to other computers in a network, causing widespread damage.	In 2021, a worm spread through a government network in Germany, causing system slowdowns and disruptions in service.
Viruses	Viruses can corrupt or delete files on your computer, and can spread to other computers via email attachments or insecure downloads.	In 2020, a virus spread through an email attachment infected thousands of personal computers in Australia, leading to loss of personal data.
Ransomware	Ransomware can encrypt your files and demand a ransom to decrypt them.	In 2022, a major hospital in the UK was hit by a ransomware attack, causing significant disruption to their operations until the ransom was paid.
Spyware	Spyware can monitor your activities on your computer and send this information to an attacker.	In 2019, a spyware attack on a telecommunications company in Canada led to the theft of user data, including call records and text messages.

3. MALWARE BEHAVIOR AND CAPABILITIES

Malware is designed to carry out a range of malicious activities with the intent of compromising the security and integrity of computer systems and data. Understanding the behavior and capabilities of malware is essential for effective analysis, detection, and mitigation. In this chapter, we explore the common behaviors exhibited by malware and the various capabilities it possesses. Table 2 differences between Windows and Linux malware based on the malicious activities and its behaviours [6].

3.1 Payload Execution

Description: Payload execution is the primary objective of most malware. Once a system is infected, the malware deploys its payload, which may include activities such as data theft, system manipulation, or further propagation.

Examples: A ransomware payload encrypts files on the victim's system, demanding a ransom for decryption. A botnet payload may include instructions to carry out DDoS attacks on specific targets.

3.2 Data Exfiltration

Description: Malware often attempts to exfiltrate sensitive data from the infected system, which can include personal information, financial data, intellectual property, or login credentials.

Examples: Spyware captures keystrokes, screenshots, or audio recordings to steal login credentials or other sensitive information. Advanced persistent threats (APTs) focus on stealthily exfiltrating valuable corporate data.

3.3 Remote Control and Command Execution

Description: Many types of malware establish a communication channel with a remote command and control (C&C) server, allowing attackers to control the infected system remotely.

Examples: Trojans and botnets can be remotely controlled to perform various tasks, such as sending spam emails, launching DDoS attacks, or downloading additional malware.

3.4 Privilege Escalation

Description: Some malware attempts to escalate its privileges on the infected system, gaining higher-level access to bypass security restrictions and install or execute more sophisticated payloads.

Examples: Rootkits and certain worms exploit vulnerabilities to gain administrative privileges, making it harder for security tools to detect and remove them.

3.5 Persistence Mechanisms

Description: To ensure long-term presence on the infected system, malware often employs persistence mechanisms, allowing it to survive system reboots and security measures.

Examples: Malware may create registry entries, startup scripts, or hidden files to ensure automatic execution on system boot.

3.6 Anti-Analysis Techniques

Description: Aware of the potential threat of analysis, many malware strains incorporate anti-analysis techniques to evade detection by security researchers and analysts.

Table 2. Representation of the differences between Windows and Linux malware

Aspect	Windows Malware	Linux Malware
Target Audience	Windows malware typically targets end-users, as Windows has a larger user base, especially in the consumer market.	Linux malware often targets servers, as Linux is widely used in server environments.
Propagation	Windows malware often spreads through email attachments, malicious downloads, and infected USB drives.	Linux malware often spreads by exploiting vulnerabilities in server software or through weak SSH credentials.
Payload	Windows malware can have a wide range of payloads, including ransomware, spyware, and Trojans.	Linux malware often includes backdoors, DDoS bots, and crypto miners.
Persistence	Windows malware often persists by modifying the registry or installing itself as a service.	Linux malware often persists by installing itself as a cron job or modifying system files.
Prevalence	Windows malware is more prevalent due to the larger user base of Windows.	Linux malware is less common but can be more sophisticated, given the nature of the systems it targets.

Examples: Malware may employ code obfuscation, encryption, or virtual machine detection to thwart analysis attempts.

3.7 Evasion and Anti-Detection

Description: To avoid detection by antivirus and security solutions, malware creators employ various evasion techniques to disguise their code and behavior.

Examples: Polymorphic malware changes its code structure with each infection, making it harder for signature-based detection to recognize it.

3.8 Self-Propagation

Description: Worms and other self-replicating malware possess the ability to spread autonomously across networks and systems, seeking new hosts to infect.

Examples: Email worms can distribute copies of themselves to the victim's contacts, while network worms exploit vulnerabilities to propagate within an organization's infrastructure.

3.9 Payload Triggering

Description: Some malware may lie dormant until specific conditions or triggers are met before executing its payload, making it harder to detect and analyze.

Examples: Malware might wait for a particular date, the presence of specific software, or user interactions before activating its malicious behavior.

By understanding the various behaviors and capabilities of malware, security professionals can better analyze and respond to potential threats effectively.

4. HOST-BASED MALWARE DETECTION

Host-based malware detection focuses on identifying and mitigating malware threats directly on individual computer systems or endpoints. This approach involves analyzing the behavior and characteristics of running processes, files, and system activities to detect and prevent malware infections [7]. In this chapter, we explore various host-based malware detection techniques and the tools used for effective endpoint security. Figure 2 shows an overview of Host Based Detection of Malware.

4.1 Antivirus Software

Description: Antivirus software is a fundamental tool for host-based malware detection. It uses signature-based detection to compare files and processes against a database of known malware signatures.

Functionality: When a file or process matches a known signature, the antivirus software quarantines or removes the threat from the system.

Figure 2. Overview of host based detection of malware

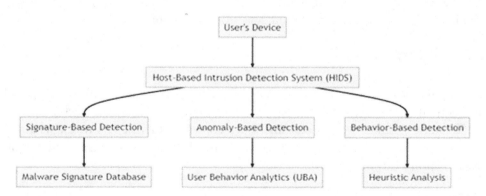

Table 3. Difference categories of malware detection their description strength and weakness

Category	Description	Strengths	Weaknesses
Signature-based Detection	Involves comparing a piece of code against a database of known malware signatures.	Fast and efficient. Highly accurate for known malware.	Can only detect known malware. Ineffective against new or modified malware.
Heuristic-based Detection	Involves analyzing the behavior or characteristics of a piece of code to determine if it is malicious.	Can detect new or modified malware that doesn't match any known signatures.	Can produce false positives. Less accurate than signature-based detection.
Behavioral-based Detection	Involves monitoring the behavior of applications and processes over time.	Can detect previously unknown malware based on suspicious behavior.	Requires significant system resources. Can produce false positives.
Sandbox Detection	Involves executing suspicious code in a safe, isolated environment and monitoring its behavior.	Can detect unknown malware by observing its behavior in a safe, isolated environment.	Can be circumvented by malware that detects when it's being run in a sandbox. Requires significant system resources.
Machine Learning-based Detection	Involves using machine learning algorithms to classify code as benign or malicious.	Can detect new and unknown malware by learning patterns that indicate malicious behavior.	Requires significant computational resources. Can produce false positives. Requires large datasets for training.

4.2 Heuristics-Based Detection

Description: Heuristics-based detection is an extension of signature-based detection, where antivirus software identifies potential malware based on suspicious behavioral patterns rather than exact signatures.

Functionality: Antivirus tools using heuristics can identify and block previously unknown malware that exhibits suspicious activities.

4.3 Behavior-Based Analysis

Description: Behavior-based analysis monitors the behavior of processes and applications on a system, looking for actions typical of malware, such as unauthorized data access or attempts to modify critical system files.

Functionality: By focusing on behavior, this approach can detect zero-day malware and previously unknown threats.

4.4 Sandboxing

Description: Sandboxing creates an isolated environment where suspicious files or processes can be executed without affecting the host system. This allows security analysts to observe the behavior of potential malware safely.

Functionality: By monitoring the actions of the sandboxed environment, analysts can determine if the file or process is malicious and take appropriate action.

4.5 Endpoint Detection and Response (EDR) Solutions

Description: EDR solutions provide real-time monitoring and response capabilities on endpoints. They collect and analyze data on system activities to detect and respond to potential threats.

Functionality: EDR tools offer a more proactive approach to host-based malware detection, allowing security teams to respond quickly to emerging threats and carry out incident response actions.

4.6 Memory Forensics

Description: Memory forensics involves analyzing the content of a system's memory to identify and investigate malicious activities that may not be visible in traditional file-based analysis.

Functionality: Memory forensics can reveal hidden malware, rootkits, and other sophisticated threats operating in the system's memory space.

4.7 Host Intrusion Detection Systems (HIDS)

Description: HIDS monitors system events and activities, looking for signs of intrusion or suspicious behavior that could indicate malware activity.

Functionality: When unusual or malicious activities are detected, HIDS generates alerts or takes automated actions to prevent further damage.

4.8 Application Whitelisting

Description: Application whitelisting allows only trusted and authorized applications to run on the system, effectively preventing unknown or unauthorized software, including malware, from executing.

Functionality: By limiting the execution of non-whitelisted applications, this approach reduces the attack surface for malware and other malicious software.

4.9 Host-Based Firewall

Description: A host-based firewall monitors incoming and outgoing network traffic on the system, controlling the data packets based on predefined rules.

Functionality: A well-configured host-based firewall can prevent unauthorized communication by malware and block attempts to exfiltrate data.

Host-based malware detection plays a critical role in protecting individual systems and endpoints from malware threats. By employing a combination of signature-based, behavior-based, and proactive detection methods, organizations can enhance their security posture and swiftly respond to emerging malware incidents. Table 3 represents the difference categories of malware detection their description strength and weakness.

5. ADVANCED MALWARE ANALYSIS TECHNIQUES

As malware creators continuously evolve their techniques to evade detection, advanced malware analysis techniques become indispensable for understanding and combating sophisticated threats [8]. In this chapter, we explore cutting-edge methods and tools used by cybersecurity professionals to gain deeper insights into malware behavior and uncover its hidden capabilities.

5.1 Analyzing Fileless Malware

Description: Fileless malware operates in memory, leaving little to no footprint on the disk. This type of malware is challenging to detect using traditional file-based analysis methods.

Techniques: Memory forensics, runtime analysis, and monitoring system API calls are essential for detecting and analyzing fileless malware.

5.2 Memory Forensics

Description: Memory forensics involves extracting and analyzing the content of a system's volatile memory (RAM) to identify malware, rootkits, and other malicious activities that may not be visible on the disk.

Techniques: Tools like Volatility and Rekall are used to analyze memory dumps and reveal hidden malware artifacts.

5.3 Behavioral Analysis on Host Systems

Description: Behavioral analysis observes and monitors the behavior of malware and its effects on the host system, focusing on actions that could indicate malicious intent.

Techniques: Sandbox environments, runtime analysis, and monitoring system calls help security analysts observe malware behavior and understand its impact on the system.

5.4 Kernel-Level Rootkit Detection

Description: Kernel-level rootkits operate at the core of an operating system, making them extremely difficult to detect and remove. Specialized techniques are required to identify and mitigate such threats.

Techniques: Kernel-level debugging, code analysis, and the use of specialized tools like GMER are essential for rootkit detection.

5.5 Dynamic Binary Instrumentation

Description: Dynamic binary instrumentation involves modifying the execution of a program during runtime to gather detailed information about its behavior.

Techniques: Tools like PIN and DynamoRIO are used to inject code into the execution flow of a program, providing insights into malware behavior.

5.6 Code Emulation and Sandboxing

Description: Code emulation and sandboxing techniques create isolated environments to execute and analyze suspicious code safely.

Techniques: Tools like Cuckoo Sandbox and Any.Run provide sandboxes for analyzing malware behavior without risking the host system.

5.7 Analyzing Packed and Obfuscated Malware

Description: Packed and obfuscated malware uses techniques to compress or scramble its code to evade traditional signature-based detection.

Techniques: Unpacking and deobfuscation techniques, such as static analysis and debugging, are used to reveal the original code and behavior of packed malware.

5.8 YARA Rules for Pattern Matching

Description: YARA is a powerful pattern matching tool used to identify and classify malware based on specific characteristics or signatures.

Techniques: Security analysts create custom YARA rules to detect known and emerging malware threats.

5.9 Machine Learning-Based Malware Analysis

Description: Machine learning algorithms are employed to analyze and classify malware based on patterns and behaviors learned from large datasets.

Techniques: Feature extraction, training machine learning models, and validating their accuracy are essential steps in machine learning-based malware analysis.

Advanced malware analysis techniques empower cybersecurity professionals to tackle the ever-evolving landscape of sophisticated threats. By combining traditional analysis methods with innovative approaches, security experts can gain a deeper understanding of malware behavior, enhance detection capabilities, and improve overall cybersecurity defense.

6. MALWARE INTELLIGENCE AND THREAT HUNTING

Malware intelligence and threat hunting play crucial roles in proactively identifying and mitigating emerging and sophisticated cyber threats [9]. In this chapter, we explore the concepts of threat intelligence, indicators of compromise (IOCs), and the strategies employed by cybersecurity professionals in threat hunting operations.

6.1 Threat Intelligence Sources

Description: Threat intelligence involves gathering and analyzing data from various sources to gain insights into emerging and existing cyber threats, including malware campaigns and threat actors.

Sources: Threat intelligence can be obtained from public repositories, security forums, dark web monitoring, vendor reports, and cybersecurity sharing communities.

6.2 Indicators of Compromise (IOCs)

Description: Indicators of Compromise are artifacts or evidence left behind by malware or threat actors during an attack. These IOCs can help identify malicious activities on compromised systems.

Types: IOCs can include IP addresses, domain names, file hashes, URLs, registry keys, and specific patterns in network traffic.

6.3 Threat Intelligence Platforms (TIPs)

Description: Threat Intelligence Platforms are tools that aggregate, analyze, and provide actionable insights from various threat intelligence sources. They aid in centralizing and automating threat intelligence operations.

Functionality: TIPs help security teams make informed decisions by correlating threat data with their organization's network and security infrastructure.

6.4 Proactive Threat Hunting Strategies

Description: Threat hunting involves actively searching for signs of malicious activity within an organization's network and endpoints, aiming to detect threats that may have evaded traditional security measures.

Techniques: Threat hunting leverages various tools, such as EDR solutions, SIEMs, network traffic analysis tools, and custom scripts, to identify anomalous behavior and potential security breaches.

6.5 Behavioral Analytics for Threat Hunting

Description: Behavioral analytics uses machine learning algorithms to establish baseline behaviors and detect deviations that could indicate suspicious or malicious activities.

Techniques: By analyzing vast amounts of data and establishing normal patterns, behavioral analytics can identify anomalies and potential security incidents.

6.6 Threat Intelligence Sharing

Description: Collaborative threat intelligence sharing involves exchanging threat data and insights among organizations and security communities to improve collective cybersecurity defenses.

Benefits: Sharing threat intelligence enables faster detection and response to emerging threats and helps others defend against similar attacks.

6.7 Cyber Threat Hunting Teams

Description: Cyber threat hunting teams are specialized groups within an organization dedicated to actively searching for and responding to advanced cyber threats.

Expertise: Threat hunting teams require a combination of cybersecurity expertise, knowledge of the organization's infrastructure, and an understanding of threat intelligence.

6.8 Incident Response and Threat Mitigation

Description: Incident response is the process of handling and mitigating cybersecurity incidents, including malware infections and other security breaches.

Techniques: Effective incident response involves containing the threat, identifying the extent of the compromise, eradicating the malware, and implementing measures to prevent similar incidents in the future.

Threat intelligence and proactive threat hunting are essential components of a robust cybersecurity strategy. By staying informed about the latest threats and actively seeking out potential risks, organizations can better defend against sophisticated malware attacks.

7. MACHINE LEARNING AND ARTIFICIAL INTELLIGENCE IN MALWARE ANALYSIS AND DETECTION

Machine learning and artificial intelligence (AI) have revolutionized the field of cybersecurity, particularly in malware analysis and detection [10-12]. In this chapter, we explore the advanced role of machine learning and AI in enhancing the effectiveness of malware analysis and detection techniques. Figure 3 illustrates the Machine Learning and AI in malware analysis and detection.

7.1 The Role of Machine Learning in Malware Analysis

Feature Extraction: Machine learning models require well-defined features to distinguish between normal and malicious files. This section explores various feature extraction techniques used in malware analysis.

Figure 3. Machine learning and AI in malware analysis and detection

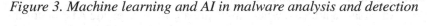
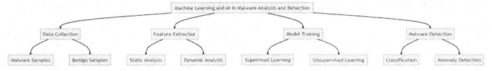

Supervised Learning: Machine learning algorithms can be trained on labeled datasets, allowing them to classify malware based on known characteristics and attributes.

Unsupervised Learning: Unsupervised learning methods help detect previously unknown patterns and anomalies, enabling the identification of novel and emerging malware threats.

7.2 Leveraging AI for Malware Detection

Behavioral Analysis: AI-driven systems can observe and learn from malware behavior, detecting patterns and deviations indicative of malicious activities [13].

Real-time Threat Detection: AI algorithms can rapidly process vast amounts of data, enabling real-time detection and response to malware threats.

7.3 AI and Endpoint Security

Endpoint Protection: AI-powered endpoint security solutions use machine learning models to identify and prevent malware and suspicious activities on individual devices.

Adaptive Defense: AI allows endpoint security systems to adapt and improve their detection capabilities as malware evolves.

7.4 AI-Enhanced Network Security

Network Traffic Analysis: AI-driven systems analyze network traffic patterns, identifying unusual behavior that may indicate malware activity or cyberattacks [14].

Intrusion Detection and Prevention: AI-based intrusion detection and prevention systems offer enhanced capabilities in recognizing and mitigating network-based malware attacks.

7.5 Advantages and Challenges of AI in Malware Analysis

Advantages: AI can handle large-scale data analysis, detect unknown threats, and improve accuracy in malware classification [15-18].

Challenges: Adversarial attacks, where malware attempts to evade AI detection, pose significant challenges to AI-driven defenses.

7.6 Human-Machine Collaboration

Hybrid Approach: Combining human expertise with AI capabilities creates a powerful defense against malware. Human analysts can provide context and insights that AI may not capture.

Empowering Analysts: AI tools can assist security analysts in processing vast amounts of data, allowing them to focus on strategic decision-making.

7.7 Ethical Considerations and Accountability

Bias and Fairness: Ensuring fairness and avoiding biases in AI models used for malware analysis is crucial to prevent false positives or negatives.

Accountability: AI-driven decisions in cybersecurity should be transparent and explainable, enabling security analysts to understand and validate results.

The integration of machine learning and artificial intelligence in malware analysis and detection has revolutionized the cybersecurity landscape. By harnessing the power of AI-driven solutions, organizations can enhance their cybersecurity defenses, detect sophisticated malware, and respond proactively to emerging threats.

8. CONCLUSION

The foundation of malware analysis and detection is a complex and evolving field that requires a deep understanding of computer systems, networks, and programming. It involves various techniques and methodologies, each with its strengths and weaknesses, to identify, analyze, and mitigate the threats posed by malware. Signature-based detection, one of the earliest methods, remains effective for known threats but falls short when dealing with new or modified malware. Heuristic-based detection, on the other hand, can identify unknown malware based on its characteristics or behavior, but it can also produce false positives. Behavioral-based detection and sandbox detection both monitor the behavior of applications and processes, either in real-time or within a controlled environment. These methods can detect previously unknown malware but require significant system resources and can be circumvented by sophisticated malware. Machine learning-based detection represents a promising avenue for future development. By learning patterns that indicate malicious behavior, machine learning algorithms can detect new and unknown malware. However, this method requires significant computational resources, can produce false positives, and requires large datasets for training. In conclusion, no single method can provide complete protection against malware. A multi-layered approach that combines different detection methods is often the most effective strategy. As malware continues to evolve, so too must our methods for detecting and analyzing it. Ongoing research and development are crucial to staying ahead of new threats and ensuring the security of our digital environments.

REFERENCES

Blanc, W., Hashem, L. G., Elish, K. O., & Hussain Almohri, M. J. (2019). Identifying Android Malware Families Using Android-Oriented Metrics. 2019 IEEE International Conference on Big Data (Big Data), (pp. 4708-4713). IEEE. 10.1109/BigData47090.2019.9005669

Calleja, J. T., & Caballero, J. (2019, December). The MalSource Dataset: Quantifying Complexity and Code Reuse in Malware Development. *IEEE Transactions on Information Forensics and Security*, *14*(12), 3175–3190. doi:10.1109/TIFS.2018.2885512

Cui, Z., Xue, F., Cai, X., Cao, Y., Wang, G., & Chen, J. (2018, July). Detection of Malicious Code Variants Based on Deep Learning. *IEEE Transactions on Industrial Informatics*, *14*(7), 3187–3196. doi:10.1109/TII.2018.2822680

Dahl, G. E., Stokes, J. W., Deng, L., & Yu, D. (2013). Large-scale malware classification using random projections and neural networks. *2013 IEEE International Conference on Acoustics, Speech and Signal Processing*, Vancouver, BC, Canada. 10.1109/ICASSP.2013.6638293

Fasano, F., Martinelli, F., Mercaldo, F., & Santone, A. (2019). Cascade Learning for Mobile Malware Families Detection through Quality and Android Metrics. *2019 International Joint Conference on Neural Networks (IJCNN)*, Budapest, Hungary. 10.1109/IJCNN.2019.8852268

Hsiao, S.-W., Sun, Y. S., & Chen, M. C. (2016). *Behavior grouping of Android malware family. 2016 IEEE International Conference on Communications (ICC)*, Kuala Lumpur, Malaysia. 10.1109/ICC.2016.7511424

Jiang, J. (2019). Android Malware Family Classification Based on Sensitive Opcode Sequence. *2019 IEEE Symposium on Computers and Communications (ISCC)*, Barcelona, Spain. 10.1109/ISCC47284.2019.8969656

Kumar, A., & Goyal, S. (2016). Advance Dynamic Malware Analysis Using Api Hooking. *International Journal of Engineering and Computer Science*, *5*(3). Advance online publication. doi:10.18535/ijecs/v5i3.32

Mohanta, A., & Saldanha, A. (2020). Malware Packers. In Apress. DOI: doi:10.1007/978-1-4842-6193-4_7

Moser, C. K., & Kirda, E. (2007). Limits of Static Analysis for Malware Detection. *Twenty-Third Annual Computer Security Applications Conference (ACSAC 2007)*, Miami Beach, FL, USA. pp. 421-430. 10.1109/ACSAC.2007.21

Omar, M. (2022). *Static Analysis of Malware*. Springer International Publishing. doi:10.1007/978-3-031-11626-1_2

Saxe, J., & Berlin, K. (2015). *Deep neural network based malware detection using two dimensional binary program features.* 2015 10th International Conference on Malicious and Unwanted Software (MALWARE), Fajardo, PR. 10.1109/ MALWARE.2015.7413680

Sethi, K., Kumar, R., Sethi, L., Bera, P., & Patra, P. K. (2019). *A Novel Machine Learning Based Malware Detection and Classification Framework*. 2019 International Conference on Cyber Security and Protection of Digital Services (Cyber Security), Oxford, UK. 10.1109/CyberSecPODS.2019.8885196

Sree Lakshmi, T., Govindarajan, M., & Sreenivasulu, A. (2022). *Malware visual resemblance analysis with minimum losses using Siamese neural networks. Theoretical Computer Science.* Elsevier BV., doi:10.1016/j.tcs.2022.07.018

Tobiyama, S., Yamaguchi, Y., Shimada, H., Ikuse, T., & Yagi, T. (2016). Malware Detection with Deep Neural Network Using Process Behavior *2016 IEEE 40th Annual Computer Software and Applications Conference (COMPSAC),* (pp. 577-582). IEEE. 10.1109/COMPSAC.2016.151

Vaishanav, L. (2017). Behavioural Analysis of Android Malware using Machine Learning. *International Journal of Engineering and Computer Science*, 6(5). doi:10.18535/ijecs/v6i5.32

Vinayakumar, R., Alazab, M., Soman, K. P., Poornachandran, P., & Venkatraman, S. (2019). Robust Intelligent Malware Detection Using Deep Learning. *IEEE Access : Practical Innovations, Open Solutions*, 7, 46717–46738. doi:10.1109/ ACCESS.2019.2906934

Zhong, F., Chen, Z., Xu, M., Zhang, G., Yu, D., & Cheng, X. (2022). Malware-on-the-Brain: Illuminating Malware Byte Codes With Images for Malware Classification. *IEEE Transactions on Computers*. doi:10.1109/TC.2022.3160357

Chapter 3
Malware Analysis and Classification

Jairaj Singh
(iD) https://orcid.org/0009-0008-1127-3553
Birla Institute of Technology, India

Kishore Kumar Kumar Senapati
Birla Institute of Technology, India

ABSTRACT

Malicious applications can be a security threat to Cyber-physical systems as these systems are composed of heterogeneous distributed systems and mostly depends on the internet, ICT services and products. The usage of ICT products and services gives the opportunity of less expensive data collection, intelligent control and decision systems using automated data mining tools. Cyber-physical systems become exposed to the internet and the public networks as they have integrated to the ICT networks for easy automated options. Cyber-attacks can lead to functional failure, blackouts, energy theft, data theft etc. and this will be a critical security concern for Cyber-physical systems. There have been many instances of cyber-attacks on CPS systems earlier, the most popular being the Stuxnet virus attack. In total there have been 7 instances of such attacks on CPS systems that have the potential to totally cripple critical infrastructures causing huge business impacts including loss of life in some cases. Earlier these CPS or process level systems used to work in an isolated manner with very less intelligence, but as the convergence between CPS and IT is increasing their cyber-attack surface is increasing for threat actors to exploit. Therefore, in this chapter, the authors shall be seeing the technical threats in the form of malware which can exploit the CPS systems and how it can be protected from cyber-attacks.

DOI: 10.4018/978-1-6684-8666-5.ch003

INTRODUCTION

Cyber-Physical system (CPS) is the new generation of intelligent, digital systems composed of physical hardware capabilities and computing software techniques. Optimizing functionality, autonomy, reliability, and safety CPS is a major step for future technology that could change and improve lives for the better.

Designed to act like a network of multiple variables with both physical input and output considered, this smart network is one where the physical and virtual worlds merge. Falling under the embedded system category, CPS can interact seamlessly with real-world systems by means of computation, communication, and control.

CPS is commonly characterized to be adaptive, robust, and user-friendly, and will eventually lead to the advanced implementation of the Internet of Things (IoT). Like IoT, every cyber-physical system is designed to support real-time applications that can manage various environmental datasets.

With CPS's huge potential in bringing about significant social benefits across domains, being able to design and build secure CPSs to deliver consistent and dependable action is of particular importance. A lot of cyber-physical systems are being used in manufacturing, transportation, health care and energy, among other industries.

CPS must have a fully integrated and connected private network that can remotely connect with other untrusted systems when necessary. The smartness of the network must be based on intelligent data available from big data analytics resulting from collected data of sensors and external devices. With the help of intelligent decision-making, the complete process of communication, control and computation will be delivered simultaneously.

By and large, every CPS is networked, has a strong sensing capability, has higher performance capability, and can work in a real-time environment with highly predictable behaviour, influencing risk mitigation and failure response effectively.

Context of the Chapter

The context of the chapter is to provide insights into the different CPS malware and its analysis that will prove a roadmap for its detection capabilities. Cyber-attacks of CPS systems using intelligent malware begin during the early 2000s where these malicious programs were targeted towards Critical infrastructure such as nuclear, aviation, electricity, and water sectors. The Triton malware was used to attack petrochemical plants in Saudi Arabia and caused it to shutdown to prevent an explosion. BlackEnergy2 and Indus-Troyer malware variants were used to take down power grids in Ukraine. The Havex rootkit was used to target CPS of different sectors by malfunctioning the underlying firmware in the PLC. Stuxnet, probably the most sophisticated malware ever built was used to attack the Iranian nuclear facilities.

Based on the different types of CPS malware discussed, the underlying functionalities are similar based upon Command-and-Control techniques and Remote Access capabilities. Based on the existing technology and methods of hacking, it can be concluded that C&C and RAT can be propagated via SMS, Bluetooth, E-mail attachments, P2P networks, covert channel attacks or any other surveillance methods.

This chapter talks about malware classification and detection techniques focusing on the different types of malwares discussed above. The malware classification for CPS would be discussed based upon fuzzy logic algorithm. There are two variants of the fuzzy logic algorithm namely Anomaly based and Signature based detection.

CPS AND INTERNET OF THINGS (IoT)

CPS has often been compared with IoT. They are often used interchangeably depending on the industrial context and framework [11]. CPS is mostly used in North American Industrial sectors while IoT is mostly used in European Industrial sectors [12]. However, it is possible to say that CPS emphasizes on the embedded part while IoT emphasizes on connectivity. Both of CPS and IoT have physical and cyber aspects. Table 1 compares both technologies based on four aspects: devices, communication/networking, connectivity levels, and applications.

TYPES OF CYBER PHYSICAL SYSTEMS

Robotics in Smart Manufacturing

Robots have become more sophisticated, with one of their main applications being within factories. In general, a robot is made from an embedded system tasked to communicate information between two components: a mechanical structure that is purpose-built to interact with its surroundings, and sensors to collect data from the environment. Together, these allow the robot to interact appropriately.

By tying together different subsystems, cyber-physical systems or embedded systems play a vital role in the functioning of almost every robot. As an example, within the Nokia Bell Labs architecture for smart manufacturing, you can combine intelligent networking with digital technologies to support innovative applications such as robots, sensors, tracking systems and smart tools with the highest security and reliability.

Intelligent Traffic Control and Smart Cars

Over the years, the number of vehicles on our roads has increased dramatically, which, in turn, has led to serious problems such as traffic jams and accidents. To address these challenges, intelligent traffic management systems have been built to effectively detect and reduce the overall density of traffic. These systems' functions are based on several modern technologies, including wireless sensor networks (WSNs), surveillance cameras and IoT.

Huawei has worked closely with ecosystem partners to develop the Intelligent Traffic Management Solution (ITMS), supporting system integration on an open platform. As one of the largest industrial cities in Saudi Arabia, Yanbu deployed Huawei's ITMS in 2019.

The solution consists of three modules — Sharp Eyes, Powerful Brain and Intelligent and

Simplified O&M. The first module replaces the traditional single functionality sensors with intelligent sensors to better detect violations and collect comprehensive traffic information, while the second module analyses the data in real-time. The last module supports the end-to-end (E2E) multi-dimensional management.

To explain, the deployment of a cyber-physical system on an intelligent traffic control design connects various smart subsystems. Sensors can be integrated in the vehicle's controller system and communicate via embedded telematics, sending command inquiries to perform desired actions through the actuators connected to the system.

Relevantly, smart cars of today and of the future will need artificial intelligence (AI), big data, cloud computing and other ICT technologies to achieve the deep integration of smart cyber-physical systems (hardware and software) for the necessary levels of safety and autonomy.

As an example, Qualcomm QCA7006AQ, a next-generation powerline communication (PLC) device, is designed to address the needs for electric vehicle (EV) charging station communications. It is compliant with the Home Plug Green PHY (HPGP) specification, which is the leading designation for implementing vehicle-to-grid (V2G) systems. By integrating smart grids, vehicles can seamlessly authenticate on the network through Plug and Charge automated payments, coordinating the EV charge timing and direction of energy to and from the grid and home.

Smart Solutions for Energy Demand

As we increase our use of technology services, networks and devices, the resultant energy consumption and emissions also surge. However, digital technologies can also be part of the solutions resolving such issues. Through cyber-physical systems, the scaling up of renewable energy markets, the support of smart power grids and smart metering for buildings, and the enabling of emissions reductions all become more feasible.

Ericsson's Global Utilities Innovation Centre is an integrated state-of-the art device testing lab where partner utilities and original equipment manufacturers (OEM) can test interoperability of their field and IoT devices over mission-critical networks. As a fully functional E2E operational lab, it contains a physical representation of a utility smart grid, enabling real-world demonstrations of E2E private networks operations across the power grid – from generation and transmission until distribution.

Moreover, 5G-ready Ericsson solutions will modernize enterprises' current communication infrastructure to simplify the communication for Ooredoo's oil and gas enterprise customers.

Advanced Medical Systems

Most medical systems use cyber-physical systems for real-time monitoring and remote sensing of patients' conditions. Through wearable sensors or non-intrusive environmental monitors, sub-optimal vital signs are recognized early and emergencies are responded to immediately. This leads to a higher quality of healthcare in hospitals, clinics or even at home, incorporating high-grade security, interoperability, and high system assurance.

Improving people's health and well-being through meaningful innovation, the infrastructure provided by du and paired with Philips' technological advancements will provide predictive analytics, data visualization and reporting capabilities to healthcare workers. This combination lets local health systems access critical patient information and make split-second life-saving decisions.

Assisting Saudi's healthcare providers in preventing the spread of COVID-19 in 2020, stc launched the "Virtual Clinic" service, a clinical engagement provided through cloud computing solutions. This service offers a medical bag to measure the patient's vital signs at their place of residence wherein a doctor is able to view and interpret results and provide medical advice accurately through a video call.

Etisalat also introduced its Business Edge Healthcare platform, offering a plethora of services dedicated to enhancing and empowering hospitals, ambulatory practices and medical staff with seamless, secure and practical solutions to better improve day-to-day operations.

Cyber-physical systems and embedded networks are projected to account for more than half of the value share in diverse sectors. One report estimates that the technical innovations of cyber-physical systems could find direct application in sectors, with the potential to grow over $80 trillion of economic output by 2025.

LEVELS OF CYBER PHYSICAL SYSTEM ARCHITECTURE

It provides a step-by- step guideline for developing and deploying a CPS for manufacturing application. In general, a CPS consists of two main functional components:

(1)   the advanced connectivity that ensures real-time data acquisition from the physical world and information feedback from the cyberspace.
(2)   intelligent data management, analytics and computational capability that constructs the cyberspace.

However, such requirement is very abstract and not specific enough for implementation purpose in general. In contrast, the 5C architecture presented here clearly defines, through a sequential workflow manner, how to construct a CPS from the initial data acquisition, to analytics, to the final value creation. The 5C represented 5 layers of the architecture namely Connection, Conversion, Cyber, Cognition and Configure. The connection involved CPS devices sensing or generating data, while the conversion layer involved the mining of these data for relevant information about the physical processes and state of the equipment.

Figure 1. AI and society today

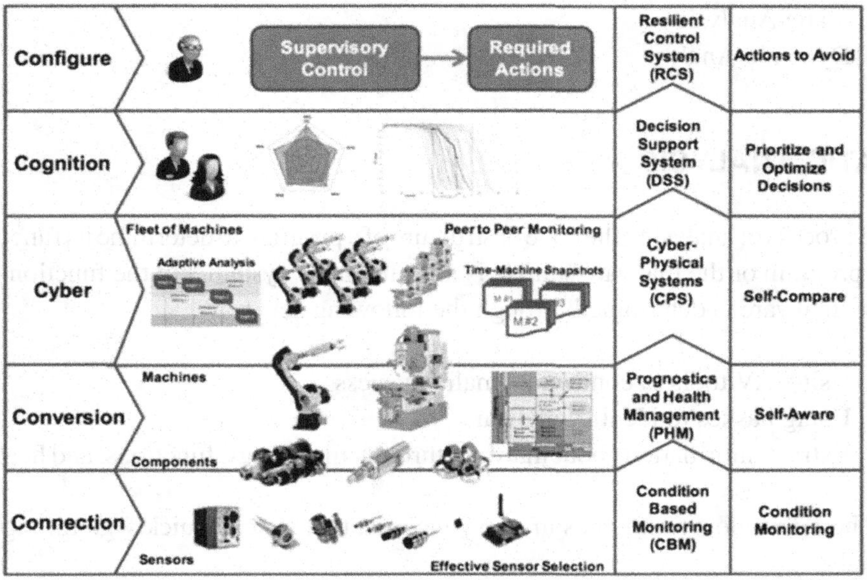

The mined data from the conversion layer is stored and further processed and analysed at the cyber layer, while at the cognition layer, the data is transformed in knowledge bases for diverse uses. Finally, the configuration layer feedbacks the acquired knowledge into the system, enabling the system to be flexible, adaptable and self-reconfigurable. Hence, the architecture involves data moving cyclically from the physical interfaces to the cyber interfaces. Figure below illustrates the essential interactions in the 5C architecture.

DETECTING MALWARE IN CYBER PHYSICAL SYSTEMS

In this chapter, we will be going through different types of malware analysis techniques and then dive deeper into dynamic analysis including Machine Learning and AI techniques to better understand the malicious behaviour observed in the CPS architecture. We shall be looking into the Purdue Model which highlights how a process works in terms of Operational Technology. Purdue Model is the way how communication is oriented in an OT Process.

Now to perform a malware analysis in such a situation, it is important to perform a malware scan of different zones or levels starting from level 1 till level 5. During the malware scanning phase, there might be different abnormalities reported in the CSOC team who would further perform analysis on the same to identify the abnormality to qualify as a malware sample.

To do this analysis there are basically two types of methods used:

- Static Analysis
- Dynamic Analysis

STATIC ANALYSIS

It is a process of analysing the code or structure of a program to determine its function. The program or the malware sample is not run on the system, but the functionality of the malware is determined through the following actions:

- Using AV tools to confirm its maliciousness
- Using hashes to identify malware
- Extract information about malware through file strings, functions, and headers

There are a few techniques in static analysis, that we can quickly go through: -

Figure 2. Purdue model: Generic CPS architecture

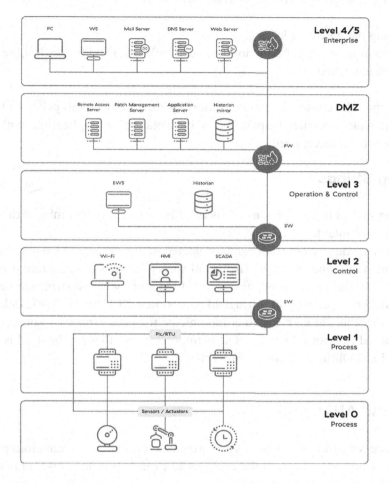

Figure 3. Hierarchal representation of Malware analysis and detection techniques

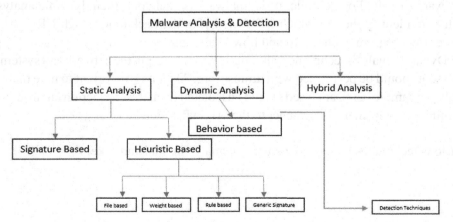

Hashing (Fingerprint on Malware)

- Using the hash as a label
- Searching the hash online in tools such as Virus Total to check if the file has been identified.

For example, the command can be: **md5deep abc_file.exe** will print out the hash of the file which can then be pasted in Virus Total online application to identify if the file has been recognized.

Finding Strings

Detecting strings in a suspicious file is an effective way to determine if the file has any malicious intent.

Strings inside any program can be detected in any program by using the **string** command. This command will display all sorts of strings the program uses. Once the command has been issued, next step is to identify what all strings are essential from a malicious standpoint. Strings like important DLL files or URL links which indicate that the file is trying to communicate to some external resource is often seen as a red flag for a malware. Other important tool that can be used is FLOSS (Fir-eye Labs Obfuscated String Solver)

DYNAMIC ANALYSIS

It is a process where examination is performed after execution of malicious program. It is performed after basic static analysis has reached a dead end, either due to obfuscation, packing or the analyst having exhausted the possibility of static analysis techniques. This is an improved technique as it examines the true nature of the malware sample. For example, if the malware is backdoor, then dynamic analysis will help identify the file which is infected with the backdoor, which URL or CC server the program connects to and how is it being controlled.

Dynamic analysis techniques, although efficient can put the network and system at risk so it should be performed with utmost care. Also, it is important to note that the malware sample being analysed should be isolated from the production environment to minimize any chance of impact to the original systems.

Various techniques which can be used in analysing malware like:-

Sandbox approach: Most malware analysts use a sandbox approach to perform basic dynamic analysis using different sandbox technologies like Norman Sandbox, GFI Sandbox, Anubis, Joe sandbox, Threat Expert, Bit Blaze, and Comodo Instant Malware Analysis.

We will be discussing one of the sandbox tools: The GFI Sandbox report has 6 main sections as follows like

- The Analysis Summary section lists all static analysis information and a high level
  overview of the dynamic analysis results.
- The File activity section lists files that are opened, created, or deleted for each process impacted by the malware.
- The Registry Activity section lists changes to the registry.
- The Network Activity section includes network activity spawned by the malware like setting up a listening port or performing a DNS request.
- The Virus Total Results section lists the results of a Virus Total scan of the malware.

Despite its advantages, the sandbox application also has the following disadvantages:

- Malware often detects when it is running on a virtual machine, and if a virtual machine is detected the malware might stop running or behave differently.
- Some malware might require the presence of certain registry keys or files on the system that might not be found in the sandbox. These might be required to contain legitimate data such as commands or encryption keys
- If the malware is a DLL based file, then it will not be invoked properly because a DLL will not run as easily as an executable does.

Function Call Monitoring

Typically, a function consists of code that performs a specific task, such as calculating factorial of a number or creating a file. The main idea of malware analysis using function call is to abstract implementation details in order to understand how the malicious program is spreading the infection. The process of intercepting function calls is termed as hooking. The analysed program is manipulated in a way that in addition to the intended function, a hook function is involved. This hook function is responsible for implementing the required analysis functionality such as recording invocation to a log file or analyse input parameters.

System Calls Monitoring

Software executing on computer systems, that run commodity off the shelf operating systems, is usually divided in two major parts. While general applications, such as word processors, or image manipulation programs are executed in so-called user-mode, the operating system is executed in kernel-mode. Only code that is executed in kernel-mode has direct access to the system state. This separation prevents user-mode processes from interacting with the system and their environment directly. It is, for example, not possible for a user-space process to directly open or create a file. Instead, the operating system provides a special well-defined API– the system call interface. Using system calls, a user-mode application can request the operating system to perform a limited set of tasks on its behalf. Thus, to create a file, a user-mode application needs to invoke the specific system call indicating the file's path, name, and access method. Once the system call is invoked, the system is switched into kernel-mode (i.e., privileged operating system code is executed). Upon verification that the calling application has sufficient access rights for the desired action, the operating system carries out the task on behalf of the user-mode applications. In the case of the file-creation example, the result the system call is a so-called file handle, where all further interaction of the user-mode application regarding this file (e.g., write to the file) is then performed through this handle. Apart from exhaustively using resources (bound by the limits of the operating system), there is usually little a malware sample can do within the bounds of its process. Therefore, malware (just as every other application) that executes in user-space and needs to communicate with its environment must invoke the respective system calls. Since system calls are the only possibility for a *user mode* process to access or interact with its environment, this interface is especially interesting for dynamic malware analysis. However, malware samples are known that manage to gain kernel-mode privileges. Such instances do not necessarily make use of the system call interface and might evade this analysis method.

ANALYSIS IN AN EMULATOR

Executing a program in an emulated environment allows an analysis component to control every aspect of program execution. Depending on which part of the execution environment is emulated, different forms of analysis are possible. Memory & CPU Emulation. Emulating the CPU and memory results in a sandbox that allows one to run potential malicious code without having to fear negative impacts on the real system. A binary is executed in this sandbox by successively reading its instructions and performing equivalent operations in the virtual emulated environment. All side

Figure 4. Malware emulator by Kaspersky to analyse malicious code

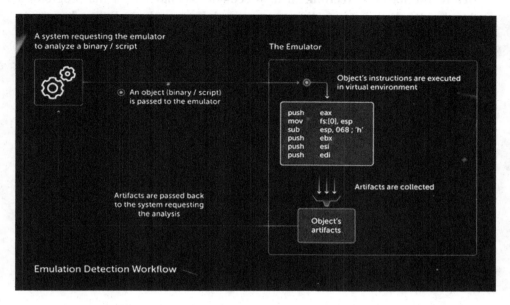

effects the binary produces are contained in the sandbox. To successfully emulate samples that rely on operating system services or shared libraries, these mechanisms need to be emulated as well.

Many AV suites employ CPU and memory emulation to overcome the hurdles imposed by packed or obfuscated binaries. To analyse a possibly packed binary, it is executed in the emulated environment. If the AV engine detects an unpacking sequence, the signatures are matched on the unencrypted memory contents contained in the emulated memory. For a malicious sample to detect that it is running in such an emulated environment, it is enough to perform an operation that requires components that are not or insufficiently emulated by the system. For example, the emulator might behave different from a real CPU in the case of a CPU bug (if this bug is not considered in the emulation).

MALWARE DETECTION METHODS

Signature based detection: Signature is a distinctive characteristic of a particular malware using which can be easily detected. The technique is also known as *pattern matching, string matching, mask matching and fingerprinting.* A signature-based detection uses bits of sequences injected in application program by malware authors that uniquely identifies malware. An example scenario can be hashing performed on the code such as SHA 256, MD5 which is used for comparison process.

Behaviour based detection: In this technique, behaviour of the program is used to decide whether it is malicious or not and does not depend on code or code sequence. The major disadvantage here is that the malware does not show its full potential in the Virtual Machine or Sandbox where it is being run and may lead to incorrect or false positive detection of the suspected program.

Heuristic based detection: It is known as a proactive technique where it is like signature-based detection technique. For detecting malware traits, it uses *opcodes, N-grams, Control Flow Graphs, and hybrid features*. The new feature enables the detection of new and novel attack vectors and undiscovered malicious traits of different virus and their signatures.

Malware detection tools: There are many available tools with a few being listed here in the table below covering both static and dynamic analysis techniques.

Next, we shall see a live malware sample to understand how a malware works and what practical steps we require to analyse it effectively using both static and dynamic analysis techniques. For sample purpose we will be taking an example of a simple Windows backdoor (Trojan) named as "*SVCHOST.exe*". This is a Windows system process used to host multiple services. It is an essential process used in the

Table 1. Static analysis tools

S. No	Tool Name	Description
1	PE id	This tool helps in identifying complicated malware. It works on the signature-based detection technique and has almost 500 fingerprints of different malware.
2	PE view	Provides information on file headers and portable executables. Various description of malware is also included like compile time and import/export functions.
3	PE explorer	Having similarity with PE view providing features such as malware packers from UPX and NS Pack can be unpacked and detected.
4	Bin text	Character strings of a binary file can be searched and displayed using this tool.
5	UPX	Malware samples can be compressed using this tool which uses the method of packing the executables.
6	Dependency Walker	The tool was developed by Microsoft for static analysis which explores the DLLs and functions imported by malware.
7	IDA Pro	A highly popular tool among malware analysts, reverse engineers and pentesters giving an interactive disassembling feature.
8	Resource Hacker	This tool is specially made and used in the Windows operating system. The tool is used to view, modify, add, and extract resources for both 32-bit and 64-bit Windows executables
9	Hex Editors	Binary files are edited using this tool in hex format. It is helpful to determine machine level execution by the malware.

Table 2. Dynamic analysis tools

S. No	Tool Name	Description
1	Process Explorer	Having similarities with task manager, this tool provides currently running process in a hierarchical view of processes.
2	Process Monitor	Real time file creation, file read, file writes, and file closure can be using this tool. This tool has other functions like – 1. Monitoring registry and activity changes, 2. Tracking processes and networks.
3	Reg Shot	Two registry snapshots are taken, one before and after the process to analyse the changes so that if any malicious activity is present, it can be easily detected by the reg shot.
4	Net cat	Tool to monitor inbound and outbound connections from the network.
5	Wireshark	This is a network packet analyser that has the potential to capture the network traffic generated by malware as soon as it was executed.
6	Olly Dbg	When the source is not available this x86 debugger is used for the binary code analysis
7	Burp Suite	Security of web applications is tested using this tool. This tool can track various server requests posted by the malware to any remote server. All the HTTP and HTTPS requests made by the malware can be intercepted by this tool using the Man in the Middle Attack
8	Sandboxes	Sandbox is a virtual container that can be used for analysing untrusted programs/malware in a virtual system (installed inside or outside the main system which is relatively a safer environment) without hurting the main system. The sandboxes use both static and dynamic approaches to analyse the programs.

essential implementation of shared service processes in Windows and is often used to load multiple DLL files to launch multiple *exe* programs. The analysis phase of the malicious SVCHOST.exe sample would be done using a Sandbox platform named **JoeSandBox Cloud**.

Static Analysis Phase

In the static analysis phase, the file was decompiled using the sandbox cloud environment and the following hashes were detected as shown below:

Once we got the hashes, we then now try and upload the MD5 hash value in Virus Total to check the status of the file.

Dynamic Analysis Phase

During the dynamic analysis phase, there were multiple steps involved since the malware (SVCHOST.exe) was run in the Sandbox environment. First, we shall go

Figure 5. SVCHOST.exe malware file signature

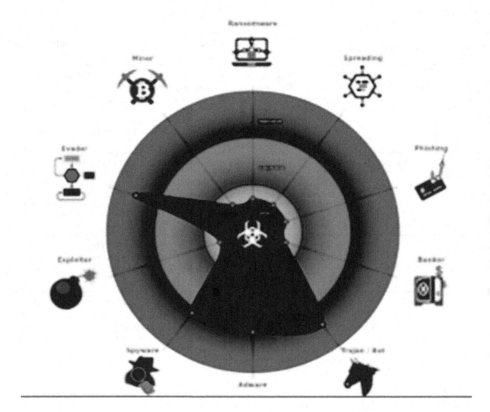

through the startup phase and see what were the different attack vectors the malicious file went through before detonating in the victim machine.

Next upon executing the malicious file an error in the Windows process gets displayed as below. This is because the malicious file has overridden the original SVCHOST.exe file running in the Windows background process tries to take over multiple legitimate processes running on the system.

To further investigate malicious strings executed by the malware, we shall check the memory dumps of the file and check executed commands by the sample.

Once we confirm that the file is malicious, we can check the overall status of the malware sample (SVCHOST.exe) by utilizing the Sandbox cloud:

From the above figure, we can see that the sandbox analysis declares this file to be malicious and having the following malware characteristics:

- Evader
- Exploiter

Figure 6. SVCHOST.exe startup phase

Sample Name:	svchost.exe ⬜
Analysis ID:	296205 ⬜
MD5:	49b8f905867aded45f1f5b... ⬜
SHA1:	0a87788428778dba56762... ⬜
SHA256:	02883009e7e310bf670bff... ⬜
Tags:	NJRAT RAT

Figure 7. Malicious SVCHOST.exe overrides legitimate process

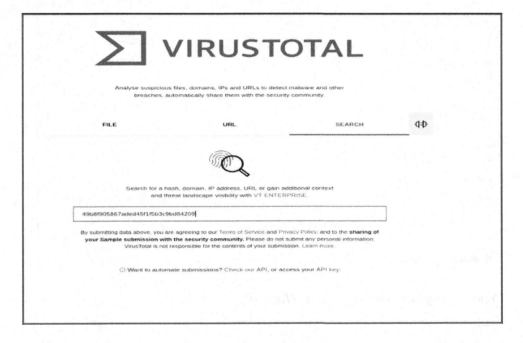

- Spyware
- Trojan/Bot

In the next section, we shall be discussing about malware classification based on some Machine Learning techniques

Figure 8. Malicious Strings executed by malware (SVCHOST.exe)

Figure 9. Overall status of SVCHOST.exe file

MALWARE CLASSIFICATION: MACHINE LEARNING APPROACH

Machine learning is a of methods that gives computers "the ability to learn without being explicitly programmed".

In simple words, a machine learning algorithm discovers and formalizes the principles that underlie the data it sees. With this knowledge, the algorithm can 'reason' the properties of previously unseen samples. In malware detection, a previously unseen sample could be a new file. Its hidden property could be malware or benign. A mathematically formalized set of principles underlying data properties is called the **model.**

Machine learning has a broad variety of approaches that it takes to a solution rather than a single method. These approaches have different capacities and different tasks that they suit best.

There are two fundamental methods for any Machine Learning algorithm to function:

- *Unsupervised Learning*: In this setting, we are given only a data set without the right answers for the task. The goal is to discover the structure of the data or the law of data generation. One important example is clustering. Clustering is a task that includes splitting a data set into groups of similar objects. Another task is representation learning – this includes building an informative feature set for objects based on their low-level description (for example, an autoencoder model).
- *Supervised Learning*: Supervised learning works on two stages. One, is that the training a model and fitting a model to available training data. Applying the trained model to new samples and obtaining predictions. Second is, we are given a set of objects where each object is represented with feature set 'X' and each object is mapped to the right answer or labelled as 'Y.' This training information is utilized during the training phase, when we search for the best model that will produce the correct label 'Y' for previously unseen objects given the feature set 'X'.

In the case of malware detection, X could be some features of file content or behaviour, for instance, file statistics and a list of used API functions. Labels Y could be malware or benign, or even a more precise classification, such as a virus, Trojan-Downloader, or adware.

During the training phase, a family of models is first selected like for example it could be neural networks or decision trees. Generally, each model in a family is determined by its parameters. Training means that we search for the model from

Figure 10. Machine learning phases for malware analysis

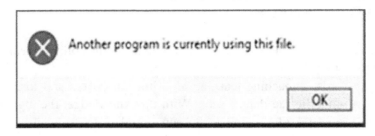

the selected family with a particular set of parameters that gives the most accurate answers for the trained model over the set of reference objects according to a particular metric. In other words, we 'learn' the optimal parameters that define valid mapping from X to Y.

After the model has been trained and verified for its efficiency, the next phase is started where we need to apply this model to new objects. In this phase, the type of the model and its parameters do not change. The model only produces predictions.

In the case of malware detection, this is the protection phase. Vendors often deliver a trained model to users where the product makes decisions based on model predictions autonomously. Mistakes can cause devastating consequences for a user – for example, removing an OS driver. It is crucial for the vendor to select a model family properly. The vendor must use an efficient training procedure to find the model with a high detection rate and a low false positive rate.

We can take one example where the model is formulated in some basic mathematical terms for a Machine Learning algorithm to perform Malware Analysis. In terms of malware classification, there are 3 main variables in the form of malware architecture, mode attack and connected asset in CPS network. These elements are correlated in the following mathematical formulations as $(A, T) = Z$. Here A represents malware classification, T represents the target asset and Z represents the detection model. If we further, elaborate the relation it can be written as $A (X + Y + V)$, $f (A_i, T_j) = Z_{ij}$. Where X represents malware behaviour, Y represents mode of attack and Z represents connected assets.

Once the relation for the malware has been established, it can be passed into different classification algorithms to determine the family for the malware. For example, in the table below it can be seen that types of malware infection which can be classified into already existing malware families:

Another, Machine Learning method which can be used is Deep Learning. Deep learning is a special machine learning approach that facilitates the extraction of features of a high level of abstraction from low-level data. Deep learning has proven successful in computer vision, speech recognition, natural language processing and

Figure 11. Table of how CPS malware can be classified based on different parameters

Source	Rule	Description	Author	Strings
00000011.00000002.324053687.0000000000012000.00000002.00020000.sdmp	JoeSecurity_Njrat	Yara detected Njrat	Joe Security	
00000011.00000002.324053687.0000000000012000.00000002.00020000.sdmp	njrat1	Identify njRat	Brian Wallace (@botnet_hunter)	• 0x693e:$a1: netsh firewall add allowedprogram • 0x690e:$a2: SEE_MASK_NOZONECHECKS • 0x6ace:$b1: {TAP} • 0x6a46:$c3: cmd.exe /c ping
00000011.00000002.324053687.0000000000012000.00000002.00020000.sdmp	Njrat	direct njRAT in memory	JPCERT/CC Incident Response Group	• 0x690e:$reg: SEE_MASK_NOZONECHECKS • 0x6bfa:$msg: Execute ERROR • 0x675a:$msg: Execute ERROR • 0x6a48:$ping: cmd.exe /c ping 0 -n 2 & del
00000014.00000000.344816193.0000000000E82000.00000002.00020000.sdmp	JoeSecurity_Njrat	Yara detected Njrat	Joe Security	
00000014.00000000.344816193.0000000000E82000.00000002.00020000.sdmp	njrat1	Identify njRat	Brian Wallace (@botnet_hunter)	• 0x693e:$a1: netsh firewall add allowedprogram • 0x690e:$a2: SEE_MASK_NOZONECHECKS • 0x6ace:$b1: {TAP} • 0x6a46:$c3: cmd.exe /c ping

other tasks. It works best when you want the machine to infer high-level meaning from low-level data.

For Deep Learning Models to be effective for malware classification they need to adhere to the following characteristics:

- ***Large representative datasets are required***: It is important to emphasize the data-driven nature of this approach. A created model depends heavily on the data it has seen during the training phase to determine which features are statistically relevant for predicting the correct label. Consider an example where collect a training set and we overlook the fact that some files larger than 20 MB are all malware samples and are not benign. (Certainly not true for real world files). While training, the model will exploit this property of the dataset, and will learn that any file larger than 20 MB is malware and will use this property for detection. When this model is applied to real world data, it will produce many ***false positives***. To prevent this outcome, we needed to add benign files with larger sizes to the training set. Then, the model will not rely on an erroneous data set property.

- ***Model should be interpretable:*** Most of the model families used currently, like deep neural networks, are called black box models. Black box models are given the input X, and they will produce Y through a complex sequence of operations that can hardly be interpreted by a human. This could pose a problem in real-life applications. For example, when a false alarm occurs, and we want to understand why it happened, we ask whether it was a problem with a training set or the model itself. The interpretability of a model determines how easy it will be for us to manage it, assess its quality and correct its operation.

- ***False positive rates must be extremely low:*** False positives happen when an algorithm mistakes a malicious label for a benign file. Our aim is to make the false positive rate as low as possible, or zero. This is not typical for a machine learning application. This is important, because even one false positive in a million benign files can create serious consequences for users. This is complicated by the fact that there are lots of clean files in the world, and they keep appearing.

- *Model must be highly robust:* After applying ML model to malware detection, we have to face the fact that data distribution is not static in the sense:
  - ○ Active adversaries (malware writers) constantly work on avoiding detections and releasing new versions of malware files that differ significantly from those that have been seen during the training phase.
  - ○ Thousands of software companies produce new types of benign executables which are significantly different from previously known types. The data on these types might be lacking in the previous set but it should be recognized them as benign.

CONCLUSION

The role of CPS is highly significant in supporting critical infrastructure operations like oil and gas, electric generation and transmission, manufacturing etc. And with the increasing convergence between CPS and IT based systems, the surface for cyber-attacks is increasing at a massive rate. Already there have been over 7 major malware the world has witnessed capable of disrupting critical infrastructure services like Stuxnet, HAVEX, Indu Stroyer and Pipedream. So, in order to protect CPS systems from cyber-attacks especially malware, it is important to analyse traffic and perform malware classification to correctly identify any suspicious data into already identified malware. This technique shall improve the detection capabilities of the organization of not only filtering traffic at the firewall but also improve the understanding of what kind of malicious traffic might be entering the organization. This might be an extra investment from an economic standpoint where a different malware analysis team would be required but can improve the overall security posture of the organization.

REFERENCES

Avira Press Center. (2007). *Avira warns: targeted malware attacks increasingly also threatening German companies.* Avira. http://www.avira.com/en/security news/ targeted attacks threatening companies.html.

Cardon, O. (2018). *Classification of cyber-physical production systems applications: Proposition of an analysis framework*. Science Direct.

Habib, M. K. (2018). *CPS: Role, Characteristics, Architectures and Future Potentials*. Science Direct.

Kaspersky Lab Machine-Learning. (2018). *Machine Learning for Malware Detection*. (Whitepaper).

Udayakumar, N. (2019). *Malware Classification Using Machine Learning Algorithms*. Research Gate.

Telecom Review. (2022). *Cyber-Physical Systems: The Integrated Form of ICT*. Telecom Review.

Chapter 4

Wrapper–Based Feature Selection for Detecting the Lexical Phishing Websites Using Ensemble Learning Algorithms

M. Gaayathri
Avinashilingam Institute for Home Science and Higher Education for Women, India

Padmavathi Ganapathi
Avinashilingam Institute for Home Science and Higher Education for Women, India

A. Roshni
Avinashilingam Institute for Home Science and Higher Education for Women, India

D. Shanmugapriya
ⓘ https://orcid.org/0000-0002-7446-6749
Avinashilingam Institute for Home Science and Higher Education for Women, India

ABSTRACT

Phishing is one of the most serious issues now-a-days, and many internet users are falling prey to it. Website phishing is a major threat that focuses on developing spoofed sites as a legal ones. Phishers develop cloned websites and distribute the uniform resource locator (URLs) to a large number of people in the form of e-mail, short message service, or through social media. In the current scenario, phishing is

DOI: 10.4018/978-1-6684-8666-5.ch004

the topmost cyber threat/cyber-attack that intrudes into the system to steal or capture sensitive information from the target. Machine learning methods, an important branch of artificial intelligence, are used to detect many critical problems. This chapter investigates the lexical features of website URLs to detect the phishing URL using wrapper-based feature selection on ensemble learning technique. To evaluate the model developed, the dataset from Mendeley repository is taken. The highest level of accuracy for the phishing websites was reached using bagging classifier with 95% accuracy compared with boosting algorithm.

1. INTRODUCTION

Cybersecurity is the process of safeguarding cyberspace from potential threats. Cyber security is concerned with defending, preventing, and recovering all web resources from cyber attacks by cabaj et al. (2018). It is incredibly difficult to identify, analyse, and control significant risk events due to the complexity of the cyber security sector, which is increasing daily stated by basit et al. (2021). During the year 2019, the UK government's Cyber Security Breaches Survey report investigated based on the frequency of occurrence, and it is noted that Phishing Attacks are the topmost ones by Alkhalil et al. (2021).

Information security is critical in protecting sensitive data from social engineering attacks like Phishing. Social engineering attempts to alter users' credentials in order to facilitate various cyber attacks. An example of a social engineering assault is phishing, which targets users' personal information using emails, SMS, voice calls, and anonymous URLs. Phishing has become a threat to many people, remarkably those ignorant of the risks they face when browsing. In FBI report (2018), between October 2013 and February 2016, a Phishing attack cost 2.3 billion dollars, according to a testimony by the Federal Bureau of Investigation (FBI). Phishing attacks can affect personal computers, smart devices, and Wi-Fi-enabled intelligent devices, among other things.

According to a Proof Point survey, approximately 90% of worldwide enterprises were targeted by Phishing attacks in 2019. Indicating that, cyber criminals continue to target individual end users. 55% of organization has been affected by Phishing attacks, out of which individuals targeted 88%, 86% in the form of social media, 84% reported in the form of SMS, 83% through Voice calls (APWG report 2020).

As per the security magazine (2020), the first six months of 2020 revealed a new side to this well-known Phishing Attack. Anti- Phishing Working Group (APWG) released eight reports in March 2020 regarding the e-Crime exchange of phishing attacks via the ZOOM video conferencing platform, which many IT employees and academicians used during CoronaVirus Disease-19 (COVID-19). In 2020, most Phishing attacks were carried out via E-mail (Security Magazine 2020). In April 2020, Google blocked 240 million COVID-related junk messages and about 18 million COVID-19 phishing emails every day. 94 percent of Phishing attacks are named with Coronavirus-related information.

E-mail, websites, SMS, and phone calls are all used in Phishing attempts. Phishing Websites are a shared network boundary for online social engineering attacks, and dozens of new web scams are constantly popping up. Many individuals fall prey to Phishing attacks for the following five reasons (Volkomer et al., 2017): (i) Users lack a fundamental knowledge of Uniform Resource Locators (URLs), (ii) do not have a clear understanding of which pages to trust, (iii) due to redirection or disguised URLs, are unable to determine the precise address of a page, (iv) alternate URLs exist or some pages may have been typed accidentally, (v) Users are unable to discern between a legitimate and a phishing web page.

This chapter's primary goal is to use Wrapper-based Feature Selection to identify Web-based Phishing attacks. The Wrapper based Feature Selection is classified into three types: Forward, Backward and Stepwise. On comparison of the three types, the one that gives the best reduced attributes is used to improve the accuracy with the help of Ensemble Learning algorithms. Significant features are identified by applying Wrapper-based feature selection methods like Forward, Backward and Stepwise Feature Selection. Based on the selected features, the ensemble model includes Bagging and AdaBoost classifiers are developed.

The following sections comprise the chapter: The introduction to Phishing attacks is presented in this section. Section 2 focuses on Ensemble Learning. Section 3 discusses the Literature Review. Section 4 encompasses the proposed methodology used to detect Phishing attacks. Section 5 presents the experimental Results and Discussions. The report concludes with recommendations for future research is discussed in Section 6. Section 7 describes some open-source malware datasets for the reader's implementation.

2. ENSEMBLE LEARNING

Ensemble methods are meta-algorithms, and they deliver high-quality predictions in a combined manner by reducing the variance and the bias due to a single machine learning model. It integrates numerous basic models to create a single predictive model that is as accurate as possible (Zhu et al., 2019). Ensemble learning algorithms are classified as follows.

- Bagging
- Boosting and
- Stacking

In this chapter Bagging and Boosting algorithm is implemented to identify Phishing websites.

The statistically flawed learning algorithm is thought to have significant variance. The algorithm is said to have computational complexity if it displays the computational problem. The algorithm that has a significant bias, on the other hand, suffers from representational difficulty. The most frequent causes of existing learning algorithms failing are these three. The ensemble techniques could minimise the bias and variance of these three defects in the conventional learning algorithms.

3. LITERATURE REVIEW

Most of the backend methods for dealing with Phishing attacks are Machine Learning techniques. Because of their excellent data handling and prediction capabilities, they are the most promising ones to automate the process of learning effectively. Table 1 presents some of the previous research based on Machine learning algorithms to detect phishing attacks.

As an overall observation, it is noted that ensemble learning methods are not explored much. Hence, this chapter focuses on devising a framework for the detection of Phishing attacks using ensemble learning methods based on the Wrapper-based feature selection technique. Figure 1 depicts the recent survey on phishing attacks, significant machine learning model and feature selection methods appropriate classification.

4. PROPOSED APPROACH

The whole design approach for Detecting Lexical-based Phishing Websites is shown in Figure 2. The following are the four steps involved:

4.1 Collection of Dataset

For detecting Phishing attacks, Phishing website datasets have been available in Mendeley data published in 2017 (Tan 2018). The Phishing website contains 48 fields with three class attributes and datasets of 10000 instances. Three kinds are

Table 1. Significant methods based on machine learning algorithms to handle phishing attacks

Reference	Observations
Sharma et al. (2020)	The Mendeley and UCI datasets are frequently used to identify phishing attempts. The decision tree algorithm yields the best F1_score of 0.94 and Execution time taken of 0.044 after an analysis of various feature selection techniques was conducted, followed by a comparison study of the affinity between Machine Learning Classification Algorithms and Feature Selection Techniques.
Tubis et al. (2020)	A study on Risk factors for cyber-attack scenarios is estimated using fuzzy theory. Seven scenarios for three mining automation levels are studied to demonstrate the method's use.
Tahir et al. (2020)	To detect the Phishing website, a hybrid model-based technique was used. Instance-based learning (IBk), Fuzzy Unordered Rule Induction (FURIA), Sequential Minimal Optimisation (SMO), Naive Bayes (NB), Bayesian Net (BN), and Random Forest (RF) classification methods are combined to increase detection accuracy. J48 + RF give the best accuracy of 97.44%.
Ali et al. (2017)	On UCI datasets, feature selection approaches are used. Back Propagation Neural Network (BPNN), Naive Bayes, Support Vector Machine, K-Nearest Neighbour, Radial Basis Function Networks, C4.5 tree-based approach is Wrapper based algorithm, Information Gain, and Principal Component Analysis are some examples of neural network techniques. The accuracy of the Back Propagation Neural Network (BPNN) algorithm is 0.96.
Fadheel et al. (2017)	The Phishing URLs websites dataset is used to select features using the Kaiser-Meyer-Olkin (KMO) test. Out of 30, 19 features were chosen by KMO. 19 attributes are implemented using the support vector machine and logistic regression technique. The SVM technique outperforms Logistic Regression with an accuracy of 0.79.
Xuan et al. (2020)	The issues and vulnerabilities around network data are discussed. To do these tasks, the URL dataset is needed. The malicious URL is found using the Random Forest technique and Support Vector Machine (SVM). The SVM method outperforms the Random Forest approach in terms of accuracy (93.39%).
Chandrasekhar et al. (2014)	The relevance of feature selection is discussed in depth in this work. Sequential Feature selection algorithm with Support Vector Machine (SVM) and *Radial basis function* (*RBF*). The Sequential Feature selection algorithm with RBF gives the best performance of 97.361% and improves predictor performance.
Singh et al. (2021)	Intrusion detection solutions are crucial because so much user-sensitive data is uploaded to the cloud every second. Ensemble learning network-based cloud IDS has been used to increase accuracy to 97.99%. Bagged trees, Boosted trees, and Random Under Sampling Boosting algorithms have all been applied.
Surwade et al. (2021)	For feature extraction, spam and phishing emails from well-known datasets like Enron, Ling Spam, PU123A, Spambase, and Phishnet, among others, can be employed. Spam and phishing emails are filtered using a combination of Origin-based Filter (OBF) and Content-based Filter (CBF).

used to categorise the 48 fields. They are Lexical-based features, Host-based features and Correlation-based features.

In this chapter, specifically, Lexical-based features are implemented. Lexical-based features have 27 features. The lexical-based feature is a valid token that could be a substring within the URL delimited by '.', '/', '?', '=', '-', '_'. Example: Num Dash, which Counts the number of "-" in the webpage URL. Figure 3 shows the sample of the phishing website dataset used in this study.

Figure 1. Survey methodology for feature selection based website phishing detection using ensemble learning

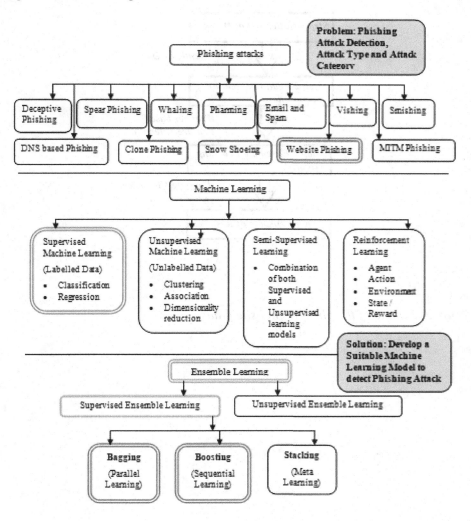

4.2 Feature Selection

The main goal of feature selection is to eliminate redundant or irrelevant features from the model. Some modelling issues involve a lot of variables, which might delay model creation (almseidin et al. 2019). Therefore, the existence of non-informative variables may increase the uncertainty of the results and reduce the overall efficacy of the model. The three categories of feature selection methods are as follows: filter-based, wrapper-based, and embedded methods (jovic et al. 2015). The wrapper-based feature selection method is used in this study to choose the momentous features for website phishing detection.

Figure 2. Overall design for detecting lexical based feature selection

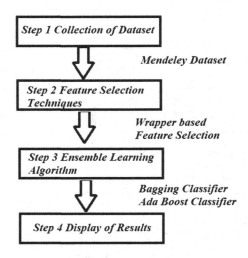

Figure 3. Sample of the phishing website dataset

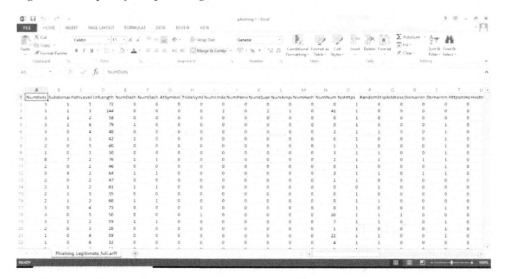

4.2.1 Wrapper-Based Feature Selection

Wrapper techniques examine a subset of features using a machine learning algorithm that searches the space of possible feature subsets using a search strategy (Zuhair et al. 2015). These algorithms are referred to as greedy algorithms since they search for the optimal feature combination that will provide the most desirable model.

Wrapper-based feature selection is considered better than filter-based and embedded methods because it evaluates the performance of a model by iteratively selecting and testing subsets of features. This technique chooses the most efficient subset of attributes by utilising a machine learning model to assess the subset's predictive power. Wrapper-based methods consider the interaction effects between features that can provide valuable information about the underlying data structure. In contrast, filter-based approaches only consider the individual relevance of each feature, which may miss meaningful relationships between them. Wrapper-based methods typically perform better than filter-based and embedded methods because they use a machine learning model to evaluate the subsets of features. The selected subset of features from Wrapper-based methods is optimal for the specific modelling problem. Wrapper-based techniques can manage non-linear relationships between features, which is not possible with filter-based methods. Wrapper-based methods are more robust to noise and outliers in the data because they evaluate the subset of features based on the model's performance rather than the features' statistical properties. Wrapper-based methods are more flexible than embedded methods because they can be applied to any machine learning model. However, embedded methods are limited to specific models.

The computational complexity of many wrapper-based feature selection techniques may prevent them from being used in extensive malware research. On the other hand, extensive malware study involves large datasets, and it is amicable to be complex in nature. Wrapper-based methods are particularly used to assess specific machine learning algorithms to obtain optimal features. Wrapper-based feature selection methods are widely employed in Intrusion Detection System applications to support complex processing and computation (Das et al., 2022).

There are 3 methods involved in Wrapper based methods: Forward Feature Selection, Backward Feature Elimination and Stepwise Feature Selection.

4.2.1.1 Forward Feature Selection

Starting with a null model, forward selection is used to fit each individual feature to the model one at a time by selecting the one with the lowest p-value. Consider fusing the feature that one previously selected with all the others that are still there in order to suit a model with two features. Repeat the process of choosing the feature with the lowest p-value. Repeat this procedure until a collection of features is picked with p-values that are lower than the desired level of significance. In forward feature selection, a logistic regression algorithm is applied to select the features in this study.

Logistic Regression

The logistic Regression (LR) model is utilized to forecast the probability of the classes once the classes are ranked based on the relative relevance of the input attributes. In this case, the LR model is used to select the features based on the ROC-AUC probabilities (i.e. ROC - Receiver Operator Characteristic, and AUC - Area under Curve). These approaches are used to remove the attributes which are irrelevant to the target variables with the help of ranking values.

$$f(e(b)) = \alpha + \beta a_1 + \gamma a_2 \tag{1}$$

From equation (1), f () is the join function, e(y) is the target attribute, and $\alpha + \beta a_1 + \gamma a_2$ is the linear predictor (α, β, γ to be predicted), respectively. The 'f' function is to 'connect' the linear predictor with the 'b' attribute. The Logistic Regression comes with a set of screening methods that help us measure the model's fitness and choose the attributes accordingly. Usually, the LR model generates the score of each attribute which help us to select the features more effectively.

4.2.1.2 Backward Feature Elimination

This procedure begins with all of the features present and gradually removes them one at a time. Backward elimination is used to first eliminate the unimportant feature with the highest p-value (>significant level), starting with the entire model with all independent variables. This approach is repeated until the final set of relevant characteristics is produced. In this, a linear regression mechanism is applied to select the features.

4.2.1.3 Stepwise Feature Selection

Similar to the forward selection, it also considers the importance of features that have previously been added in addition to introducing a new feature. Backward elimination is used to simply eliminate any previously chosen qualities that turn out to be unimportant. It is, therefore, a mix of forward elimination and backward elimination. It is vital to note that sequential backward selection (SBS) does not remove features that have already been selected by sequential forward selection (SFS). SFS does not introduce features that SBS has already removed. In this study, a linear regression mechanism is applied to select the features.

Linear Regression

The link between a dependent variable (y) and at least one independent variable (x) is established using a linear regression model. The parameter of a linear regression model is frequently estimated using the Ordinary Least Squares (OLS) approach. In OLS Model, add the constant to the variable (i.e.) Target Variable.

$$C = x + yA \tag{2}$$

From equation (2), indicates where C is the descriptive attribute, and A is the dependent attribute. The slope of the line is x, and y is the intercept (the value of C when y = 0).

4.2.1.4 Advantages and Limitations of Wrapper-Based Feature Selection Technique

As discussed above, the wrapper-based feature selection methods consist of forward selection, backward elimination, and stepwise selection. Table 2 describes the advantages and limitations of wrapper-based feature selection techniques.

Due to the evolving nature of Malware tremendously in recent days, novel variants appear regularly. Feature Selection methods play a significant role in dealing with Malware's dynamic nature. In particular, Wrapper-based feature selection methods can handle static and dynamic Malware with variant signature patterns (Guendouz et al., 2022).

4.2.1.5 Suitable Feature Selection Methods for Specific Datasets

The types of datasets or malware families influence the feature selection techniques. To choose the best feature selection method for a particular set of data, Table 3 suggests some of the suitable feature selection methods for a dataset.

Table 2. Pros and cons of wrapper-based feature selection methods

Wrapper-based Feature Selection Method	Advantages	Limitations
Forward Selection	• It is simple and fast to execute and enables the model's performance to be enhanced. • The method process one feature at a time, adding the feature that improves the efficiency of the model. • This process is repeated until the desired level of accuracy is achieved. • Also, it helps to reduce the computational complexity of the model. • By eliminating irrelevant or redundant features, the model can significantly reduce the number of variables and simplifies the same.	• It can be prone to overfitting. • Overfitting happens when an algorithm loses its ability to generalize because it becomes too specialized to the training data. • When dealing with large datasets, it is computationally expensive. • The technique has to evaluate the performance of the model for each feature, which is a time-consuming one. • Sometimes, it fails to detect the best subset of features.
Backward Elimination	• By starting with all of the features and deleting the least significant one at a time, backward elimination improves the model's performance. • Repeat the step until there is no improvement is observed in removal of features. • Lower Complexity • Improves the performance of the model • Less prone to overfitting	• The main lacuna of the backward elimination method is that once the feature is eliminated from the model, it is not possible to re-enter again. • Sometimes, a dropped feature becomes significant in a while in the final. • Due to its attaining insignificance, it is impossible to determine which predictor caused the rejection of another predictor. • No feature can be selected again after it has been removed from a model using a backward elimination process. In other words, backward elimination cannot be used in a flexible manner to add or remove features.
Stepwise Selection	• Stepwise selection can be done in both forward and backward selection processes. • This technique is easy to interpret. • Less prone to overfitting. • It is computationally efficient. • It is faster than other automatic model selection methods.	• It is unreliable or inconsistent. • Stepwise selection is sensitive to the data sample size, the order of the variables, the Correlation among the variables and the significance level.

Table 3. Suitable feature selection methods for specific datasets

Feature Selection Method	Types of Feature Selection Methods	Type of Problem/ Dataset	E.g.: Malware Family	Merits	Demerits
Filter-Based Feature Selection	• Correlation • Chi-Square • ANOVA • Information Gain	• Use Proxy Measure • Supports High Dimensional Data • Numerical Generic Dataset • Statistical Modelling	• General Malware Classification / Malware Detection • Phishing Dataset (Numerical)	• Computationally cheaper compared to Wrapper and embedded methods • Fastest Run Time • Avoids Overfitting • The ability to Good Generalization	• No interaction with the classification model for feature selection • Ignores Feature Dependencies • Consider each feature as a univariate one • Sometimes fails to select the best feature • Low performance
Wrapper-Based Feature Selection	• Forward Selection • Backward Elimination • Stepwise Selection	• Predictive Modelling • Dataset with more features • Supports Categorical and Numerical Data	• General Malware Classification / Malware Detection • Phishing, Cross-site Scripting, Adware, Spyware, Ransomware, Trojan horse, any malware etc…	• Interacts with classifier for feature selection • A more comprehensive search of feature set space • Consider feature dependencies • Performs with better generalization than the filter method	• High Computational Cost • Longer running time • High risk of overfitting compared to filter and embedded • More computationally unfeasible with the increased number of features • No guarantee of optimality of the solution if predicted with another classifier
Embedded Feature Selection	• LASSO • Elastic Net • Ridge Regression	• Supports High Dimensional Data • Suits for both Numerical, Categorical and Temporal Data	• General Malware Classification / Malware Detection • Supports all classes of Malware	• Less computationally intensive as compared to Wrapper • Faster run time compared to Wrapper • Interacts with the classification model for feature selection • Lower risk of overfitting compared to Wrapper • Outperforms filter in generalization error with the increased number of data points	• Problematic in the identification of the small set of features

4.3 Ensemble Learning Algorithm

Ensemble approaches aim to improve a statistical learning or model fitting technique's performance. Rather than using a single fit of the approach, the overall principle of ensemble techniques is to develop a linear combination of some model fitting method. Because it is learned and then utilized to make predictions, an ensemble is a supervised learning algorithm. Ensemble approaches combine one or more classifiers to produce a more accurate prediction than a single classifier (Huang et al., 2009). Ensemble learning methods dispel the notion that combining the predictions of numerous classifiers will improve performance by either increasing prediction accuracy or lowering bias and variance (Mohanty et al., 2022; Almomani et al., 2022; Moedjahedy et al., 2022; Nugraha et al., 2022; Khatun et al., 2022; Ghaleb et al., 2022).

4.3.1 Bagging Classifier

In the bagging method, homogenous weak learners are evaluated, learned in parallel, and then combined using a deterministic averaging method. Weak learners (also known as base models) are models that can be used to create more complicated models. These fundamental models frequently underperform on their own, either due to bias (poor degree of freedom models) or an excessive amount of variance (high degree of freedom models), which makes them unreliable. Bagging compares one or more weak learners to enhance the model's accuracy.

4.3.2 Boosting Algorithm

A technique for ensemble modelling called "boosting" creates a robust classifier from a group of weak ones. By sequentially constructing a model out of weak models, this is accomplished. The training data is used to build a model as a starting point. Then, a second model is developed to address the issues with the original model. Until the maximum number of models has been added, or the complete training set has been successfully predicted, this process is repeated.

4.3.2.1 AdaBoost Algorithm

AdaBoost was the first functional boosting algorithm created specifically for binary classification. A standard boosting method known as AdaBoost, or adaptive boosting, combines multiple "weak classifiers" into a single "strong classifier." One of the few boosting techniques is AdaBoost or adaptive boosting. In modelling, decision trees are frequently used.

Pseudo Code for Ensemble learning classifier

```
Let N be the training set's size
for each iteration of t:
        N replacement instances from the original training set
```

```
are sampled
      Apply the sample to the learning algorithm
      The generated classifier should be saved
Put an end to it.
```

5. RESULTS AND DISCUSSION

This session discusses the results of the proposed approach in order to demonstrate its effectiveness and reliability. In this work, the Wrapper-based Feature Selection techniques are applied to the Mendeley dataset. The parameters that were used to select the best subsets of attributes are shown in Table 4.

Table 4. Parameters that were used to select the best subsets of features

Wrapper-based Algorithms	Parameters
Forward Feature Selection (Logistic Regression)	ROC AUC is employed for choosing the subset of features within the dataset. ROC AUC values between 0.89-0.9 values are selected.
Backward Feature Selection (Linear Regression)	The parameter used here is the P-value. P-value stands for probability measure given for statistical model is search out the hypnosis of null values. The features that meet the p-value>0.05 features are eliminated.
Stepwise Feature Selection (Linear Regression)	The parameters used are the P-value. If the feature attains a P-value of 0.05, the feature gets added, and if the feature attains a p-value bigger than 0.05 gets removed.

The parameters that were used to Detecting the Phishing Websites are Accuracy metric (A), are

$$A = \frac{TP + TN}{TP + TN + FP + FN} \tag{3}$$

Precision (P), Recall (R) and F1 score (F_1) the classifier's performance was also examined using metrics where:

$$P = \frac{TP}{TP + FP} \tag{4}$$

$$R = \frac{TP}{TP + FP} \tag{5}$$

$$F_1 = \frac{2*P*R}{P + B} \tag{6}$$

Figure 4 illustrates the overall results of the proposed approaches, in which Wrapper-based Feature selection techniques; Forward Feature selection gives the best reduction percentages when compared to Backward and Stepwise Feature selection. Figure 5 shows the Bagging Classifier algorithm gives the best accuracy than the Boosting algorithm in ensemble modelling.

Figure 4. Wrapper-based feature selection reduction percentages

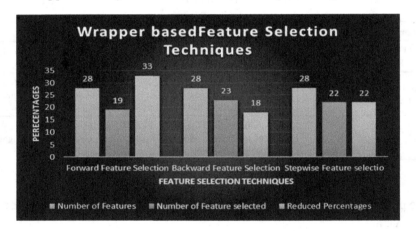

Figure 5. Performance comparison of ensemble learning algorithms

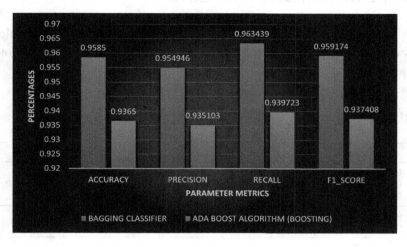

6. CONCLUSION AND FUTURE SCOPE

Constant monitoring of security risks is essential in all automated and semi-automated industries. Remote maintenance has been an integral part of mining industries. Many security models are available to monitor security risks. Phishing attacks are one of the targeted attacks of major industries, where the attackers steal user credential information in the form of websites, e-mails, SMS, or through phone calls. In this chapter, the Mendeley dataset is utilized to detect Phishing Websites. Wrapper-based Feature selection techniques are segregated into three types, namely Forward, Backward and Stepwise. In which Forward Feature selection with Logistic Regression algorithm gives the best reduction of the attributes, nearly 33% of attributes are reduced from the dataset. In order to assess the model's performance, ensemble learning algorithms are used. To recognise phishing websites, Bagging and Boosting ensemble models are developed. Based on the performance evaluation metrics, the Bagging Classifier provides the best accuracy of 95% than Boosting algorithms in phishing website detection.

In future, to detect Phishing Websites using other attributes like Host-based and Correlation- based attributes can be applied with various feature selection techniques. A Hybrid Ensemble learning approach will be carried out to enhance the robustness of the model. This study will also be extended by developing adaptive feature selection systems and successfully selecting relevant features in real time.

7. FUTURE RESEARCH PROSPECTS

Table 5 presents some of the other open-source malware datasets available with reference to the prospective web links that may be useful to the readers for their implementations.

Table 5. Open source datasets as future research prospects

S.No.	Dataset	Source	Weblink
1.	Phishing Website Dataset for Feature Evaluation	Mendeley Data	https://data.mendeley.com/datasets/h3cgnj8hft/1
2.	Phishing Website Dataset	Mendeley Data	https://data.mendeley.com/datasets/72ptz43s9v/1
3.	Phishing Website Dataset	Mendeley Data	https://data.mendeley.com/datasets/n96ncsr5g4/1
4.	Webpage Phishing Detection Dataset	Mendeley Data	https://data.mendeley.com/datasets/c2gw7fy2j4/1
5.	CICMalDroid Dataset	UNB - CIC	https://www.unb.ca/cic/datasets/maldroid-2020.html
6.	Darknet Dataset	UNB - CIC	https://www.unb.ca/cic/datasets/darknet2020.html
7.	DNS Over HTTPS Dataset	UNB - CIC	https://www.unb.ca/cic/datasets/dohbrw-2020.html
8.	DDoS Evaluation Dataset	UNB - CIC	https://www.unb.ca/cic/datasets/ddos-2019.html
9.	CIC Malware Memory Analysis Dataset	UNB - CIC	https://www.unb.ca/cic/datasets/malmem-2022.html
10.	CIC Android Malware Dataset	UNB - CIC	https://www.unb.ca/cic/datasets/invesandmal2019.html

ACKNOWLEDGMENT

This work is supported by DST-CURIE-AI project during 2021–2023 by Centre for Cyber Intelligence established under Centre for Machine Learning and Intelligence, Avinashilingam Institute for Home Science and Higher Education for Women, Coimbatore - 43, Tamilnadu, India.

Declaration of Competing Interest: None.

REFERENCES

Ali, W. (2017). Phishing Website Detection based on Supervised Machine Learning with Wrapper Features Selection. *International Journal of Advanced Computer Science and Applications*, *8*(9). doi:10.14569/IJACSA.2017.080910

Alkhalil, Z., Hewage, C. T. E. R., Nawaf, L., & Khan, I. (2021). Phishing Attacks: A Recent Comprehensive Study and a New Anatomy. *Frontiers of Computer Science*, *3*, 563060. Advance online publication. doi:10.3389/fcomp.2021.563060

Almomani, A., Alauthman, M., Shatnawi, M. T., Alweshah, M., Alrosan, A., Alomoush, W., Gupta, B. B., Gupta, B. B., & Gupta, B. B. (2022). Phishing website detection with semantic features based on machine learning classifiers. *International Journal on Semantic Web and Information Systems*, *18*(1), 1–24. doi:10.4018/IJSWIS.297032

Almseidin, M., Zuraiq, A. A., Alkasassbeh, M., & Alnidami, N. (2019). Phishing Detection Based on Machine Learning and Feature Selection Methods. *International Journal of Interactive Mobile Technologies*, *13*(12), 171. doi:10.3991/ijim.v13i12.11411

APWG. (2019). *APWG trend Report*. APWG. https://docs.apwg.org/reports/apwg_trends_report_q3_2019.pdfAccessed from 20 July 2020.

Basit, A., Zafar, M., Liu, X., Javed, A. R., Jalil, Z., & Kifayat, K. (2021b). A comprehensive survey of AI-enabled phishing attacks detection techniques. *Telecommunication Systems*, *76*(1), 139–154. doi:10.100711235-020-00733-2 PMID:33110340

Cabaj, K., Domingos, D., Kotulski, Z., & Respício, A. (2018). Cybersecurity education: Evolution of the discipline and analysis of master programs. *Computers & Security*, *75*, 24–35. doi:10.1016/j.cose.2018.01.015

Chandrashekar, G., & Sahin, F. (2014). A survey on feature selection methods. *Computers & Electrical Engineering*, *40*(1), 16–28. doi:10.1016/j.compeleceng.2013.11.024

Das, A., Pramod, & S, S. B. (2022). An efficient feature selection approach for Intrusion Detection System using decision tree. *International Journal of Advanced Computer Science and Applications*, *13*(2). doi:10.14569/IJACSA.2022.0130276

Fadheel, W., Abusharkh, M., & Abdel-Qader, I. (2017). *On Feature Selection for the Prediction of Phishing Websites*. Dependable Autonomic and Secure Computing., doi:10.1109/DASC-PICom-DataCom-CyberSciTec.2017.146

FBI Warns of Dramatic Increase in Business E-Mail Compromise (BEC) Schemes. (2018b, June 27). FBI. https://www.fbi.gov/contact-us/field-offices/memphis/news/press-releases/fbi-warns-of-dramatic-increase-in-business-e-mail-compromise-bec-schemes

Ghaleb Al-Mekhlafi, Z., Abdulkarem Mohammed, B., Al-Sarem, M., Saeed, F., Al-Hadhrami, T., & Alshammari, T., M., Alreshidi, A., & Sarheed Alshammari, T. (. (2022). Phishing websites detection by using optimized stacking ensemble model. *Computer Systems Science and Engineering*, *41*(1), 109–125. doi:10.32604/csse.2022.020414

Guendouz, M., & Amine, A. (2022). A new wrapper-based feature selection technique with fireworks algorithm for Android Malware detection. *International Journal of Software Science and Computational Intelligence*, *14*(1), 1–19. doi:10.4018/IJSSCI.312554

Huang, F., Xie, G., & Xiao, R. (2009). Research on Ensemble Learning. *International Conference on Artificial Intelligence and Computational Intelligence.* IEEE. 10.1109/AICI.2009.235

Jovic, A., Brkić, K., & Bogunović, N. (2015). A review of feature selection methods with applications. *International Convention on Information and Communication Technology, Electronics and Microelectronics.* IEEE. 10.1109/MIPRO.2015.7160458

Khatun, M., Mozumder, M. A., Polash, M., Hasan, M. R., Ahammad, K., & Shaiham, M. D. S. (2022). An approach to detect phishing websites with features selection method and Ensemble Learning. *International Journal of Advanced Computer Science and Applications*, *13*(8). doi:10.14569/IJACSA.2022.0130888

Moedjahedy, J., Setyanto, A., Alarfaj, F. K., & Alreshoodi, M. (2022). CCrFS: Combine correlation features selection for detecting phishing websites using machine learning. *Future Internet*, *14*(8), 229. doi:10.3390/fi14080229

Mohanty, S., Sahoo, M., & Acharya, A. A. (2022). Predicting phishing URL using filter based univariate feature selection technique. *2022 Second International Conference on Computer Science, Engineering and Applications (ICCSEA).* IEEE. 10.1109/ICCSEA54677.2022.9936298

Nugraha, A. F., Tama, D. A., Istiqomah, D. A., Ramadhani, S. T., Kusuma, B. N., & Windarni, V. A. (2022). Feature selection technique for improving classification performance in the web-phishing detection process. *Conference Series*, *4*, 25–31. doi:10.34306/conferenceseries.v4i1.667

Security Magazine. (n.d.). https://www.securitymagazine.com/articles/92157-coronavirus-related-spear-phishing-attacks-see-667-increase-in-march-2020

Sharma, S. R., Parthasarathy, R., & Honnavalli, P. B. (2020). A Feature Selection Comparative Study for Web Phishing Datasets. *IEEE International Conference on Electronics, Computing and Communication Technologies*. IEEE. 10.1109/CONECCT50063.2020.9198349

Singh, P., & Ranga, V. (2021). Attack and intrusion detection in cloud computing using an ensemble learning approach. *International Journal of Information Technology : an Official Journal of Bharati Vidyapeeth's Institute of Computer Applications and Management*, *13*(2), 565–571. doi:10.100741870-020-00583-w

Surwade, A. P. (2020). Phishing e-mail is an increasing menace. *International Journal of Information Technology : an Official Journal of Bharati Vidyapeeth's Institute of Computer Applications and Management*, *12*(2), 611–617. doi:10.100741870-019-00407-6

Tahir, M., Asghar, S., Zafar, A., & Gillani, S. (2016). A Hybrid Model to Detect Phishing-Sites Using Supervised Learning Algorithms. *International Conference on Computational Science*. IEEE. 10.1109/CSCI.2016.0214

TanC. S. (2018, March 24). *Phishing Dataset for Machine Learning: Feature Evaluation*. doi:10.17632/h3cgnj8hft.1

Tubis, A., Werbińska-Wojciechowska, S., Góralczyk, M., Wróblewski, A., & Ziętek, B. (2020). Cyber-Attacks Risk Analysis Method for Different Levels of Automation of Mining Processes in Mines Based on Fuzzy Theory Use. *Sensors (Basel)*, *20*(24), 7210. doi:10.339020247210 PMID:33339301

Volkamer, M., Renaud, K., Reinheimer, B., & Kunz, A. (2017). User experiences of TORPEDO: TOoltip-poweRed Phishing E-mail DetectiOn. *Computers & Security*, *71*, 100–113. doi:10.1016/j.cose.2017.02.004

Xuan, C. D., Nguyen, H. L., & Nikolaevich, T. V. (2020). Malicious URL Detection based on Machine Learning. *International Journal of Advanced Computer Science and Applications*, *11*(1). Advance online publication. doi:10.14569/IJACSA.2020.0110119

Zhu, E., Chen, Y., Ye, C., Li, X., & Liu, F. (2019). OFS-NN: An Effective Phishing Websites Detection Model Based on Optimal Feature Selection and Neural Network. *IEEE Access : Practical Innovations, Open Solutions*, *7*, 73271–73284. doi:10.1109/ACCESS.2019.2920655

Zuhair, H., Selmat, A., & Salleh, M. (2015). The Effect of Feature Selection on Phish Website Detection. *International Journal of Advanced Computer Science and Applications*, *6*(10). doi:10.14569/IJACSA.2015.061031

Chapter 5
Classification of Firewall Log Files Using Supervised Machine Learning Techniques

Sri Danalaksmi
Avinashilingam Institute for Home Science and Higher Education for Women, India

Geethalakshmi
Avinashilingam Institute for Home Science and Higher Education for Women, India

A. Roshni
Avinashilingam Institute for Home Science and Higher Education for Women, India

Padmavathi Ganapathi
Avinashilingam Institute for Home Science and Higher Education for Women, India

ABSTRACT

A firewall prevents traffic entering and departing the domain it was supposed to protect. The logging feature keeps track of how the firewall handles different sorts of traffic. Monitoring and analyzing log files can assist IT businesses in improving the end-user reliability of their systems. This book chapter investigates and classifies the firewall log files using supervised machine learning algorithms. The main objective of this chapter is to examine firewall security by analyzing the firewall log files. Supervised machine learning classifiers such as support vector machine (SVM), Naïve Bayes, logistic regression and k-nearest neighbor (KNN) models are developed to classify the firewall log files. Feature selection using Ranker

DOI: 10.4018/978-1-6684-8666-5.ch005

and Info_Gain_Attribute_Eval methods within the Weka tool is applied to derive the robust features from the data. Finally, a comparative analysis is performed to evaluate the efficiency of the supervised machine learning models. Results that, the Naïve Bayes Classifier attains the highest accuracy of 99.26% for the classification of firewall log files.

1. INTRODUCTION

A firewall is a security access management point that controls access to computer networks and ensures safe network connectivity. A network firewall is a device or collection of systems that control access between two networks - a trustworthy network and an untrusted network—by using pre-configured rules or filters by As-Suhbani et al. (2019). The outcomes of firewall rules can be audited, verified, and evaluated via monitoring. The analyzing and classifying of the firewall checks and decides the packets to pass it or not. It can improve security purposes even more by allowing based on the required protocols. Internet traffic kinds that are allowed or forbidden are specified by firewall rules. Figure 1 shows the Firewall security which allows the traffic and denies it.

Each firewall profile includes a set of firewall rules; these rules cannot be changed. The ability to create new rules is therefore limited to a few profiles. It is also possible to build your own rules using a profile with no predefined ones. The firewall profile will also impact how important the rules are compared to predefined rules, so make one selection carefully (Allagi et al., 2019).

Inbound traffic from the Internet to the computer or outbound traffic from the computer to the Internet can both be blocked by a firewall rule. A rule may be applied simultaneously in both directions. For instance, firewalls are security tools designed to prevent or restrict unauthorized access to intranets and other private networks connected to the Internet. Firewall policies that outline the only traffic that is permitted on the network forbid any extra traffic from connecting. At the network's front end, network firewalls act as a communication channel between internal and external devices (Ertam et al., 2018).

Figure 1. A phase of firewall in a network

Without firewalls, any network service currently running on a device with a publicly visible IP - for instance, if it is linked directly to the Internet through ethernet - may become accessible to the public. Any computer network that has an internet connection is open to cyber attacks. These networks become open to hostile attacks if a firewall is not there. Some malware is built to get network access in order to access confidential information like customer information or other proprietary data like credit card numbers and bank account information (Sharma et al., 2021).

Other kinds of malware are created with the sole purpose of destroying data or bringing networks to a halt. Hackers can easily interrupt the network if it is public IP. The classification of a Firewall is far more important than attackers are less for breaching the network threats.

The survey's findings show that network engineering teams are devoting more time and effort to firewall maintenance and that their duties are becoming more difficult. According to over 45 per cent of respondents, most of these chores are still done by hand. It is challenging to keep up with everything since most teams deal with a multi-vendor environment with inherent complexity (Winding et al., 2006). The Key Findings and Trends in Firewalls are:

- Increased spending on firewalls and network security
- The use of several vendors has become the standard
- There is a demand for firewall engineers with particular knowledge
- Network automation is becoming more popular
- Firewall Management to be enhanced

This chapter contributes to the automation of the classification of firewall log files using various supervised machine learning models and suggests the suitable one for precise mechanisms. This study aims to explore the significance of a Firewall in a network to safeguard user credentials and develop supervised learning models to classify it appropriately.

This chapter is organized as the introduction of Firewall, and its significance was specified in Section 1. Section 2 deals with the classification of firewall log files. Section 3 describes similar existing literature works. Section 4 encompasses the proposed methodology for firewall log file classification. Section 5 highlights the open challenges in Network Firewall Security. Followed by section 6 concludes with the future scope of the study.

2. CLASSIFICATION OF FIREWALL LOG FILES

This section deals with the classification of firewall log files and the steps involved in processing them. Firewall log files can be classified based on the following factors (Kowalski et al., 2006):

i.   **Type of Firewall**: There are various kinds of firewalls, including network firewalls, application firewalls, host-based firewalls, and cloud-based firewalls. Each type of Firewall generates different types of log files.

ii.   **Data Format**: Firewall log files can be generated in different data formats such as CSV, JSON, Syslog, or XML. The data format can determine the type of log analysis tools required.

iii.   **Level of Detail**: Firewall logs can range from basic information about network traffic to detailed information about individual packets. The level of detail can be adjusted according to the requirements of the organization.

iv.   **Purpose**: Firewall log files can be used for various purposes, such as network troubleshooting, intrusion detection, compliance monitoring, and security analysis. The classification of firewall log files can be based on their specific purpose.

v.   **Time Frame**: Firewall log files can be classified based on the time frame they cover, such as daily, weekly, monthly, or yearly logs.

vi.   **Source and Destination IP Address**: Firewall logs can be categorized based on the source and destination IP addresses. This makes it easier to spot trends in network traffic and potential security issues.

vii.   **Protocol and Port**: Firewall logs can be classified based on the protocol and port used in network traffic. This can help identify potential security threats and patterns in network traffic.

viii.   **Severity Level**: Firewall logs can be classified based on the severity level of the event, such as critical, high, medium, or low severity. This can help prioritize security incidents and focus on the most critical issues.

ix.   **User Identity**: Firewall logs can be classified based on the user identity associated with network traffic. This can help identify unauthorized access attempts and track user activity on the network.

2.1 Log Files

Log files in network firewalls are generated due to the Firewall's activity in processing network traffic (Nimbalkar et al., 2016). Firewalls typically generate log files that record information about events such as:

i.   **Blocked traffic**: The source and destination IP addresses, protocol, port number, and the reason for blocking the traffic are all recorded in a log entry that is created whenever the Firewall stops any network traffic.

ii. **Allowed traffic**: The Firewall also generates log entries for traffic that are allowed to pass through it. This log entry contains similar information to the one generated for blocked traffic.

iii. **Intrusion attempts**: If the Firewall detects any attempted intrusion into the network, it generates a log entry that contains information about the type of attack, source IP address, and any other relevant information about the attack.

iv. **Configuration changes**: Whenever a change is made to the Firewall's configuration, it generates a log entry that records the user who made the change, the time and date of the change, and any other relevant details.

The log files help monitor network traffic, detect and prevent unauthorized access, troubleshoot network issues, and ensure compliance with security policies and regulations. They can also be used for forensic analysis and investigations.

2.2 Identify Attack in Log Files

Identifying attacks in firewall log files can be a complex task, as there are many log entries to analyze and many different types of attacks to look for (Hommes et al., 2012; Shaheed et al., 2022). However, several steps can be taken to help identify attacks in firewall log files:

Step 1: Analyze the log files regularly
Step 2: Look for Patterns
Step 3: Use Automated Tools
Step 4: Check for Known attacks
Step 5: Look for anomalies

Step 1: Analyze the log files regularly: Regularly reviewing the firewall log files is an important step in identifying potential attacks. This will help to identify any anomalies or suspicious activity that may indicate an attack.

Step 2: Look for patterns: Many attacks follow a specific pattern or use specific techniques that can be identified in the firewall log files. By analyzing the log files for patterns or commonalities, it may be possible to identify potential attacks.

Step 3: Use automated tools: There are several tools available that can help to analyze firewall log files for potential attacks. These technologies look for trends and abnormalities that can point to an attack using machine learning and other methods.

Step 4: Check for known attacks: Firewalls often have built-in rules and signatures for known attacks. By checking the log files against these rules and signatures, it may be possible to identify known attacks.

Step 5: Look for anomalies: Anomalies or unusual activity in the firewall log files may indicate an attack. For example, a sudden spike in traffic from a specific IP address or unusual traffic patterns may be a sign of an attack.

It is important to note that no single approach can guarantee the detection of all attacks and that a combination of techniques and strategies is often needed to identify potential attacks in firewall log files.

3. RELATED WORKS

In this section, details of the previous works carried out by other researchers in dealing with the classification of firewall log files using machine learning techniques are discussed below.

Hajar Esmail As Suhnbani et al. (2019) have analyzed a firewall log dataset using data mining approaches such as feature selection and redundancy removal. Then, to speed up the process, they employ WEKA's machine learning classifiers, which include Naive Bayes, kNN, One R, and J48. They also contrasted the performance of these algorithms' classification accuracy and F-measure. And they also performed a 10-fold cross-validation test. In terms of accuracy, the required model has performed admirably.

ShridharAllagi, RashmiRachh et al. (2019) used a network log data collection generated by a corporation for research. Several million entries make up the log data set. Only 5% of the data appears to be abnormal behaviour. This exposes the system to an issue of class imbalance, in which one sort of cluster is insignificant compared to others. They suggest using k-means (k=2) to create two groups, normal and abnormal, and a self-organizing feature map (SOFM) of an artificial neural network with neurons in the input and output layers. It focuses on linguistic information in log data, with a particular emphasis on bigram words (for example, "ACCESS DENIED," "401 ERROR," "INVALID PASSCODE," and so on). They evaluated the system using a sizable dataset of network records and a supervised machine learning methodology. The trial's findings showed that deviant behaviour may be predicted with a high level of acceptability.

FatihErtam et al. (2018) obtained log data through the Firewall. The log logs were obtained from Firat University's Palo Alto 5020 Firewall device. The receiving log record is the result of about 30 seconds' worth of recording and is made up of thousands of records. Priority is given to the characteristics of the port, byte, packet, and time information in the receiving log. The action attribute of the class can be one of the following: "allow," "deny," "drop," or "reset-both." Along with the SVM classifier, the activation functions linear, polynomial, RBF, and sigmoid were used. The results were contrasted using the ROC curves, F1 score, recall, precision, and precision.

Deepanshu Sharma et al. (2021) examined the performance of machine learning classification models for firewall log data. It also attempted to improve classification by comparing the outcomes of all the models utilizing heterogeneous ensemble classification models. The dataset was first put into the workspace, where data pre-processing was carried out. The feature selection was made once the multi-labels were encoded into numeric values. The data were then scaled to make the selected features uniform in nature. The dataset was separated afterwards, and the model was built.

Robert Winding et al. (2006) used several analysis methodologies to investigate system anomaly detection. Firewall log data is also subject to this type of statistical analysis. Boxplots were used to choose meaningful features from aggregations of the data, look at the distribution of selected features, spot individual data records, and examine outliers for some features. A classification model was constructed as a result of clustering the destination perspective vector.

Kazimierz Kowalski, and Mohsen Beheshti (2006), present their study towards establishing general and systematic intrusion prevention strategies. The main concept is to find repeating patterns in system variables that describe user and programme activity using data mining techniques. Server systems routinely generate extensive activity logs and are useful for detecting intrusion. Unfortunately, manufacturing volumes outweigh the traditional technique's capacity and manageability. In this work, they suggested examining intersections between log files from various firewalls and apps installed on the same computer and intersections between log files from other machines. Full log files are substantially larger than intersections of log files, which contain entries demonstrating anomalies in accessing a single computer or a collection of computers.

PiyushNimbalkar et al. (2016) assume that this approach makes use of the framework for determining the semantics of information stored in tables and portraying it as RDF Linked Data. The Tabulate module analyses the log file's structure and finds it. The module establishes a table-like structure for the log by dividing it into columns and rows. After identifying the types of values in each column, a sorted list of potential semantic classes is generated from ontology by the Decode module. The Relationship Generator module constructs a set of relationships between the columns in the log file using the ontology and this ranked list of classes. In order to create an RDF Linked Data representation of the content of the log file, the Generate RDF module employs the inferred schema.

Stefan Hommes et al. (2012), this study described an automated method for log file analysis. A chart tracking system identifies the most obvious fraudulent behaviour in the first phase. In a second optional phase, a human operator can confirm the results. The first phase involves tracking temporal changes between grouped instances in successive windows. Utilizing relevant set-specific distances and information theoretical measurements, the difference is computed. Then, using statistical process control techniques, outliers that might be anomalies are discovered. Evaluation of our method's performance in the presence of a large-scale tagged ground truth is its most difficult component. They were unable to complete this job because no such tagged dataset exists; nonetheless, our approach might be applied in this situation.

Hayder Naser Khraib Behadili et al. (2021), the categorization approach is based on generalizing powerful decision trees. One of the most common machine learning methods for transparency is the DT algorithm (interpretable). To build the classification model, DT employs a separate-and-conquer strategy. Quinlan defined the approach as creating an upside-down tree with roots at the top from D instances in the input. The "leaves" linked with the most common class in D are the D instances of firewall log activity. For each feature, the DT generates a feature list and attributes. The gain ratio is an information-based measurement that takes into account various numbers (and probabilities) of test results of attributes for each feature in a decision tree. As a result, the maximum gain ratio is discovered.

Kazunori Kamiya et al. (2015) provide a mechanism for identifying hosts that are compromised with malware by looking at both Firewall and Proxy logs. It demonstrates that the approach can discover malware-infected hosts that are missed by HTTP-based harmful lists. When compared to solitary Proxy-based detection, the strategy delivers a 6% improvement in accuracy. As a result, they demonstrate that multi-layer analysis can help to improve malware detection.

Based on the relevant literature works discussed above, the following are the research gaps identified are discussed.

- In related works, most of the proposed models do not achieve the maximum performance in the classification of firewall log files.
- Fails to attempt significant feature selection methods before model development for firewall log file classification.
- Comparison between the supervised machine learning models is not appropriately carried out using the validation measures such as accuracy, train_accuracy, test_accuracy, precision, recall and F1_score.

This chapter concentrates on overcoming the above-mentioned research gaps by implementing properly supervised machine learning models based on the feature selection methods for firewall log file classification. The developed models are further assessed by significant performance evaluation metrics and suggest the most suitable model for the chosen problem.

4. PROPOSED METHODOLOGY

The proposed methodology consists of six phases to develop significant firewall log file classification models using supervised machine learning methods. Figure 2 represents the proposed, designed methodology.

Figure 2. Proposed methodology

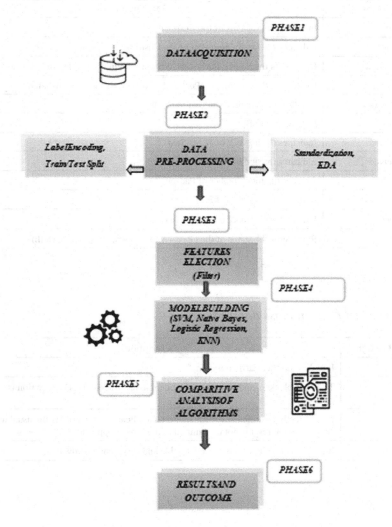

4.1 Dataset

Internet traffic records from the Palo Alto 5020 Firewall system at Firat University were used to compile the Internet Firewall data collection. There are 12 features and 65533 records in all. The class "action feature" is employed. There are a total of 4 classes. These are the classes allow, action, drop, and reset.

Table 1 shows the Dataset features and their description.

Table 2 represents the Dataset classes for firewall log file classification.

Table 1. Dataset feature description

Attribute	Description
Source Port	Indicates Source Port of the Customer
Destination Port	Indicates the Destination Port of the Customer
NAT Source Port	Represents the Source Port of the Network Address Translation
NAT Destination Port	Represents the Destination Port of the Network Address Translation
Elapsed time (sec)	Denotes the stream of the Elapsed Time
Bytes	Denotes entire Bytes
Bytes Sent	Indicates the number of Bytes Sent
Bytes Received	Indicates the number of Bytes Received
Packets	Denotes the total number of Packets
pkts_sent	Indicates the number of Packets Sent
pkts_recieved	Indicates the number of Packets Received
Action	Represents the status of the Class (Allow, Deny, Drop, Reset-Both)

Table 2. Dataset firewall class description

Firewall Action	Description
Allow	It makes internet traffic possible.
Deny	Traffic is blocked, and the application-denial-specific default Deny Action is enforced.
Drop	By discreetly terminating the traffic for an application, it overrides the usual deny action. A TCP reset is not transmitted to the host or application.
Reset - Both	It transmits a TCP reset to the client-side and server-side hardware.

4.2 Data Pre-Processing

A critical stage in machine learning is data preparation, which improves the reliability of the data and makes it simpler to glean insights that can be put to use. In order to make raw data suitable for developing and refining Machine Learning models, it must first be organized and managed. The first step in creating a machine learning model will be data preparation, and this is where the process will begin. Real-world data is usually incomplete, inconsistent, inaccurate (owing to outliers or errors), missing in specific attribute values, and lacking in trends. In this process, label encoding, Train and Test Split and Standardization steps are applied to refine the data.

4.2.1 Label Encoding

Label encoding is a process used in supervised machine learning to convert categorical data into numerical form. In this process, each unique category in the categorical variable is assigned a unique numerical value. This allows the algorithm to work with numerical data, which is often easier to process and analyze. In machine learning methods like support vector machines, Naive Bayes, K-Nearest Neighbour, Decision trees, Random forests, and Logistic regression, it is frequently used for categorical variables. But it is crucial to keep in mind that label encoding might not be the ideal choice for all kinds of categorical data, as it may introduce an artificial order or hierarchy that does not exist in the original data. In such cases, one may consider using one-hot encoding or other encoding techniques instead.

4.2.2 Train and Test Split

In supervised machine learning, the train-test split strategy is used to assess a model's performance. The provided dataset is divided into a training set and a test set. In contrast to the training set, which is used to train the model, the test set is used to evaluate how well the model performs when applied to fresh data. Ideally, the test set should include data the model will encounter in the real world.

The first portion of the data is reserved for training, and the second portion is used for testing. It is common practice to divide the train and test randomly. Generally speaking, 70–80% of the data is used for training, and 20% is used for testing. The actual split may change based on the size and composition of the dataset. Overfitting is when a model performs well on training data but poorly on fresh, untested data. The train-test divide can assist in preventing this. Analyzing a model's performance on the test set can help one understand how well it generalizes to new data.

It is important to note that train-test split is an essential technique and may need to be revised for complex models or datasets. In such cases, cross-validation or stratified sampling techniques may be used for more accurate evaluation. In this study, the dataset is split into 80% for training and 20% for testing.

4.2.3 Standardization

In order to standardize input data for machine learning, it must be changed to have a mean of 0 and a standard deviation of 1. This is also known as "feature scaling" or "data normalization". Standardization aims to ensure that each feature in the input data is treated equally in the machine learning algorithm. When the input data has different ranges for different features, some features may dominate others, leading to biased or skewed results. Standardization helps to avoid this problem by scaling each feature to have the same range (Aljabri et al., 2022).

Both the input data (i.e., the independent variables) and the output data (i.e., the dependent variable) can be standardized. However, standardizing the input data is usually only necessary, as the output data is often a categorical variable that does not require scaling (Abu AI-Haija et al., 2021).

Several methods, including z-score normalization, min-max normalization, and unit normalization, can be used to standardize data. The most popular approach to Z-score normalization is dividing the result by the standard deviation after removing the mean of each feature from the feature values. Each feature is scaled to a range between 0 and 1 in the min-max normalization process. Scaling each feature to have a unit norm or a length of 1 is known as unit normalization. Since it helps to ensure that the input data is properly prepared for the algorithm to create accurate and unbiased predictions, standardization is typically viewed as a vital pre-processing step in machine learning.

4.3 Feature Selection Using Ranker and Info_ Gain_Attribute_Eval Methods in WEKA Tool

When a database has a huge number of attributes, some of them will be irrelevant to the analysis, looking for. As a result, removing undesirable attributes from the dataset has become a necessary stage in creating a good machine learning model. This could be a still over for databases with many characteristics, but it can visually analyze the entire dataset and remove the pointless features. Fortunately, WEKA has an automated feature selection tool. Weka is a software term used to cover visualization tools and algorithms for feature selection and classification, as well as graphical user interfaces enabling quick access to these features. In the Weka tool, using ranker and infogain_attribute_evaluator methods are used to select the best features of the data (Naryanto et al., 2022; Skazin et al., 2021; Pavlychev et al., 2021).

4.3.1 Ranker

Individual evaluations are used to rank attributes. When combined with attribute valuators, it is a strong option (ReliefF, GainRatio, Entropyetc).

4.3.2 Info_Gain_Attribute_Eval

It measures the information gain with respect to the class to determine the value of an attribute. It is calculated as,

InfoGain(Class,Attribute) = H(Class) - H(Class|Attribute).

4.4 Model Building

In order to develop predictions and various classifications to achieve its objective, a machine learning model is created by learning from training data, generalizing that information, and then applying that knowledge to brand-new data that it has never seen before. With the necessary classification and performance criteria, the SVM, Naive Bayes, Logistic Regression, and K-NN models are constructed (Taher et al., 2019; Gajda et al., 2022; Pawar et al., 2022; Wang et al., 2021; Nawir et al., 2019; Kazim et al., 2019; Li et al., 2019; Zhang et al., 2019; Ndichu et al., 2023).

4.4.1 Support Vector Machine

The Support Vector Machine (SVM) is a powerful machine learning technique for classification and regression analysis. Based on previously categorized data, data can be evaluated and classified using a supervised learning method called SVM. The SVM method aims to find the best decision border that separates multiple data classes by maximizing the margin between them. The margin is the distance between the judgment's outer limit and each class's closest available data points. With a more considerable margin, the model becomes more general.

SVM transforms the input data into a high-dimensional space, which makes it easier to identify a hyperplane that separates the various classes. This is accomplished by mapping the initial data into a new space using a kernel function. SVM is beneficial when dealing with high-dimensional data, where other algorithms may struggle to find a reasonable decision boundary. SVM works well with noisy data because it can effectively manage outliers. Regression analysis and binary and multi-class classification issues can both be solved with SVM. There are different types of SVM, including linear SVM, non-linear SVM, and support vector regression (SVR).

While SVM is a powerful algorithm, it does have some limitations. SVM can need much processing, especially when working with huge datasets. SVM can also be sensitive to the kernel function, and hyperparameters used, which can affect the model's performance. SVM is a flexible and powerful machine learning algorithm, especially when working with high-dimensional and noisy data.

4.4.1.1 Working of Support Vector Machine (SVM)

The following is the step-by-step explanation of how Support Vector Machines (SVMs) algorithm work:

Step 1: Data Preparation

A labelled training dataset should contain samples (x1, y1), (x2, y2),..., (xn, yn), where xi is the feature vector for the i-th example, and yi stands for the correct class label (+1 or -1).

Step 2: Feature Mapping

Choose a suitable kernel function, indicated as K(x, x'), to convert the input data into a higher-dimensional feature space. The kernel function determines the degree of similarity between two feature vectors, x and x'.

Step 3: Optimization

To determine the best hyperplane that most effectively divides the classes while maximizing the margin between them, formulate the SVM problem as an optimization challenge. The optimization problem can be defined as:

Minimize: $\frac{1}{2}w^2 + C\sum \xi_i$

Subject to: $y_i(w \cdot \Phi(x_i) + b) \geq 1 - \xi_i$ for all training examples (x_i, y_i)

Here, w is the weight vector, b is the bias term, $\Phi(.)$ is the feature mapping function, ξ_i represents slack variables, and C is the regularization parameter.

Step 4: Lagrange Multipliers

Use the Lagrange multiplier approach to solve the optimization problem and obtain the dual form of the issue. The dual problem involves maximizing the following expression:

Maximize: $\Sigma\alpha_i - \frac{1}{2}\Sigma\Sigma\alpha_i\alpha_jy_iy_jK(x_i, x_j)$

Subject to: $\Sigma\alpha_iy_i = 0$

$0 \leq \alpha_i \leq C$ for all training examples (x_i, y_i)

Here, α_i is the Lagrange multiplier associated with each training example.

Step 5: Support Vectors

The solution of the dual problem provides the optimal values of α_i. Identify the support vectors, which are the training examples with non-zero α_i values. These examples lie on or inside the margin. Only support vectors contribute to the definition of the hyperplane.

Step 6: Classification

Given a new test example x, the class label y can be predicted using the following equation: $y = \text{sign}(\Sigma\alpha_iy_iK(x_i, x) + b)$

Here, sign(.) is the sign function, α_i are the Lagrange multipliers obtained from the dual problem, and b is the bias term.

These steps summarize the working of Support Vector Machines. It is important to remain in that SVMs can be modified and extended in various ways, such as kernel selection and soft-margin SVMs, which can improve their performance and usefulness.

4.4.2 Naïve Bayes

It is a popular machine learning technique for categorization tasks. It is founded on Bayes' theorem, a probability theorem that assesses the likelihood of a hypothesis in light of available data. Since Naive Bayes is a supervised learning system, labelled training data are necessary. After computing the conditional probabilities of each feature given each class label, Bayes applies the Bayes theorem to ascertain the probability of each class given the features. The algorithm is referred regarded as "naive" since it thinks the features are independent of one another. There are various versions of Naive Bayes, including:

Multinomial Naive Bayes: utilized for discrete data, such as text data, where each feature denotes the frequency of a particular word in a document.

Gaussian Naive Bayes: utilized for continuous data with Gaussian-distributed features.

Bernoulli Naive Bayes: used for binary data, where each feature indicates if another characteristic is present or not.

The ease of use and effectiveness of Naive Bayes, which only needs a small quantity of training data to work well, are two of its key features. Additionally, it excels at multi-class classification issues and has good high-dimensional data handling capabilities. The assumption made by Naive Bayes, however, is that the qualities are always independent of one another. It also assumes that the data is normally distributed, which may not be the case for some datasets. Nonetheless, Naive Bayes remains a powerful and widely used algorithm in machine learning. This study implements Gaussian Naïve Bayes to classify the firewall log files.

4.4.2.1 Working of Naïve Bayes (NB)

The following is the step-by-step explanation of how the Naïve Bayes (NB) algorithm works:

Step 1: Data Preparation

In a labelled training dataset, collect samples $(x1, y1)$, $(x2, y2)$,..., (xn, yn), where xi is the feature vector for the i-th example, and yi is the matching class label.

Step 2: Feature Independence Assumption

Naive Bayes bases its analysis on the premise that all features in the dataset are independent of one another given the class label. Using what is referred to as the "naive" assumption simplifies calculations.

Step 3: Calculate Class Priors

Determine each class label's prior probability using the training dataset. To do this, divide the total number of training examples by the count of examples of class y.

Step 4: Calculate Feature Probabilities

For each feature x_j and each class label y, calculate the conditional probability $P(x_j|y)$. This represents the probability of feature x_j occurring given the class label y. Different probability estimation methods can be used depending on the type of features (categorical or continuous). Common methods include:

For categorical features: Use the frequency of feature x_j in class y divided by the count of examples in class y.

For continuous features: Assume a probability distribution (e.g., Gaussian) and estimate the distribution's parameters (mean and variance) for each class label.

Step 5: Make Predictions

Calculate the posterior probability of each class label for each new test example x given the feature vector x using Bayes' theorem.

$$P(y|x) = (P(x|y) * P(y)) / P(x)$$

Where P(y) is the prior probability of the class label, P(x) is the evidence probability (a normalization constant), and P(y|x) is the product of the conditional probabilities of each feature given the class label.

Step 6: Choose the Predicted Class

Choose the projected class for the provided test instance with the highest posterior probability.

These steps summarize the working of the Naive Bayes algorithm. It is known for its simplicity, efficiency, and ability to handle high-dimensional feature spaces. Although the independence assumption may not hold true in all cases, Naive Bayes can still perform well in practice and is widely used in various applications, such as text classification and spam filtering.

4.4.3 Logistic Regression

When using one or more independent variables to predict the likelihood of a categorical dependent variable, a classification method known as logistic regression is applied. It is a regression analysis that works well for forecasting outcomes that fall into one of two categories, such as true or false, yes or no, or success or failure. A logistic function, also referred to as a sigmoid function, is fitted to the training set of data by the logistic regression procedure. This function transforms any input value into a number between 0 and 1, which represents the likelihood of being in a positive class. The logistic function has the following mathematical formula:

$$p = \frac{1}{1 + e^{\Delta}(-Z)}$$

(1)

If z is the input value, e is a mathematical constant roughly equal to 2.718, and p is the probability of the positive class.

To select the coefficients that minimize the difference between the projected probabilities and the actual values in the training data for the logistic regression model, the method employs a maximum likelihood estimation strategy. This is typically accomplished using an optimization technique like gradient descent. The logistic regression model can predict the probability of the positive class for incoming input data after training. The input value is identified as belonging to the positive class if the probability exceeds a predefined threshold, often 0.5; otherwise, it is classed as belonging to the negative class.

4.4.3.1 Working of Logistic Regression (LR)

The following is the step-by-step explanation of how the Logistic Regression (LR) algorithm works:

Step 1: Data Preparation

Gather instances of (x1, y1), (x2, y2),..., (xn, yn), where xi is the feature vector for the i-th sample, and yi stands for the matching class label (0 or 1).

Step 2: Initialize Model Parameters

Assign the bias term b and the weight vector w tiny random values as initial values.

Step 3: Define the Logistic Function (Sigmoid)

Define the logistic function, often known as the sigmoid function, which yields a probability between 0 and 1 from the output of a linear combination of data and model parameters. It is defined as: $\sigma(z) = 1 / (1 + e^{\wedge}(-z))$, where $z = w \cdot x + b$.

Step 4: Hypothesis Calculation

Using the logistic function, calculate the hypothesis $h_A(x)$ for a given example x.

$h_A(x) = \sigma(w \cdot x + b)$, where $\sigma(.)$ is the sigmoid function.

Step 5: Cost Function

Make a cost function that measures the discrepancy between the actual class labels and the predicted likelihood. The binary cross-entropy loss is a frequently employed cost function for logistic regression and is defined as follows:

$J(w, b) = -1/n * \Sigma[y_i\log(h_A(x_i)) + (1-y_i)\log(1-h_A(x_i))]$, where n is the number of training examples.

Step 6: Gradient Descent Optimization

Use gradient descent optimization to iteratively update the model's w and b parameters and minimize the cost function. Determine the cost function's gradients with respect to w and b:

$\partial J/\partial w = 1/n * \Sigma[(h_A(x_i) - y_i) * x_i]$

$\partial J/\partial b = 1/n * \Sigma[h_A(x_i) - y_i]$

Update the model parameters using the gradients and a learning rate α:

$w := w - \alpha * \partial J/\partial w$

$b := b - \alpha * \partial J/\partial b$

Step 7: Repeat Steps 4-6

Up to convergence or a predetermined number of iterations, repeat Steps 4 through 6 as necessary. Convergence is typically determined by comparing the change in the cost function across iterations or when the model parameters reach a stable state.

Step 8: Make Predictions

Given a new test example x, calculate the hypothesis $h_A(x)$ using the learned model parameters. If $h_A(x)$ is greater than or equal to 0.5, predict the positive class (1). Otherwise, predict the negative class (0).

These actions encapsulate how the Logistic Regression algorithm functions. With methods like one-vs.-rest or softmax regression, the widely used approach for binary classification tasks known as logistic regression can also be expanded to tackle multi-class classification challenges. It provides interpretable results and can handle both categorical and numerical features.

4.4.4 K – Nearest Neighbor

K-Nearest Neighbors (K-NN), a supervised machine learning technique, can be used for classification or regression issues. The non-parametric approach produces predictions based on the proximity of a new instance to the tagged examples in the training set. The hyperparameter k's value (a positive integer) determines how many nearest neighbours should be considered when forecasting a new instance. The Euclidean distance or another distance metric is typically used to calculate the distance between two instances. The K-NN algorithm works as follows:

- Load the training data into memory.
- Calculate how far apart each new instance is from each other instance in the training set.
- Select the k nearest neighbours based on the estimated distances.
- If there are classification problems, determine the new instance's class based on its k nearest neighbors' dominant class. For regression tasks, forecast the goal value of the new instance as the average of the target values of the k neighbours.
- Repeat steps 2-4 for all new instances in the test set.

The K-NN algorithm has several advantages, including its simplicity, interpretability, and flexibility to handle non-linear decision boundaries. The choice of k can have a big impact on the algorithm's performance, and it can be computationally expensive for big datasets.

4.4.4.1 Working of K – Nearest Neighbor (K-NN)

The following is the step-by-step explanation of how the K-Nearest Neighbor (K-NN) algorithm works:

Step 1: Data Preparation

In a labelled training dataset, collect samples $(x1, y1), (x2, y2),..., (xn, yn)$, where xi is the feature vector for the i-th example, and yi signifies a compatible class label.

Step 2: Choose the Number of Neighbors (k)

Choose how many neighbours (k) to take into account while making forecasts. This is a hyperparameter that needs to be determined based on the problem and dataset.

Step 3: Distance Calculation

Establish a distance metric (such as the Euclidean distance or Manhattan distance) to gauge how similar two feature vectors are to one another. Determine the separation between each training example in the dataset and the test example.

Step 4: Select the Nearest Neighbors

Find the k training examples that are most similar (closest) to the test example based on the chosen distance metric. These nearest neighbors will influence the prediction for the test example.

Step 5: Class Label Voting

The k closest neighbors' class labels should be counted. Find out which class is most prevalent among the neighbours.

Step 6: Make a Prediction

Assign the majority class label as the predicted class for the test example.

Step 7: Repeat Steps 3-6 for each Test Example

For all test examples in the dataset, repeat Steps 3 to 6.

Step 8: Evaluate Performance

On a different validation or test dataset, evaluate the performance of the k-NN method using the proper evaluation metrics (e.g., accuracy, precision, recall, F1-score).

Step 9: Hyperparameter Tuning

Experiment with different values of k and evaluate the performance to select the optimal value that yields the best results.

The k-Nearest Neighbour algorithm is explained in these steps. It is a straightforward technique that can be used for classification and regression applications. It has the benefit of not requiring training time as the complete training dataset is saved for making predictions, despite the fact that it might be computationally expensive for large datasets. Additionally, it is important to normalize or scale the features to ensure that no single feature dominates the distance calculation.

4.5 Performance Evaluation

Accuracy is the most crucial measure for a classification machine learning model. By dividing the entire number of data points in the test dataset by the total number of accurate predictions, the accuracy of a prediction is determined. Accuracy is one way to judge a model's performance, but there are other ways as well. The ratio of True Positives to all of the Positives predicted by the model is how accuracy is measured. Recall is defined as the proportion of True Positives to all other Positives in the dataset. The F1 score's means are recall and precision. When compared to other metrics, accuracy provides the most accurate representation of a model's performance for a particular dataset. The utilized metrics are used to assess a model's performance. Table 3 presents the model's significant performance metrics with its formula.

In the formulas above, the following terms are used:

TP (True Positive): The percentage of cases where a good outcome was correctly predicted.

TN (True Negative): The percentage of adverse events that were accurately predicted.

FP (False Positive): The percentage of events that were incorrectly rated as favorable.

FN (False Negative): The number of times where a negative outcome was incorrectly predicted

Table 3. Performance evaluation metrics with its formula

Performance Metrics	Formula
Accuracy	(TP + TN) / (TP + TN + FP + FN) 1.
Precision	TP / (TP + FP) 2.
Recall	TP / (TP + FN) 3.
F1-Score	2 * (Precision * Recall) / (Precision + Recall) 4.

These metrics are commonly used in evaluating the performance of classification models. Recall calculates the percentage of properly identified positive instances, accuracy analyses the overall accuracy of predictions, precision examines the accuracy of positive predictions, and the F1-score offers a single metric that strikes a compromise between precision and recall.

Figure 3 shows the level of the machine learning model precision score.

Figure 4 shows the level of accuracy in the f1 score.

Figure 5 shows the level of accuracy in the recall score.

Figure 3. Model precision score

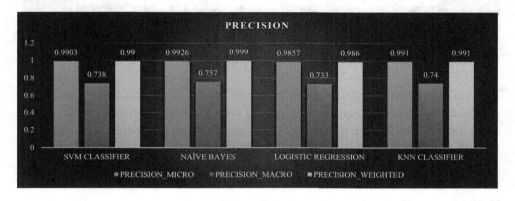

Figure 4. Model F1 – score

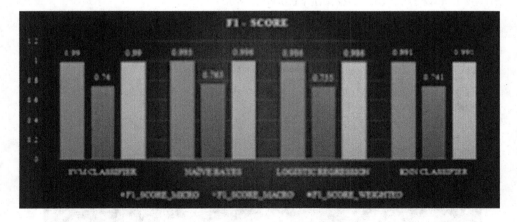

Figure 5. Model recall score

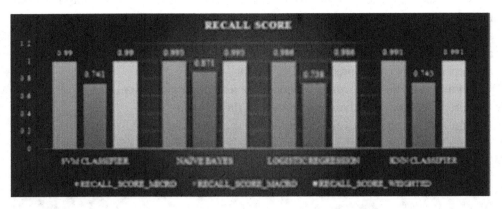

4.6 Experimental Results and Discussion

The four supervised algorithms are compared based on their accuracy level and classification metrics precision score, recall score, and f1 score. Since it is a multi-class dataset, Evaluation metrics such as 'micro, macro and weighted' based on Classification metrics these evaluation measures are also calculated for both train and test datasets. And finally, based on the higher level of test accuracy, the model is chosen as the best model to fit. One model is chosen to be the best one. Based on their performance, the accuracy is improved.

Action (Allow, Deny, Drop, Reset -Both), Source Port, Destination Port, NAT Source Port, NAT Destination Port, and Bytes are the five main features considered.

Figure 6. Overall Model Accuracy Comparison

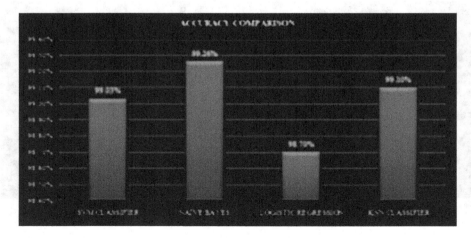

Figure 7. Relative analysis of supervised machine learning models

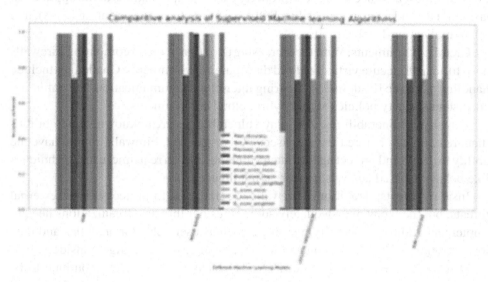

The Naive Bayes algorithm outperformed the other in-model classification techniques. The Naive Bayes classifier was determined to have the greatest Accuracy value, at 99.26%.

Figure 6 shows the level of accuracy in the overall algorithms used.

Figure 7 shows the Classification and performance metrics comparison.

Based on the accuracy, precision micro, macro, and weighted; f1-score micro, macro, and weight; and recall score micro, macro, and weight, the above results compare different algorithms.

5. OPEN CHALLENGES IN NETWORK FIREWALL SECURITY

Network firewall security faces several open challenges, including:

Advanced Persistent Threats (APTs): APTs are sophisticated, targeted assaults to break into a network without authorization. Firewalls must be constantly updated to detect and prevent such evolving threats effectively.

Encrypted Traffic Inspection: As more and more network traffic is encrypted using protocols like HTTPS, it becomes challenging for firewalls to inspect the content of encrypted packets. Firewalls need to develop techniques to inspect encrypted traffic without compromising user privacy.

Application Layer Attacks: Traditional firewalls primarily focus on network-layer filtering. However, modern attacks often target application-layer vulnerabilities.

Firewalls must advance in order to properly examine applications at the application layer and defend against attacks like SQL injection, cross-site scripting (XSS), and other application-level exploits.

Cloud Environments: With the increasing adoption of cloud computing, firewalls need to adapt to secure virtualized and distributed environments. Challenges include handling dynamic IP addresses, securing inter-cloud communication, and enforcing consistent security policies across hybrid cloud environments.

Zero-Day Vulnerabilities: Zero-day vulnerabilities are unknown vulnerabilities that are exploited before they are discovered or patched. Firewalls should have the ability to detect and protect against such vulnerabilities in real time, using techniques like behavior-based analysis and threat intelligence.

Insider Threats: Traditional firewalls are designed to protect against external threats, but they may not adequately address insider threats. Organizations need to implement additional security measures, such as user behavior analytics and data loss prevention (DLP), to mitigate risks from malicious or negligent insiders.

Distributed Denial of Service (DDoS) Attacks: DDoS attacks continue to be a significant threat, and firewalls play a crucial role in mitigating such attacks. However, attackers continuously develop new techniques to bypass traditional DDoS mitigation strategies, requiring firewalls to employ advanced anomaly detection and rate-limiting techniques.

Security Policy Complexity: Organizations often have complex network environments with multiple firewalls and security policies. Managing and maintaining these policies can be challenging, leading to misconfigurations and security gaps. Simplifying policy management and ensuring consistent policy enforcement is an ongoing challenge.

Evolving Threat Landscape: With new attack channels, malware varieties, and evasion strategies regularly appearing, the threat landscape is constantly changing. To effectively fight against new threats, firewalls must keep up with the most recent threat intelligence and regularly update their rule sets.

Addressing these challenges requires a combination of technological advancements, threat intelligence sharing, collaboration between security vendors, and ongoing research and development efforts in the field of network firewall security.

6. CONCLUSION AND FUTURE SCOPE

One of the most critical parts of a network is the Firewall, and there should be no inconsistencies in the security measures that are being used because doing so would expose the network to security risks. So, all people should be aware of the risks employed in all the components. Network technology and applications continually evolve, yet network security lags behind. Many computer security threats originate from networking, while others are amplified by it. The secure network is dependent on secure computing, and vice versa. Unsurprisingly, as networking technology becomes more vulnerable, individuals are beginning to take network security more seriously. The usage of these methods in a real network with many scenarios in the future to analyze the depth and classify the threats based on their level of vulnerability. This chapter investigates the classification of firewall log files using four different machine learning models to suggest a suitable model for the problem. Based on the comparative analysis between the models such as SVM, NB, LR and K-NN, it is observed that the Naïve Bayesian classifier outperforms with the highest accuracy of 99.26%. In future, the model can be developed using other different deep learning methods which can provide higher-end solutions for real-time data.

ACKNOWLEDGMENT

This work is supported by the DST-CURIE-AI project during 2021 – 2023 by the Centre for Cyber Intelligence established under Centre for Machine Learning and Intelligence, Avinashilingam Institute for Home Science and Higher Education for Women, Coimbatore – 43, Tamilnadu, INDIA.
    Declaration of Competing Interest: None.

REFERENCES

Abu Al-Haija, Q., & Ishtaiwi, A. (2021). Machine learning-based model to identify firewall decisions to improve Cyber-Defense. *International Journal on Advanced Science, Engineering and Information Technology*, *11*(4), 1688. doi:10.18517/ijaseit.11.4.14608

Al-Behadili, H. N. K. (2021). Decision Tree for Multi-class Classification of Firewall Access. *International Journal of Intelligent Engineering and Systems*, *14*(3), 294–302. doi:10.22266/ijies2021.0630.25

Aljabri, M., Alahmadi, A. A., Mohammad, R. M., Aboulnour, M., Alomari, D. M., & Almotiri, S. H. (2022). Classification of firewall log data using multi-class machine learning models. *Electronics (Basel)*, *11*(12), 1851. doi:10.3390/electronics11121851

Allagi, S., & Rachh, R. R. (2019). Analysis of Network log data using Machine Learning. *International Conference for Convergence for Technology*. IEEE. 10.1109/I2CT45611.2019.9033737

As-Suhabni, H. E. Q., & Khamitkar, S. D. Dr. (2020a, February 25). Discovering anomalous rules in firewall logs using data mining and machine learning classifiers. *International Journal of Scientific & Technology Research.* https://www.ijstr.org/paper-references.php?ref=IJSTR-0120-29748.

As-Suhbani, H. E., & Khamitkar, S. (2019). Classification of Firewall Logs Using Supervised Machine Learning Algorithms. *International Journal on Computer Science and Engineering, 7*(8), 301–304. doi:10.26438/ijcse/v7i8.301304

Ertam, F., & Kaya, M. (2018). Classification of firewall log files with multi-class support vector machine. *2018 6th International Symposium on Digital Forensic and Security (ISDFS).* IEEE. 10.1109/ISDFS.2018.8355382

Gajda, J., Kwiecien, J., & Chmiel, W. (2022). Machine learning methods for anomaly detection in computer networks. *2022 26th International Conference on Methods and Models in Automation and Robotics (MMAR).* IEEE. 10.1109/MMAR55195.2022.9874341

Hommes, S., State, R., & Engel, T. (2012). A distance-based method to detect anomalous attributes in log files. *Network Operations and Management Symposium.* IEEE. 10.1109/NOMS.2012.6211940

Internet firewall data. UCI Machine Learning Repository. (n.d.). https://archive.ics.uci.edu/ml/datasets/Internet+Firewall+Data. Last accessed: July 11, 2023

Kamiya, K., Aoki, K., Nakata, K., Sato, T., Kurakami, H., & Tanikawa, M. (2015). The method of detecting malware-infected hosts is analyzing firewall and proxy logs. *Asia-Pacific Symposium on Information and Telecommunication Technologies.* IEEE. 10.1109/APSITT.2015.7217113

Kazim, M., & Doreswamy. (2019). Machine Learning Based Network Anomaly Detection. *International Journal of Recent Technology and Engineering (IJRTE), 8*(4), 542–548. doi:10.35940/ijrte.D7271.118419

Kowalski, K., & Geinitz, H. (2006). Analysis of Log Files Intersections for Security Enhancement. *International Conference on Information Technology: New Generations.* IEEE. 10.1109/ITNG.2006.32

Li, Z., Rios, A. L., Xu, G., & Trajkovic, L. (2019). Machine learning techniques for classifying network anomalies and intrusions. *2019 IEEE International Symposium on Circuits and Systems (ISCAS).* IEEE. 10.1109/ISCAS.2019.8702583

Machine Learning-Driven Firewall. (n.d.). KDnuggets.https://www.kdnuggets.com/2017/02/machine-learning-driven-firewall.html.

Martinez, L. F. M. (2021, August 19). How data science could make cybersecurity troubleshooting easier: Firewall logs analysis. *Medium*. https://towardsdatascience. com/how-data-science-could-make-cybersecurity-troubleshooting-easier-firewall-logs-analysis-591e4832f7e6.

Naryanto, R. F., & Delimayanti, M. K. (2022). Machine learning technique for classification of internet firewall data using rapid miner. *2022 6th International Conference on Electrical, Telecommunication and Computer Engineering (ELTICOM)*. IEEE. 10.1109/ELTICOM57747.2022.10037798

Nawir, M., Amir, A., Yaakob, N., & Bi Lynn, O. (2019). Effective and efficient network anomaly detection system using machine learning algorithm. *Bulletin of Electrical Engineering and Informatics*, *8*(1), 46–51. doi:10.11591/eei.v8i1.1387

Ndichu, S., McOyowo, S., Okoyo, H., & Wekesa, C. (2023). Detecting Remote Access Network attacks using supervised machine learning methods. *International Journal of Computer Network and Information Security*, *15*(2), 48–61. doi:10.5815/ijcnis.2023.02.04

Newman, M. (2023, May 9). *Firewall logging & monitoring*. HOBSoft. https://www.loganalysis.org/firewall-logging/.

Nimbalkar, P., Mulwad, V., Puranik, N., Joshi, A., & Finin, T. (2016). Semantic Interpretation of Structured Log Files. *2016 IEEE 17th International Conference on Information Reuse and Integration (IRI)*. IEEE. 10.1109/IRI.2016.81

Patil, S. (2021a, June 29). Routing network traffic based on firewall logs using machine learning. *Medium*. https://medium.com/mlearning-ai/routing-network-traffic-based-on-firewall-logs-using-machine-learning-dc5e5c8c6bb3.

Pavlychev, A. V., Soldatov, K. S., & Skazin, V. A. (2021). Network anomaly detection in the Microsoft Windows system logs using machine learning methods. *Proceedings of Tomsk State University of Control Systems and Radio Electronics*, *24*(4), 27–32. doi:10.21293/1818-0442-2021-24-4-27-32

Pawar, S. L., & Hiwarkar, T. (2022). Analysis of various machine learning approaches to detect anomalies from Network Traffic. *International Journal of Computer Science and Mobile Computing*, *11*(6), 137–151. doi:10.47760/ijcsmc.2022.v11i06.011

Shaheed, A., & Kurdy, M. H. D. B. (2022). Web Application Firewall Using Machine Learning and Features Engineering. *Security and Communication Networks*, *2022*, 1–14. doi:10.1155/2022/5280158

Sharma, D., Wason, V., & Johri, P. (2021). Optimized Classification of Firewall Log Data using Heterogeneous Ensemble Techniques. *2021 International Conference on Advance Computing and Innovative Technologies in Engineering (ICACITE)*. IEEE. 10.1109/ICACITE51222.2021.9404732

Skazin, V. A., Pavlychev, A. V., & Zotov, S. S. (2021). Detection of network anomalies in log files using machine learning methods. *IOP Conference Series. Materials Science and Engineering*, *1069*(1), 012021. doi:10.1088/1757-899X/1069/1/012021

Taher, K. A., Mohammed Yasin Jisan, B., & Rahman, Md. M. (2019). Network intrusion detection using supervised machine learning technique with feature selection. *2019 International Conference on Robotics, Electrical and Signal Processing Techniques (ICREST)*. IEEE. 10.1109/ICREST.2019.8644161

The significance and role of firewall logs. (2023, June 9). Exabeam. https://www.exabeam.com/siem-guide/siem-concepts/firewall-logs.

Wang, S., Balarezo, J. F., Kandeepan, S., Al-Hourani, A., Chavez, K. G., & Rubinstein, B. (2021). Machine learning in network anomaly detection: A survey. *IEEE Access : Practical Innovations, Open Solutions*, *9*, 152379–152396. doi:10.1109/ACCESS.2021.3126834

Winding, R., Wright, T., & Chapple, M. (2006). System Anomaly Detection: Mining Firewall Logs. *2006 Securecomm and Workshops*. IEEE. doi:10.1109/SECCOMW.2006.359572

Zhang, J., Gardner, R., & Vukotic, I. (2019). Anomaly detection in wide area network meshes using two machine learning algorithms. *Future Generation Computer Systems*, *93*, 418–426. doi:10.1016/j.future.2018.07.023

Chapter 6
Discernment and Perusal of Software Vulnerability

Guneet Kaur
Dr. B.R. Ambedkar National Institute of Technology, India

Urvashi Bansal
Dr. B.R. Ambedkar National Institute of Technology, India

Harsh K. Verma
Dr. B.R. Ambedkar National Institute of Technology, India

Geeta Sikka
National Institute of Technology, Delhi, India

Lalit K. Awasthi
National Institute of Technology, Srinagar, India

ABSTRACT

The examination of vulnerabilities is vital to network security, and finding the route to the flaw's source is essential for the analysis and mitigation of software vulnerabilities that attackers can exploit. The automation of secure software development can be easily achieved by using vulnerability ID. Prior to this, manually tagged communications with vulnerability ID was a laborious process that had scalability problems and room for human mistakes. To facilitate code examination, several vulnerability detection techniques have been developed and to support code inspection, several vulnerability detection techniques have been developed. A series of research that uses machine learning approaches and provide encouraging outcomes are among these strategies. This chapter discusses recent research trend that uses deep learning to identify vulnerabilities and demonstrates how cutting-edge neural approaches are used to identify potentially problematic code patterns. It also highlights a few publications from research that have analyzed vulnerability identification using deep learning.

DOI: 10.4018/978-1-6684-8666-5.ch006

INTRODUCTION

For securing the network from attacks, discernment and perusal of software vulnerabilities have become an important aspects. Now, what is meant by discernment and perusal? The word discernment means identifying the vulnerabilities and understanding the weaknesses in the network, that could be exploited by the attacker. This process involves various activities like scanning of the network, reviewing the code, and security testing, whereas perusal means, once vulnerabilities are identified, they need to be thoroughly examined to access the impact and the potential risk. This process includes vulnerability prioritization and verification and risk mitigation. To maintain network security, a productive Vulnerability Management Framework (VMF) (Chhillar and Shrivastava, 2021) has become essential. A network's vulnerabilities keep growing quickly, thus they must be remedied quickly and effectively. Identification, classification, prioritization, repair, and mitigation of vulnerabilities in a network are all part of the cyclical Network Vulnerability Management (NVM) process. Vulnerability scanners are used to find and classify vulnerabilities. Networks, programs, and machines may all be accessed by vulnerability scanners to check for known flaws. A router, application server, firewall, web server, and other assets are only a few examples of the types of assets whose programming flaws or incorrect configurations can make a network vulnerable.

The network's security policy may be changed, patches can be installed, and users can be informed about network security and software reconfiguration to help mitigate vulnerabilities. VM discovers flaws in a network and assesses the threat posed by those vulnerabilities. This assessment also aids in reducing or eliminating flaws. A bug must be fixed as quickly as possible so that the threat involved gets reduced. VM is a more inclusive word than vulnerability scanning. Along with vulnerability scanning, VM also takes into account, factors like risk assessment, vulnerability repair, and so on. The concept of Vulnerability Management process and Vulnerability Scanning have been discussed below.

Vulnerability Management Process

A traditional management method has become essential to guarantee the network's security. Everyone is aware that vulnerabilities are constantly expanding and come in so many different forms that it is hard to address them manually. Thus, the network requires an automated administration method that is well-planned and step-by- step. The foremost goal of this procedure is to quickly identify and address that vulnerability. To keep track of vulnerabilities and to guarantee the veracity and integrity of data in a network, periodic network scanning is required. The stages of the vulnerability management process are defined in Figure 1. The initial stage

Figure 1. Vulnerability management process

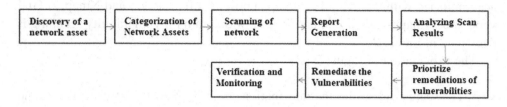

identifies the software or hardware assets using automation. Once the assets have been discovered, categorizing and classifying those assets is the next important step. Thereafter, analysis of scanned results is performed on the basis of asset criticality, its cvss score, and vulnerability threat. In the next step, vulnerabilities are prioritized and fixed on the basis of their business risk and severity level. In the end, verify if the threats have been eliminated or not.

Vulnerability Scanning

It is the method of locating weak points in a network. Various scanning programs, including Burp Suite, GFI Languard, Nexpose, Nessus, Nmap, OpenVAS, Advanced IP scanner, and many more, may be used to do this. These tools guard the system against strange activity and identify network problems. It is an easy method of protecting the computer network. Today, network tools play a crucial part in network security. Information about the network is gathered using the techniques used for network mapping. Port scanning, operating system identification, and a

Figure 2. Vulnerability scanning process

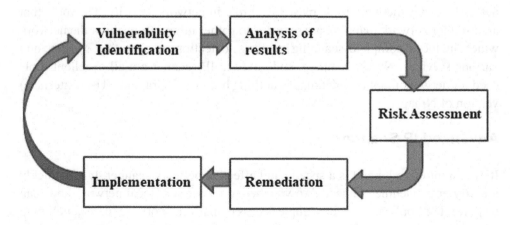

number of services are all included in network mapping. Network mapping may be accomplished with the help of Zenmap, a powerful IP scanner, and Nmap. A GUI version of Nmap is called Zenmap. The flow diagram for vulnerability scanning is described in Figure 2.

The explanation of Figure 2 is:

- The scanner identifies the information about open ports, software assets, and devices. Also, correlates the collected data with known vulnerabilities, which can be fetched from databases.
- The scanned results are usually in the form of pdf which is provided to the security team for study. It also includes false positive information which does not need any remediation but is good to know.
- Risk Assessments prioritizes the vulnerabilities on the basis of their severity level for remediation with a reasonable buffer. Then the detected vulnerability which is vulnerable to a network is remediated using different algorithms.

The remaining work is structured as follows: Section 2 explains recent trends and tools used for detecting vulnerabilities in any network. The relevant study that was previously carried out by researchers and the outcomes of the study is covered in Section 3 and 4. Section 5 elaborates proposed methodology. Section 6 depicts discussion. Finally, Section 8 and 9 concludes the article and highlights the future Scope and Conclusion in this field.

TRENDS AND TOOLS FOR VULNERABILITY SCANNING

Scanning tools are programs that are designed to find network flaws and safeguard the system against unusual activity. It is an easy method of protecting your computer network. Today, network tools play a vital role in network security. The tools that are used for network mapping are required to gather information about the network which includes complete scanning of ports, detection of operating system, and various services. Nmap, Zenmap, and advance IP scanner are all excellent tools used for network mapping. Zenmap is nothing but a GUI(Graphical User Interface) version of Nmap.

Advanced IP Scanner

It has an intuitive UI and is a speedy and effective network scanner. It can quickly identify any machine connected to your wired or wireless local network and scan its ports. The application offers simple access to many network resources, including

Figure 3. Advanced IP scanner

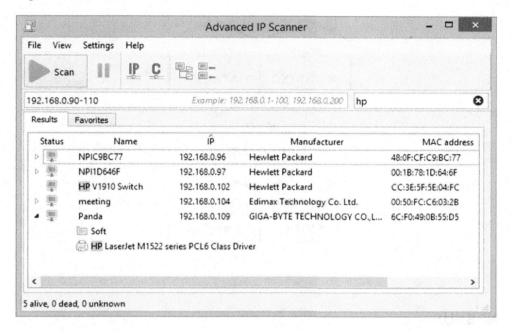

shared folders, HTTP, FTP, and HTTPS. Scanning report of advanced ip scanner is shown in Figure 3.

Nmap

By sending packets and examining the answers, a network scanner called Nmap (Network Mapper) may be used to locate hosts and find out the services that is running on a computer network (Lyon, 2014). It provides a range of features for exploring the networks, such as discovery of host, which service is running on that network, and OS detection. Scripts that provide more complicated service discovery, detection of vulnerability, and many other features may be used to expand these attributes. Nmap can adapt in changing network conditions, which are latency and congestion while performing a scan. The most important features of Nmap are shown in Figure 4.

Figure 4. Important features of Nmap

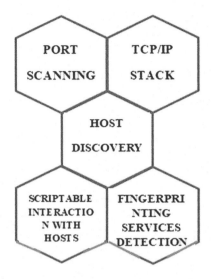

NESSUS

One of the numerous vulnerability scanners used for penetration testing, malicious attacks, and vulnerability assessment is Nessus. During scans, Nessus uses plug-ins to run against every network host and keep track of vulnerabilities. It performs a series of actions when a scan is begun. The procedures used during scanning are summarized Figure 5.

Figure 5. Scanning steps in Nessus

Figure 6. Example of complete vulnerability scan

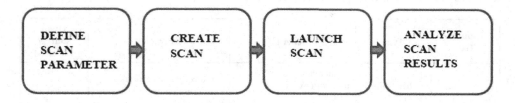

Nessus follows a series of stages when starting a scan.

- **Step 1:** The scan settings will be retrieved by Nessus and Which port is to be inspected will be determined by the settings.
- **Step 2:** To find out which hosts are online, it then performs host discovery. The host discovery process will use the following protocols: TCP, ICMP, ARP, and UDP. These can be specified in accordance with personal preference.
- **Step 3:** Afterwards, complete scanning of ports of each single host that it comes across is performed. One can also define which ports one wants to be scanned.
- **Step 4:** The next step is service detection, which identifies the services that are active behind each port that a host encounters.
- **Step 5:** It then detects which operating system is running on the network.
- **Step 6:** Once each step has been completed, Nessus checks each host against a list of known bugs to determine which hosts are vulnerable.

An example of a complete vulnerability scan is shown in Figure 6.

The different vulnerability scanning tools, static code analysis tools, and dynamic code analysis tools are listed below in a tabular manner, along with information about their advantages, disadvantages, and whether they are open source or licensed.

RELATED WORK

With an increase in the menace of vulnerabilities, researchers seemingly have gained significant interest in knowing the level of vulnerability, its risk score, and precise knowledge of effective patches for network hardening. Stiffler and Jack introduced the idea of vulnerability assessment and analysis in 1981 (Stiffler, 1981) representing the relationships among different vulnerabilities and a significant number of work that has been published since then. The most significant flaws in network systems are the portrayal of vulnerabilities and the availability of official data that has been

Table 1. This table showcases a meticulously curated compendium encompassing a diverse array of highly sophisticated scanning tools

Scanning Tool	Type	Benefit	Drawback	Open source/ Licensed
Nessus	Vulnerability Scanner	Comprehensive scanning tool with extensive reporting capabilities	it is a comprehensive tool with lim- ited features in a trial version	licensed
Nexpose	Vulnerability Scanner	Accurate scanning tool with wide coverage of flaws and Network	It is a commercial tool	licensed
Acunetix	Dynamic Code Analysis	The tool is easy to use and the accuracy of this detection tool is very good	It is a commercial tool which gives limited features in its trial pack	Licensed
Burp Suite	Dynamic Code Analysis	It is a powerful vulnerability scan ner with interactive capabilities to test the network and generate comprehensive report	The primarily focus of this tool is on web application security and also it requires manual interaction	Licensed
OWASP We-BGoat	Dynamic Code Analysis	It is designed for the educational purpose as it provides a web application for learning and testing the network	It is not a general purpose scan- ning tool	Open source
OWASP ZAP	Vulnerability Scanner	It is an Open source tool which is maintained by OWASP	This tool requires a technical background personnel to configure and use the tool	Open Source
OpenVas	Vulnerability Scanner	It is an alternative to Nessus, which regularly updates the vulnerability tests and also per- forms customized Scans	Its interface is not user friendly and the set up is com plex	Open Source
SonarQube	Static Code Analysis	This tool offers security vulnerability detection and com- plete code analysis. Also, it sup- ports multiple languages.	It may produce false positive but with proper tuning and configuration accuracy can be achieved.	Open source

collected such as CVE (Common Vulnerabilities and Exposures), which enables users to utilize them to estimate the most likely attack vectors. However, even when fixes are offered, they cannot be quickly implemented due to resource shortages and corporate restrictions. Managers of network security must thus cope with a variety of vulnerabilities. In order to address the problem, Marco Angelini et al. (Angelini et al., 2019) discussed VULNUS (VULNerabilities visUal assessment), which dynamically evaluates vulnerabilities present in the network, swiftly ascertains network condition, and visually categorizes nodes depending on their vulnerabilities. Additionally, it simulates the impact of eliminating one or more vulnerabilities such that a sub-optimal patching approach may be investigated, computing the estimated optimal sequence of patches that can stop all attack pathways. Experts in the field assessed the suggested remedy to VULNUS through lab tests that looked at its efficacy and efficiency.

A detection model based on the attack graph has been proposed by Shiman Yang et al. (Yang et al., 2019), which utilizes quasi-destructive assets to analyze and examine various components and systems along with comparing CNVD and CVE to inculcate the vulnerability and generated the asset's threat list. An examination was then optimized to find the best attack path. For vulnerability scanning and information collection Kismat Chillar et al. have used different scanning tools in their sudy (Chhillar and Shrivastava, 2021). They also identified the hosts that were most vulnerable by examining the scan results, and decisions about prioritization and repair were made in light of those findings.

With the advancement of automation in vulnerabilities, a risk analysis program has been launched by Wenhao He et. al and Drew Malzahn et. al in (He et al., 2019) (Malzahn et al., 2020) that follows a specific attack path to find the vulnerabilies also, confirms if the specified path is accessible by the attacker. In addition to this, they examined the directed graph model from three angles, including benefits, drawbacks, and solutions. Meanwhile, security metrics for directed graph models-based assessments of unknown vulnerability risk are compiled and categorized. Moreover, some work has been done in the field of online Vulnerability finder which uses MulVAL to construct the attack graph based on different vulnerabilities (Alnafrani and Wijesekera, 2022) and offers various users, current risks and vulnerabilities from each component using reliable datasets. To find out the total time to exploit the attack path a real-time network has been created by the researcher which has prioritized attack paths approaching the target (Zhang et al., 2019). Present research on the vulnerability discovery model demonstrates that an application's vulnerability may be related to distinctive features.

However, Bolun Wu and Futai Zou (Wu et al., 2022) give a thorough explanation of the backdrop as well as several early techniques for finding code vulnerabilities. They classify recent works according to sequence-based and graph-based techniques, explicitly review and compare the various detection frameworks and strategies, and present the argument that while graph-based models utilize the intricate structural details of the code, sequence- based methods can capture extensive semantic characteristics. The difficulties with code encoding, code embedding techniques, model choice, fine-grained vulnerability identification and dataset were also explored by the researcher. The model has also been extended in a way that enables it to readily react as the network environment changes. Meanwhile, researchers showed a contrast of methodologies based on two attack graphs and also did the CVSS metrics (Wang et al., 2020). The suggested methodology offers accuracy equivalent to the BAG-based method but at a lower computing complexity, as evidenced by the experiment simulation results, and can more accurately estimate the danger of susceptibility in a particular network than CVSS approaches or AssetRank can.

(Alperin et al., 2020)Combination of visualizations and analytics have also been created to give a more com- prehensible visual encoding as a decision making tool for evaluating vulnerabilities, the issue of creating datasets has also been taken into account by analyzing each vulnerability's individual score using an explainable Artificial Intelligence toolkit embedded with different technologies like SonarQube, ZAP-API, and Jenkins tools. The IAST technique (Interactive Application Security Testing)has also been addressed by some researchers for security test- ing and for establishing a website-based vulnerability analysis method for government software projects(Setiawan et al., 2020).

"Remediating a vulnerability as it has given a high CVSS score (Shi et al., 2022) (Mell et al., 2006)is the same as picking a vulnerability to remediate at random," the statement reads. It is not an accurate portrayal of an exploit. CVSS is designed to gauge vulnerability severity and should not be used in isolation to determine risk(Allodi and Massacci, 2014). Existing techniques based on machine learning and deep learning evaluates risk by calculating the relationships between vulnerability attributes and actual exploits(Jacobs et al., 2020). A new approach called LICALITY (Zeng et al., 2021) has been proposed, that captures the attackers based on preferences to exploit vulnerabilities via threat modeling techniques and also tries to learn threat values that contribute in vulnerability extortion, as the approximation of risk changes depending upon datasets, deep learning, and machine learning techniques used.

A solution has been proposed to address the cold start issue that several ML-based vulnerability testing methods regularly encounter in real-world situations(Lin et al., 2021). As shown in the case of many less well-known open- source projects, the cold-start problem is specifically related to the issue of a lack or even a lack of ground truth vulnerability data during the early phases of software project development.

Using the representation learning capabilities of deep learning algorithms, Guanjun Lin and colleagues developed a way to automatically extract high-level representations that are indicative of susceptible patterns from suitable sensitive data sources(Lin et al., 2021). In order to manage data of multiple types and formats, they developed a Bi-LSTM network. Also produced unified representations that are useful in identifying potentially susceptible functions on the data set. This helped to bridge the gaps between the cross-domain data sources. The empirical investigation demonstrated that it was possible to transfer the information found in susceptible data sources can aid in the development of algorithms for detecting actual code vulnerabilities. The outcomes also show the suggested methodology beat the benchmark tool Flawfinder utilising a test software project, even in the absence of labeled data.

Neuro-symbolic models with neural networks (NN) and probabilistic logic (PLP) programming approaches have been used to understand the characteristics of such threats (Zeng et al., 2021). Recent ground-breaking deep learning applications to voice recognition and machine translation show the enormous potential of neural models' ability to comprehend spoken language, because of which academics have been prompted in the realms of cybersecurity and software development to employ deep learning to make the network learn and comprehend the patterns and semantics that define susceptible code(Lin et al., 2020a). Fang Wu used deep learning techniques to identify gaps in his research. He published three deep learning models, which are Convolutional Neural Network (CNN), Long-Short-Term Memory (LSTM), and Convolutional Neural Network-Long-Short-Term Memory (CNN- LSTM). He collects dynamic information from his 9872 binaries and trains multiple deep-learning models to find vulnerabilities in order to evaluate the effectiveness of this method. Compared to conventional techniques like MLP, this is substantially greater (MultiLayer Perceptron).

In order to check for flaws in image recognition models,(Chu et al., 2020) DNN security assessment system SecureAS was introduced by Yan Chu et al. SecureAS assesses current DNN vulnerabilities both locally and remotely in a black-box way in comparison to existing attack/defense platforms. The MAS index, which is used to quantitatively evaluate the security risks of models, is the foundation of SecureAS. The security of deep learning models for image identification may be directly measured by the MAS index. He also offers two enhanced techniques for producing inconsistent instances. Higher-quality examples may be produced using the Fast Gradient Norm Method (FGNM) and Peak Iteration Norm Method (PINM). Researchers have conducted extensive experiments to ensure that the system can examine things well and assess vulnerabilities and risks in DNN models. A unique graph- based technique called Flow sensitive vulnerability code detection model(Wang et al., 2021) which extends standard neural graph networks to simulate several key code interactions for modeling program structure for vulnerability identification. It uses probabilistic learning and statistical evaluation for gathering code snippets automatically derived from an open-source database in order to give enough training data.

Wentao Wang et al. (Wang et al., 2022)enhanced vulnerability findings by concentrating on their interdepen- dencies rather than only on the interdependencies of various security criteria in order to address the problem. To discover needs dependencies, the team suggested a semi-automatic method that integrated horizontal and vertical traceability. The dependencies' usage in security testing to find vulnerabilities was then shown. The strategy greatly enhances recollection at 81 percent when compared to the baseline techniques. Additional risks may also result from dependencies between security requirements(Wang et al., 2022). Four

Table 2. Related work

Author	Year and Dataset	Methodology	Performance
Shiman Yang et al.	(2019) Non-destructive asset profiling and their open service communication protocol	search engine segment matching method	game attack graph based on risk assessment model and find rule-based attack network information with comparing the vulnerabilities CNVD and CVE(Common Vulnerability Exposure).
Wenhao He et al.	(2019) Network level data and system level data of node	exploit process, directed graph models and security matrices	Perform directed model graph in the summarized form and classify its vulnerability.
Drew Malzahn et al.	(2020) Host and net-working information	AVRA tools for detection of automated vulnerability and risk analysis	Automated vulnerability and risk analysis and generate attack graphs for end to end process.
Rami Alnafrani et al.	(2022) Components of IoT devices and gad-gets	SUS (System Usability Scale), MULVAL and customize OVF tool	This model emphasized the automated framework by utilizing publicly known vulnerability.
Mengyuan Zhang et al.	(2019) 9 feature sub-Sets	7 feature selection method and machine learning models	large-scale empirical investigation of the relationship between various applications and weaknesses.
Kenneth B. Alperin et al.	(2020) Multi-Scale Dataset	AI and ML-based vul-nerability Assessment	Detected CVSS score features for Multi-level vulnerabilities.
Bolun Wu and Futai Zou	(2020) Source Code to the repository	Deep learning based approach for graph model	Code vulnerability de-tection
Wenrui Wang et al.	(2020) Heterogeneous information of the net-work and device vul-nerability (CERT)	CVSS metrics for scor-ing vulnerability risk	Vulnerability risk model based on Heterogeneous infor-mation is created
Herman Seti-awan et al.	(2020) Source Code to the repository	IAST based approach, ZAP and SonarQube have been used for se-curity tests	Identification of 249 vulnerability risks

previously undiscovered vulner- abilities were also found thanks to a case study on Scholar@UC, improving the general security of the Samvera Hyrax community.

Effective vulnerability management is crucial, given the rising trend of cybercrime and events connected to vulnerabilities. For this, a statistical framework is suggested (Tang et al., 2019), in which the existence of volatility clustering and the GARCH model is thoroughly examined and tested. In place of source code, Shigang Liu et al. (Liu et al., 2020) suggested a deep learning method for detecting software vulnerabilities in IoT devices. He was one of the pioneers in the creation of a system that employs deep learning to find flaws in binary machine code. They built a binary instruction-attention model for learning high-level feature representations using IDA Pro to do this. Then, a prediction model is developed using the high-level representations as a basis. Observations were made during experiments based on actual IoT-related initiatives. Experimental findings demonstrate that the proposed technique outperforms the baselines, highlighting that the proposed technique is useful and adaptable to security issues in the real world. Zhe Yu et al. (Yu et al., 2021) presented a HARMLESS learning-based prediction framework that focuses on reducing the cost of a recall and effectively correcting a human mistake in order to decrease software security risk.

OUTCOME OF RELATED WORK

The section highlights numerous research findings and suggestions for identifying and addressing vulnerabilities in network systems. The results and contributions of each study are highlighted:

- **VULNUS:** To find the best sequences, Marco Angelini and colleagues created VULNUS, a system that assesses vulnerabilities, classifies nodes, and simulates the effects of patching flaws.
- **Attack Graph-based Detection Model:** Shiman Yang et al. put forth a model that evaluates systems and components, contrasts vulnerability data sources, and optimises to discover the most effective attack path.
- **Identification of Vulnerable Hosts and Information Gathering:** Based on scan findings, Kismat Chillar et al. employed scanning technologies to identify vulnerable hosts and prioritise repairs.
- **Risk Analysis Programme:** Wenhao He et al. and Drew Malzahn et al. created a programme that tracks attack routes, discovers vulnerabilities, and calculates the projected ideal sequence of fixes. Additionally, they classified security metrics and examined directed graph models.

- **Online Vulnerability Finder:** Researchers created an attack graph based on vulnerabilities using MulVAL and presented users with the most recent risks and vulnerabilities from each component.

- **Vulnerability Discovery Model:** Researchers discovered that a vulnerability in an application may be con- nected to distinguishing characteristics.

- **Code Vulnerability Detection strategies:** Bolun Wu and Futai Zou examined difficulties in code analysis and assessed code vulnerability detection strategies. They also categorised new efforts.

- **Visualisations and Analytics for Vulnerability Evaluation:** Researchers used visualisations and analytics to develop a tool for assessing vulnerabilities and took into account the generation of datasets and the score of individual vulnerabilities.

- **Interactive Application Security Testing (IAST):** Scientists investigated IAST for security testing and created a vulnerability analysis approach for government software projects.

- **CVSS Evaluation and Risk Calculation:** The article cautions readers against depending entirely on CVSS ratings and emphasises the usage of machine learning and deep learning for risk assessment.

- **LICALITY Approach:** Using threat modelling methodologies, LICALITY collects attacker preferences for exploiting vulnerabilities and uses deep learning and machine learning for risk approximation.

- **Deep Learning for Vulnerability Detection:** Researchers extracted high-level representations from sensitive data sources and successfully detected vulnerabilities using deep learning methods.

- **Neuro-symbolic Models and Deep Learning:** To grasp danger features, neuro-symbolic models incorporating neural networks and probabilistic logic programming were applied.

- **Image Recognition Model Vulnerability Detection:** Researchers developed SecureAS, a system that analyses image recognition model vulnerabilities using the MAS index.

- **Flow Sensitive Vulnerability Code Detection Model:** To mimic code interactions for vulnerability detection, a graph-based method was adopted

PROPOSED METHODOLOGY

To design a detection model, the foremost thing is to make the model learn all the historical and synthetic datasets, for which the training phase is the first step. After that, using that training model the detection model can itself bifurcate which code is vulnerable and which is not.

Figure 7. Detection model illustrating two different phases

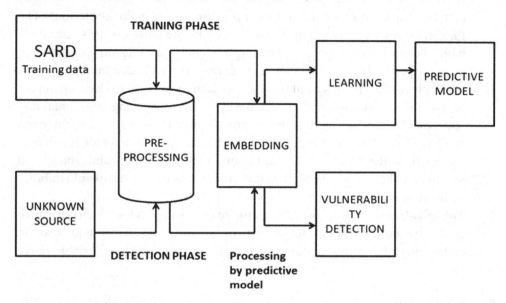

The detection model is divided into two different phases:

- Training phase
- Detection phase

The training phase is designed in such a way that a detection model can learn different datasets, whereas the detection phase, on the contrary uses that trained model to find the vulnerability. As emphasized in Figure 7, both phases use the identical process for embedding the input data after the source code gets preprocessed and the activity includes a program named, slicing step with subtask for choosing the slicing criteria. The steps of detection model are explained further.

- **Preprocessing:** The source code contains flaws in a number of code statements. As a result, it is not necessary to review the full code to determine a vulnerability. The location where the vulnerability occurs is surrounded by a series of code statements that are connected to data and control flow and are extracted and inspected. The flow diagram of the preprocessing activity is shown in Figure 8, and it is further detailed. Preprocessing activity includes program slicing and tokenization.
- **Program slicing**: It is the set of program statements, that simplify the program using slicing criteria which can be used to remove the vulnerabilities

from the source code. It is a method for identifying a group of assertions that are impacted or influenced by a program's goal point (criterion). The fundamental goal of program slicing is to eliminate unnecessary source code while keeping the program's meaning intact. Depending on the direction of the trip, program slicing may also be divided into backward and forward categories (Weiser, 1984). All the program statements that can have an impact on the slicing criterion and aid the developer in identifying bug-containing code blocks are included in backward slicing. Forward slicing forecasts the code block that will be modified and includes the program statements impacted by the slicing criterion. Finding the root of the vulnerability and identifying the impacted code block is crucial when it comes to vulnerability identification.

- **Tokenization:** It is the process to vectorize code snippets for which the source code must be divided into token units. Depending on the technique used in embedding, the symbolic image of task goal is reducing the variable range

Figure 8. Preprocessing activity: Tokenization is ready for embedding vector after slicing the source sample

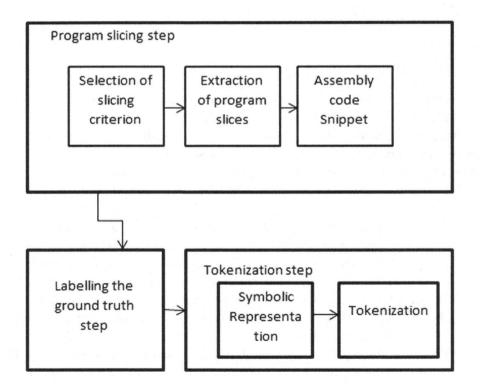

Figure 9. Embedding activity

of variables or functions may not be successful. As a result, the symbolic representation task in this study was made optional.

- **Embedding:** In this, vector representation can be generated and used as data sources for deep learning and neural models. The embedding activity is explained in Figure 9.

To sum up, a quick comparison between the proposed work and the existing work is given which illustrates that the proposed work which explains how a detection model for finding flaws in code was created. The training phase and the detection phase are the two phases of the model. The model learns from different datasets during the training phase, and it uses the learned model to find vulnerabilities during the detection phase whereas the existing study describes numerous methods and procedures for analysing and assessing vulnerabilities in network security. It draws attention to the difficulties that researchers and professionals confront while trying to find vulnerabilities, decide which fixes to apply first, and reduce risks. Numerous methodologies are investigated, including vulnerability visualisation, attack graph analysis, vulnerability scanning, risk analysis software, and machine learning-based solutions. Additionally, it concentrated on creating approaches and tools for identifying and analysing vulnerabilities. Examples include using MulVAL to build attack graphs, real-time networks to predict attack pathways, and combining visualisations and analytics to assess vulnerabilities and examines the use of deep learning approaches for identifying vulnerabilities and analysing threats, including representation learning and neuro-symbolic models.

DISCUSSION

In the present scenario, most vulnerability detection and assessment models are using search engine segment- matching methods, directed graph models with security matrices, AVRA tool for automated vulnerabilities. For security tests, ZAP and SONARQube with IAST approaches are being used. For calculating risk score matrices, CVSS technique is being used in the majority of research. But with each passing day, the need for the enhancement of the security of any network becomes more challenging, and to combat with, integration of machine learning with artificial intelligence is the best solution that comes across, also which is suitable for network safety. In addition to this, releasing patches of vulnerability would be another solution, which will make the network more versatile and flaw free. An automated risk detection model is the most effective approach and has been used in several research since it results in a network that is less vulnerable.

CHALLENGES AND FUTURE DIRECTIONS

By studying various vulnerability patterns using a training dataset, DLVP approaches seek to identify undiscovered vulnerabilities in the target software. The three steps of the majority of common DLVP techniques are data gathering, model construction, and evaluation. Data is first gathered for training, after which a suitable model is selected based on the design objective and available resources. The pre-processing of the training data takes into account the preferred format of the selected model. The model is then taught to reduce a loss function and is designed in a way that it can be applied in practical settings. Performance on unused test instances is analyzed to gauge the model's efficacy.

Existing Dataset

A collection of annotated code is required that can be tagged as neutral or vulnerable in such a way that a vulnerability prediction model can be trained. It should be possible for the model to learn from the high number of vulnerable pieces of code. For DLVP, researchers drew from a range of data sources (see Figure 10) (Chakraborty et al., 2021).

Figure 10. Various DLVP datasets and their realistic/synthetic status. The dataset's growing realism is represented by colors. Green is the most realistic color, whereas red is the most artificial

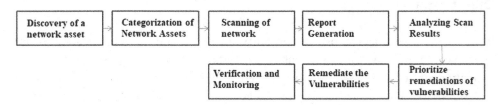

We categorize the code samples into the following groups based on how they were gathered and annotated:

Synthetic Data

An annotated sequence sample and vulnerable code example were made up. These datasets include SARD (Black, 2018) and SATE IV Juliet (Okun et al., 2013). In this case, instances are built by fusing well-known weaknesses. These datasets were initially intended to predict vulnerability algorithms based on static analysis and dynamic evaluation.

Semi-Synthetic Data

In this case, either the sequence samples or the interpretation is artificially derived. Russell et al. (Russell et al., 2018) suggested the Draper dataset which incorporates functions that are gathered from open-source but validated using static calibration. Despite being more complex than synthetic ones, samples from the National Vulnerability Database (Booth et al., 2013) and SARD dataset(Black, 2018) are created from production code, however they are typically altered to take the vulnerability out of its original context in order to show it these datasets do not accurately reflect the complexity of vulnerabilities in the actual world since they have been separated and simplified.

Actual Data

Here, both the vulnerability annotations and the source samples were obtained from reliable sources. For example, the Devign dataset, which contains previous flaws from different open-source projects, two of which are accessible to the general public(Zhou et al., 2019). There is still a long way to go, despite the reviewed research's recommendations for various feature set kinds and use of diverse network topologies to close the semantic gap. In this section, we'll talk about the difficulties and upcoming duties and offer some thoughts.

LARGE-SCALE GROUND TRUTH DATA SETS

The main obstacle preventing this field's advancement is the data sets. At this time, all of the suggested neural network-based vulnerability detection methods have been tested on their own sets of data. The ground truth datasets created by earlier investigations include various levels of labeling (designated at the function level, for instance, or at the line-of-code level) due to different techniques aiming for differing detection granularity (Li et al., 2019). The data sets employed in current research are either synthesized artificially or gathered from real systems. It is absolutely important to establish a standard benchmarking data set in order to assess and compare the effectiveness of offered alternatives. A lot of data sources provide synthetic vulnerability samples. The Software Assurance Metrics and Tool Evaluation (SAMATE) project was created by the National Institute of Standards and Technology (NIST) for the assessment of automated ways to guarantee software quality. The Static Analysis Tool Exposition (SATE) data sets for the evaluation of static analysis tools are one of the data sets that make up the SAMATE project. Other data sets include the Juliet Test Suite, the SARD, the Securely Taking On New Executable Software of Uncertain Provenance (STONESOUP) project by the Intelligence Advanced Research Projects Activity (IARPA), and the Static Analysis Tool Exposition (SARD).

ANALYSIS OF CODE AND NEURAL LEARNING

After careful analysis, it was discovered that network models were becoming increasingly complex and expres- sive in order to better comprehend the semantics of weak code snippets. The changing network structure has demonstrated the study effort that has been made to look at the possibilities of neural networks for understanding about the semantics of code and rich correlations for improving vulnerability finding. Earlier research employed MLPs, more recent studies CNNs or LSTMs, and most recent studies memory networks. Modern methodologies and approaches for source code for vulnerability finding have been adopted by researchers in the ML and NLP fields. The effort required for code analysis decreases as network complexity rises, which is another pattern that may be seen. The study used MLP to learn input validation and sanitization code patterns using handmade fea- tures from both CFGs and DDGs. It takes a lot of code analysis work and feature-deriving knowledge to extract CFGs and DDGs. While more recent memory network experiments take source code as input without needing to analyze it, later studies using CNN were able to directly learn features from laxed source code with minimal effort. However, it is still necessary to define meaningful and useful features from the software engineering and cyber security domains to direct the network architecture's design for the improved discovery of hidden and complicated vulnerable semantics and patterns (Li et al., 2019).

NEURAL MODEL WITH SEMANTIC RESERVATION

Using programming language to help a neural network model perform more efficiently in order to close the semantic gap. Semantic detection is a significant advancement in the use of NN for vulnerability identification. The algorithmic-semantic gap can be closed by creating an expressive and capable model for learning syntactic along with semantic structures. Despite the tendency for network used in the reviewed research to become more complex, the state-of-the-art implementation, such as the memory network, was shown to perform well (achieving) 91.7 percent of the F1-score) only on synthetic data sets with simplified code samples as opposed to real-time code samples. Despite this, scientists are actively investigating the possibilities of sophisticated brain models. A recent research that employed generative adversarial networks (GAN) to fix vulnerabilities on samples of synthetic C/C++ code demonstrated the neural model's capacity to understand the logic and semantics of code. (Lin et al., 2020b). Another problem needs to be solve is the application of tree/graph-based neural networks for vulnerability identification. Software representations commonly employ trees or graphs. A tree structure is one way that the AST, for instance, expresses code components. The CFG and PDG are the two graphs, in which CFG is a directed graph that shows the control flows in a software, whereas PDG defines the data and also controls the relationship programs. These program representations are used in existing research, however they are "flattened" and analysed using FCN, CNN, or RNNs in a "sequential" manner, which may inevitably lose the hierarchical and/or structural information encoding potentially susceptible code semantics. (Lin et al., 2020b).

MODEL INTERPRETIBILITY FOR HUMAN UNDERSTANDING

Machine learning models, especially NN models, are "black boxes", which means that practitioners are unaware of the criteria used to classify or predict data. The majority of the papers that were analyzed did not attempt to explain the behavior of the model. In the realm of vulnerability detection, a model's usefulness may be called into doubt if it is unclear how it forecasts whether a given line of code is either vulnerable or not (Li et al., 2019). Are there any concerns about the model's reliability? Or is the accuracy of this (individual) prediction/classification? One of the challenges to the practical use of NN-based models for the detection of vulnerability can be the inability to comprehend a model's behavior.

In contrast to linear models, neural networks incorporate nonlinearity, and their layered topologies make it more difficult to comprehend the models. The characteristics that are produced when applying neural networks for automatic learning of higher-level representations as features, are abstract and unintelligible to humans. LIME10 was offered as a solution to this problem, offering explicable for any model by learning an uncomplicated and unambiguous model locally around the forecasting samples. But when neural network models are utilized to find the characteristics, and those characteristics are then applied to train a classifier, LIME is not applicable (Li et al., 2019).

The ML discipline is rapidly expanding, and significant advances in ML and deep learning will be valuable additions to the arsenal for vulnerability identification. Aiming to close the gap between interpreters and understands the vulnerability and the obtained semantics that a neural network model can learn from, we reviewed existing studies that applied neural networks for vulnerability detection and identification. These studies demonstrated the trend of neural network structures being adopted for better learning and found the characteristics of vulnerable code snippets. More researchers will be encouraged to contribute to this promising subject because of the representation learning capabilities of neural network models and their adaptable structure, which offers intriguing potential for automated learning of complicated susceptible code patterns.

FUTURE RESEARCH AND DIRECTION

On studying various papers we find that vulnerability analysis and detection are in infancy state. To do the advancement in detection of vulnerabilities, we are designing a hardware and working on the model to get the accurate detection and analysis result.

CONCLUSION

This study examines current research on machine learning and deep learning for vulnerability identification and highlights various pillars in the area. By bringing new concepts and methods to the area of deep learning-based vulnerability identification, these pillars provide innovation. In order to give researchers an ordered overview of this developing topic, we classify pertinent research papers. Based on various methodologies and potential future research paths, this study offers knowledge of vulnerability detection accomplishments and research trends. Our key finding from the study of previous research work is that the use of deep learning techniques for software vulnerability analysis and detection is still in its infancy. Significant advancements in machine learning and deep learning will continually raise the value of vulnerability identification with the rapid development of data-driven methodologies (Chakraborty et al., 2021).

ACKNOWLEDGMENT

I would like to thank the Department of Science and Technology, India for funding the research work under Device Development Program. The sanction number of the project entitled, "An intelligent network analyzer cum patcher for advanced security hardening of the organizational network" is DST/TDT/DDP-30/2021.

REFERENCES

Allodi, L., & Massacci, F. (2014). Comparing vulnerability severity and exploits using case-control studies. [TISSEC]. *ACM Transactions on Information and System Security*, *17*(1), 1–20. doi:10.1145/2630069

Alnafrani, R., & Wijesekera, D. (2022). An automated framework for generating attack graphs using known security threats. In *2022 10th International Symposium on Digital Forensics and Security (ISDFS)*, pages 1–6. 10.1109/ISDFS55398.2022.9800833

Alperin, K. B., Wollaber, A. B., & Gomez, S. R. (2020). Improving interpretability for cyber vulnerability assessment using focus and context visualizations. In *2020 IEEE Symposium on Visualization for Cyber Security (VizSec)*, (pp. 30–39). IEEE. 10.1109/VizSec51108.2020.00011

Angelini, M., Blasilli, G., Catarci, T., Lenti, S., & Santucci, G. (2019). Vulnus: Visual vulnerability analysis for network security. *IEEE Transactions on Visualization and Computer Graphics*, *25*(1), 183–192. doi:10.1109/TVCG.2018.2865028 PMID:30136974

Black, P. E. (2018). A software assurance reference dataset: Thousands of programs with known bugs. *Journal of Research of the National Institute of Standards and Technology*, *123*, 1. doi:10.6028/jres.123.005 PMID:34877127

Booth, H., Rike, D., & Witte, G. A. (2013). *The national vulnerability database (nvd)*. Overview.

Chakraborty, S., Krishna, R., Ding, Y., & Ray, B. (2021). Deep learning based vulnerability detection: Are we there yet. *IEEE Transactions on Software Engineering*.

Chhillar, K., & Shrivastava, S. (2021). Vulnerability scanning and management of university computer network. In *2021 10th International Conference on Internet of Everything, Microwave Engineering, Communication and Networks (IEMECON)*, (pp. 01–06). IEEE. 10.1109/IEMECON53809.2021.9689207

Chu, Y., Yue, X., Wang, Q., & Wang, Z. (2020). Secureas: A vulnerability assessment system for deep neural network based on adversarial examples. *IEEE Access : Practical Innovations, Open Solutions*, *8*, 109156–109167. doi:10.1109/ACCESS.2020.3001730

He, W., Li, H., & Li, J. (2019). Unknown vulnerability risk assessment based on directed graph models: A survey. *IEEE Access : Practical Innovations, Open Solutions*, *7*, 168201–168225. doi:10.1109/ACCESS.2019.2954092

Jacobs, J., Romanosky, S., Adjerid, I., & Baker, W. (2020). Improving vulnerability remediation through better exploit prediction. *Journal of Cybersecurity*, *6*(1), tyaa015. doi:10.1093/cybsec/tyaa015

Li, Z., Zou, D., Tang, J., Zhang, Z., Sun, M., & Jin, H. (2019). A comparative study of deep learning-based vulnerability detection system. *IEEE Access : Practical Innovations, Open Solutions*, *7*, 103184–103197. doi:10.1109/ACCESS.2019.2930578

Lin, G., Wen, S., Han, Q.-L., Zhang, J., & Xiang, Y. (2020a). Software vulnerability detection using deep neural networks: A survey. *Proceedings of the IEEE*, *108*(10), 1825–1848. doi:10.1109/JPROC.2020.2993293

Lin, G., Wen, S., Han, Q.-L., Zhang, J., & Xiang, Y. (2020b). Software vulnerability detection using deep neural networks: A survey. *Proceedings of the IEEE*, *108*(10), 1825–1848. doi:10.1109/JPROC.2020.2993293

Lin, G., Zhang, J., Luo, W., Pan, L., De Vel, O., Montague, P., & Xiang, Y. (2021). Software vulnerability discovery via learning multi-domain knowledge bases. *IEEE Transactions on Dependable and Secure Computing*, *18*(5), 2469–2485. doi:10.1109/TDSC.2019.2954088

Liu, S., Dibaei, M., Tai, Y., Chen, C., Zhang, J., & Xiang, Y. (2020). Cyber vulnerability intelligence for internet of things binary. *IEEE Transactions on Industrial Informatics*, *16*(3), 2154–2163. doi:10.1109/TII.2019.2942800

Lyon, G. (2014). Nmap security scanner. *l'ınea] URL:* http://nmap. org/*[Consulta: 8 de junio de 2012].*

Malzahn, D., Birnbaum, Z., & Wright-Hamor, C. (2020). Automated vulnerability testing via executable attack graphs. In *2020 International Conference on Cyber Security and Protection of Digital Services (Cyber Security)*, (pp. 1–10). IEEE. 10.1109/CyberSecurity49315.2020.9138852

Mell, P., Scarfone, K., & Romanosky, S. (2006). Common vulnerability scoring system. *IEEE Security and Privacy*, *4*(6), 85–89. doi:10.1109/MSP.2006.145

Okun, V., Delaitre, A., & Black, P. E. (2013). Report on the static analysis tool exposition (sate) iv. *NIST Special Publication*, *500*, 297. doi:10.6028/NIST.SP.500-297

Russell, R., Kim, L., Hamilton, L., Lazovich, T., Harer, J., Ozdemir, O., Ellingwood, P., & McConley, M. (2018). Automated vulnerability detection in source code using deep representation learning. In *2018 17th IEEE international conference on machine learning and applications (ICMLA)*, pages 757–762. IEEE. 10.1109/ICMLA.2018.00120

Setiawan, H., Erlangga, L. E., & Baskoro, I. (2020). Vulnerability analysis using the interactive application security testing (iast) approach for government x website applications. In *2020 3rd International Conference on Information and Communications Technology (ICOIACT)*, (pp. 471–475). IEEE.

Shi, F., Kai, S., Zheng, J., & Zhong, Y. (2022). Xlnet-based prediction model for cvss metric values. *Applied Sciences (Basel, Switzerland)*, *12*(18), 8983. doi:10.3390/app12188983

Stiffler, J. J. (1981). The vulnerability of computers: Malfunctions may be due to "illegal" operations, to hardware failures, or to combinations of hardware and software failures that simply elude pinpointing. *IEEE Spectrum*, *18*(10), 44–45. doi:10.1109/MSPEC.1981.6369634

Tang, M., Alazab, M., & Luo, Y. (2019). Big data for cybersecurity: Vulnerability disclosure trends and depen- dencies. *IEEE Transactions on Big Data*, *5*(3), 317–329. doi:10.1109/TBDATA.2017.2723570

Wang, H., Ye, G., Tang, Z., Tan, S. H., Huang, S., Fang, D., Feng, Y., Bian, L., & Wang, Z. (2021). Combining graph-based learning with automated data collection for code vulnerability detection. *IEEE Transactions on Information Forensics and Security*, *16*, 1943–1958. doi:10.1109/TIFS.2020.3044773

Wang, W., Dumont, F., Niu, N., & Horton, G. (2022). Detecting software security vulnerabilities via requirements dependency analysis. *IEEE Transactions on Software Engineering*, *48*(5), 1665–1675. doi:10.1109/TSE.2020.3030745

Wang, W., Shi, F., Zhang, M., Xu, C., & Zheng, J. (2020). A vulnerability risk assessment method based on heterogeneous information network. *IEEE Access : Practical Innovations, Open Solutions*, *8*, 148315–148330. doi:10.1109/ACCESS.2020.3015551

Weiser, M. (1984). Program slicing. *IEEE Transactions on Software Engineering, SE-10*(4), 352–357. doi:10.1109/TSE.1984.5010248

Wu, B., & Zou, F. (2022). Code vulnerability detection based on deep sequence and graph models: A survey. *Security and Communication Networks, 2022*, 2022. doi:10.1155/2022/1176898

Yang, S., Shi, Y., & Guo, F. (2019). Risk assessment of industrial internet system by using game-attack graphs. In *2019 IEEE 5th International Conference on Computer and Communications (ICCC)*, pages 1660–1663. IEEE. 10.1109/ICCC47050.2019.9064444

Yu, Z., Theisen, C., Williams, L., & Menzies, T. (2021). Improving vulnerability inspection efficiency using active learning. *IEEE Transactions on Software Engineering, 47*(11), 2401–2420. doi:10.1109/TSE.2019.2949275

Zeng, Z., Yang, Z., Huang, D., & Chung, C.-J. (2021). Licality–likelihood and criticality: Vulnerability risk prior- itization through logical reasoning and deep learning. *IEEE Transactions on Network and Service Management.*

Zhang, M., de Carn'e de Carnavalet, X., Wang, L., & Ragab, A. (2019). Large-scale empirical study of important features indicative of discovered vulnerabilities to assess application security. *IEEE Transactions on Information Forensics and Security, 14*(9), 2315–2330. doi:10.1109/TIFS.2019.2895963

Zhou, Y., Liu, S., Siow, J., Du, X., & Liu, Y. (2019). Devign: Effective vulnerability identification by learning comprehensive program semantics via graph neural networks. *Advances in Neural Information Processing Systems, 32.*

Chapter 7
Knowledge Repository on Cyber Security

Kunal Sinha

iD https://orcid.org/0000-0002-2347-1791
Artificial Computing Machines, India

Kishore Kumar Senapati
Birla Institute of Technology, India

ABSTRACT

Cyber-attacks are serious problems for the IT sector. According to a survey, 66 percent of businesses have experienced these attacks. It's difficult and tiresome to fend against these attacks. Cyber analysts are now studying hacker intentions and purposes for incidents in addition to analysing cyber occurrences as a result of the rise in cyberattacks. DBMS may also establish itself as a key technology in the field of computer security and addressing cyber threats among the several technologies being designed and developed to avoid cybercrime. Research on cybercrime and hacker's interpretation can be honed with the use of DBMS. Through its logical and physical models and query processing, it aids in supplying sufficient knowledge to understand upcoming cyber-attacks.

INTRODUCTION

The repository's main idea is the creation of a database model that helps move society closer to cyber security by answering end users' questions about cybercrime and preparing them for upcoming threats by retrieving various data on cybercrime.

DOI: 10.4018/978-1-6684-8666-5.ch007

By developing prototypes that will be converted into a data model and input into a database, it aids in the decision-making and response related to cyberspace. This gives the database a defensive capacity that serves as a teaching tool for cyber threat and supports the present cyber security algorithms.

DATA PRIVACY AND DATA BREACH

Data privacy, security and its protection are a major challenge in the modern computer era of network systems. Gathering information of users has become easy for cyber-criminals if certain concerns are overlooked. This negligence due to insufficient knowledge and or ignorance of security mandates invites cyber-criminals for practicing illegal activities.

Some of the problems related to it, may be defined as - Carelessness in the use of an information system or network system in respect of personal or official data protection; Ignorance of security policy and security practices that results in destruction of information and service; non-enforcement of policy and procedures in work culture and while development of applications and products. Distribution of personal data over social networks systems leading to an unknown data breach etc.

ELEMENTS OF CYBER DATABASE

Database is a cluster of related data. Context to this cyber database is a collection of related cyber data. The assembly of cyber data is predicted as cyber database that constitutes of information related to a specific subject (Here, Cyber Crime). This collection of data can be of various nature, it may be a crime data, data related to a specific application or hackers, victim's data etc.

The system is formulated and developed to govern a massive body of collected information. Data management includes establishing structure for information warehousing and preparing a mechanism that assists in an interpretation of stored data. Management of data also includes development of technical strategies for incidents like system crashes, unauthorized access and faulty results.

It privileges its end-users to explore and understand cyber data. The fundamental objective of cyber DBMS is to deliver a methodology that store and fetches information's in appropriate and structured way.

Technically cyber DBMS is a software program that access databases by through data queries used to store and fetch data in database management system. These queries are an information retrieval in nature or used for insertion of new data in the database management system.

There are various different database management system application programs available in the computer science industry for the use commercial and personal use of databases. Each of these application programs has one or more unique features with a basic similarity of fundamentals of DBMS i.e., information storage, information retrieval, information transaction and information security and ease of access while in use with frontend application programs of various categories and nature. Some examples of database application systems are ORACLE, MYSQL, SQL SERVER, POSTGRES SQL, NOSQL, MONGODB etc.

CHARACTERISTICS OF CYBER DATABASE

In computer, earlier before the use of database approach there was a primitive approach of writing customized programs to access data stored in a file, it was known as traditional file processing. In this approach required files are defined and implemented by the users in specific software's during the programming of applications. On the other hand, cyber database provides an exclusive repository that is used to maintain overall data, which are defined once and accessed by many users through data queries, data transactions and software's programs for which it is being used.

Major characteristics of cyber database technique are - Self-exploratory property, Segregation between programs, data and data abstraction, providing multiple views of information's, Data sharing, Redundancy control, Unauthorized access restriction, Uninterrupted storage for objects of programs, Structured warehousing and mining techniques using robust query processing, Data backup and data recovery mechanisms, Multiple end-user's interfaces, Illustration of relationships among the data, Allowing interfacing and activities through regulations and triggers, Reducing application development time, Flexibility and Up-to-date information availability

Actors of Cyber Database

A cyber database can be large in nature. Databases that are large in nature and encompasses numerous users. The different users that are involved in different jobs in large database are called as the actors of the database. Some of the actors of cyber database are as follows:-

Cyber Data Administrators

In databases the principle means are database and secondary is the database related applications and software's. Administration of these is done by cyber data administrator. These are the peoples are authorized for database access, databases use monitoring and buying software's and hardware's as needed. It is the cyber data administrator who are responsible for security breaches and poor response time while the use of cyber database systems (Ramez & Shamakant, 2019) (Abraham et al., 2006).

Cyber Database Designers

They are the persons authorized for identification of cyber data's that needs to be saved in a database. They choose significant organization for cyber data representation and storage. It is the cyber database designers that are responsible to reach all the potential end-users of database to recognize the requirement's before designing and developing a cyber database (Ramez & Shamakant, 2019) (Abraham et al., 2006).

END USERS

They are the persons engaged in accessing the designed database. This access is related to information enquiry, information upgrade and report generations etc. End users are of several types, these are:-

1. **Casual End Users** – Occasionally access when information's are required.
2. **Naive or Parametric** – Their jobs involve in regular querying and updating a database using standard queries and updates.
3. **Sophisticated End Users** – They are the end users like engineers, analysts etc. who familiarize themselves from the features of a Cyber DBMS to implement in their own applications which meets with its complex requirements.
4. **Standalone End Users** – They are the users who maintains their personal databases using readymade programs which provides user friendly interfaces (Ramez & Shamakant, 2019) (Abraham et al., 2006).

Database System Architecture

The database system architectures are dependent upon computer systems on which it is executed. Particularly the computer architectures are classified as network system, parallel system and distributed system.

Network or Client Server Architectures

Network computers or client server architectures are systems where few tasks are carried over at server system and few tasks are carried in client system. This classification of system laid the client-server database system. It's a system were high-performance database runs on a high-end server. The functionality is distributed in environments of server systems, containing the database and a several client systems engaged in query processing and transactions (Abraham et al., 2006).

Figure 1. Client server system

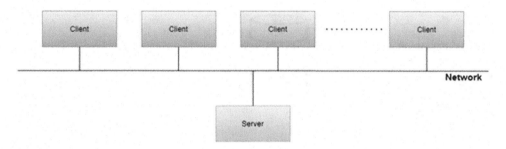

Parallel Database Architecture

Parallel processing in computers allows database to speed up executions and response in transactions. This parallel query processing system laid the parallel DBMS. There are various models available for parallel systems. Among these some important models of architectures are (Abraham et al., 2006):-

Shared Memory – In this architecture all processors share one common memory (Figure 2).

Shared Disks – In this architecture all processors share common sets of disks, this system is also known as clusters (Figure 3).

Shared Nothing – In this architecture the no processors share common memory or a common disk (Figure 4).

Hierarchical – It is a hybrid design of the all the architectures i.e., shared memory, shared disk and shared nothing (Figure 5).

Figure 2. Shared memory

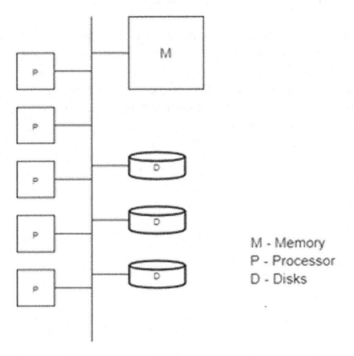

Figure 3. Shared disk

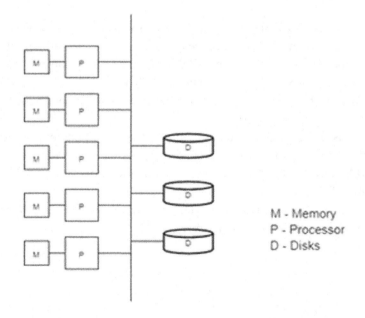

Figure 4. Shared nothing

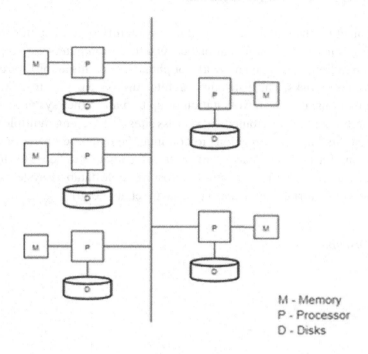

Figure 5. Hierarchical

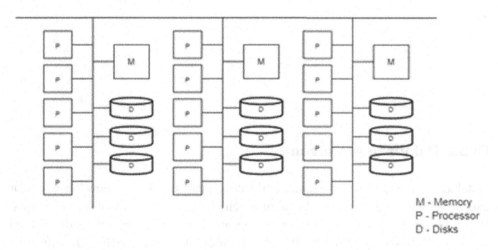

Distributed Database Architecture

In this architecture the database is stored in several different computers located at different locations. The communication between these computers with one another is done through lightning speed networks or phone lines. This architecture does not share memories or disks. The distributed architecture system may differ in different sizes and functions, may be a workstation or up to mainframes systems.

In this architecture a distributed data across sites and keeping multiple copies of database benefits large organizations to continue the database operations even on non-operation of a site due to natural disaster or technical glitches. This has laid to distributed database system that is spread across multiple database systems (udemy) (geeksforgeeks) (tutorialspoints.com) (Abraham et al., 2006).

Figure 6. Distributed system

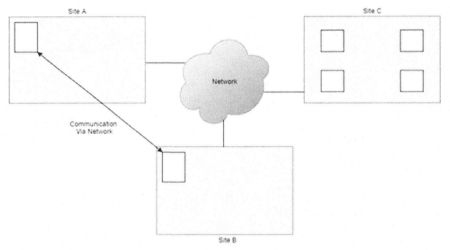

Cyber Database Architecture

Database architectures are significantly dependent on the systems on which it executes. It may be a centralized system which processes on behalf of several clients. It can be designed for parallel computing architecture and can be a distributed database. Database systems are divided into different modules each dealing discrete responsibilities making an overall system. The various component for this database system and connections among them are depicted in Figure 7.

Figure 7. Database architecture

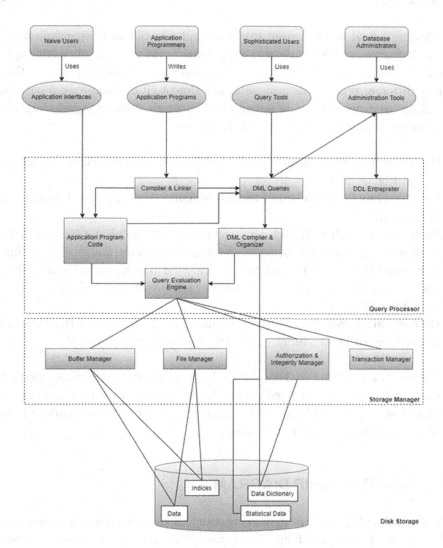

Operational component of cyber-DBMS can be divided into three functions i.e., **Query Processor** for simplifying and accessing data, **Storage Manager** and **Disk Storage**. Disk storage becomes important for this architecture because the current database typically requires large amount of storage space. The DBMS is responsible for translating queries and updates in non-procedural languages to an organized physical operations flow at the logical level.

DATA MODEL

It is a technological concept used to describe the layout and organization of a database. It discusses the various data kinds, connections, and restrictions that apply to database data. It provides the tools we need to accomplish abstraction. There are many different types of data models, and almost all of them have a basic set of operations to express database updates and retrievals. (udemy) (geeksforgeeks) (tutorialspoints) (Abraham et al., 2006). These are:

1. **High Level or Conceptual Data Model** – explains the ideas behind user recognition of data.
2. **Low Level or Physical Data Model** – explains the principles of data storage in a system.
3. **Entity Relationship Model** – a conceptual data model at a high level that explains the relationships between an entity, its qualities, and its relationships.
4. **Relational Data Model** – This displays database as groupings of relationships. Each row of a table represents a group of related values in a relation, which is a table with values.
5. **Hierarchal Model** – the data representation model that uses a tree structure.
6. **Record Based Data Model** – consists of record structures used to represent data..
7. **Object Data Model** – These are object-oriented programming models. Programme space is expanded to include object management and shareability.
8. **Self-Describing Data Models** – It is a data model that combines the description of the data with the actual data values.

ENTITY RELATIONSHIP DIAGRAM

The development of database designs using entity relationship diagrams, also known as ERDs, allows for the sketching of schemas, which describe the overall database structure of a certain subject or issue. The database structure is improved with a better entity relationship diagram. Entity, Attribute, and Relationship are the three essential parts of an ER diagram.

Entity

An entity is anything that actually exists in the real world and for which data must be kept. Entities can be anything that is associated in a system, including people, places, actions, or items. Role, Event, Location, and Anything Tangible are the five different categories of entities that can exist.

Attributes

An attribute is made up of both an entity and an attribute. An attribute may be shared by several entities or it may be a part of one specific entity.

Relationship

A relationship both shows the connections between the entities and their relationships with one another.

INSTANCES AND SCHEMAS

An instance is the collective collection of data that is kept in a database at a specific point in time. And a schema is the name given to the full design. The programming language used to create a programme will determine the instances and schemas that are used. Schemas and programme variable declarations are connected. Variables have a defined value right now. A schema instance and the values of programme variables at a given time are related.

A database system may contain several different types of schemas. These schemas describe designs at physical levels and are physical in nature. logical schemas that describe logically levelled designs. Databases have numerous additional schemas at the view level that are referred to as sub schemas and explain the various views of a database. (udemy) (geeksforgeeks) (tutorialspoints) (Abraham et al., 2006).

Mathematical Modelling

Mathematical modelling is increasingly being acknowledged as a crucial tool for proof synthesis and teaching cyber security, especially when information from earlier research' systematic evaluations is insufficient to answer some of the questions. However, due to a lack of a common grasp of concepts and terminology between evidence synthesis experts and mathematical modellers, systematic observers and rules developers may have trouble using the results of modelling research. Common nomenclature usages for modelling studies covering many cyber research areas that address a variety of cybercrimes. The professionals in research and other computer-related fields will be able to employ terms in the studies of mathematical modelling that are especially significant for evidence synthesis and knowledge translation in the Cyber domain with the help of the characterization, comparison, and usage of mathematical modelling studies. Mathematical models are "mathematical framework representing variables and its interrelationships to describe observed occurrences or predicting future events". We describe mathematical modelling research as a study that uses a mathematical model to answer specific concerns about cybercrime. The framework of the mathematical model, which represents the correlations between adversaries, cyberspace, victims, crimes, information or software, actions, physical systems, and extrinsic (all of these are variables), is most appropriate for modelling studies that involve evidence synthesis and decision-making in cybercrime. Their correlations are often defined in terms of their motive, objective, firewall, service provider, infrastructure, browser, technology, name, and age to establish these parameters, mathematical modellers may utilise a variety of techniques, including the use of theoretical values, values that are provided in (Teegwende et al., 2018)

This chapter won't use any of these model strategies until all of its schemas, entities (variables), methods, and procedures have been properly developed. The various operators of the relational database theory will then correlate to the rule of evidence combination. After the model has fully developed, the interpretation of the variables and their relationships will fit to any of the models. The databases will be enhanced and prepared for reference by the research communities using the model. Additionally, the various tables will connect with various capabilities.

Approach of Knowledge Repository

The key concern when creating a "*knowledge repository*" is how to depict a cyberattack. The goal is to create a representation that explains precisely what cyberattacks and related ideas entail. Additionally, the created representation of a cyberattack must be able to describe such attacks using publicly available information from any source, including the internet.

The representation must be capable of: Getting rid of ambiguities and contradictions in various theories of how cyberattacks are used; Creating a multidisciplinary theory of cyberattacks that can be used to comprehend and predict upcoming attacks; and Creating databases for cyberattacks that contain theory development.

In order to conceptualise and comprehend database design and development procedures, it is necessary to gather and study previously observed and recorded cyberattacks in order to understand the various forms of cyberattacks and how an attacker selects a victim.

Methodology

The figure 8 below shows the methodology and approach for creating the respective knowledge repository.

Figure 8. Methodology

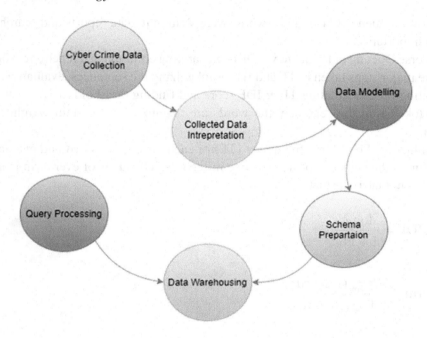

Data Collection

In data collection phase, relevant data are collected from various online and offline sources. This data is stored as raw data in a system. After collection the next phase is the approach of pre-processing which helps in overcoming noisy information from the raw data. An extraction process takes place. By doing so, high-dimensional data can be transformed into low-dimensional data. Pre-processed data are beneficial for data visualisation because composite data can organise better when complicated data is translated into fewer dimensions. (Rupa et al., 2020).

For Example, below is the content based feature of classifying cyber-crime (Rupa et al., 2020):-

Content Based Feature
Crime
Cyber Criminal/Hacker
Damages
Year
Victim

Term Frequency (TF) – How words were written in data reports and searching for its importance.

Inverse Document Frequency (IDF) – Separating common and repetitive words.

The major steps taken in TF and IDF is tokenizing the sentences, evaluating TF, evaluating IDF, calculating TF & IDF score and finding threshold.

In tokenizing the sentence, the words are tokenized and certain weights are assigned.

Evaluating TF – Term frequency (TF) or each term is recorded and evaluated based upon the statistics of its presence in records. TF values of ever term is then recorded in matrix format.

$$TF - IDF = \frac{\log N}{1 + N_w}$$

$$TF(term) = \frac{N_{term}(Record)}{T_{term}(Record)}$$

Where, N_{term} = No of times terms appeared and T^{term} = Total No of terms in record. X^2
Evaluating IDF and storing it in matrix Format

$$\sum_{i=1}^{N} X^2 \left(\frac{0 - E}{E} IDF(term) = \log \frac{N}{1 + N_{term}} \right)$$

Where N = total number of records; N_{term} = total number of terms in records. Calculation of TF – IDF score is estimated by considering individual matrices of both frequencies.

TF – IDF (term) = TF (term) x IDF (term)

Scoring the record sentence: TF – IDF is taken into consideration for allotting score to the terms of sentences that belongs to a record. Average of TF – IDF of all terms of sentences becomes score of sentences.

Finding Threshold: Average score of all sentences in the record is taken as threshold. This value helps in finding corelated terms in data.

The (X^2) measure is utilized in finding out corelation between the categorial attributes of the data. It verifies whether relationships between two variables reflect on cyber-crime data set or not.

$$\sum \frac{(O-E)^2}{E}$$

Where O = Observed count of cyber-crime incidents and E is the expected count of cyber-crime incidents (Rupa et al., 2020).

Data Interpretation

the method of reviewing data using a few methods that are predefined and that are helpful in providing a meaning to data to reach a conclusion relevant to objective is termed as data interpretation. The process involves taking results of data analysis, making inferences on studied relations and using it for relevant conclusion.

Usually, the first step for any data interpretation is the process of organization, categorization, manipulation and summarization of the collected data to obtain the research questions. This process needs to be completed properly. Various methods have been recognized for data interpretation and it is categorized as:-

- Qualitative
- Quantitative

A. **Qualitative Interpretation** – This is a categorical interpretation. In this text data is gathered by employing wide variety of techniques like:-
   - **Observation** – Detailing behavioural patterns.
   - **Focus** – Selecting relevant questions to generate collaborative discussions.
   - **Secondary Research** – Division and coding of document based upon material.
   - **Interviews** – Collection of methods for narrative data.

After the process of data collection, data interpretation is followed by defined methods like:-

1. **Content Analysis** – This is method is used to identify frequencies and recurring words, subjects and concepts present in image, video, or audio. It transforms qualitative information into quantitative, thus helping in discovery of trends and conclusions may support in vital research queries.

2. **Thematic Analysis** – This method is a exploratory technique that helps in analysing qualitative data to identify common patterns and separate it into different groups according to found similarities. For example, imagine you want to analyze what customers think about your restaurant.

3. **Narrative Analysis** – Used to analyze stories and discover the meaning behind them. These can in form of testimonials, case studies and interviews etc. This method is valuable technique as it helps to understand preferences.

4. **Discourse Analysis** – It is used to understand how data context can affect the way language is laid out and is understood. It is time consuming as the data needs to be analysed until no new perception emerge.

5. **Grounded Theory Analysis** – This analysis aims in discovering a new theory through carefully testing and evaluating the data available. It helps in extractions, conclusions and building hypotheses from data.

B. **Quantitative Interpretation** – This is a numerical data type interpretation. This type of interpretation involves statistical modelling like:-

   ○ **Mean** – It represents a numerical average for a set of data.
   ○ **Standard Deviation** – It describes distribution of responses around the mean.
   ○ **Frequency Distribution** – It measure the rate of response appearance within a data set.

Correlation analyses between two or more significant variables are used to measure quantitative data. Several methods for interpreting data include:-

1. **Regression Analysis** – It makes use of historical data to understand the relationship between a dependent variable and one or more independent factors.

2. **Cohort Analysis** – It helps in identifying groups that share common characteristics during a particular time period.

3. **Predictive Analysis** – This is a predictive method that aims to predict future developments by analysing historical and current data.

4. **Prescriptive Analysis** – This approach uses methods like graphs, complicated event processing, neural networks, etc. to solve and correct the repercussions of future actions before they are ever made.

5. **Conjoint Analysis** – This survey-style analysis is used to examine consumer perceptions of various product features.

6.   **Cluster Analysis** – This method used is used to group objects into categories. This method is useful to find hidden trends and patterns in the data.

Understanding Cyber Threat

Understanding the distinctions between data, information, and intelligence is essential to comprehending the cyber threat. (NakHyun et al., 2017).

1.   **Data** – A single item that has atomicity.
2.   **Information** - a manipulated data.
3.   **Intelligence** - Facts about how to recognise and fend off cyberattacks and threats.

The definition above can be expressed in terms of a cyber threat by (NakHyun et al., 2017):-

4.   **Data** - Information that can be gathered from the Internet or a network: IP, domain, URL, and email etc.
5.   **Information** - A domain that distributed malicious code, a URL used for phishing, and an IP address used for connection.
6.   **Intelligence** - The thorough analysis's output that details a cyber event or crime.

Thus, an analysis of these statistics, their related information, and their intelligence to construct a repository that helps in an explanation of how and why a cyberattack becomes a threat is offered in the development of a new information security field. This work may provide an enhanced theoretical and practical reference that can help in understanding cyber-crime patterns, process and overcoming it in any further attempt.

CYBER CRIME CHARACTERIZATION

On the basis of the aforementioned findings, a methodology to describe and model cyber dangers is carried out. It is discovered that no one existing approach completely meets all of the specifications for a cyber threat model while building a data model for cyber threat. A framework for characterising cyber threats is presented and used to create the data model based on an existing survey.

Design And Development of Cyber Data Repository

The characterization of elements of cyber threat, its approaches and according to the constructed threat model, identification of entities and their attributes are obtained. This provides us a path for data modelling. This data modelling is further constituted for the cyber database schema preparation and ends with a model cyber threat database creation.

Indexing techniques are utilized in the created database for optimization of the performance of designed cyber threat database. The indexing technique provides a helping hand in seamless query processing to understand the assessment of occurred attacks and predicting the future attacks.

Potential Mapping of The Threat

Table 1. Mapping of characterization

Data Model Objects	Threat Characterization Categories
Actor	Adversary/Type
	Adversary/Commitment
	Adversary/Resources
Adversary	Adversary/Motivation (non-hostile)
	Attack / Delivery mechanisms
	Attack/Tools
	Attack/Automation
Significant Incident	Attack/Actions
Intent	Adversary/Motivation (hostile)
	Effect / Cyber effects
Impact	Effect
Resource	Asset/Container
	Asset/Vulnerability
Target	Asset/Profile
Victim	Suffer/Loss

Data Repository Preparing Techniques

To better understand the various cyberattack classes and create the cyberattack data model, an analysis based on observations of cyberattacks is carried out. The

Table 2. Steps of repository preparation

SL No	STEPS	DESCRIPTION OF STEPS
1	Identification of entities	Determine the function, circumstance, setting, and ideas of the subject
2	Identification of attributes	Provide entity information
3	Finding relationships	Find connections between different entities
4	Sketching an ERD	Following the guidelines for drawing the ER Diagram
5	Preparing schema based upon ERD	creation of a schema that includes key identification

study's acknowledgment of cyber-attack ideas is a crucial step. In order to illustrate these concepts of cybercrime, ER Diagrams were created and utilized to explore the concepts of cyberattacks. The collected literature and information gleaned from the internet are used to identify entities and gain understanding of cybercrime.

The purpose of this study, which is exploratory in nature, is to present and address various theories and methods of cyber-attacks. The study makes an effort to classify online data on cyberattacks into entities, their characteristics, and their connections.

In this study, the adversary was defined as the assailant. Attack recognized as the attacker's delivery method. Hardware, software, network systems, information, and managed physical assets are all considered assets. The person or group affected by an attack is referred to as the victim.

An attacker's adversary may use cyberspace, which may be impacted by elements both within and external to their organizations. Any establishment or a person's assets that are impacted by attacks on the victim may be intrinsic or extrinsic.

Reference Graph

An Entity Relationship model can be represented as graphs i.e., $G = \{V, E\}$. This is known as referenced graph. Here, V is a set of entities and E is a set of relationships. This reference graph is described as directed graph. The set V moreover encompasses m: n relationship. There is an *id* key set which consists primary keys of all sets of system. A set that represents an entity or relationship in the set V contains two subsets – set of identifying attributes (Keys) *id* and set of describing attributes *D* (Subhrajyoti & Bichitra, 2013).

Unary Relationship

It is an Entity that is correlated with itself. Therefore, it becomes important to specify the role of contributor in a relationship (Subhrajyoti & Bichitra, 2013). Example: -

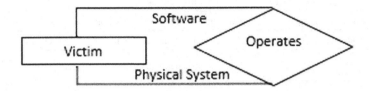

Ternary Relationship

An ERD with ternary relationship with its corresponding reference graph is shown below (Subhrajyoti & Bichitra, 2013): -

Table 3. Entities

SL No	Cyber-Attack Definition	Entities
1	Actions that compromise a computer system's functioning	• Action • Adversary • Net or System
2	Using methods to damage or impair a computer system	• Action • Adversary • Victim • Net or System • Info and Software
3	Operations carried out to interfere with or destroy a computer system as well as a personal or professional network.	• Action • Adversary • Victim • Extrinsic • Physical • Net or System • Info and SW
4	Illegal use of cyberspace for unauthorized access	• Cyberspace • Net or Systems • Info and Software
5	Aggressive technological use to disrupt and undermine a cyber system, its resources, and its functions	• Action • Adversary • Victim • Cyberspace
6	Efforts destroy a cyber system, its assets and functions	• Action • Net or System • Info and Software

Table 4. Attributes

SL No	Cyber-Attack Definition	Attributes
1	Actions that compromise a computer system's functioning	• Type • Objective • Durations
2	Use of actions to disrupt or destroy a computer system	• Software Name • License Type • Apps • Type • Network Hardware
3	Operations carried out to interfere with or destroy a computer system as well as a personal or professional network.	• Software Name • License Type • Apps • Costs
4	Illegal use of cyberspace for unauthorized access	• Firewall • Service Provider • Infrastructure • Technology • Browser
5	Aggressive technological use to disrupt and undermine a cyber system, its resources, and its functions	• Origin • Type • Date and Time • Type • Degree
6	Efforts destroy a cyber system, its assets and functions	• Software Name • License Type • Apps • Type • Network Hardware • Costs

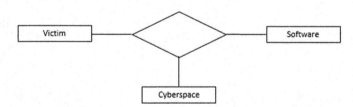

Identification of Entities (Table 3)

Identification of Attributes (Table 4)

Relationship Among Entity and Attributes (Table 5)

Table 5. Relationship

SL No	Cyber-Attack Definition	Relationship
1	Actions that compromise a computer system's functioning	Adversary executes Actions damages Net or Systems
2	Use of actions to disrupt or destroy a computer system	Adversary executes Actions damages Net or Systems Action damages Software Net or System run transit Info and Software
3	Operations carried out to interfere with or destroy a computer system as well as a personal or professional network.	Adversary executes Action damages Net or Systems Action damages Info and Software Action damages Physical System Action Damages Extrinsic
4	Illegal use of cyberspace for unauthorized access	Adversary uses Cyberspace damages Net or System Action damages Info and Software
5	Aggressive technological use to disrupt and undermine a cyber system, its resources, and its functions	Adversary executes Action Adversary uses Cyberspace Action damages Net or Systems Action damages Info and Software
6	Efforts destroy a cyber system, its assets and functions	Adversary execute Action Action damages Net or System

Figure 9. Schema

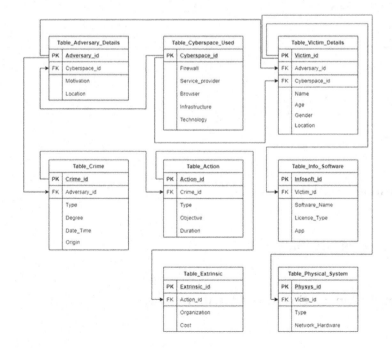

Specimen Schema of Repository (Figure 9)

QUERY PROCESSING

Query processing in database model helps its users to insert data into the designed tables of the database and accordingly fetch any desired outcomes based upon the schema of the designed database. In the dissertation the data model is studied and designed to give it users a response to know the different questions regarding the cyber-crime.

A sample of is taken to understand the exploratory uses of the designed data model:-

```
SELECT Adversary_Details.Location, Victim_Details.Name
FROM Adversary_Details INNER JOIN
Victim_Details ON Adversary_Details.Adversary_ID = Victim_Details.Adversary_
    ID
WHERE Victim_Details.Name = 'Name'
```

Machine Configuration of Repository Experimentation

The repository was designed and tested using a set of training data with Intel CORE 5 8th Generation i5-8250 CPU @ 1.60 Ghz 1.80 Ghz, X64-based processor having 8 GB of RAM as hardware and database tools used was Microsoft SQL Server 2008 R2.

REFERENCES

Agana, M. A., & Inyiama, H. C. (2015). Cyber Crime Detection and Control Using the Cyber User Identification Model. *IRACST – International Journal of Computer Science and Information Technology & Security(IJCSITS)*, 5(5).

Bordoloi, S., & Kalita, B. (2013). E-R Model to an Abstract Mathematical Model for Database Schema Using Reference Graph. *International Journal of Engineering Research and Development*, 6(4).

Boulahia-Cuppens, N., Cuppens, F., Gabillon, A., & Yazdanian, K. (1992). MultiView model for object-oriented database. *Proceedings of 9th Annual Computer Security Applications Conference*. Springer.

Ch, R., Gadekallu, T., Abidi M., & Al-Ahmari, A. (2020). *Computational System to classify Cyber Crime Offences using Machine Learning*. MPDI.

Choi, D.-L., Kim, B.-W., Lee, Y.-J., Um, Y., & Chung, M. (2011). Design and Creation of Dysarthric Speech Database for Development of QoLT Software Technology. *2011 International Conference on Speech Database and Assessments (Oriental COCOSDA)*. IEEE. 10.1109/ICSDA.2011.6085978

Elmasri, R., & Navathe, S. B. (2019). *Fundamentals of Database Systems* (7th ed.). Pearson.

Griffin, M. P., & Mitchell, R. J. (1992). Regenerating Database Techniques for Real-time Creation and Maintenance of Very Large Scale Databases. *IEEE Colloquium on Using Virtual Worlds*. IEEE.

Hyeisum, S. L., Kim, B., & Lee, T. (2016). The Data Indexing for Cyber Threat Resources. *IEEE Eighth International Conference on Ubiquitous and Future Networks (ICUFN)*. IEEE. 10.1109/ICUFN.2016.7536960

Jing, S., Liu, X., Cheng, C., Shang, X. Q., & Xiong, G. (2014). Study on a Process Safety Management System Design of a Chemical Accident Database. *IEEE International Conference on Service Operations and Logistics, and Informatics*. IEEE. 10.1109/SOLI.2014.6960736

Kadivar, M. (2015). *Entity Relationship Diagram Approach to Defining Cyber Attacks* [Thesis, Carleton University].

Kao-ming, B., & Geng-guo, C. (2009). Design the Database of Laboratory Management System. *IEEE First International Conference on Information Science and Engineering*. IEEE.

Kellette M. & Bernier, M. (2016). Cyber Threat Data Model high level model and use cases. *Defence Research and Development Canada, Reference Document*. Defense Canada.

Kim, N., Kim, B., Lee, S., Cho, H., & Park, J. (2017). Design of a Cyber Threat Intelligence Framework. *International Journal of Innovation Research in Technology & Science (IJIRTS), 5*(6).

Komarkova, J., Lastovicka, M., Husak, M., & Tovarnak, D. (2018). CRUSOE: Data Model for Cyber Situational Awareness. *International Conference on Availability, Reliability, and Security*. ACM.

Ponniah, P. (2019). *Data Warehousing Fundamentals for IT Professionals*. Wiley.

Porgo, T. V., Norris, S. L., Salanti, G., Johnson, L. F., Simpson, J. A., Low, N., Egger, M., & Althaus, C. L. (2018). *The Use of Mathematical Modeling Studies for Evidence Synthesis and Guideline Development: A Glossary.* Research Synthesis Methods, Published by John Wiley & Sons Ltd.

Silberschatz, A., Forth, H. F., & Sudarshan, S. (2006). *Database System* (5th ed.). McGraw - Hill.

Telnarova, Z. (2010). Relational Database as a Source of Ontology Creation. *Proceedings of the International Multiconference on Computer Science and Information Technology.* UDEMY. www.google.co.in www.udemy.com www.geeksforgeeks.com www.tutorialspoints.com

Chapter 8
Impact of Information Leakage and Conserving Digital Privacy

Kishore Kumar Senapati
Birla Institute of Technology, India

Abhishek Kumar
Birla Institute of Technology, India

Kunal Sinha
(iD) https://orcid.org/0000-0002-2347-1791
Artificial Computing Machines, India

ABSTRACT

The rise of globally integrated technology with a pace in technical intervention in diversified fields of social, financial, governmental, and defense services the world today is transforming into data age. This scientific development of storing and processing tasks within software territory had invaded the privacy of the users and individuals through technical attacks of existing and innovated technical solutions to discover and mine related information that may use for illegal and legal activities as per demand. Such a data, if extracted from a secured system, may harm a user or an individual in various ways depending on culprit's intention. It therefore becomes important to learn and understand the technical art of safeguarding their data while going digital. Privacy conserved data publishing should be an essential precondition for all data driven technologies. Keeping data safe and legal is another aspect. Existing protection mechanisms may not help in privacy mechanism due to unbalanced research in legal and illegal related technical innovations.

DOI: 10.4018/978-1-6684-8666-5.ch008

INTRODUCTION

Information Leakage is a technical flaw in data storage where sensitive data are revealed and collected by real world end users which may be used to make benefits or illegal use. These data can be technical details of any web application or user-specific data. Any sensitive data may be used by a concern end user or a hacker to exploit the owner, its hosting network and related users. Therefore, leakage of sensitive data should be prevented from misuse. An information Leakage may be a result of many conditions – technical or no-technical, like, failure in encrypting HTML or script containing sensitive information, improper configurations and carelessness in sharing vital information in digital world.

Historically, Information leakage, both in the online and offline world, is a longstanding problem in a variety of contexts. Here's the leak history in both areas:

OFFLINE WORLD

In the pre-digital age, information leakage mainly occurs through physical means. Here are some notable examples:

Spy

Throughout history, governments and intelligence agencies have engaged in information leakage through espionage. Spies are responsible for collecting and disclosing classified information for the benefit of their country or organization.

Leaks on Paper

Information leakage also occurs through physical documents. Examples include whistleblowers who disclose classified documents, leaked memos or sensitive information accidentally left in public places.

Social Engineering

In offline situations, social engineering techniques have been used to manipulate individuals and extract sensitive information. Techniques such as impersonation, pretence and seduction have been used to gain unauthorized access to confidential data.

ONLINE WORLD

With the advent of the Internet and digital technologies, information leakage has spread to the online world. Here are the important steps:

Hacks and Data Breaches

The rise in hacks and data breaches has drawn attention to online information leaks. Notable incidents include serious breaches of the 2000s, such as the 2008 Heartland Payment System breach and the 2011 Sony PlayStation Network breach.

Warning Platform

Platforms like WikiLeaks have become known, allowing whistleblowers to anonymously leak sensitive documents and information to the public. These platforms have served as outlets for exposing corporate or government misconduct.

Insider Threats

Insider leaks have become a significant concern, with employees or insiders intentionally or unintentionally leaking sensitive data. Notable cases include Edward Snowden's leak of classified NSA documents in 2013. (Isabel et al., 2022)

Privacy and Social Media Concerns

The rise of social media platforms has brought new challenges related to information leakage. Users have unknowingly shared personal information, leading to privacy issues and the potential for misuse or abuse of personal data.

PRIVACY POLICY

Governments around the world have introduced privacy regulations to prevent information leakage. Examples include the European Union's General Data Protection Regulation (GDPR) implemented in 2018 and the California Consumer Privacy Act (CCPA) in 2020.

Cloud and Third-Party Risks

As organizations increasingly rely on cloud services and third-party providers, the risk of information leakage due to incorrect configurations, data breaches, or inadequate security practices has increased. . The historical background of information leakage spans centuries, evolving from an offline to an online context as technology has evolved. The ongoing challenge is to develop robust security and awareness measures to reduce risk and protect sensitive information in both areas.

protecting information is important and it requires specific procedural and behavioural activities. Other than any aspect of system security, information security requires data to be properly created, labelled, stored, and backed up. Any usable files by other users should constitute a significant secured undertaking of safety. Proper and accurate risk assessments that include identification of sensitive information should be maintained. Finally, information retention and disposal should be taken into consideration. Every data or information has a finite life cycle, and hence mechanisms should be in place to ensure that data that is no longer of use is properly disposed of.

SOCIAL SURVEILLANCE

The advent of modern technology and communications has flooded the amount and speed at which information is available to everyone. It effects like an invention of microscope which makes invisible visible, if analysed thoroughly. It also acts like a mirror that allows an observer to zoom in and look at various hierarchy of information. Seldomly there may be loses of few artifacts and originality of the data points, but aggregated results are good.

Referencing the same a one major subject to it is social surveillance, which refers to the collection and processing of personal data extracted from digital platforms. Often through modern digital technology that grants real-time aggregation, organization, and analysis of data, metadata and contents. People across the globe use these digital platforms nowadays to communicate with loved ones, connect with friends and express their beliefs of any nature. Even the individuals who seldomly utilizes such services, their information may also be available that may be collected and worked out to gain valuable information. These surveillance holds tremendous value for different class of society. On the other hand, it may be boon for law agencies and intelligence as well.

Protecting Digital Privacy

Advances in artificial intelligence and its allied technologies had unfolded new possibilities for automated large scale surveillance. Sophisticated monitoring systems can quickly map user's relationships through analysis. Assign meanings of social media posts using natural-language processing. Machine learning enables systems to search for patterns that may be invisible to humans and deep neural networks can identify and suggest a whole new category of patterns for further investigation. Accurate or inaccurate, conclusions made about an individual may have serious consequences.

Technology is more effective or other means of security, is debatable considering social surveillance. Social media activities such as original content, likes, shares, speeches and videos in slang or local languages are open to misinterpretation. Research estimates that accuracy rate of natural language processing tools is approximately between 70 - 80 percent. While this technology is justified to reduce human errors, it may establish racial discrimination because of inaccurate or biased data. The resulting false positives can add innocent people to government watch lists, often without their knowledge.

At least this social surveillance or social media surveillance needs more attention. The implementation of these programs should be transparent and must involve dialogue between law agencies and affected communities. Civil rights oversight should be carried out. Authorities should be held accountable when tools are being misused and victims should be given proper treatment. Online surveillance technology should not be used to monitor the planning and participation of peaceful communication, protest activities by individuals or groups. Governments needs to update existing privacy laws to address the proper use technology. (Senthil et al., 2015)

TYPES OF INFORMATION LEAKAGE

Malicious Insiders

A disappointed employee or business partner who leaves the organization may attempt to steal the data and leak it to a competitor or sell it on the black market for large sums.

Physical Exposure

Storage devices with sensitive contents are often left ignored by employees, leaving data at risk.

Electronic Communication

Many organizations enforce bring-your-own-device policies and encourage employees to use their own devices at work. Hackers use this to trick users into clicking generic links, giving them access to their devices and data.

Accidental Leakage

The most common cause of data breaches is the human factor. Common failures include employees sending emails containing sensitive information to the wrong recipients, weak security policies such as excessive access to sensitive files, and exposure of sensitive data due to unpatched software vulnerabilities. (Adwait et al., 2013)

TARGETED BREACH

A data leakage may be a result of a blameless mistake. Actual damages occurs if an unauthorized entity gains access to a computer system; steals and sells personally identifiable information or organizational sensitive data for money raising or to do some harm.

Cyber-criminals are inclined towards a fundamental pattern, this is, either by targeting organizations for a data leakage or a person for illegal gains which takes planning to execute the both. Cyber criminals research their victims to learn where the vulnerabilities and loopholes exist. For example, a missing or failed update or an employee susceptibility to phishing campaigns.

Cyber Criminals are known to target's weak points. They develop campaigns to get an insider to download malwares mistakenly. Sometimes they try these directly in networks. Once accessible, these cyber criminals get the privilege to search the information needed — they even take time to do it. On an average some breaches take more than a couple of months to detect.

Some of the common weakness and loopholes attacked by cyber criminals includes following:-

Weak credentials. A majority of data leakages are the result of stolen and weak credentials. If cyber-criminals have a username and password combination, then the doors are open into the network. It is because most of the people reuse their passwords in different places. Cyber criminals often use technically harsh attacks to access the controls of emails, websites, bank accounts, and other sources of PII and financial information.

Stolen credentials. Leakages that are caused by phishing attacks is one of a major security issue and if cyber-criminals get grips of any personal information, then through this they definitely use it to access confidential information like financial online accounts.

Compromised assets. These are different malware attacks; these are used to revoke systematic authentication processes that are normally used to protect a computer's privacy. These are in practice targeting a person or an organization.

Payment Card Frauds. Fraudsters attach a card skimmer to fuel pumps and at ATM machines to steal user data of swiped cards.

Third Party Access. Everyone tries to keep everything possible to keep their system, network and data secured; even though cyber-criminals use various third-party vendors' applications to make their path into targeted systems.

Mobile Devices. When in organization an employee is allowed to use their personal electronic devices in their workplace, it becomes easy for hackers to download some malware loaded application through these unsecured devices thus giving them path to gain access to sensitive data stored organizations device and also to create a copy of data in employee's devices for more easy access later. These often include work emails and files as well as the owner's and organizations personal and official information.

Impact

Impact of data breach has diversified losses. Any end user who suffers this can be harmed in various ways. Information leakage may be personal, social and organizational. Out of the overwhelming list of information leakage losses the top four kind of losses are:-

- Revenue Loss and its impact on finance
- Downfall of brand value and reputation
- Operational Downtime
- Litigation and risk of legal action

CASE STUDIES

Through services like email, blogs, and most recently Online Social Networks, the act of exchanging information on the Internet has been made easier (OSNs). This kind of communication has many benefits, but it also has certain risks, including the speed at which information may be posted in one location and the convenience of having it reach a large audience at once. The tremendous popularity of social media platforms such as Facebook and Twitter at a worldwide and local scale gives it a success, but at the same point brings its users, more prone to information leakage and eventually be the potential targets of cybercriminals. Information leakage is the unintended dissemination of information to users with whom it was not originally intended to share this information. The simplicity, invisibility and imprecise nature of the Internet, combined with the poor default security settings of social media platforms, have fuelled a lucrative cybercrime industry. Hence, a correct user knowledge is important for preventing breaches of information in an online context.

Twitter Information Leak

An enormous database purported to contain basic information on more than 230 million Twitter users, including email addresses and screen names, was made public in January 2023 by an anonymous user on a hacker forum.

Politicians, journalists, bankers, and other people are listed in the database along with their names and email addresses. According to the experts, Twitter's software had a bug that caused information to leak.

An error in the platform's operating code led to the information leak in this case. This is not a one-time occurrence, though. Peiter "Mudge" Zatko, the former head of security for Twitter, described the platform to lawmakers and regulators in September 2022 as having outdated software and a reactive security policy that had engineers running "from fire."

The Equifax Data Leak

Over 145 million Americans' personal data were exposed in 2017 due to a significant data leak at Equifax, one of the biggest credit reporting companies in the country. The leak happened when hackers broke into the company's network by taking advantage of a flaw in Equifax's website. Names, addresses, Social Security numbers, dates of birth, and other private data were all stolen by the hackers.

The Ashley Madison Data Leak

A data leak at the extramarital affairs website Ashley Madison in 2015 resulted in the exposure of over 30 million users' personal data. The leak happened when hackers used a flaw in Ashley Madison's website to access the company's network. Names, addresses, email addresses, and other private information were all stolen by the hackers.

The Yahoo Data Leak

One of the biggest email service providers in the US, Yahoo, experienced a data leak in 2016 that exposed the personal data of over 500 million users. The leak happened when hackers used a flaw in the company's website to access Yahoo's network. Names, addresses, email addresses, phone numbers, and other private information were all taken by the hackers.

The Uber Data Leak

Uber, a ride-sharing company, experienced a data leak in 2016 that resulted in the exposure of over 50 million customers' personal data. Due to a flaw in the company's website, hackers were able to access Uber's network and cause the leak. Names, addresses, email addresses, phone numbers, and other private information were all taken by the hackers.

The Facebook Data Leak

Social media company Facebook experienced a data leak in 2018 that resulted in the exposure of over 87 million users' personal data. Through a flaw in the company's website, hackers were able to access Facebook's network and cause the leak. Names, addresses, phone numbers, email addresses, and other private data were all stolen by the hackers.

Inadvertent Leak of Information on Twitter

For this case study, the PII (Personal Identifiable information) has been redacted

Ms. Sundari is a social media user sharing her thoughts on various topics including current affairs, economics, stock market, and foreign affairs. She is an avid Twitter user with more than 500K followers and she is often quick to respond to the comments on her tweets.

A test was run to check for information leakage out of her tweets.

Following information, if leaked, was considered to be Information Leakage.

1) Phone Number
2) House Address
3) Vehicle Number
4) Family information

As part of the investigation to check for information leakage, her tweets were analysed for the last few months.

American Airlines Data Breach

In June 2023, Hackers allegedly stole the personal information of "thousands" of pilots applying for positions at American Airlines and Southwest Airlines. Instead of being extracted directly from either airline, the information is extracted from a database maintained by a recruitment company. About 8,000 pilots are believed to have been affected, including 2,200 represented by the Allied Pilots Association.

TYPES OF ATTACK

Botnets

It is networks of private computers that infect systems with malwares and are controlled externally by remote hackers without the knowledge of owners. Spams are then forwarded to user's systems using botnets. Botnets may be used as malware to perform hostile tasks. (Kunal & Kishore, 2021) (Kunal et al., 2021)

DDoS Attacks

DDos are attacks that interrupt online services by making it unavailable. It brings down networks by sending huge traffics to sites. Further, by embedding malwares in user's systems, Botnets are created and systems are hacked when networks are down. (Kunal & Kishore, 2021) (Kunal et al., 2021)

Identity Thefts

Identity theft is the breach of personal information of users. This may lead to various illegal activities and practice frauds. Using identity thefts, a cyber-criminal may access various users accounts and play foul activities. It is done by bringing out passwords by hacking, gaining information from social media and phishing's etc. (Kunal & Kishore, 2021) (Kunal et al., 2021)

Cyberstalking

Cyberstalking is a crime where targeted users are harassed through online messages and emails. Social media websites and search engines are especially used to frighten and establish fear. Generally, a cyber-stalker targets a known user or victim to make them feel afraid and safe. (Kunal & Kishore, 2021) (Kunal et al., 2021)

Social Engineering

In Social engineering cyber-criminals directly contact the users by phone or email. Their intentions are to obtain users' confidence as a customer service agent or etc. to get users valid information. This information are user's passwords, professional or financial information etc. Cyber-criminals after gaining the information's uses it in ill activities like adding friends in user's social media, selling these information and hacks accounts of users. (Kunal & Kishore, 2021) (Kunal et al., 2021)

PUPs

PUPS or Potentially Unwanted Programs are a kind of malwares. It uninstalls important computers such as search engines and applications etc. Pups may include spyware or adware. An Antivirus may help in avoiding these downloads. (Kunal & Kishore, 2021) (Kunal et al., 2021)

Phishing

Phishing attacks are malicious emails attachments or URLs to send to users to get information of their various online or offline accounts. Users are confused through emails that look alike as valid sources and trapped persons send, change or do whatever instructed related to their personal information, thus giving criminals an access to their accounts. (Kunal & Kishore, 2021) (Kunal et al., 2021)

Prohibited/Illegal Content

This cyber-crime involves distributing and sharing unsuitable contents which may be embarrassing and insulting. It may include sexual activities, violent videos and clips of crimes etc. Illegal contents may include matters related to terrorism and child or women exploitations. These exist both on the general internet and the dark web. (Kunal & Kishore, 2021) (Kunal et al., 2021)

Online Scams

Online scams are online advertisements or emails ensuring users some exciting awards. It is designed in such a manner that pretends to be true and as accessed by users it can lead to installing malwares and or leak of personal confidential information. (Kunal & Kishore, 2021) (Kunal et al., 2021)

Exploit Kits

These are vulnerable software's like bugs designed for corrupting a software program etc. It is used to gain control of users' PCs. It also may be a tool that cyber-criminals can purchase to use against any system or user. Exploit kits are regularly updated as software and are easily available on dark net. (Kunal & Kishore, 2021) (Kunal et al., 2021)

PREVENTION TECHNIQUES

Malicious Insiders

Performing Risk Assessments

Identify critical assets, the kind of vulnerabilities and the threats that can affect it. Always try to include the risks imposed by insider threats. Further prioritize the risks based on priority and continuously improve your IT security infrastructure. (K.S. Wagh, 2018)

Documenting and Enforce Policies and Controls

Software security solutions and instruments should have separate management policies and configurations documented. Working with the human resources department to develop such policies regarding the IT environment for almost all employees. For example, defining the following:

- Common Data Protection Regulation
- Response Policies for Incidents occurred
- Access Policy for Third Parties
- Accounts Management Policy
- Users Policy Monitoring
- Password Policy Management

All these policies must be controlled by the legal wings, should be verified and authorized by the executives. If a policy is violated and your investigation identifies the culprit, it becomes vital to document the actions to be taken and the penalties that shall be applied. (Otgonpurev et al., 2020) (Arden et al., 2012)

Establishing Physical Security in Work Environment

A professional security team following all security guidelines must be there to prevent suspicious personnel from entry to critical computing objects (such as servers and with switches). They should check everyone at the entrance labs and document any discrepancy found considering the security baseline. Check cell phones and cameras activity. Remember to lock all labs. (K.S. Wagh, 2018)

Implementing Security Software and Equipment

Properly install and configure the following software:

- Active Directory System
- Endpoint Protection
- Intrusion Prevention and Detection System
- Web Filters
- Traffic Monitoring Applications
- Spam Filters
- Encrypted Access Management Application
- Password Management Policy
- Two-Factor Authentication
- Call Manager
- Data Loss and Prevention System

Must enable mailbox journaling in Exchange servers, ideally with an installed eDiscovery application.

Implementing Password and Account Management Practices

All the users must only use the system by entering respective credentials that identifies them; each user must have an ID and password. Following and practicing such policies are must. (K. Podins et al., 2013) (Arden et al., 2012)

Monitoring and Controlling Remote Access and Mobile Devices

Install wireless intrusion detection/prevention systems and mobile data interception systems. Periodically check for employee's requirement for remote access and mobile devices. Termination of remote access should be confirmed before leaving the office premises. (Mathieu & Maurice, 2011)

Strengthen Network Perimeter Security

Configure firewalls. Use only whitelisted hosts and ports. Setup demilitarized zone. Avoid VPN or FTP; Do not connect critical systems directly to the Internet. Divide the network in VLANs defined by department and prevent users from freely using the network. A baseline of normal network device behaviour should be established.

Surveillance

Monitor all critical facilities with high quality and feature cameras. Enable session screen capture technology on all critical servers and devices. (Xiaokui et al., 2016)

Separation of Duties and Least Privilege Policy

Dual user permissions should be required to copy data to removable devices. Two system administrators must approve deletion of critical data or configuration changes. Implement role-based access controls. Set group policies to prevent employees from accessing services not necessary for their jobs. Ensure employees under administrator roles have unique and distinct accounts for their activities.

Recycle or Dispose Old Hardware's and Documents Properly

Before disposing or recycling a disk, thoroughly erase all the information on it and ensure that the data can't be recovered. Old hard drives and other computer equipment containing critical information must be physically destroyed; specific computer engineers are in charge of personally controlling the process.

. Use a Log Correlation Engine or Security Information and Event Management (SIEM) System to Record, Monitor, and Audit Employee Behaviour

Retaining devices logs of every year to aid incident investigations due to available historical evidence. Implementing log management and change auditing software also provides enterprise-wide visibility. Organizations should monitor and document every significant change in the IT environment. (sharyar et al., 2020)

Implementing Secure Backup, Archive and Restore Processes

Introduce strategies to Implement and configure file, mailbox archiving and backups. A disaster recovery plan is always an added benefit. But, be aware that is If parts of the backup and recovery process are outsourced, the possibility of a malicious insider being hired by a trusted business partner increase.

Identify Risky Actors and React Immediately to Suspicious Behaviour

Monitor the security systems continuously and respond to any suspicious behaviour according to the defined and planned response strategies of the organization. Monitor and control remote access to organizational infrastructure. Configure alerts for all critical systems and events, and ensure that alerts alert you through multiple channels. By implementing User Behaviour Analysis (UBA) techniques, you can spot bad actors more effectively. (Fan Yang et al., 2013)

Set Clear Security Protocols for any Cloud Service, Especially Access Restrictions and Monitoring Capabilities

Cloud services extend an organization's network periphery and allow paths for new attacks for malicious insiders. Performing risk assessments of the data that are outsourced to a cloud service especially if it is sensitive information. Ensure that service providers give a permissible level of risk and meet the organization's security practices. Learn data security works. Confirm who is responsible for guiding technical access to organizational resources in the cloud. Monitor and control all changes that are made in clouds. (sharyar et al., 2020)

Comprehensive Employee Termination Procedures

Exercise with Human Resources professionals to develop a strong user elimination program that shall protect the organization both legally and technically from ex-employees. Try to follow best practices for user eliminations.

Include Insider Threat Awareness in Regular Security Training for all Employees

Organize security awareness training programs for all new employees and users before giving access to computer systems. Train and examine employees against social engineering attacks, active shootouts, and exposure to sensitive data. E.g., carrying out phishing attacks programs in their mailboxes or social engineering attacks through phone. Additional training should be a must for failures. Ask employees to not to ignore reporting security issues. Offer incentives to reward those who follow best security practices. It is important to understand that complete elimination of insider threats is not possible and hence implementing insider threat detection solutions should be in regular practice.

Physical Exposure

Ensure appropriate physical security of sensitive data available at any location.

- Lock workstations and laptops.
- Secure files and portable devices before leaving.
- Do not leave documents, computers or other equipment in an open and free area.
- Destroy important papers or documents before disposing.
- Do not leave sensitive information unprotected, this includes printers, storage devices etc.

Laptops should be kept secured. Lock it before moving anywhere while in work. Security solutions must be applied to all portable devices and electronic media that consist sensitive or critical information, like:-

- Encryption
- Physical security
- Portable devices and media should also be strictly secured.

Securely delete personal identification information and other sensitive data when no longer needed. Remember reducing the size of sensitive data reduces the risks.

Password Hacked or Revealed

- Use tough passwords which are hard to guess.
- Never share passwords, even with people you trust.
- Use different passwords in different places.
- Each account must have a unique password.
- Change and reset passwords frequently.

Missing Patches and Updates

Ensure that all networked systems have "patches" and security updates in operating systems and applications.

Dealing Infected Computers

Use a good antivirus to make sure it's always up to date.

Stop clicking on unknown links and attachments.

Don't open files sent via chat/IM or P2P software on systems containing sensitive data – virus scan often bypasses these files.

Improperly Configured or Risky Software

Don't install unknown and suspicious programs on computers. It can hide a computer virus behind and may open a "back door" that allows external access to computers without knowledge. Stop posting sensitive information where access rights are wide. (Kafle et al., 2021)

Electronic Communication

Apply Rules-Based Enterprise Rights Management to Email Attachments

People use mail application software to send sensitive documents. This is risky as one may lose control of company documents and data. But there's no other way out. Even if anyone transmits sensitive information to co-workers, some documents can be accidentally shared with unintended recipients. If this happens and eDRM is not applied, then there is no way to block access and track the document location.

Use Data Loss Prevention (DLP) Content Classification to Determine the Sensitivity of Email Attachments

Content-aware DLP is an effective method to identify sensitive data, classify it on specific parameters, and then perform appropriate enforcement on administrator-defined content classification. DLP and DRM are of the same category: scanning email attachments with a content-aware DLP engine ensures information requiring the highest security is always automatically closed through DRM, which helps avoiding accidental loss. Highly confidential and valuable crowns should be blocked immediately, while certain important information should be protected automatically by DRM controls. Normal information can be transmitted usually. DRM solutions should be integrated with popular DLP solutions from companies that provide such facilities. (K. Podins et al., 2013)

Replace Oversized Attachments With Secure Links

The Enterprise File Synchronization and Sharing Solutions replaces email attachments with secure links. This allows to send large attachments than email platforms support. It gives more control over document access rights. In absence of such kind of solutions, employees turn to consumer cloud-based file sharing solutions which can introduce significant risk because there is no system control.

Audit Trails to Meet Compliances

After protection levels and security settings have been applied to mail attachments, administrators should be able to monitor all kinds of operations performed on documents and data as well as information or reports available in the form of audit trail. This becomes helpful in breach investigation or compliance. Leaving security and protection of sensitive email attachments for employees, implement preventative methods to protect organizations from accidental leaks and theft.

Accidental Leakage

Limiting Access to Valuable Data

Most organizations are forced to move to trust less security architecture, it makes a sense to at least limit the access the valuable data. One must implement an information-sharing architecture were sensitive data is accessible to only those who actually need it. It is important to ensure that critical and sensitive information is shared strictly on a need-to-know basis.

Evaluate Third-Party Risks

Even if all necessary precautions to protect the business are taken for possible data breaches. There may still be significant risks from possibly inadequate IT security practices by organizations outside business partners. (Sultan et al., 2016)

Develop own vendor risk assessment criteria or ensure that third parties meet regulatory standards such as HIPAA, PCI-DSS or GDPR. Meeting risk management requirements may be a tedious task if the network of third-party cloud services is large.

Portable Encryption

To prevent accidental data losses, software based encryption should be used always. If any employees misplace removable physical storage assets containing sensitive information the business should not be affected. All time-sensitive data that leaves your network area should be encrypted automatically.

Third-Party Compliance

Establish a clear security framework for third-party's stakeholders or vendors. Additionally, organizations should limit access based on the service required. Make sure the stakeholders, partners absolutely share information that complies with privacy and data laws regulations. Insist on thorough background checks of third-parties.

Use of Difficult-to-Decipher Passwords

Password policy must be enforced. Start security awareness training programs on a regular basis so that employees understand the importance of changing passwords and make them hard to guess or remember.

Regularly Secure Back-Ups

In case of data breach, having a fully functional and accessible backup can save you. But remember that backups are also vulnerable to intruders, so multiple backups should be kept. Encrypting backup is necessary to protect your valuable data. Regularly test backup validity. Additionally, organizations must ensure that backup servers are not publicly visible, thus preventing hackers access.

Conduct Security Awareness Training Programs

Humans always remain weak in following the data security rules. Employees sometimes may be manipulated by social engineering techniques etc. Embedding cybersecurity in organization's and organizing regular security awareness training ensure that the team is ready to respond to breaches and that each individual worker has a designated role to ensure secure work continuity.

Checkout the Permissions

One best way to improve data loss is to turn the organization into a zero-trust environment. This involves checking all of the permissions to ensure that the critical data is inaccessible to users other than those who need it. Permissions should only be granted to authorized persons and critical data that needs to be classified should have control access. Access to these data should be limited to specific and trustworthy employees that have the required security clearances.

SYSTEM FRAMEWORK FOR PREVENTION

Data leakage is an ongoing process. Understanding data leakage is horrifying as due to the consequences a user faces if trapped into some illegal use of disclosed personal data of any nature. Prevention techniques help us to understand the technical strategies to safeguard data. Simultaneously there should be a technical architecture that should be in practice to encrypt data from leakage. The architecture, if followed, helps the end users to extract the vital contents of data and apply encryption techniques for

Figure 1. System framework

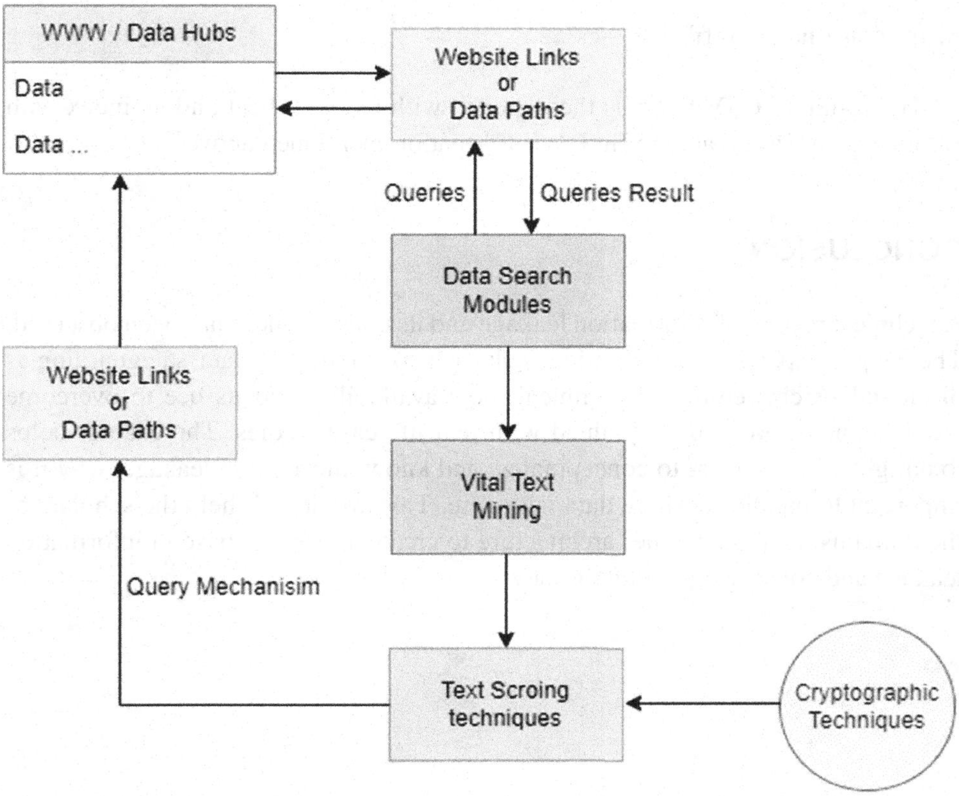

safeguarding it. There can be many numbers of possible architecture out of which we have conceptualize it:-

Data is collected from the world wide web or using technical paths from data hubs in an intranet using data fetching query mechanism. This query mechanism can be either technical or non-technical in nature based upon the category of information required. Collection of information from such queries if followed by mining of such contents of texts which may contain any information that may be misused if leaked. Cryptographic techniques are applied to those mined contents for encryption to safeguard it and further processed to save it in the required places of world wide web or data hubs in a secured manner.

Tools

An open source tool Twint was used to analyze the tweets of Ms. Sundari. The tool took her twitter ID as input, and scrapped the tweets along with other information (such as any links, any other twitter users who are mentioned, and any hashtags which are used, etc). Following command was used to scrap the tweets into a CSV file

```
twint -u username -o file.csv --csv
```

The resultant CSV file was then opened with Google sheet and an index with Elasticsearch was created to find the information mentioned above.

CONCLUSION

A technical review of information leakage and its consequences has been observed. The major impacts of information leakage and vitality of data safeguarding is discussed. Architecture and technical tools availability and its use to overcome incidents are thoroughly explained with real life case studies. The chapter helps to enlighten the readers to conceptualize and know information leakage, why it is important to handle sensitive data with care. This article will help the scholars of the domains to create further architecture to create a research base in information leakage and conserving digital privacy.

REFERENCES

Alneyadi, S., Sithirasenan, E., & Muthukkumarasamy, V. (2016, February). A survey on data leakage prevention system. *Journal of Network and Computer Applications*, *62*, 137–152. doi:10.1016/j.jnca.2016.01.008

Arden, O., George, M. D., Liu, J., Vikram, K., Askarov, A., & Myers, A. C. (2012). Sharing Mobile Code Securely With Information Flow Control. In *Proceedings of the IEEE Symposium on Security and Privacy*. IEEE. 10.1109/SP.2012.22

Boue, M. (2011). Inspire Ontology Handler: automatically building and managing a knowledge base for Critical Information Infrastructure Protection. 12th IFIP/IEEE 1M, Poster Session. IEEE.

Kafle K, Moran K, Manandhar S, Nadkarni A and Poshyvanyk D. (2020). Security in Centralized Data Store-based Home Automation Platforms. *ACM Transactions on Cyber-Physical Systems*, (pp. 1-27). ACM.

Kunal Sinha, K. K. (2022). *Creation of Novel Database for Knowledge Repository on Cyber Security*. In: First International Conference on Cyber Warfare, Security and Space Research. Thapar University.

SpacSec. (2021). *Communications in Computer and Information Science*, (vol 1599). Springer, Cham

Mendsaikhan, O., Shimada, H., Hasegawa, H., Yamaguchi, Y., & Shimada, H. (2020, September 28). Quantifying the Significance and Relevance of Cyber-Security Text Through Textual Similarity and Cyber-Security Knowledge Graph. *IEEE Access : Practical Innovations, Open Solutions*, *8*, 177041–177052. doi:10.1109/ ACCESS.2020.3027321

Nadkarni, A., & Enck, W. (2013). Preventing accidental data disclosure in modern operating system. *Proceedings of 2013 ACM SIGSAC Conference on Computer & Communication Security*. ACM. 10.1145/2508859.2516677

Podins, K., Stinissen, J., & Maybaum, M. (2013). Towards Improved Cyber Security Information Sharing. *L Requirements for a Cyber Security Data Exchange and Collaboration Infrastructure*. (CDXI)uc.

Dandurand, O. (2013). *5th International Conference on Cyber Conflict*. NATO CCD COE Publications, Tallinn.

Senthil Kumar, N., Saravanakumar, K., & Deepa, K. (2015).On Privacy and Security in Social Media – A Comprehensive Study. *International Conference on Information Security & Privacy (ICISP2015)*. Elsevier

Shu, X., Zhang, J. Danfeng, D., & Feng, W. C. (2016). Fast Detection of Transformed Data Leaks. IEEE Transactions on Information Forensics and Security. IEEE.

Sinha, K. & Senapati, K. (2021). *Design and Development of Data Model for Cyber Threat*. Lambert Academic Publishing.

Wagh, K. S. (2018). A Survey: Data Leakge Detection Techniques. *International Journal of Electrical and Computer Engineering (IJECE), 8*(4).

Wani, S., & Mohd, T. Sembok, T., & Wahiddin, M. (2022). Constructing a knowledge base for Al-Qur' an utilizing principles of human communication. Fourth International Conference on Information Retrieval and Knowledge Management. Springer.

Yang, F., Wu, J., Tang, S., & Zhang, H. (2013). Dynamic Knowledge Repository-based Security Auxiliary System of User behavior. *IEEE International Conference on Green Computing and Communications and IEEE Internet of Things and IEEE Cyber, Physical and Social Computing*. IEEE. 10.1109/GreenCom-iThings-CPSCom.2013.390

Chapter 9
Intrusion Detection in Cyber Physical Systems Using Multichain

C. M. Nalayini
iD https://orcid.org/0000-0002-3138-8584
Velammal Engineering College, India

Jeevaa Katiravan
Velammal Engineering College, India

V. Sathya
Panimalar Engineering College, India

ABSTRACT

Distributed denial of service attack is a kind of cyber smack. Though this attack is known by everyone, its severity is increasing day by day. It denies the services of the network or online services by flooding with unwanted data and makes things unavailable. The impact of DDoS is very high, always. Recently, Twitter, Spotify, Amazon, and Paypal were severely affected by this DDoS. This made the services unavailable to their customers. Blockchain is one of the trending technology can be used to find the misbehaving nodes alias bots from the peer to peer networks. Due to lack of interoperability in blockchain, Multichain is proposed in this chapter to detect DDoS attacks along with cross chain technology. It is designed to communicate with multiple networks and the cross chain technology is built to have the flow between the different chains using smart contract. Deep learning models such as CNN and LSTM are trained and tested with CICDDOS2019 dataset and selected LSTM as the best model and installed at Multichain for detecting the malicious activity and blacklisting it immediately.

DOI: 10.4018/978-1-6684-8666-5.ch009

INTRODUCTION

In real world scenario, physically handling patient records, doctor appointments, administration data, etc becoming a difficult task due to lack of security. Electronic Health Records (EHR) minimizes the data replication and disorganization. As population gets increased, technology gets increased, food habits get changed, diseases also gets increased. In the present scenario, large volume of electronic health records needs to be addressed with full security. A study stating that patient's sensitive information are stolen widely due to lack of security (Nalayini, 2022). EHR with single chain is developed to improve the security in all aspects say decentralized, immutable, transparent and distributed. It works well for individual organizations. EHR system faces challenges such as interoperability, privacy and health related transaction processing issues using single blockchain environment. Sharing of health information among various sectors, interoperability should be involved. Interoperability is the one which focuses on heterogeneous in hardware, software, structure and deployment. But single chain does not support interoperability. If an hospital has multiple branches at different locations and they need to share hospital information dealing with either doctor or patient or any administration information with other sectors, then Multichain is the solution to be used along with cross chain technology. Further smart contracts are deployed in Ethereum MainNet to handle storage and retrieval with full security.

EHealth chain was developed for managing health records using Hyper ledger fabric. The adapter component works as the intermediary between Blockchain and application. The adapter gets the data from the application and stores in the Blockchain and whenever data is requested from the application the adapter retrieves it from the Blockchain. Mirtskhulava (2021) deals with how to solve the security problems in 5G, Mobile IOT and particularly storing electronic health records in online, have analyzed hashing based post quantum signatures, also used quantum technology to improve the security. As each study gives us a new concept and idea, Peterson (2016) provides the new consensus algorithm Proof of Interoperability. It also explains about FHIR - Fast Healthcare Interoperability Resources. The FHIR facilitates by making the workflow customized and flexible. The EHR is structured with data structures known as resources. Prokofieva (2019) explained that a systematic review was conducted on Blockchain in healthcare. There are some companies which provide Blockchain service in Healthcare such as Nebula Genomics (Blockchain Healthcare Today, n.d.), Secure Health Chain, Doc-AI. Another experiment was conducted by Anton Hasselgren (2020), it concluded that e-health records and individual health records are the main targets of the Blockchain Expertise. Thomas McGhin (2019) explains the major focuses in healthcare industry application related to blockchain are smart contracts, identity verification, fraud/fault detection, etc.

Figure1. General view of a blockchain

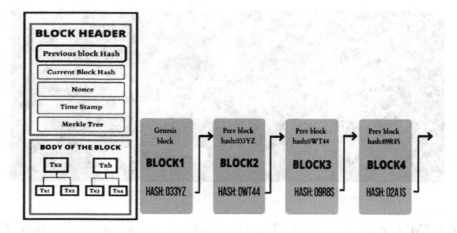

BLOCKCHAIN

Blockchain is a Distributed, Decentralized, Immutable ledger which stores record of transactions/data. In Blockchain, blocks are connected in a chain like structure which is shown in Figure 1. Each block is connected to other block using the feature called Hash (Nalayini et al 2023). Hash is of fixed length which is the output of the Hashing algorithm. There are many hashing algorithms such as Secure Hash Algorithm (SHA), Rivest, Shamir, Adleman (RSA) etc. Blockchain's drawback is Interoperability i.e., communication between the different Blockchain applications. This can be overcome by Multichain.

MULTICHAIN

Multichain was developed from Bitcoin core. Multichain provides us the ability to communicate with other Blockchain. This is especially useful where a single organization has multiple Blockchains and need communication between them. It is mainly built for the interaction between cross chains. On July 20,2020 Multichain was introduced as Anyswap (Multichain, n.d.). Using multichain, communication between any chains is possible regardless to whatever chain it is and it is also an open source framework (Multichain, n.d.). Multichain is a cross router protocol (CRP) (Academy, n.d.). It makes use of nodes called SMPC nodes. SMPC stands for Secure Multiparty computation. These are the nodes which are not present outside the blockchain to sign the transactions and it does group work only (Multichain,

Figure 2. General view of a multichain

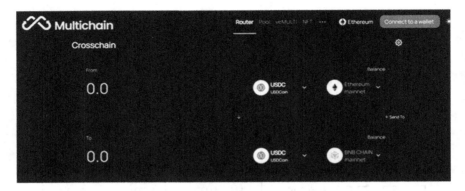

n.d.). SMPC nodes implement TSS Distributed Key Generation algorithm. TSS stands for Threshold Signature Schemes. Multichain supports many chains such as EVM chains, EVM Layer2 chains, Bitcoin like chains and other chains. EVM Blockchains include Avalanche C chain, Binance smart chain, Ethereum, Fantom, Kucoin, Moondriver, Moonbeam, Polygon, Telosetc. EVM Layer2 Blockchain includes Arbitrum, Boba. Bitcoin like chains include Bitcoin, Litecoin, etc. Currently multichain supports more than 70 Blockchains. Multichain supports 2000 transactions per second (Zebpay, n.d.). Unlike other Blockchains, Multichain shares the data to the nodes with permissions. It does not share data to all the nodes in the chain. Figure 2 shows the overview of the Multichain.

Need of Multichain

Considering a hospital with multiple sectors such as clinical labs, research dept, blood /organ transplant, Operation department, Bio medical equipment department, Human resources department and lot more. Each sector can form a Blockchain and can communicate with other chains via multichain. As EHR is stored in Blockchain, patients can give access to whom they want to share data in other chain, They can send their EHR from general patient chain to surgery department chain for surgery so that they can view the past history of patients, the prescription can be shared to other pharmacy chain, where the patients can give access to them to view only the prescription and the payment can also be done to pharmacy via Blockchain using wallets. First whoever needs access to EHR of the patient should request them via Blockchain, and then patient will grant them access. By implementing the technology in this way, patients can control their data and track the accessibility of the data. We can also make use of other multichain features such as streams, tokens, assets, etc. depending on our requirements.

Terminologies of Multichain

- **Streams**: Streams are nothing but the collection of items. Each item contains and identity, a time stamp, digital signature, etc. They are used to store and retrieve the data. Streams can be in the form of text, Binary format, JSON, etc. Each content in the stream can have more than 1 key. The streams can be open or closed based on the permission given to the nodes.
- **Assets**: Assets are nothing but native tokens of the Blockchain.
- **Tokens**: Tokens are the representation of assets/rights to access.
- **Bridge**: It is the connection between 2 chains. We can send assets from one chain to other using bridges.
- **Handshaking**: When two nodes connect with each other and form a multichain Blockchain, this process is known as Handshaking.

We can transfer our assets via multichain by Cross chain bridges and Cross chain routers. Transfer of tokens/assets can be done in 2 ways:

- Bridging - whenever we want to transfer (bridge) a token from one chain to other. First the token will be locked in the current chain and then it will mint the pegged token on other chain. This was the first service offered by multichain.
- Swapping - Coins which cannot be bridged can be swapped with the help of liquidity pool. But someone have to liquefy the asset/token so that it can get swapped.

Routers will accept the user's request and provides the service either by swapping or bridging.

Polygon

Polygon is one of the frameworks of multichain. Smart contracts are implemented using Ethereum Blockchain. It provides an alternative solution for storing PMHCR (Patient centric multichain healthcare record). PMHCR is stored in IPFS- Inter Planetary File system. IPFS is protocol or distributed storage system where we can share and store data. Whenever we store any file in IPFS-, the files are split into sub files which are hashed using various cryptographic algorithms. Then each and every sub file is allocated a unique fingerprint in terms of Content identifier. In polygon we can write smart contracts as it is compatible with Ethereum and it provides the feature of interoperability as it is the framework of multichain.

Malware Types in Multichain Routing

Malware is any software that was created specifically with the goal to harm a computer, a movable device, data, or an individual. Our dataset contained five different kinds of malware. Malware can come in more than one type, and each type has its own unique traits. Backdoors are fundamentally made to get around authentication processes, weakening the system. Following the bypass, other backdoors might be installed, giving the attacker access in the future without the user being aware of it. Malware called a rootkit is designed to be "imperceptible" to users and security programmes. It makes an attempt to obtain remote access or take over a computer. The most prevalent kind of malware is undoubtedly a trojan horse. Through "camouflage," this virus attempts to pass like common cleanware or another programme that the user is persuaded to download. After that, the computer on which it is installed will have unrestricted access, which can be used to monitor user behaviour, steal data, alter files, incorporate the machine into a botnet, and other things (Nalayini et al 2023). The virus has the ability to replicate many times. For instance, it can infect many computers that are part of the same network and propagate when a user unknowingly runs malicious software.The worm, one of the most destructive kinds of malware, spreads swiftly over a network of computers by taking advantage of flaws in the operating system. The worm can replicate itself as well, but unlike viruses, it doesn't require user programme execution to do so. In essence, there are two forms of malware analysis: static and dynamic (dynamic is for code analysis, while static is for behavioral analysis).

Related Work

In Yu et al. (2019), smart contracts are implemented in 3 platforms – Multichain, Hyperledger fabric and Ethereum. Types of smart contract, Programming language, Network permission, Open source licensing and Applications are considered as technical features in their paper. Three Blockchain platforms were tested based on doing transactions and executing the smart contracts. To compare the learning time, Ethereum took 7 days, Hyperledger fabric took 14 days and Multichain took 2 days. To speak about development time, Ethereum and Multichain took 30 mins while Hyperledger fabric took 45 mins.

Khezr et al. (2019) explained the implementation of Blockchain in Healthcare technology. It categories the usage of Blockchain Technology in healthcare into 3 domains. It starts with Data management, followed by supply chain and ends with Internet of Things. The workflow includes layers such as Healthcare applications, Blockchain Technology, Health care raw data. Blockchain is used to store, transfer data and also for transferring crypto currencies. Explained how EHR can be used in Blockchain Technology.

Galvan (n.d.) explained the healthcare Blockchain. Galvan provides the ability to buy and set up node within 5 minutes. The nodes will facilitate distributing an ERC-20 token. But these tokens can be used only to buy Galvan products.

Rai et al. (2022) explained that each patient should own their medical records and those records should be managed by them. Patients should have full control of their records. Patients should be able to give access to their records whenever needed. Proposed a concept called Patient centric multichain healthcare record (PCMHR) In PMHCR health reports are maintained with the help of Smart contracts and Polygon.

Kshirsagar et al. (2020) explained how Multichain is secure for storing electronic health records. In addition to multichain, authors have suggested a way to combine machine learning with Multichain. Each patient is provided with a digital wallet, in Multichain streams are considered. The security is provided by encrypting the data and the node which has key can only access the data. It also provides us the relationship between patient and hospital.

$$tx = (WUm, Hn)$$

Where tx denotes a single transaction, W denotes the set of streams/wallets, H is the vector consisting of the details of the hospital. U is the vector with the details of the users .The data retrieved from the stream is represented in text, image or pdf etc. But we have size limitations. In onchain we can use up to 64MB only but in offchain we can use upto 1GB.The proposed system starts working with registration of the user by biometric or any other means. After verification, the wallet is provided to them. The data in digital wallet is anonymized and the analysis or prediction is done with the help of machine learning. After verifying this data, hash is calculated and appended to the wallet of the patient. User can view the data by logging in to their portal. The analysis will help the patient as well as doctor in treatment.

Greenspan (2019) explained that SAP (System Analysis Program Development), is the company which produces software for managing data and business models. They have developed a multichain based Blockchain solution for keeping track of drugs and pharmaceuticals. In this concept, every box of packed drugs will be attached a barcode. Each barcode is considered as an item in the streams of multichain. In the chain, manufacturers of drug/medicine and whole sale persons will act as node. Using this multichain it is easy for them to track the location of packed drugs and it also solves the problem of double spending. This system is already in existence and was successfully tested which resulted in scalability of 1.5 billion recorded barcodes and 30 million verification per year.

Rapidqube (n.d.) deals with the Electronic medical record system. To store medical records of the patients, streams of multichain is used. This system is used at present and it was developed by an IT company called RapidQube. In early production itself it has stored nearly 2 million records, of which 50000 currently supports only text formats and yet to support rich data such as images, video.

Syafiq et al. (2022) proposed a multichannel method for Healthcare systems but using Hyperledger. Created a Blockchain consortium which is managed by group of organizations such as Governments, Financial organizations and hospitals. The proposed system provides the feature of interoperability between them using multichannel.

Malika Achary et al. (2020) proposed a Proof of existence in Multichain. Created a webpage which generates the link of Proof of Existence attached with timestamp. A hash code is also generated with the help of jQuery, which can be used to create digital wallet. Streams are used to store the data.

Pravin Pawar et al. (2021) explained that Ehealthchain was developed for managing health records using Hyperledger fabric. The adapter component works as the intermediary between Blockchain and application. The adapter gets the data from the application and stores in the Blockchain and whenever data is requested from the application the adapter retrieves it from the Blockchain.

Deep learning algorithms can identify malware with high correctness as its feature set keeps growing. In a Multichain Platform, deep learning methods such as GRU, DBNs, CNNs, LSTM, and their varieties may successfully identify malicious software. By evaluating the existing detection methods, Convolutional Neural Networks and LSTM have received a lot of attention and attained usually good accuracy. To train, understand, and detect new malware as well as developing cyberattacking patterns and methodologies, deep learning-based malware detection models require frequently updated malware datasets. E. Amer et al. (2022) states that Precision, Recall, F1-Score, and Accuracy were achieved using the LSTM model using the Android Malware and Goodware dataset. The model is unable to include fresh behavioral-driven heuristics that would enable it to adjust to fresh, undiscovered threats from malicious software. Z. Wang et al. (2022) states that Accuracy was 99.56% using CNN model, VirusShare, and Drebin datasets. It is necessary to increase the dynamic analysis coverage and dynamic feature extraction. J. Kim et al. (2022) states that Accuracy 91.27% produced using CNN and the VirusShare dataset. The model didn't include applications that were obfuscated and couldn't extract Flowdroid's API call graphs. N. Lu et al. (2021) states that Accuracy- 95.83% Precision- 95.24% Recall- 96.15% F1-score- 95.69% produced using the CNN and LSTM models, the VirusTotal dataset, and the Drebin dataset. Based on hybridized image-based features, the model was unable to identify malicious Android software samples. K. Bakour et al. (2021) produced 98.96% accuracy rate using CNN . Some code concealment was difficult for the model to recognise. Imtiaz et al. (2021) states that accuracy of 93.4% F1-score- 93.2% Recall- 93.4% Precision- 93.5% were achieved using the Deep Neural Networks (DNN) model using the CICInvesAndMal2019 and CICAndMal2017 datasets. Before downloading, the model was unable to identify programmes that were harmful or benign.

PROPOSED WORK

Every Electronic Health record (EHR) involves objects such as patient, Doctor, hospital administration team in all aspects (billing, lab tests, appointments, etc.). With the help of Mutlichain architecture, one hospital can share the treatment information or shifting patient's health records to other hospitals or other vendors.

Figure 3. Proposed architecture

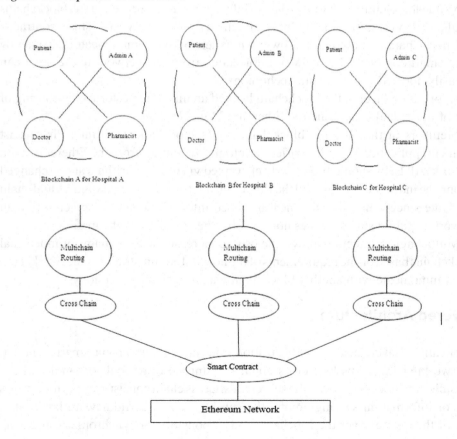

Patient details, doctor details, appointment details, doctor availability are obtained via web3.js. Patients can access their health records and also checks for appointment and availability. Doctor can have access to patient details under limited constraints. Hospital administration can have access to both patients and doctors details. Every blockchain is created with these details using web3.js as the very first step.

Next Multichain Routing takes care of interoperability among the various chains connected to the environment via cross chain technology. It permits private blockchains which allows only the authorized members to access the health information. This architecture involves multichains to handle various operations to be executed with ease and improves the processing speed. Individual blockchains for Hospital A, Hospital B and C are dependent with each other. Sharing of health information among these blockchains are done via multichain routing in aligned with cross chain technology. Each Blockchain say A, B and C performs their own business logic and stores the health reports individually as shown in Figure 3.

Interoperability: It allows different sub blockchains to communicate with each other.

Multicahin Routing: Sharing of health information among different sub blockchains should travel via multichain routing. Multichain supports only basic smart contracts.

Cross-Chain Technology: It allows various networks to communicate conveniently using smart contracts. The flow of information from one network to the other can be easily notified in cross chain technology.

Application layer in the blockchain layered architecture performs the sharing of data of individual chains and the Ethereum Main Network.

Members of the Hospital blockchain say Doctor, Patient, Admin, Pharmacist login via application layer. It verifies their login credentials from the Ethereum main network. All EHR should be properly encrypted via hash algorithms and exchanged among the individual chains and the Ethereum main network. Every individual chain is private since it has sensitive health related information and the ethereum main network is public since it stores non sensitive health related information.

Multichain architecture allows the user to increase the Sub-chains or individual blockchains based on the requirements of the hospital administration. One Blockchain can communicate with another blockchain via cross chain technology.

Layered Architecture

Application Layer handles authorization and authentication via smart contract. Interworking layer involves cross chain transmission protocol to handle all the transmission process between the sub-chains. Cross chain consistency protocol takes care of information sharing among the sub blockchains. Middleware layer takes care of the queries over the subchains and responsible for synchronization during

Figure 4. Multichain layered architecture

Application Layer(Authorization, Authentication, smart contract)
Interworking Layer(Multichain Routing and Cross Chain)
Middleware Layer(Synchronization)
Blockchain Layer(Private and Public)
Platform Layer(Web3, Truffle, Ganache, VMWare, AWS cloud)

transactions inside the sub chains. It also supervises Hashing, Digital signature, block creation, voting, validation and verification. Bockchain Layer is responsible for blockchain implementation using Ethereum, Hyperledger etc. Platform Layer is responsible for selecting the front end tools and backend tools. Figure 4 shows the Multichain Layered architecture.

DDoS and Tampering EHR are the main issues in Cyber Physical systems. Distributed Denial of Service attack(DDoS) is one of the popular vulnerable attack in healthcare. It sends unwanted information from different bots to overwhelm the server and thereby denying the legitimate nodes. During DDoS (Nalayini, 2022), Health record forgery and false medical reports are easily processed by the hackers. Tampering patient's sensitive information is also done due poor authentication.

Different sub-blockchains constructed and health information shared conveniently via multichain routing through cross chain technology. Every node's requests and response should happen through Ethereum mainnet via Mutichain routing and cross chain technology. In order to detect Intrusion effectively in the respective blockchains, best performing deep learning model is installed at the Multichain routing to detect the intrusion and block the respective malicious node immediately.

Any programme or group of instructions known as malware is intended to harm computer networks or any other type of company and jeopardize user security. Its mission statement is to gain unauthorized access, steal personal information, and obstruct the system's normal operation. Due to reliance on the internet, a significant number of people were impacted by data breaches and cyber-attacks. Malware attackers have created automated malware-generating toolkits that allow for the rapid creation of risky programmes with an endless number of variants that are easily able to circumvent detection by conventional pattern matching. A revolutionary deep learning method has been developed to counter the surge of dangerous programming.

Deep Learning General Model

Deep Learning is the subset of machine learning. It produces accurate predictions for large volume of data. Most of the applications started using Deep Learning for its self-learning nature. Input layer, Hidden Layer and output layer are the general flow of any deep learning models as shown in Figure 5. CICDDoS2019 Dataset is used to train and test the CNN and LSTM classification models (Nalayini, 2023).

Input layer: Initial data is given as the input to the neural network
Hidden Layer: Also called Intermediate Layers, responsible for computation
Output Layer: predicts the output for the given input

CNN: It is very popular for image processing in all aspects. It is also useful for time series data prediction. 1DConv supports time series data. DDoS dataset is in the time series format, So 1DConv is used for implementation. It consists of multiple layers for effective classification. It builds all possible patterns from the input dataset and better classification. It uses convolution layer for performing convolution operation. It uses ReLuLayer (Rectified Linear Unit) to obtain efficient feature map. It gives the feature map obtained from ReLu as input to the Pooling layer to reduce the dimensions of the feature map. ReLu converts the input matrix into flattened output. This flattened output is given as the input to the fully connected layer to perform the classification accurately.

Figure 5. Deep learning general model

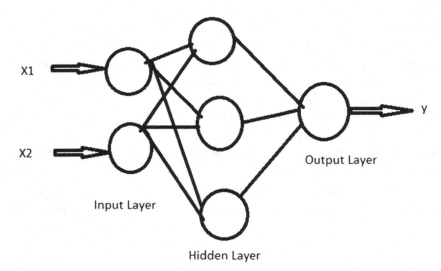

LSTM: It is a type of RNN (Recurrent Neural Network). It retains all the learned information for a longer period of time. It is very popular for time series data since it remembers the previous input for effective classification. Due to their ability to maintain states over extended periods of time, the memory cells found in LSTMs were designed to address this issue. Local spatial correlations are captured by LSTM neurons, which also learn from subsequent long-term relationships. The characteristic of an algorithm where the dataset size remains constant while undergoing numerous transformations is called spatial invariance, also known as symmetry. As a result, the task of classifying malware is aided by the programmed mining of elevated construct and demonstration. The method includes binary classification for detection as well as multiclass classification. About 128 neurons make up the LSTM layer, which is in charge of taking in inputs from the layer above and producing outputs using a linear activation function. Following multiple experiments, the network's features, time steps, and number of neurons were decided upon. The time steps and features fit the reading of the LSTM. In reality, the "dropout layer" is a method for reducing overfitting in neural networks. For t = 1 to T, the following recursive equations are used to estimate the hidden vector sequence xi = (xi1, xi2,...,xin) and the output vector sequence o = (o1, o2,..., on) from the extracted feature sequences of benign and malicious apps, respectively, of arbitrary length. $wq_{xi}q + w_{xixi}xi + e = Ki(q, x)$. LSTM typically receives a sequence of features as input, and as a result, continuously estimates gates like the input gate, output gate, and forget gate while also updating the activations of memory cells (ml) in an iterative fashion from t = 1 to T.

It consists of a cell, forget state, input and output gate. Cell is the memory blocks arranged in a chain like structure. Three gates control the flow of information of the cell. Input gate is used to modify the memory. A sigmoid function selectively permits the information to flow and permits 0 or 1. The tanh() is used to assign weight to the data to determine the significance with a level of -1 to 1. Forget gate concludes the details to be removed from memory block or cell. Sigmoid function decides the threshold that if the produced number is 0 removes it otherwise keeps it.

Figure 6. Input, forget, and output gate

Input, Forget and Output

$$i_t = \sigma(W_i . [h_t - 1, x_t] + bi)$$
$$C_t = \tanh (W_C . [h_t - 1, x_t] + b_C)$$
$$f_t = \sigma(W_f . [h_t - 1, x_t] + b_f)$$
$$O_t = \sigma(W_o [h_t - 1, x_t] + b_o$$
$$h_t = o_t \cdot \tanh(C_t)$$

Output gate is used to find the output. With the use of sigmoid and tanh functions, final output is obtained as shown in Figure 6.

Sigmoid Activation Function and Stochastic gradient descent Optimization algorithm considered for the proposed work. CNN and LSTM are the models selected for detecting the DDoS (Nalayini, 2017, 2018) in the Health care system deployed using multi chain. These models are trained with n partitions of the dataset. Initial weight is same and learning rate is common to all the users.

RESULTS AND DISCUSSION

Need to create Metamask account for all the stakeholders involved in the EHR systems. Metamask account created for Patient, Doctor and Admin is shown in Figure 7.

Once the Metamask account is created for the stakeholder, the account address is copied and pasted in the goerli Faucet to obtain ethers for deploying the respective smart contracts. Web3.js is used to design the front end where the details of all the stakeholders such as patients, Doctor, Admin, Pharmacist, etc. details are obtained and stored in the distributed ledger after proper validation and verification by consensus mechanisms. Patient details are shown in Figure 8.

Figure 7. Metamask account creation

Figure 8. Patient details

Doctor details are added and viewed as shown in Figure 9. Doctor can views the patients details based on the authorized permissions.

Patients can consult doctors based on the appointment as shown in Figure 10. All these information are stored securely in the respective blockchains for effective information sharing among various sectors via Mutichain and cross chain technology.

Create different Blockchains with the help of the following command

multichain-util create blockchain1

Same way create other blockchains based on the requirement as shown in Figure 11.
Create genesis block using the following command as shown in the Figure 12.
Multichain d blockchain1 -daemon

Create proper streams as shown in Figure 13 to have proper permissions to share information from one blockchain to the other.

Likewise all the blockchains are created and connected under Multichain environment as shown in the Figure 14. Every record in the EHR is properly validated and verified by proper wallet aligned with EthereumMainNet.

Figure 9. Doctor details

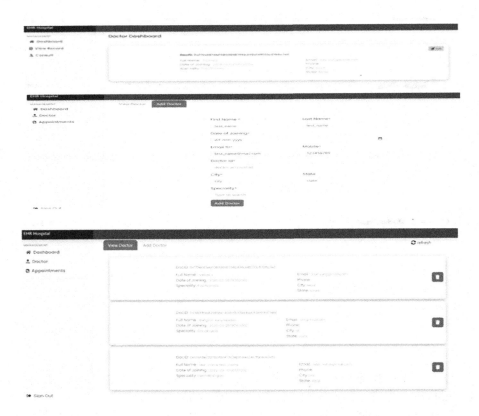

Proper Communication among various sectors can be linked via Web3.js, Ganache, Wallet and EthereumMainNet as shown in the Figure 15.

Deep learning classification models such as CNN and LSTM are trained and tested with different partitions of the datasets for effective learning. CICDDoS2019 Dataset is used to train and test the models (Sharafaldin, 2019). CICDoS2019 contains the most current, harmless DDoS attacks that closely resemble PCAPs of real world data. The output of the CICFlowMeter-V3 network traffic analysis is also incorporated. The tagged flows are based on the time stamp, protocols, attack (CSV files), source and destination IP addresses, source and destination ports. This dataset involves the HTTP, HTTPS, FTP, SSH, and email protocols to generate the conceptual deeds of 25 individuals. This dataset contains reflected DDoS attacks on PortMap, NetBIOS, LDAP, MSSQL, UDP, UDP-Lag, SYN, NTP, DNS, and SNMP, among other modern protocols. Twelve DDoS attacks were launched on the training day, comprising assaults against NTP, DNS, LDAP, MSSQL, NetBIOS,

Figure 10. Appointment details

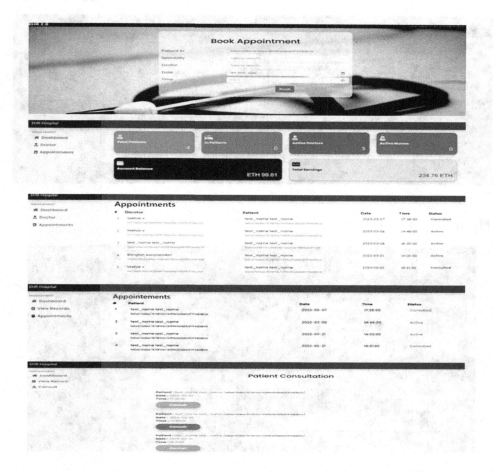

Figure 11. Creating individual blockchain

```
sahana@DESKTOP-2NM8UC7:~$ multichain-util create blockchain1

MultiChain 2.3 Utilities (latest protocol 20013)

Blockchain parameter set was successfully generated.
You can edit it in /home/sahana/.multichain/blockchain1/params.dat before running multichaind for the first time.

To generate blockchain please run "multichaind blockchain1 -daemon".
sahana@DESKTOP-2NM8UC7:~$
```

Figure 12. Creating genesis block

```
sahana@DESKTOP-2NM8UC7:~$ multichain-util create blockchain1

MultiChain 2.3 Utilities (latest protocol 20013)

Blockchain parameter set was successfully generated.
You can edit it in /home/sahana/.multichain/blockchain1/params.dat before running multichaind for the first time.

To generate blockchain please run "multichaind blockchain1 -daemon".
sahana@DESKTOP-2NM8UC7:~$ multichaind blockchain1 -daemon

MultiChain 2.3 Daemon (Enterprise Demo Edition, latest protocol 20013)

NOTE! THIS DEMO VERSION CAN BE USED DURING THE FIRST 3 MONTHS OF A BLOCKCHAIN.

Starting up node...

Looking for genesis block...
Genesis block found

Other nodes can connect to this node using:
```

Figure 13. Creating streams

```
{"method":"getinfo","params":[],"id":"26716657-1670129430","chain_name":"blockchain1"}

{
    "version" : "2.3",
    "nodeversion" : 20300901,
    "edition" : "Enterprise Demo",
    "protocolversion" : 20013,
    "chainname" : "blockchain1",
    "description" : "MultiChain blockchain1",
    "protocol" : "multichain",
    "port" : 4787,
    "setupblocks" : 60,
    "nodeaddress" : "blockchain1@192.168.191.108:4787",
    "burnaddress" : "1XXXXXXWoJXXXXXXkqXXXXXXVNXXXXXXVkmwUE",
    "incomingpaused" : false,
    "miningpaused" : false,
    "offchainpaused" : false,
    "walletversion" : 60000,
    "balance" : 0,
    "walletdbversion" : 3,
```

Figure 14. List of blockchains

```
blockchain1: listblocks -10
{"method":"listblocks","params":["-10"],"id":"12408078-1670131453","chain_name":"blockchain1"}

[
    {
        "hash" : "006e83bf648c5268fb1d04e467637679b069f3405ffc1a78fddb7afc2b7c77ac",
        "miner" : "1QcWmXJtUwmnRkjoRQNTrWDyt9yuU1JonkBBQ1",
        "confirmations" : 10,
        "height" : 61,
        "time" : 1670131174,
        "txcount" : 1
    },
    {
        "hash" : "003101169ed7d88b0ffff4dd537bff9eb1dc4142ffe25b98e63b09d89bed53cb",
        "miner" : "1QcWmXJtUwmnRkjoRQNTrWDyt9yuU1JonkBBQ1",
        "confirmations" : 9,
        "height" : 62,
```

Figure 15. Web3.js, ganache and ethereum network interconnection

```
elcot@boss:~$ npm -v
8.19.3
elcot@boss:~$ node -v
v16.19.1
elcot@boss:~$ mkdir -p ethereum_DDOS_dapp/chapter1/
elcot@boss:~$ cd ethereum_DDOS_dapp/chapter1
elcot@boss:~/ethereum_DDOS_dapp/chapter1$ node_modules/.bin/ganache-cli

Ganache CLI v6.12.2 (ganache-core: 2.13.2)

Available Accounts
==================
(0) 0xc6A76Bf6A6a730Ad5be485Abd542904FdB4a5865 (100 ETH)
(1) 0x46306d8a4efD702Cd1d9b8050cb8d57e96858681 (100 ETH)
(2) 0xD1c8E3D1047167c72a13fDb6A70b83Db20B75349 (100 ETH)
(3) 0x7e15970f893f3cBf9437FcBBb10480354330d4B0 (100 ETH)
(4) 0x841FBB7023C33eEA0AD966E528FE1A426134a888 (100 ETH)
(5) 0x3c9Ff0e88776D91811c395eBd082185fd5059621 (100 ETH)
(6) 0x642C065ec6A88bD20E4c01a96e105B2467F57DC5 (100 ETH)
(7) 0x855f73C7711b8256C4E4D452fc5F1736067ca9e5 (100 ETH)
(8) 0x3290fe598F338b7D5c66b39F7b4edC0f2c2B40f9 (100 ETH)
(9) 0xc93F8C35C81e13CBa26Fdc13cd0432B6251e4E5A (100 ETH)

Private Keys
==================
(0) 0xd896ff6cdd907c3f6b6524f2a5e79cc227b71d714461a27cc319f45f8d9f83c8
(1) 0x368f1bd0185436319f28b5236dba55383f46d9a575e7359070662d2934725206
(2) 0xaff6555bfbf7fbfb207bac8f4d3c92814137403a224c2b43bbe27c6eea4787f6
(3) 0x362c62518c77cc0d58d8e2cd03b2aeed755f54074379ac6cb4c699ef58990909
(4) 0x0806f83499cd1e56417fc896f110719d3733cd79b69716ade18fdec934ce2ab3
(5) 0xae143e88512b4934e8a02b970709f84f7bcb27c22b41771cd64007b2219f976b
(6) 0x0ca5ef003c590df2512552d18d2fb1930d2174199381c0ad35b21e391253cd51
(7) 0x5782ceb4415fd02ec2b5d645acda5b1706d456702983677049220e2d74c71ff3
(8) 0x717dbdabc2d758444e996dc3157f7beaf76223f22fcd7ffdb466b3e846bf17fb
(9) 0x950834417843287a8fcbf73fc0fa01a9a748469050fb326b93edd0af477dc4bf

HD Wallet
==================
Mnemonic:      oven rude guess monitor hundred fat know group silk hand nuclear floor
Base HD Path:  m/44'/60'/0'/0/{account_index}

Gas Price
==================
20000000000

Gas Limit
==================
6721975

Call Gas Limit
==================
9007199254740991

Listening on 127.0.0.1:8545
```

SNMP, SSDP, UDP, UDP-Lag, WebDDoS, SYN, and TFTP. 7 attacks were launched on the testing day with assaults against PortScan, NetBIOS, LDAP, MSSQL, UDP, and SYN. network traffic (Pcaps) and event logs for each machine (Windows and Ubuntu event logs) were included in the raw data for each day. We were able to store more than 80 traffic features as CSV files for each computer by using the CICFlowMeter-V3 to extract features from the raw data.

Starting with a moderately-sized LSTM, experiments were conducted to determine the proper LSTM network parameters. There are three layers in it: an input layer with x neurons for minimal feature sets, a hidden layer with y memory blocks, and an output layer with two neurons, one for benign behavior and the other for malicious behavior. All instances are initially mapped to the range (Mirtskhulava et al., 2021). For LSTM training with multiple parameter and structural setups, we utilized all features. The LSTM's epoch parameter value is set to 200 during training and executed for 500 epochs maximum. According to the observed results from the numerous experiments, the hidden layer with the higher number of LSTM memory blocks functioned well and produced superior classification results. In instance, choosing a lower 0.1 learning rate results in improved performance. 0.1 using Single LSTM layer. However, occasionally dangerous apps are mislabeled as safe. The network has to iterate more frequently to understand all of the behavioral patterns for harmful apps. For dynamic analysis, the malware detection rate ranges from 0.01 to 0.5 with a variable learning rate. The LSTM network is run for up to 1000 epochs to prevent this.

This dataset has all types of DDoS attacks. Null/NAN values are replaced with mean values and nominal features are removed. Normal traffic belong to class 0 and attack traffic belong to class 1. To normalize high dimensional attributes, MinMAxScalar function is used. Random Split with 80% training and 20% testing. Full Features set is considered for best learning of the models. CNN has produced 98.87% accuracy, 98.38% detection rate and 40% False alarm rate. LSTM has produced 99.97% accuracy, 100% detection rate and 10% False alarm rate. When comparing these two models LSTM has produced high Accuracy as shown in Figure 16.

Figure 16. Accuracy of CNN and LSTM

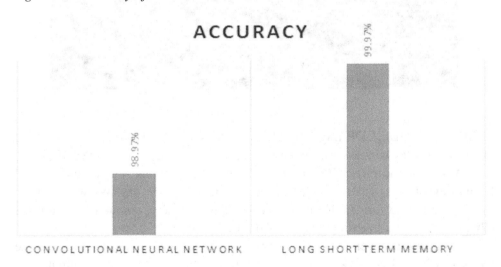

As LSTM is very popular for time series data, it proved that by producing high detection rate and low false alarm rate. Hence LSTM model is selected as the best Intrusion detection model and installed at the Multichain Routing Environment. If any of the malicious activity has taken place say bombarding the server with unwanted messages and try to change the medical report means, immediately the respective set of nodes are identified by the LSTM model at the Multichain routing and those nodes are blocked immediately for further communication as shown in Figure 17

Our proposed model is compared with the existing models to prove our model is the best among all. O. Yaman (2020) used SVM and KNN models to produce 91.25% accuracy. (J.M. Tracy, 2020) used RF and logistic regression models to produce 90.1% accuracy. R. Sheibani (2019) used Ensemble method to produce 90.6% accuracy. H. Kuresan (2019) used SVM and HMM to produce 95.16% accuracy. D. Sztaho (2019) used ANN and DNN to produce 89.3% accuracy. Our proposed

Figure 17. Malicious activity detected and blocked

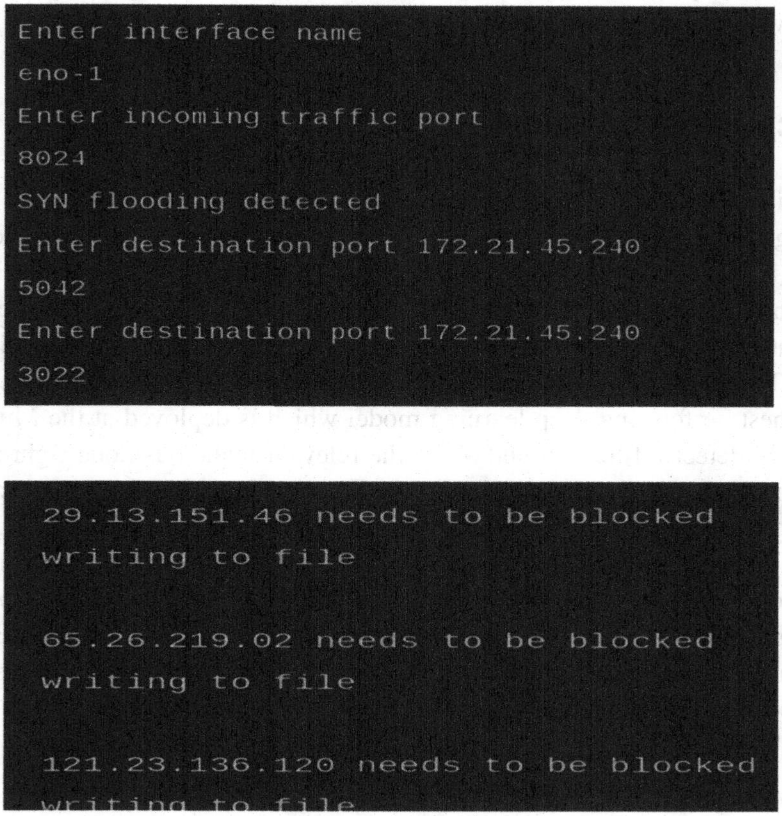

```
Enter interface name
eno-1
Enter incoming traffic port
8024
SYN flooding detected
Enter destination port 172.21.45.240
5042
Enter destination port 172.21.45.240
3022
```

```
29.13.151.46 needs to be blocked
writing to file

65.26.219.02 needs to be blocked
writing to file

121.23.136.120 needs to be blocked
writing to file
```

Figure 18. Comparison of existing models and proposed model

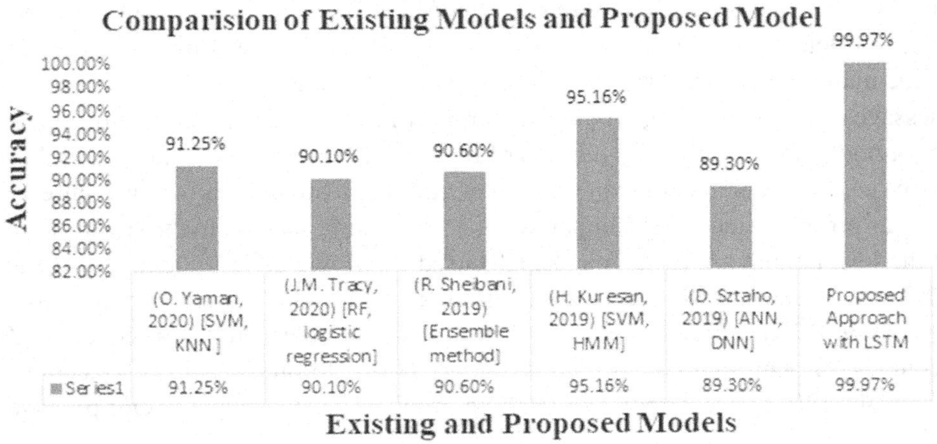

model LSTM produced 99.97 as the highest accuracy. Comparison of proposed LSTM with existing models is shown in the Figure 18.

CONCLUSION

Constructed various sub-blockchains and convenient multichain routing for the exchange of health information among different sectors. Requests from each node should be routed through the Ethereum mainnet using multichain routing and cross-chain technologies. CNN and LSTM models are experimented to detect the different malware attacks and also compared with other existing models and found that LSTM performed well to detect the health related malware attacks. LSTM is the highest performing deep learning model which is deployed at the Multichain routing to detect infiltration and block the relevant malicious node right away in order to efficiently detect intrusion in the separate blockchains. In general, deep learning techniques, especially LSTM and its variations, are effective in finding hidden malware patterns in a lot of different apps. Although the LSTM network has produced impressive results with the available data sets, there is still potential for improvement. Single layer LSTM is experimented with dynamic analysis by increasing the memory blocks and number of epochs to achieve better results. In future stacked layer LSTM is planned to improve the performance level.

REFERENCES

Academy. (n.d.). https://academy.binance.com/en/articles/what-is-multichain-multi

Acharya, M. (2020). *Proof of Document using Multichain and Ethereum, (vol. 07)*. IOP Publishing. www.irjet.net doi:10.1007/s12243-021-00868-6

Amer, E., & El-Sappagh, S. (2022). Robust deep learning early alarm prediction model based on the behavioural smell for android malware. *Computers & Security, 116*, 102670. doi:10.1016/j.cose.2022.102670

Bakour, K., & Ünver, H. M. (2021). DeepVisDroid: Android malware detection by hybridizing image-based features with deep learning techniques. *Neural Computing & Applications, 33*(18), 11499–11516. doi:10.100700521-021-05816-y

Blockchain Healthcare Today. (n.d.). https://blockchainhealthcaretoday.com/index. php/journal/article/view/34

Galvan. (n.d.-a). https://www.galvan.health/nodes

Galvan. (n.d.-b). *A New Kind of Node*. Galavan Nodes. https://www.galvan.health/ nodes

Greenspan, G. (2019). *Ten Enterprise Blockchains that Actually Work*. Multichain. https://www.multichain.com/blog/2019/06/ten-enterprise-blockchains/

Hasselgren, A., Kralevska, K., Gligoroski, D., & Pedersen, S. A. (2020). Blockchain in healthcare and health sciences—A scoping review. *International Journal of Medical Informatics, 134*. doi:10.1016/j.ijmedinf.2019.104040

Imtiaz, S. I., Rehman, S., Javed, A. R., Jalil, Z., Liu, X., & Alnumay, W. S. (2021). DeepAMD: Detection and identification of Android malware using high-efficient Deep Artificial Neural Network. *Future Generation Computer Systems, 115*, 844–856. doi:10.1016/j.future.2020.10.008

Khezr, S., Moniruzzaman, M., Yassine, A., & Benlamri, R. (2019). Blockchain Technology in Healthcare: A Comprehensive Review and Directions for Future Research. *Applied Sciences 9*(9), 1736. doi:10.3390/app9091736

Kim, J., Ban, Y., Ko, E., Cho, H., & Yi, J. H. (2022). MAPAS: A practical deep learningbased android malware detection system. *International Journal of Information Security*, 1–14. doi:10.100710207-020-00537-0

Kshirsagar, M., Patil, A., Deshmukh, S., Vaidya, G., Rahangdale, M., Kulkarni, C., & Kshirsagar, V. (2020). *Mutichain Enabled EHR Management System and Predictive Analytics*. Springer. ,. doi:10.1007/978-981-15-0077-0_19

Kuresan, H., Samiappan, D., & Masunda, S. (2019). Fusion of wpt and mfcc feature extraction in parkinsons disease diagnosis. *Technology and Health Care, 27*(4), 363–372. doi:10.3233/THC-181306 PMID:30664511

Lu, N., Li, D., Shi, W., Vijayakumar, P., Piccialli, F., & Chang, V. (2021). An efficient combined deep neural network based malware detection framework in 5G environment. *Computer Networks, 189*, 107932. doi:10.1016/j.comnet.2021.107932

McGhin, T., Choo, K.-K. R., Liu, C. Z., & He, D. (2019). Blockchain in healthcare applications: Research challenges and opportunities. *Journal of Network and Computer Applications, 135*, 62-75. doi:10.1016/j.jnca.2019.02.027

Mirtskhulava, L., Iavich, M., Razmadze, M., & Gulua, N. (2021). Securing Medical Data in 5G and 6G via MultichainBlockchain Technology using Post-Quantum Signatures. *2021 IEEE International Conference on Information and Telecommunication Technologies and Radio Electronics (UkrMiCo),* (pp. 72-75). IEEE. 10.1109/UkrMiCo52950.2021.9716595

Multichain. (n.d.). https://docs.multichain.org/getting-started/introduction

Nalayini, C. MKatiravan, J. (2022). Detection of DDoS Attack using Machine Learning Algorithms. *Journal of Emerging Technologies and Innovative Research, 9*(7).

Nalayini, C. M. & Katiravan, J. (2023). A New IDS for Detecting DDoS Attacks in Wireless Networks using Spotted Hyena Optimization and Fuzzy Temporal CNN. *Journal of Internet Technology, 1*(24).

Nalayini, C. M., & Gayathri, T. (2022). A Comparative Analysis of Standard Classifiers with CHDTC to Detect Credit Card Fraudulent Transactions. In A. Sivasubramanian (Ed.), *Shastry, in Electrical Engineering* (Vol. 792). Springer. doi:10.1007/978-981-16-4625-6_99

Nalayini, C. M., Katiravan, J., & Prasad, A. (2017). Flooding Attack on MANET – A Survey. *International Journal of Trend in Research and Development (IJTRD).*

Nalayini, C. M., & Katiravan, JImogen, PSahana, J. M. (2023). *A Study on Digital Signature in Blockchain Technology.* IEEE Explore. doi:10.1109/ICAIS56108.2023.10073680

Nalayini, C. M., & Katiravan, J. (2018). Block Link Flooding Algorithm for TCP SYN Flooding Attack. *International Conference on Computer Networks and Communication Technologies. Lecture Notes on Data Engineering and Communications Technologies.* Springer. 10.1007/978-981-10-8681-6_83

Nalayini, C. M., Katiravan, J., Sathyabama, A. R., Rajasuganya, P. V., & Abirami, K. (2023). Identification and Detection of Credit Card Frauds Using CNN. In M. Mishra, N. Kesswani, & I. Brigui (Eds.), *Applications of Computational Intelligence in Management & Mathematics. ICCM 2022. Springer Proceedings in Mathematics & Statistics* (Vol. 417). Springer. doi:10.1007/978-3-031-25194-8_22

Peterson, K., Deeduvanu, R., Kanjamala, P., Boles, K., & Mayo Clinic. (2016). *A Blockchain-Based Approach to Health Information Exchange Networks.* Mayo Clinic.

Prokofieva, M., & Miah, S. (2019). Blockchain in healthcare. *AJIS. Australasian Journal of Information Systems*, *23*. Advance online publication. doi:10.3127/ajis.v23i0.2203

Rai, B. K., Fatima, S., & Satyarth, K. (2022). Patient-Centric Multichain Healthcare Record. *International Journal of E-Health and Medical Communications*, *13*(4), 1–14. doi:10.4018/IJEHMC.309439

Rapidqube. (n.d.). https://www.rapidqube.com/

Sharafaldin, I., Lashkari, A., Hakak, S., & Ghorbani, A. (2019). Developing Realistic Distributed Denial of Service (DDoS) Attack Dataset and Taxonomy. *IEEE 53rd International Carnahan Conference on Security Technology.* IEEE.

Sheibani, R., Nikookar, E., & Alavi, S. (2019). An ensemble method for diagnosis of Parkinson's disease based on voice measurements. *Journal of Medical Signals and Sensors*, *9*(4), 221. doi:10.4103/jmss.JMSS_57_18 PMID:31737550

Syafiq, M. & Soewitob, B. (2022). A Blockchain For Secure Data Storing With Multi Chain On Smart Healthcare System. *Journal of Theoretical and Applied Information Technology, 100*(13).

Sztaho, D., Valalik, I., & Vicsi, K. (2019). Parkinson's disease severity estimation on hungarian speech using various speech tasks. In: *10th Int. Conf. Speech Technol. Human-Computer Dialogue.* SpeD. 10.1109/SPED.2019.8906277

Tracy, J. M., Özkanca, Y., Atkins, D. C., & Hosseini Ghomi, R. (2020). Investigating voice as a biomarker: Deep phenotyping methods for early detection of Parkinson's disease. *Journal of Biomedical Informatics*, *104*, 103362. doi:10.1016/j.jbi.2019.103362 PMID:31866434

Wang, Z., Li, G., Zhuo, Z., Ren, X., Lin, Y., & Gu, J. (2022). A deep learning method for android application classification using semantic features. *Security and Communication Networks*, *2022*, 1–16. doi:10.1155/2022/1289175

Yaman, O., Ertam, F., & Tuncer, T. (2020). Automated Parkinson's disease recognition based on statistical pooling method using acoustic features. *Medical Hypotheses*, *135*, 109483. doi:10.1016/j.mehy.2019.109483 PMID:31954340

Yu, H., Sun, H., Wu, D., & Kuo, T. T. (2019). Comparison of Smart Contract Blockchains for Healthcare Applications. *AMIA Symposium*, (pp.1266-1275). AMIA.

Zebpay. (n.d.). https://zebpay.com/blog/what-is-multichain

Chapter 10
Malware Analysis With Machine Learning:
Methods, Challenges, and Future Directions

Ravi Singh
National Institute of Technology, Patna, India

Piyush Kumar
National Institute of Technology, Patna, India

ABSTRACT

Malware attacks are growing years after years because of increasing android, IOT along with traditional computing devices. To protect all these devices malware analysis is necessary so that interest of the organizations and individuals can be protected. There are different approaches of malware analysis like static, dynamic and heuristic. As the technology is advancing malware authors also use the advanced malware attacking techniques like obfuscation and packing techniques, which cannot be detect by signature based on static approaches. To overcome all these problems behavior of malware must be analyzed using dynamic approaches. Now a days malware author using some more advanced evasion techniques in which malware suspends its malicious behavior after detecting virtual environment. So, evasion techniques give a new challenge to malware analysis because even dynamic approach some time fails to detect and analyze the malwares.

DOI: 10.4018/978-1-6684-8666-5.ch010

1. INTRODUCTION

Malware is any malicious code that can perform some action on the devices without consent of the user. The device may window based devices, android devices or IOT devices. Malware can perform action like information theft or hide, information can encrypt, utilize the system resources like battery, memory and CPU, control the whole system using command and control techniques and some malware can damage the hardware of the devices. So, we can say that malware is big threat to system security because the devices directly or indirectly connected to local network or internet. Nowadays Malware is also using advanced techniques like obfuscation, emulation evasion and crypter and packer so challenges to detect and analyze the malware also becomes tough to cyber security day by day.

In starting machine learning techniques are cast-off for malware detection and classification for known type of malware detection in which whole data set is separated into two parts training dataset and testing dataset. After splitting of data model is trained with training dataset and tested with the testing dataset. Some time dataset is not homogeneous in nature so that to make correct prediction we use k-fold cross validation to understand overall pattern of the dataset by the model.

In traditional machine learning there are different approach for feature extraction which is root parameter of classifier development like static, dynamic and hybrid. In static approach generally we study the structure of malware binaries without execution and for this no need of virtual environment. In dynamic analysis, we look at how malware binaries behave once they've been run. And for the study of behavior of malware analysis safe virtual environment is required. Virtual environment protects the host computer from malware binaries. In hybrid approach we use a combination of both static and dynamic approach. But the problem with hybrid approach is that it enhances the complexity of model.

In Classification we categorize the data points into different classes whatever is exist in that data pattern. In general, different classes is labelled with some label called target or category. In ML model is trained by set of data called training data that may be labelled or un labelled, depends on we are developing supervised model or unsupervised model and accuracy of the model is checked by another set of data called testing data set. In this study we found that different malware detection models gave different techniques as best in extraction, detection, classification, evaluation.

Yet among all these many strategies are:

- Ranking and choosing features by determining feature significance scores.
- Dimensionality reduction reduces bias and noise by transforming features into a lower dimension.

- Ensemble models, which can be combined with either of the preceding two methods, integrate the output of various base models to improve the overall classification performance.

As we know the impact of machine learning techniques are growing exponentially in solving different real time problems like object identification, text recognition, speech recognition and so on in the same way demand of ML model is also increasing in malware detection system because malware authors are using day by day advanced malware development techniques like obfuscation, encryption, packing, evasion etc. And all these advanced malware techniques cannot be defended by traditional malware detection system. Hence now a days we are focusing over advanced machine learning techniques to neutralized the advanced malware development techniques. The problem with machine learning technique is that there is no common consensus i.e., generalization of classification, detection and evaluation. The absence of a common consensus creates misunderstanding, lead to half-true or even wrong simplifications, and even misinform future work. To mitigate these issues, this work full fill following objectives:

- Provides a thorough mapping of the modern ML methods for the Android malware detection system that have been put forth in the literature.
- Classifies each contribution according to four different criteria: the metrics selected, the age of the dataset, the classification models, and the performance improvement methods.
- Gives motivation to researchers to develop a common approach in every aspect including detection, classification and evaluation for malware detection system.

Now a days internet is the basic need of society to fulfill the day-to-day requirements. Because without internet it is almost impossible to do financial transaction, social interaction, health management, transport management, business transaction government agencies interaction. So in short we can say that all these things shifted from physical word to cyberspace. In the same way physical crime is also shifted towards cybercrime by which they steal the valuable information. Cybercriminal can remotely access the victim system by which they can change, encrypt, steal the information. By malware attack victim devices like desktop, laptop, mobile devices and network component can be destroyed. These malware attacks are of different types like virus, worms, trojan horse, adware, rootkit, ransomware, crypter and packers.

This article reviews the literature on existing malware detection and classification techniques, discusses the difficulties associated with advanced malware attacks, and

Table 1. Analysis type and corresponding feature extraction method

Analysis Technique	Feature Extraction Approaches	Extracted Features
Static	Manifest analysis Code analysis Opcode analysis Signature Analysis	Package name, Intents, Activities, permissions, Services, Providers, Information flow, APIs, Clear text analysis, Native code, opcode
Dynamic	Network traffic analysis System call analysis PE analysis API traffic analysis System resource analysis	IPs of communicating devices, Network Protocols, Non-encrypted data, Certificate, traffics analysis, System calls, APIs, CPU usage, Battery usage, Memory usage, Buttons, Icons, Events
Heuristic	Manifest analysis Code analysis Opcode analysis PE analysis API analysis Network traffic analysis	Package name, Intents, permissions, Services, Providers, Information flow, APIs, Clear text analysis, Native code, opcode, Network Protocols, String data Analysis, Certificate, traffics Analysis, System calls, API calls, CPU usage, Battery usage, Memory usage Buttons, Icons, Events

provides researchers with a direction for the future. Thus, the review's contribution is as follows:

- Outlines how to overcome evasion attacks, obfuscation, crypter, and packer problems.
- Investigates the probability of detecting malware.
- Gives advanced detection and evaluation approaches
- Gives present challenges of classification model new assumption for all these challenges

Nowadays malware attacks are increasing exponentially day by day and it targets to business organizations, research organization, government organizations along with individual attacks for different purposes like stealing the information, hiding the information, disturbing the services, utilizing the resources of the devices along with annoying the individual by adware, so overcome to all these problems a strong malware detection system is required. Malware authors are using advanced techniques to bypass the emulation environment using evasion techniques.

To protect the interest of different organizations and individuals a strong detection, prevention and analysis system is required. Malware analysis often uses two approaches: a static method and a dynamic one. In static approach malwares are analyzed without executing it using different techniques like signature mapping of previously stored unique hash values in database or reverse engineering. Static malware analysis is effective to known malware but not effective for zero-day malware, hence to protect from zero-day malware dynamic approach is used. Factors affect static analysis:

- Packing
- Resource obfuscation
- Anti-disassembly techniques
- Dynamically download data

In dynamic approach of malware analysis code of malware is executed to see the behavior of malware monitoring network traffic, API calls, restricted permissions, registry changes, unauthorized access demand, but the complexity of malware detection system also increases comparatively to static approach-based malware detection system, so some times we use heuristic approach which is effective for both known and unknown malwares.

1.1 Naive Bayes Classifier

The Bayesian algorithm is the foundation of the statistical probabilistic classifier known as the naive bayes classifier.it is used to find the probability of finding a binary file belong to malware or benign ware depending on several metrics obtained from the training dataset.

P(BENIGN/BINARY) = P(BINARY/BENIGN) P(BINIGN)
P(MALWARE/BINARY) = P(BINARY/MALWARE) P(MALWARE)

Challenges of naïve bayes classifiers are:

- If the test data set has a categorical variable of category that was not present in the training data set, the naïve bayes model will allotted it zero probability and will not be able to make any predictions, this is known as 'Zero Frequency'.
- It undertakes that all the features are independent but in real life some features like manifest feature of course will be related to hash value.

1.2 Support Vector Machine

Support vector machine is linear classifier hence it is used for malware detection and classification. As we know there are different categories of malware like virus, worm, trojan, adware, rootkit, ransomware. Support vector machine classify that particular binary belong to which categories of malware after training the model.

Linear SVM is used to reduce feature which is not important for malware classification using feature ranking.

1.3 Logistic Regression

Logistic regression is probabilistic classifier which is used in binary as well as multi label classifier, it finds probability between 0 and 1 to find a data point belong to particular a class among many classes but it is based on one assumption that data is normally distributed. In case, of binary classification sigmoid function used for classification and in case of multiclass softmax classifier is used, but in general logistic regression is most suitable for binary classification. Logistic regression is used as classifier as well as regressor but in case malware it is used as binary classifier i.e., it classifies that a particular given binary is malware or benign ware after the training by labeled dataset. The gradient descent algorithm is used to decide the boundary between malware and benign ware. Features with positive weights are assumed to be malware.

1.4. K-Nearest Neighbor Classifier

K-nearest neighbor is supervised learning-based classifier where k is a hyper parameter denotes the number of neighbors. In k-nearest neighbors we calculate the distance of given binary sample from the data elements of training dataset and then filter the least k distances and if majority among it belong to malware, then unknown binary belongs to malware class otherwise it belongs to benign ware.

1.5. Decision Tree Classifier

Decision tree is also supervised learning-based classifier which classify the unknown binary is malware or benign ware on the basis of selected features and it solves the problem of overfitting in decision tree the decision of feature to be used as root is decided by entropy or gini index and at every node of the tree a question is employed to decide whether sample is malware or benign ware. Both classification and regression can be done using decision trees. In decision tree most important task is to decide which feature will be the root node, Actual classification is done on leaf node, at the root node entropy or degree of randomness is zero or near to zero. There are many criteria for choosing the root node's attributes in a decision tree, including entropy, information gain, gini index, gini ratio, variance reduction, and chi square. Decision tree classifier faces the problem of over fitting and this can be solved by:

- Pruning Decision Tree

- Random Forest

If the dependent and independent variable are linearly related then linear regression classification model will we suitable and if dependent and independent variables having nonlinear relation then decision tree classifier will be suitable.

1.6 Random Forest Classifier

There is different classifier in traditional machine learning model like logistic, SVM, K-Means. The problem with these malware classifiers is that these models suffer from overfitting problem. In general Decision Tree and Random Forest classifier is not affected by overfitting problem. Random forest is collection of decision tree. Implementation of random forest is very complex but it gives maximum accuracy

Figure 1. Ensemble technique for malware classification

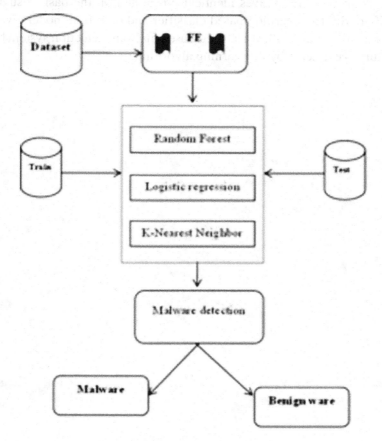

in shallow machine learning techniques. As we know forest is collection of similar or dissimilar types of trees using this concept ensemble technique can be used for malware detection and classification.

1.6 Deep Neural Network

The problem with traditional machine learning is that model takes decision only on the basis of pre decided features i.e., model in itself does not decide which feature will be used for model development. In case of deep learning model itself drive high label features for malware detection and classification which gives more accuracy and less false reporting i.e., less false positive and less false negative. And for automatic malware identification and classification, deep learning CNN is utilized. The raw bytes model eliminates the need for feature extraction, feature selection i.e., feature engineering. It performs end-to-end malware detection and classification in real-time environment. In this approach image of malware binary is created. Malware of same category generally gives identical image and on the basis visualization it is classified. So deep learning-based classifier and detection model gives more accurate prediction than shallow learning-based malware detection system because in this feature is extracted by the learning algorithm.

Figure 2. Neural network

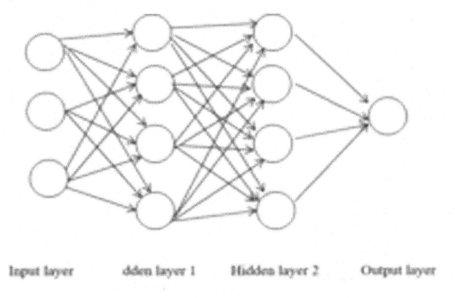

Input layer   dden layer 1   Hidden layer 2   Output layer

1.7 Adversarial Machine Learning

In adversarial malware attacks attacker generate adversarial malware just by manipulation in existing malware. So, to detect these types of malwares is very tough by detection and classification system. Adversarial malware attacks are based on the machine learning techniques that is known as adversarial machine learning. Adversarial machine learning is used to create adversarial data i.e., artificial data generation. There are so many fields where sufficient size data set for model training is not sufficient and availability of data is almost impossible in that cases, we take help od adversarial data generator. Adversarial data generator generate artificial data for dataset looks like real data.

In machine learning, choosing the best features from a large pool of features is difficult since not all features are useful for model training or model learning. If we take into account all the features, the model's complexity will rise and it will become overfit. Therefore, in machine learning, we employ several feature selection techniques to address the overfit problem. Traditional machine learning employs a technique called dimensionality reduction, while deep learning refers to it as dropout. In a wide range of application fields, including object classification, digit identification, speech recognition, document classification, and analysis of computational biology data, it was discovered that this technique enhanced the performance of neural networks. This shows that dropping out is a common strategy.

2. LITERATURE REVIEW

As of today, malware classification and detection system using machine learning technique has taken a plenty of attention in the literature because traditional fingerprint based are not sufficient to detect and analyze against advanced malware techniques like obfuscation and packing. In this section, contribution of literature is placed in my work as s it is.

Moubarak et al. (2020) compare the different traditional machine learning techniques like random forest, logistic regression, naïve bayes, SVM and k-nearest neighbors and got the best result in random forest with 92% true positive rate and 0.01 false positive rate.

Chowdhury et al. (2018) address the problem of traditional machine learning techniques like SVM, naïve bayes, decision tree and random forest for increasing false positive rate and these needs many training samples to develop the classifier and for this they proposed a hybrid malware classification framework with the amalgamation of binary associative memory (BAM) and multi-layer perceptron (MLP) neural network which is used for both static means signature based analysis and dynamic means behavior based or anomaly analysis. For signature-based analysis n-gram approach is used and for behavior-based analysis application program interfaces (APIs) are used.

Catak et al. (2020) in their study contributed a novel deep-learning-based architecture which can detect and classify different categories of malwares by knowledge transfer deep learning technique in which two pre-trained network models are used in an optimization manner. In this study different approaches of feature selection, analysis, detections, model evaluation metrics along with limitation of hybrid model is addressed in a systematic manner. In this work evaluation metrics used are accuracy, sensitivity, specificity, f-score for Alexnet Network, Resnet-50 network and proposed hybrid model separately for the different Microsoft BIG 2015, Malimg, Malevis datasets, after comparison it is observed that the proposed model out performed to existing state-of-the-art studies. In this study at last nine malware variants (rammit, lollipop, kelihos-ver1, kelihos-ver3, vundo, simda, tracur, obfuscator.acy and gatak) investigated along with confusion metrices using Microsoft BIG 2015 datasets here also accuracy rate of projected hybrid model is better than the other two models.

Aslan et al. (2017) presents an approach for acquiring knowledge of the popular malware analysis and detection tools, these tools were used in different well known malware detection and classification systems. In this study these tools are used over the sample of 100 malware and 100 benign ware and conclusion of this study is that only single tools & technique is not sufficient to detect malware. So, a combination of tools and techniques-based malware detection system is secure against malware attacks.

Catak et al. (2012) analyze API calls made by diverse types of malwares on the system to build a collection of malware-based API calls and this dataset is utilized for behavior-based malware identification techniques. The research's overall contribution is as follows:

- A new dataset has been created for the Windows operating system's malware detection and classification. In this field, there is seldom any data of this kind.
- Malware was examined, and API calls were documented by executing it in an virtual sandbox environment.
- The detection model for the type of malware was created by modelling the detection as a text classification problem and using the LSTM algorithm, which is frequently discarded for text classification problems.

Gong et al. (2020) build a malware detection system named APICHECKER using API, permissions and intents as features. In this work 426 key APIs are used as feature and for classification and detection light weight Random Forest machine learning algorithm is used for dynamic behavior analysis. APICHECKER is working since 2018 in market commercially with precision 98.9% and recall 98.1%, it detects an app in 0.9 minutes which is less than googles BOUNCER which takes 5 minutes for scanning an app. For the model comparison in this work collected logs are feed to nine mainstream machine learning algorithms to perceive the detection and classification performance, Naïve bayes (NB), CART decision tree, logistic regression (LR), k-nearest neighbor (kNN), support vector machine (SVM), gradient boosting decision tree (GBDT), artificial neural network (ANN), deep neural network (DNN), and random forest (RF) and after comparison it is found that APICHECKER is giving the best performance.

Darshan et al. (2020) proposes a conventional neural network (CNN). This model uses execution time of portable executable (PE) files for the behavior analysis. To ensure dataset homogeneity in this model, 10-fold cross validation is employed. The feature selection relief approach is used to choose the most noticeable features from a feature set. Application programming interface (API) calls and their category (CAT) are used as dynamic features in this work. It attains 97.968 percent accuracy. The final feature set consists of topmost N-grams features. These features are used to construct an image for visual analysis.

Natraj et al. (2019) proposes a malware classification technique using images of malware binaries visualization. Most important thing of this work is that classification is done without disassembly and execution of code. For the classification k-nearest neighbor approach with Euclidean distance is used. For making the data homogeneous 10-fold cross validation with 90% training data and 10% for testing. This computer vision-based technique is also helpful for malware classification which uses advanced techniques like obfuscation to some extent. In this work 9,458 samples of 25 families are used which gave 98% classification accuracy.

Albelwi et al. (2011) a new optimization objective function that aggregates the error rate and knowledge gained by a collection of feature maps using deconvolutional networks is provided. The new goal function directs the CNN through enhanced visualization of learned features using deconvnet, allowing the hyperparameters of the CNN architecture to be optimized in a way that enhances performance. This work contributes to automatically finding high performance CNN architecture. This work also introduces the concept of objective function that exploits the error rate on the validation set and the quality of the feature visualization via decovnet. One of the advantages of objective function is that it did not get fixed in local minima using Nelder-Mead Method (NMM).

Srivastava et al. (2022) show that dropout enhances the performance deep neural network (DNN) on supervised learning tasks in vision, speech recognition, document classification and computational biology. In this work following data sets has been used

- MNIST: A standard hand written digits.
- TIMIT: Speech recognition data sets.
- CIFAR-10 and CIFAR-100: Tiny natural images data sets of 10 and 100 categories.
- Street View House Number (SVHN) data set.
- ImageNet: A large collection of natural Images.
- Reuters-RCV1.

And in this work using diverse data sets it is proved that dropout is general technique to improve neural networks instead of application specific.

Aboaoja et al. (2019) discussed different feature engineering, detection, classification techniques on the different datatypes. Different types of data with same technique gives different accuracy and different techniques with same dataset will also different accuracy. In this work latest advanced techniques like obfuscation and evasion are addressed in detail. There are a number of methods that have been suggested for detecting evasive malware, including creating API-based evasive malware signatures, observing evasion behaviors using different execution contexts, and using well-known evasion techniques. Therefore, this survey's key result is that it offered a complete evaluation of the evolution and current trends in malware analysis and detection approaches.

Darshan et al. (2021) addresses the challenges of shallow learning in case of sophisticated malware which is based on obfuscation and evasion techniques. So, in this paper a window-based malware detection system is projected using Convolutional Neural Network (CNN). CNN is trained by back propagation as a means of stochastic Gradient Descent to calculate weight and bias so that difference between actual output and calculated output can be minimized i.e., loss can be minimized. In this paper, the CNN-based windows malware detector has been projected that uses Application programming Interface (API) calls and their corresponding category (CAT) as dynamic feature (API-CAT). In the proposed work the execution time behavior feature of Portable Executable (PE) is used to spot and classify obscure malware. The model is trained using the entire pattern of the data set using the 10-fold cross-validation. The N-gram approach is utilized in this work to extract features. For the feature selection all the four selection techniques like Relief, Information gain, Mutual Information gain and Chi-Square is compared and best result is obtained by Relief feature selection technique with 97.968% detection accuracy.

Li et al. (2019) proposes a malware detection system that uses deep neural networks to defend against attacks that aim to evade legitimate spyware. Machine learning-based solutions, as we are aware, are weak against adversarial malware attacks because the attacker is free to change malicious instances into good ones. The context of this study is realistic because genuine attacker specifications, such as attack strategies, manipulation sets, and specific adversarial cases, are not known by defenses. The challenge's realistic environment and the problem's significance in protecting against adversarial malware instances serve as the inspiration for the current study. This framework gives an average 98.49% average accuracy with Drebin Android malware dataset. In this work attacks are classified into three categories grey-box attack, black-box attack, white-box attack. In grey-box attack where attackers know something about defense system and defender gives 98.49%. In a white-box attack, where the attacker is fully aware of the defence mechanism, the defender has a detection accuracy of 89.14%. 76.02 percent in a black-box attack where the attacker is unaware of the defense system.

Rafiqe et al. (2018) proposes deep learning malware detection and classification system using hybrid dataset which is prepared ASM file and byte file. ASM file is malware file in which all instructions are in assembly language. In byte file malware executables are in hexadecimal format. ASM files are used to calculate the count of opcode or words present in assemble source code file. In this work CNN is used for feature extraction. As we know that after detection of malware the most important task is to decide detected malware belongs to which category i.e., classification is also important. Different category of malware performs different type of malicious activities. There are different malware classification approaches like static, dynamic and hybrid. But in this proposed DLMD model static approach is fallowed. In this work hybrid data structure is used after the feature engineering of two type of files like ASM and byte files. ASM. First, features are extracted from byte files using two different Deep Convolutional Neural Networks (CNN). After that, essential and discriminative opcode features are selected using a wrapper-based mechanism, where Support Vector Machine (SVM) is used as a classifier.

3. DISCUSSIONS

In this section key findings of literature study are discussed for malware detection system starts from datasets, data preprocessing, feature selection, detection techniques, classification techniques and evaluation techniques in following orders:

- As for as the dataset is concerned in initial stages when detection system was based on traditional based model Drebin, Malgenome, DroidBench were used but now a days Microsoft BIG 2015, VirusShare are used frequently for developing complex detection system.
- In most of the literature along with normal procedure of data preprocessing like missing value handling, textual to numeric conversion using one hot

Table 2. Outline of the surveyed works

Work	Analysis	Methods	Feature(s)	Dataset(s)	ML Technique(s)
(Moubarak & Feghali, 2020)	Static and Dynamic		API, System calls, Network Inspection	System log files, historical data on IP addresses, honeypots, system and user behaviors	KNN, SVM, LR, NB,
(Chowdhury et al., 2018)	Hybrid	BAM, MLP	N-Gram Features	VX Heaven	NB, Random Forest, SVM, J48
(Aslan & Yilmaz, 2021)	Hybrid	CNN		Microsoft BIG 2015, Malimg, Malevis	Deep Learning
(Aslan & Samet, 2017)	Static, Dynamic, Hybrid detection system	Base machine learning models	Manifest, permissions, API calls	Contagio, malware dump, malshare, open malware	ML, DL
(Allix, Bissyande, Klein, & Le Traon, 2014)	Dynamic, static	ML, DL	API calls	Virushare, malzenome	ML, DL
(Catak, Yazı, Elezaj, & Ahmed, 2020)	Dynamic	Deep learning	API calls	Mal-API-2019, virus total	LSTM (Long Short-Term Memory)
(Catak, Yazı, Elezaj, & Ahmed, 2020)	Dynamic	Traditional ML	API	T-market data	Random Forest
(Allix, Bissyande, Klein, & Le Traon, 2014)	Dynamic	N-GRAM sequence	CAT-API	Malheur dataset	CNN
(Nataraj et al., 2011)	Dynamic	Deconvnet	Images	ImageNet, MNIST, CIFAR-10, CIFAR-100	CNN
(Aboaoja et al., 2022)	Dynamic and static analysis	Conv Net + max pooling	Images	MNIST, TIMIT, CIFAR, SVHN, ImageNet, Reuters-RCV1	CNN
(SL, 2019)	Static, dynamic and heuristic	API calls, API Sequence, Permissions, Op-code, Intents etc.	TF-IDF	Total Virus, MNIST, Microsoft BIG2015, Malzenome	ML, DL
(Rafique et al., 2019)	Dynamic analysis	Adversarial Malware Detection	Android Manifest, APK classes	Drebin Android malware dataset	Adversarial Machine Learning,
(Ni et al., 2018)	Static Analysis	DLMD	Opcode	Microsoft BIG2015	CNN

encoder maximum weightage is given to data scaling to make the data zero centric for the better prediction of model.

- The majority of studies found that traditional machine learning-based malware detection systems work best with random forests, decision trees, support vector machines, and naive bayes, whereas complex hybrid, dynamic analysis-based detection models used ensemble techniques in addition to multilayer perceptron techniques of deep learning for detection and classification.

The problem with traditional machine learning is that model takes decision only on the basis of pre decided features i.e., model in itself does not decide which feature will be used for model development. In case of deep learning model itself drive high label features for malware detection and classification which gives more accuracy and less false reporting i.e., less false positive and less false negative. And deep learning CNN technique is used for automatic malware detection and classification. The raw bytes model eliminates the need for feature extraction, feature selection i.e., feature engineering. It performs end-to-end malware detection and classification in real- time environment. In this approach image of malware binary is created. Malware of same category generally gives identical image and on the basis visualization it is classified. So deep learning-based classifier and detection model gives more accurate prediction than shallow learning-based malware detection system because in this feature is extracted by the learning algorithm.

Now a days adversarial malware attack is also a challenge to machine learning based malware detection and classification system. In adversarial malware attacks attacker generate adversarial malware just by manipulation in existing malware. So, to detect these types of malwares is very tough by detection and classification system. When malicious software tries to escape the virtual environment, the attack is referred to as an evasive adversarial attack. Attacks using malicious viruses are based on a type of machine learning called adversarial machine learning. Artificial data production using adversarial machine learning yields adversarial data. There are so many fields where sufficient size data set for model training is not sufficient and availability of data is almost impossible in that cases, we take help od adversarial data generator. Adversarial data generator generate artificial data for dataset looks like real data.

In machine learning there is a big challenge for feature selection from so many features because all features are not helpful to train the model or for the learning of model. if we will consider all the features complexity of model will be increased and model will be overfit. So, in machine learning to overcome the overfit problem we use different feature selection technique. In traditional machine learning it uses dimensionality reduction technique like PCA and in deep learning auto encoders are used. Problem of feature selection is sort out by using deep learning techniques, because deep neural network automatically select the hidden featured for model trainings.

As for as evaluation techniques are concerned to find the accuracy and performance of the malware detection system precision, recall, F1-Score, AUC, detection rate and confusion matrix are used in maximum studies.

This section also describes that during study we got that work for malware detection is constructed on static analysis which is good for known malware detection but signature identification-based detection system is not good for new malware detection so need of the time is focused over optimized dynamic malware detection or hybrid detection system so that system can be protected from zero-day malware. During the study of different literature study, it is observed following important observation can we made about performance optimization:

- Make generalization by using Ensemble techniques
- By ranking the features so that most important feature can be selected for model development
- Using dimensionality reduction techniques so that complexity of model can be reduced

Ensemble techniques in starting used for static analysis for generalize view among the different view of different models using bagging, boosting and gradient descent methods according to requirement but right now it is also used for dynamic and heuristic approach of malware detection and classification for updated dataset like Androzoo and Virusshare.

It is observed that most the studies shows that source code analysis is most preferred technique. However most preferred classification and detection features are Permissions, Intents, Opcode, API calls for different malware detection approaches like static, dynamic and hybrid.

Previous work also shows that extraction multiple feature categories from big dataset also substantially large. So, selection of most suitable features from a group of extracted features is also big challenge because quality of feature will also affect the performance and accuracy of the model. It also reduces the complexity and cost of the model along with avoid the overfit tendency of the model by using feature ranking and dimensionality reduction techniques.

After the development of model evaluation of model performance is important because performance of any model depends how much it predicts correctly. There are several variables that are used as evaluation variables. Precision, recall, F1-Score, and area under the curve (AUC), Confusion matrix, Detection rate (DR), True Positive Rate (TPR), False Positive Rate, and others (FPR). But the problem

Figure 3. Block diagram of working of machine learning and deep learning-based models

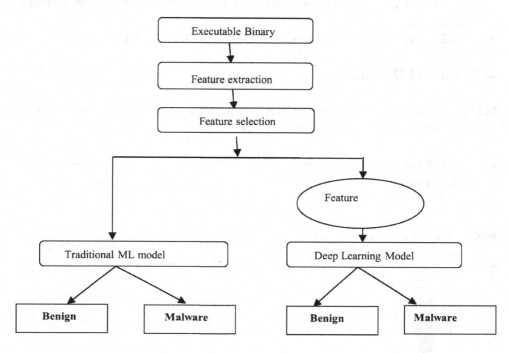

with evaluation techniques is that there is no common evaluation technique, which is suitable for all malware detection and classification model. An evaluation technique is suitable for a particular model and dataset it is not necessary that it will be suitable for another an environment also.

4. EXPERIMENT

According to this prediction, the kind and size of the dataset would affect the methodologies used to construct malware detection and classification models. Traditional machine learning approaches like decision trees, random forests, and logistic regression will work effectively if the dataset volume is limited.If the dataset contains sufficient number of records, then deep learning-based techniques perform well comparatively to shallow machine learning techniques. As for as the nature of dataset is concerned means dataset is homogeneous or non-homogeneous in nature. Nature of dataset also decide which algorithm will perform well, for example in this experiment data is non homogeneous hence logistic regression performance is poor. Hence overall objective of this experiment is as follows:

- Built a model which uses traditional machine learning models like random forest and logistic regression and one deep learning model for malware detection.
- Make a comparison of all model and select the best model.

4. 1 Dataset Details

Malware dataset is taken from GitHub which contains 1380047 records with 56 features, link of dataset is given in reference

- 41,323 binaries - legitimate
- 96,724 malware files

Figure 4. Dataset distribution pattern

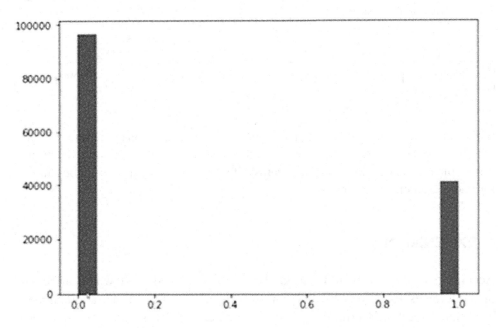

4. 2 Result and Discussions

As clear from the above table random forest is best classifier in traditional machine learning while logistic regression is not good for non-homogeneous pattern of data that is why f1-score is zero. Neural network is also giving better result, f1-score 91%.

Table 3. Performance comparison of different classifiers

Model	Training accuracy	Testing accuracy	F1-score	Position
Random forest	0.982	0.983	0.973	1st
Logistic regression	0.70%	0.69%	0.0	3rd
Neural network	0.951%	0.953	0.91	2nd

5. CONCLUSION

Malware authors are using advanced techniques like obfuscation, packing, polymorphism and metamorphism. To address all these advanced cyberattacks a powerful malware detection system is also necessary. So, in this study different approaches of malware detection and classification is described along with pros and cons. In this work it is observed that different approaches use different parameters, different detection techniques, different classification techniques, different evaluation techniques. So, objective of this study is to motivate for developing a common approach which is suitable against different types of malware attack.

REFERENCES

Github. (n.d.). [Data set]. https://raw.githubusercontent.com/PacktPublishing/ Mastering-Machine-Learning-for-Penetration-Testing/master/Chapter03/Chapter3- Practice/dataset.csv

Aboaoja, F. A., Zainal, A., Ghaleb, F. A., Al-rimy, B. A. S., Eisa, T. A. E., & Elnour, A. A. H. (2022). Malware detection issues, challenges, and future directions: A survey. *Applied Sciences (Basel, Switzerland)*, *12*(17), 8482. doi:10.3390/app12178482

Allix, K., Bissyande, T. F. D. A., Klein, J., & Le Traon, Y. (2014). *Machine learning-based malware detection for Android applications: History matters!*. University of Luxembourg, SnT.

Aslan, Ö., & Samet, R. (2017, October). Investigation of possibilities to detect malware using existing tools. In *2017 IEEE/ACS 14th International Conference on Computer Systems and Applications (AICCSA)* (pp. 1277-1284). IEEE. 10.1109/AICCSA.2017.24

Aslan, Ö., & Yilmaz, A. A. (2021). A new malware classification framework based on deep learning algorithms. *IEEE Access : Practical Innovations, Open Solutions, 9,* 87936–87951. doi:10.1109/ACCESS.2021.3089586

Baldangombo, U., Jambaljav, N., & Horng, S. J. (2013). A static malware detection system using data mining methods. arXiv preprint arXiv:1308.2831.

Cakir, B., & Dogdu, E. (2018, March). Malware classification using deep learning methods. In *Proceedings of the ACMSE 2018 Conference* (pp. 1-5). ACMSE.

Catak, F. O., Yazı, A. F., Elezaj, O., & Ahmed, J. (2020). Deep learning based Sequential model for malware analysis using Windows exe API Calls. *PeerJ. Computer Science, 6,* e285. doi:10.7717/peerj-cs.285 PMID:33816936

Chen, L., Ye, Y., & Bourlai, T. (2017, September). Adversarial machine learning in malware detection: Arms race between evasion attack and defense. In *2017 European intelligence and security informatics conference (EISIC)* (pp. 99-106). IEEE.

Chowdhury, M., Rahman, A., & Islam, R. (2018). Malware analysis and detection using data mining and machine learning classification. In *International conference on applications and techniques in cyber security and intelligence: applications and techniques in cyber security and intelligence* (pp. 266-274). Springer International Publishing. 10.1007/978-3-319-67071-3_33

Dahl, G. E., Stokes, J. W., Deng, L., & Yu, D. (2013, May). Large-scale malware classification using random projections and neural networks. In *2013 IEEE International Conference on Acoustics, Speech and Signal Processing* (pp. 3422-3426). IEEE 10.1109/ICASSP.2013.6638293

Dekel, O., & Shamir, O. (2008, July). Learning to classify with missing and corrupted features. In *Proceedings of the 25th international conference on Machine learning* (pp. 216-223). ACM. 10.1145/1390156.1390184

Drew, J., Moore, T., & Hahsler, M. (2016, May). Polymorphic malware detection using sequence classification methods. In 2016 IEEE Security and Privacy Workshops (SPW) (pp. 81-87). IEEE. doi:10.1109/SPW.2016.30

Enck, W., Octeau, D., McDaniel, P. D., & Chaudhuri, S. (2011, August). A study of android application security. In USENIX security symposium (Vol. 2). William Enck.

Feng, R., Sen Chen, X. X., Meng, G., Lin, S.-W., & Liu, Y. (2020, September). A performance-sensitive malware detection system using deep learning on mobile devices. *IEEE Transactions on Information Forensics and Security, 16*, 1563–1578. doi:10.1109/TIFS.2020.3025436

Firdausi, I., Erwin, A., & Nugroho, A. S. (2010, December). Analysis of machine learning techniques used in behavior-based malware detection. In *2010 second international conference on advances in computing, control, and telecommunication technologies* (pp. 201-203). IEEE. 10.1109/ACT.2010.33

Gong, L., Li, Z., Qian, F., Zhang, Z., Chen, Q. A., Qian, Z., & Liu, Y. (2020, April). Experiences of landing machine learning onto market-scale mobile malware detection. In *Proceedings of the Fifteenth European Conference on Computer Systems* (pp. 1-14). ACM. 10.1145/3342195.3387530

Gong, L., Lin, H., Li, Z., Qian, F., Li, Y., Ma, X., & Liu, Y. (2020). Systematically landing machine learning onto market-scale mobile malware detection. *IEEE Transactions on Parallel and Distributed Systems, 32*(7), 1615–1628. doi:10.1109/TPDS.2020.3046092

Han, K. S., Lim, J. H., Kang, B., & Im, E. G. (2015). Malware analysis using visualized images and entropy graphs. *International Journal of Information Security, 14*(1), 1–14. doi:10.100710207-014-0242-0

Hardy, W., Chen, L., Hou, S., Ye, Y., & Li, X. (2016). DL4MD: A deep learning framework for intelligent malware detection. In *Proceedings of the International Conference on Data Science (ICDATA)* (p. 61). The Steering Committee of The World Congress in Computer Science, Computer Engineering and Applied Computing (WorldComp).

Hosseini, S., Nezhad, A. E., & Seilani, H. (2021). Android malware classification using convolutional neural network and LSTM. *Journal of Computer Virology and Hacking Techniques, 17*(4), 307–318. doi:10.100711416-021-00385-z

Islam, R., Tian, R., Batten, L., & Versteeg, S. (2010, July). Classification of malware based on string and function feature selection. In *2010 Second Cybercrime and Trustworthy Computing Workshop* (pp. 9-17). IEEE. 10.1109/CTC.2010.11

Komashinskiy, D., & Kotenko, I. (2010, February). Malware detection by data mining techniques based on positionally dependent features. In *2010 18th Euromicro Conference on Parallel, Distributed and Network-based Processing* (pp. 617-623). IEEE. 10.1109/PDP.2010.30

Kumar, A., Kuppusamy, K. S., & Aghila, G. (2019). A learning model to detect maliciousness of portable executable using integrated feature set. *Journal of King Saud University-Computer and Information Sciences*, *31*(2), 252–265. doi:10.1016/j.jksuci.2017.01.003

Li, D., Li, Q., Ye, Y., & Xu, S. (2021). A framework for enhancing deep neural networks against adversarial malware. *IEEE Transactions on Network Science and Engineering*, *8*(1), 736–750. doi:10.1109/TNSE.2021.3051354

Mahmoud, B. S., & Garko, A. B. (2022). A Machine Learning Model for Malware Detection Using Recursive Feature Elimination (RFE) For Feature Selection and Ensemble Technique. IOS Journals.

Milosevic, N., Dehghantanha, A., & Choo, K. K. R. (2017). Machine learning aided Android malware classification. *Computers & Electrical Engineering*, *61*, 266–274. doi:10.1016/j.compeleceng.2017.02.013

Moubarak, J., & Feghali, T. (2020). Comparing Machine Learning Techniques for Malware Detection. *ICISSP*, *10*, 0009373708440851. doi:10.5220/0009373708440851

Nataraj, L., Karthikeyan, S., Jacob, G., & Manjunath, B. S. (2011, July). Malware images: visualization and automatic classification. In *Proceedings of the 8th international symposium on visualization for cyber security* (pp. 1-7). ACM.

Naway, A., & Li, Y. (2019). Using deep neural network for Android malware detection. arXiv preprint arXiv:1904.00736.

Ni, S., Qian, Q., & Zhang, R. (2018). Malware identification using visualization images and deep learning. *Computers & Security*, *77*, 871–885. doi:10.1016/j.cose.2018.04.005

Rafique, M. F., Ali, M., Qureshi, A. S., Khan, A., & Mirza, A. M. (2019). Malware classification using deep learning-based feature extraction and wrapper-based feature selection technique. arXiv preprint arXiv:1910.10958.

Shang, S., Zheng, N., Xu, J., Xu, M., & Zhang, H. (2010, October). Detecting malware variants via function-call graph similarity. In *2010 5th International Conference on Malicious and Unwanted Software* (pp. 113-120). IEEE. 10.1109/MALWARE.2010.5665787

Sikorski, M., & Honig, A. (2012). *Practical malware analysis: the hands-on guide to dissecting malicious software*. No Starch Press.

SL, S. D., & Jaidhar, C. D. (2019). Windows malware detector using convolutional neural network based on visualization images. *IEEE Transactions on Emerging Topics in Computing*, *9*(2), 1057–1069.

Urmila, T. S. (2022). Machine learning-based malware detection on Android devices using behavioral features. *Materials Today: Proceedings*, *62*, 4659–4664. doi:10.1016/j.matpr.2022.03.121

Chapter 11
Malware Forensics Analysis and Detection in Cyber Physical Systems

T. Sarath
Vellore Institute of Technology, India

K. Brindha
Vellore Institute of Technology, India

Sudha Senthilkumar
Vellore Institute of Technology, India

ABSTRACT

In day to day life, the internet is becoming an essential part for making use of services like online banking or advertising. On the internet, just as in the real world, there are those who wish to harm others by taking advantage of trustworthy individuals anytime whenever money is exchanged. For accomplishing their goals, people intent with malicious software to harm the internet and this attack is named as Malware. The malware denotes as malevolent software which is installed in computer or mobile without awareness of owner or user. As a result, by looking into this malicious software, the IT team is better able to assess a security incident and help stop more infections from spreading to the victim's computer or server. For this kind of performance, IT responders typically look for solutions known technically as malware forensics. The importance of malware forensics has grown as the cybercrime community targets financial institutions, technological companies, and retail businesses with malicious software. This virus can be broken down into two categories: static malware and dynamic malware. While dynamic malware analysis offers various tools and code, static malware analysis has several limitations. As a result, dynamic malware analysis is often preferred in most contexts. This chapter

DOI: 10.4018/978-1-6684-8666-5.ch011

deals with the study of malware types, how it is affecting the users, static malware limitations, and dynamic malware tools that are used for analyzing malicious software. Further focuses on issues, challenges that are facing in malware analysis and available online malware analysis tools that work on cloud along with feature research prospects.

1. INTRODUCTION

Malicious software is known as malware, and as its name suggests, malwares are created to harm computers and their users by stealing data, corrupting files, or just acting naughtily to annoy them. According to reports, malware is becoming more and more prevalent, and computer security incidents are skyrocketing (Adelstein et al., 2002; Bergeron, 2001). Network expansion is halted by malware. malware targets the internet-based applications. Since almost every part of life today depends on the internet to improve its level of service and prevent any negative impacts that these malwares might have, it is more important than ever to identify and stop malware as soon as possible. Malware that has the potential to propagate is difficult to defend against because it lacks centralised management. According to studies (William, 2008), malware is among the largest threats to computer security. They design malware so that it changes itself on a regular basis to avoid being easily found.

Malware developers continuously work to produce programmes that are challenging to detect, and over time, they have successfully enhanced the strategies they employ to hide or morph the bad code. Beginning with simple encryption, these ideas move on to polymorphic, oligomorphic and metamorphic viruses.

One method of identifying some of these malwares is through antivirus scanners, although with improvements in malware development methods, malware detectors now employ a number of techniques to lessen the detrimental effects of this software. Due to the limits of the present malware detection approaches, machine learning and data mining techniques are combined with the current detection techniques to boost the detection process' efficiency (Wang et al., 2021). Even though signature-based detection techniques are good at catching known malware, polymorphic and unidentified threats might change their signatures, making them ineffective in catching these threats. Furthermore, signature-based detection is unable to identify new malware because no signatures for it have yet been created. The ability to locate new, well-known, and unknown viruses is provided by heuristic-based detection methods, but their high rate of false positives and negatives encourages us to develop more accurate methods. Due to the exponential proliferation of polymorphic malware, heuristic-based detection techniques are combined with machine learning techniques to increase malware detection efficiency and accuracy.

This chapter deals with study of malwares, types, how it affecting the users, static malware limitations, dynamic malware tools that used for analyzing malicious software. Further focuses on issues, challenges that facing in malware analysis and available online malware analysis tools that work on cloud and future research prospects of cyber physical systems.

2. TYPES OF MALWARE

Malware can take many various forms, but it can be broadly divided into the following kinds. Despite the fact that many of them fall under more than one class, they are not mutually exclusive.

- **Virus:** A virus replicates itself in order to infect computers and other files. Due to its inability to function independently, it joins files with another files that are specifically executable files and applications because of replication capabilities, it spreads between files and even computers across a network. Performance system and Denial of service degradation are the results (Spafford, 1989).
- **Worms:** are independently existing malicious computer code. This have the ability to duplicate themselves and spread via email and storage media, they also use up network and computer resources, which lowers system performance. Antivirus scanners can recognise these codes due to their ability, to produce numerous copies of themselves. (Li & Stafford, 2014)
- **Trojan Horse:** is a helpful application that serves at malicious ends. It duplicates on itself, and these are downloaded into a computer through online activity. It can destroy, change or corrupt files on the system as well as steal important data and watch user activities. (Idika & Mathur, 2007)
- **Spyware:** Spyware is used to track user activity or steal someone's personal information. Without the system owner's awareness, it is installed, and discreetly gathers information before sending it back to its maker. Even well-known corporations like Google utilise spyware to gather the necessary customer data (Yin, 2007).
- **Adware:** Most of the time, adware is pretty bothersome because it plays advertisements on the user's computer without their consent and interferes with their present task. The primary goal of adware is generating profit. It is just damaging as other malware.
- **Cookies:** it is in text files format that a user's web browser stores on their computer for later use and include information. Supposedly cookies are safe, but when certain spyware uses them, they pose a problem.

- **Sniffers** are pieces of software that monitor and capture network communication. They examine various packet fields and gather data in order to get ready for a virus attack.
- **Botnet:** is a piece of software which enables the attacker to command a compromised machine. a collection of compromised machines that are managed by hackers or other attackers and used for nefarious purposes without the owner's knowledge. They launch assaults with denial-of-service, spam messages can be send and data can be steal.
- **Keyloggers** is a type of spyware used to capture keystrokes in order to steal credit card numbers, sensitive information and passwords. These can enter computer when user viewed a website that was infected or installed some other malicious software.
- **Spam:** Another name for spams is junk emails. These are sent through emails and made numerous inheritors. That uses up a lot of bandwidth and makes the system slower.
- **Ransomware** is currently the biggest threat to the internet sector. Ransomware is a type of software that encrypts your data, disables various applications, and prevents you from using your operating system until you pay the ransom. Most requests are expressed in monetary terms. Even after paying money, there is no assurance that you will regain authority.

2.1. Camouflage Evolution in Malware

Studying malware camouflage is highly advised in order to comprehend and build malware analysis and detection strategies. Malware camouflage is the term for concealing malware in order to keep it away from malware detectors for as long as feasible. Malware authors employ a variety of tactics, ranging from straightforward ones like encryption to sophisticated ones like metamorphic (Wang et al., 2021).

2.1.1. Encryption

Malware authors constantly strive to make programmes less noticeable to detectable by scanners of malware. Encryption is the method they employ to blend in the best. It is the first method for malware concealing (You & Yim, 2010). It has modules for encryption and decryption. Whereas decryption uses the same key every time, encryption uses a different key every time. As the decryption method does not guarantee uniqueness, their detection is possible. The first encrypted malware, CASCADE, originally surfaced in 1987 (Beaucamps, 2007). Figure 1 depicts the virus's structure.

Figure 1. Encrypted virus structure

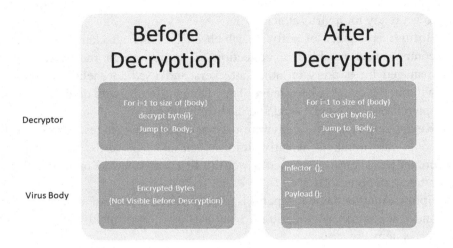

This method's primary goal is to prevent static code analysis and antivirus detection. This approach also causes the inquiry process to lag.

2.1.2. Oligiomorphism

The first oligiomorphic virus, known as Whale and a DOS virus, first surfaced in 1990 (Szor, 2005). This is seen as a development in malware camouflage. In contrast to oligiomorphism different decryptor are used for every infection, the decryptor in encryption stays the same for every infection. It is also regarded as a development in the semi-polymorphic encryption method. Although oligiomorphism offers different decryptor for each fresh attack from a list of decryption, there is still potential that antivirus software will detect the attack by scanning all the decryptors.

2.1.3. Polymorphic

Mark Washburn created first polymorphic Virus 1260 in 1990. Although polymorphic is more complicated than other viruses because it combines encryption with oligiomorphism. Antiviruses have a tough time detecting them because they alter their look with each copy. There is no cap on the number of decryptors they can produce. These viruses alter their appearance by using various obfuscation techniques. The mutation engine is responsible for this process of change.

2.1.4. Metamorphism

In this generation of metamorphic viruses, the malware's content changes rather than being encrypted. Because of this a decryptor is not required. It also uses mutation engine similar to polymorphism instead of changing the decryptor, it changes the entire body. The fundamental infection thought that a syntax changes with semantics of new copy which stays same even if virus appears to change with apiece of function that does not change. The ACG is the first metamorphic virus created for DOS in 1998.

3. MALWARE OBFUSCATION TECHNIQUES

Obfuscation is a technique that is used by writers of malware to create their code inspiring to read and comprehend. This method's primary goal is to mask malware's damaging activity. Several investigators have different categories for obfuscation strategies. The six categories listed below break down the most popular techniques (You & Yim,).

3.1. Insertion Dead Code

This is the naivest method for altering code without altering its intent. Through employing NOP statements, push, and pop statements, trash code are introduced into code via this technique. These statements are used in a manner that preserves code of semantics.

3.2. Replacement of Instruction

This method substitutes instructions with others that produce the similar meaning, much like replacements do in normal languages. For instance, the register eax is affected the same by the following commands. The register value was set to zero by each instruction.

```
move eax,0
xor eax, eax
and eax,0
sub eax,eax
```

Instructions are replaced with equivalent instructions in this strategy which makes it difficult to detect these malwares.

3.3. Register Reassignment

This method redistributes registers across each replica without altering the semantics of virus's. Although it is simple method, it can exceedingly challenge to detect when combined with other techniques.

3.4. Subroutine Reordering

This approach permutes a sequence of commands in a section of code so that behaviour is unaffected while the appearance changes. The following is an instance of subroutine followed by the situation reordering:

```
//Subroutine
mov eax, 0A
push ecx
add esi, ebx
//reordering
add esi, ebx
mov eax,0A
push ecx
```

3.5. Transposition Code

With this method, original piece of code's commands is reorganised so that their semantics are preserved (Christodorescu & Jha, 2006). To transpose codes, there are two methods that can be applied. One way involves randomly rearranging the instructions, recovering the inventive code using jumps and unconditional statements, while alternative involves selecting and rearranging independent instructions that have no bearing on other instructions. Although the second strategy is challenging to put into practise it is far more successful than the first.

3.6. Code Integration

As the name suggests, malicious code is integrated within software that wants to be unnatural in malware obfuscation technique. This method, which decompiles the original programme and inserts malicious code such that it cannot be easily discovered, is particularly effective (Konstantinou & Wolthusen, 2008).

4. MALWARE DETECTOR

Malware detector is a programme created to identify harmful software and code. The basic malware detection process is defined as in below equation 1

$$D(P) = \begin{cases} malicous & if\ p\ contains\ malicious\ code \\ begin & otherwise \end{cases}$$

D is a function that determines whether a programme or application (p) is harmful or not.

$$D(P) = \begin{cases} malicous & if\ p\ contains\ malcode \\ begin & if\ p\ is\ a\ normal\ program \\ undecidable & if\ D\ fails\ to\ determine\ P \end{cases}$$

We can modify the above-described function equation 2 as follows when D is unable to determine whether a programme is hazardous or harmless since the virus is a recent innovation and cannot be recognised by malware detector.

4.1. Techniques of Malware Analysis

The first step in detecting malware is malware analysis. In order to create the defensive feature of malware detectors, the developers must first understand how malware operates and what drives its development. This type of expertise about malware will help us identify malware. Based on the method and time malware analysis are categorised into three groups.

4.1.1. Analysis of Static

Static analysis is often called as code analysis that refers to process of analysing software or a section of code without actually running it. To ascertain the software holds harmful code, static data that is collected from the source code. In this method software is using reverse engineering tools, the malicious code's structure is examined to determine how it functions. Debuggers, disassemblers, decompiles, and source code analysers are some of the tools that can be used to perform static analysis. AV Scanning, File Format Inspection, Disassembly, Fingerprinting and String Extraction are techniques used in static analysis.

For instance, if the source code is accessible, it is possible to extract a variety of useful information including data structures and used functions. Further investigation is hampered by the fact that this info is lost once the basis program has been converted into an executable binary.

Static malware analysis uses a variety of methodologies. This is a description of a few.

- **File fingerprinting** comprises activities on the file level like computing cryptographic hash (like md5) of the binary to identify it from other binary files and to confirm that it has not been modified, in addition to looking at the binary's obvious exterior features.
- **File format:** is a helpful information that retrieved by utilising the metadata of certain file format. This also applies to UNIX system's magic number used to identify the file type. For instance, a lot of data may be gleaned from a Windows binary, which is normally in PE format (portable executable), including the time of compilation, functions that were imported and exported, icons, menus and strings.
- **AV scanning:** is a binary examination is normally known as malware, one or more AV scanners are very likely to find it. Using one or more antivirus scanners takes time, but there are instances when it is necessary.
- **Packer detection:** These days, malware is sometimes disseminated in an obscured format, such as one that is compressed or encrypted. A packer is employed to accomplish this algorithm are used for modification.

Static analysis shows that the programme looks very different after packing, making it difficult to recover the logic and other metadata. While some unpackers, such PEiD2, exist there isn't a universal unpacker, which makes static malware analysis extremely difficult.

- **Disassembly:** Typically, disassembling a particular binary is the main component of static analysis. This is done with the use of programmes like IDA Pro that can reverse machine code into assembly language. An analyst can then study the programme logic as a result look into the program's goal using the reconstruction of the assembly code. Static malware analysis's key benefit is enables examination thorough a specific binary. Therefore, it can cover potential sample malware execution pathways and source code is really not run, dynamic analysis is not safer than static analysis. Yet, it can take a lot of time and hence calls for knowledge.

4.1.1.1. Limitations of Static Malware Analysis

Malware sample source codes are typically not easily accessible. This limits relevant static analysis methods for analysing malware to those extract data from the binary malwares represents are considers fact that the majority of malware attacks use hosts that are running the IA32 instruction set. The binary usages self-modifying code methods, the results of such programmes' disassembly could be unclear.

4.1.2. Analysis of Dynamic

Dynamic or behavioural analysis is the procedure of examining and executing software functions (Elhadi et al., 2012). It can accomplish through tracking the calls by function, controlling flows, scrutinising function instructions and parameters. In order to monitor its behaviour and create countermeasures, malicious program is run in virtual environment. RegShot, Sandbox, emulators, Process Explorer and imulator are the tools used for dynamic analysis. As this technique infected programme is effected on a virtual computer for the purpose of monitoring, analysing dynamic is more effective than analysing static. This makes a variety of malware types easily detectable. This form of analysis requires more time because we need to create the execution and testing environment for a malicious software.

If the analytic environment is improperly separated and damaging third-party systems malware samples are not performed in controlled analysis environment may change their behaviour or stop completely. The fundamental methods of analysing dynamic malware has two methods, which are as follows:

- *Analysing the difference between defined points:* Comparing the changes made to the system to its starting state allows for the analysis of differences between definite points after a malware sample run for predetermined amount of time. With this method a comparison report describes malware behaviour.
- **Monitoring runtime behaviour:** In this method, harmful operations carried out by the malicious application are kept track of while they are in progress using a specific tool. Regshot tool is an illustration of the first strategy. Uses the Regshot to take a snapshot of the registry before running the programme. After running the binary, 2nd shot button will click to take a second snapshot, then click the comparison button to compare the two snapshots. The results receive the analysis in a text file including information on the added and modified files. The most promising method at the moment involves watching an application's behaviour during runtime. A controlled runtime environment that is divided off from the rest of the system in order to isolate the malicious

process referred to "sandbox" in this context. On some level, this partitioning is often accomplished utilising virtualization techniques.

4.1.3. Hybrid

It mixes dynamic and static analytic methods in order to profit from both strategies. A software is first examined through the analysis of code by looking for malware signatures and then it is launched in a virtual environment to watch how it behaves in real life.

In Table 1, a comparison of dynamic and static analysis methods is presented.

Table 1. Comparison of Dynamic and Static

Analysis of Static	Analysis of Dynamic
Safe and Fast	Consumed Time and Vulnerable
It is good for analysis of Multipath malware	It is difficult for analysis of Multipath malware
It cannot analyse the polymorphic malware and Obfuscated	It cannot analyse the polymorphic malware and Obfuscated
False positive level is Low	False positive level is High

5. TECHNIQUES OF MALWARE DETECTION

The three primary kinds of malware detection techniques are signature-based, specification-based and heuristic-based. These methods locate, recognise the malware to take action against protect computer from resource loss and potential data.

Below is summary of the methods and resources that are currently available for analysing unfamiliar and potentially harmful software. An analyst can learn lot about the activities taken by sample from reports analysis produced by section of tools. These reports offer the groundwork for an immediate and thorough comprehension of the sample.

- **FileMon:** The FileMon application is excellent for detecting file system changes. Additionally, the binary will be able to recognise and record any searches it conducts. This utility is quite loud and detects changes in files made by Windows that appears to inactive. Thus, make sure to "stop capture" around 10 seconds after starting the tool and to "clean the tool" before running the binary.

- **Norman Sandbox:** This tool executes samples in a strictly regulated virtual environment that mimics Windows operating system. A host computer associated local area network, Internet connectivity are simulated in this environment. The Norman Sandbox's main principle is to mimic all functionality that is necessary for an assessed sample in order to replace it with actual functionality. Hence, supporting operating system related mechanisms like multithreading support and memory protection must be provided by the simulated system. To give sample false impression in operating on real system, all necessary APIs must provide. Packaged or obfuscated executables are not a hindrance to the study itself because malware is executed in counterfeit system. Norman Sandbox focuses on identification of viruses that attempt to propagate across network shares, email, or P2P networks.
- **JoeBox:** JoeBox generates a log during the dynamic examination of a possibly harmful sample that comprises high level details of the operations conducted in relation to file, system, and registry processes. JoeBox was created from the ground up to run actual hardware, without the use of any virtualization or emulation software. The structure is built using a client-server architecture, where single controller illustration can manage a number of clients who are in charge of carrying out the analysis. Consequently, by adding additional analysing clients to the system, it is simple to raise the throughput of entire system. The machine in charge of collecting the data gathers all analysis data.

5.1. Detection Based on Signature

As malware is created a string of bits commonly referred as a signature inserted into the code that can later use to determine which members of malware family. Most antivirus products employ the signature-based detection method. The antivirus tool analyses infected file's code and looks for patterns that are characteristic of a certain malware family (Landage & Wankhade, 2013). Malware signatures are kept up to date in databases and then utilised for comparison during the detection process. String or pattern scanning or matching are other names for this type of detection method. It may also be static, dynamic, or hybrid.

5.2. Detection Based on Heuristic

Detection of Heuristic-based picks up on distinguishes among system's normal and anomalous behaviour in order to finally find and stop known and unidentified malware threats. Two steps make up detection of heuristic-based method. The system's behaviour is first observed when an attack is not present, and crucial data is recorded so it may be checked and validated in the incident of a round. In the next stage distinction is scrutinised to find malware belonging to a specific family. The three main parts of a behaviour detector labouring in a technique heuristic-based are as follows.

- **Collection of Data:** As its name advises, this part is concerned with gathering both dynamic or static data.
- **Interpretation of Data:** This step transforms data into an intermediate format after being interpreted by the data gathering component.
- **Algorithm for matching:** In the interpretation component, converted information is compared with behaviour signature using matching algorithm component. Figure 2 depicts the behaviour detector, which demonstrates how all of these parts function as a unit.

Although detection of heuristic-based is an effective technique also has the drawbacks to the technique, including higher level of false positives and higher resource requirement. This approach is often referred to as a proactive strategy, behaviour analysis, or anomaly identification. Before using heuristic-based detection

Figure 2. Detector behaviour
(Jacob et al., 2008)

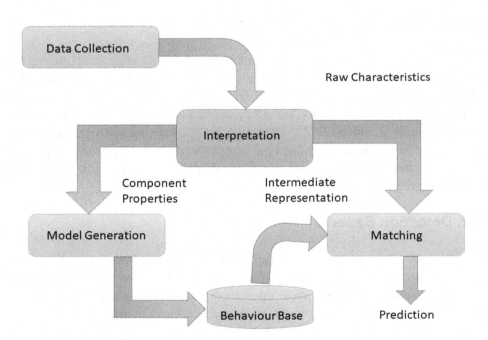

many types of analysis, including rule-based, file-based, generic signature, and weight-based analysis are conducted

5.3. Detection Based on Specification

Applications are monitored in accordance with their specifications in specification-based detection techniques, which look for both normal and anomalous behaviour. This method derivative from techniques of heuristic-based is a key distinction between the two: while techniques of heuristic-based detection using AI methods to detect legitimate and fraudulent activity of legitimate programme, detection based on specification techniques are analysed based on behaviour of the system specification (Yaacoub et al., 2020). This process is somehow done by physical comparison of normal actions of some system. By reducing level of false positives and raising the level of false negatives, it gets around the drawback of heuristic-based approaches. Table 2 displays the benefits and drawbacks of the three detection methods.

Figure 3 illustrates the classification and relationships between malware analysis and detection techniques. Detection of Malware methods can be static, hybrid, or dynamic, and specification based methods are developed from heuristic-based methods.

Figure 3. The classification and relationships

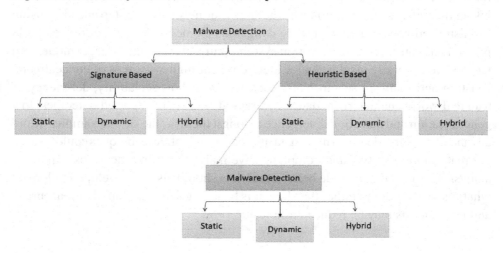

Table 2. The benefits and drawbacks of the three detection methods

	Advantages	Disadvantages
Detection based on Signature	• Known malwares can be detected easily • Used less resources as compared to other techniques	• It cannot detect Unknown malwares
Detection based on Heuristic	• Known and unknown novel malware can be detected	• The unknown and new malwares update is need for data. • In terms of space and time need more resources. • Level of false positive is high
Detection based on Specification	• Unknown, Known and novel malware can be detected • Low in Level of false positive	• Level of false negative is high • Not efficient in detection of new malwares. • Specification development is time consuming

6. ISSUES AND CHALLENGES IN MALWARE

The continually developing demand of minimalized catastrophe rates of anti-malware results have unlocked up urgent investigation opportunities and trials to be determined yet.

6.1. Anti-Malware Methods Existing Issues

Future challenges will be more challenging as malware remains to dramatically increase in complexity. The majority of previous static, dynamic and hybrid approaches require virtual environments and are time-consuming, respectively do not effort for innovative, unidentified, or zero-day marks. Virtual environments nonetheless losing their effectiveness as malware authors routinely stay one step ahead by using sophisticated new strategies to hide dangerous elements. Despite efforts to build parallel and multi-level dispensation systems, current anti-malware techniques and tackles are generally insufficient or ineffective for higher degrees of concealment. Existing anti-malware schemes also look issues such as scalability, deficiency of true real world characteristic datasets, irreproducibility of reported outcomes, low generalisation and detection divergence amongst them for the similar samples. More advanced machine/deep learning, data mining, and adaptive techniques could be used to create more effective and comprehensive malware countermeasures. Anomaly analysis methods that include behavioural data should also be developed to look at what the virus is doing rather than how it is behaving. The likelihood of inaccuracy and false alarms may be reduced as a result.

6.2. Techniques for Anti-Malware in Advanced Machine Learning (AML)

Quintessential anti-malwares are vulnerable to overfitting and have lower overall reliability because they frequently rely on non-linear opponent categorical models and skilled domain information. Instead using explicit models, systems or attacks, AML approaches try to emulate attackers using varied material, settings, etc. Although there have few preliminary investigations on the usage of shallow AML for anti-malware, much work has to be done in this area. AML patterns like exposed set gratitude, more compound and remaining data mining dictionary learning and deep learning should investigate aimed at feature segmentation/ illustration selection/ learning /classification and figuring out temporal relations inside and amid malware segments in order to improve accuracy, scalability and flexibility on wide-ranging and unidentified samples.

6.3. Mobile Device Malwares

The number of internet-connected smart gadgets is increasing rapidly are the malware threats they face (particularly through third-party apps). Malware for mobile devices has been the subject of insufficient research. Furthermore, due to their high computing costs and/or the complexity of the features they use for analysis, the majority of current anti-malware techniques are not actual and inappropriate for mobile devices. Bayesian classification-based real-time lightweight mobile antimalware is thus an intriguing research area to investigate. Various data from built-in sensors, like accelerometer may improve the effectiveness of mobile anti-malware. Another issue that requires careful investigation is the detection and eradication of mobile hardware malware. Early mobile anti-malware techniques will have big impact on how smart gadgets are designed. However, strong countermeasures should be used to combat smart device malware. The security and privacy standards of their apps should be upheld according to app creators. Administrators of app marketplaces should inspect and eliminate questionable apps. Users should use reputable apps and use advanced anti-malware programmes. Overall, malware and anti-malware for wearable and mobile devices are a new area of study in cybersecurity with pressing issues that merit investigation.

6.4. Large-Scale Benchmark Databases

The public disposal of thorough standard datasets with precise contexts and labels is essential for the advancement of malware research. The majority of current databases suffer from drawbacks including short size, missing information or features, unbalanced classifications, and not being accessible to the general public. Research on malware has been hampered by a lack of sufficient large-scale public datasets. Benchmark unrestricted datasets will help to associate different anti-malware programmes, identify the correlations among security contravention phenomena and combine malware discoveries to make statistically significant assumptions. Nonetheless, due to the diversity of malware traits, forms, and behaviours, compiling large-scale heterogeneous marked databases is difficult for time and resource overriding. Using crowdsourcing gather various large-scale annotated data sets may be beneficial.

6.5. Graph Based Malware Analysis

The majority of malware today uses concealments to avoid detection by traditional anti-malware programmes, which mostly ignore learning and recognising the underlying links between samples and variations as well as contextual data. Data, data program, call graphs, control flow graphs and control dependence graphs are a few examples of graph-based relationship representations and features that offer interesting possibilities even when malware code is changed because they make it easier to trace the history of malware in various contexts. The development of graph-based anti-malwares still faces challenges related to data heterogeneity, inaccurate and noisy labelling computational expense during real-time detection. Such problems can extent is solved decentralized. Usage of several undirected and directed graphs, heterogeneous networks, multi-view spectral clustering, dynamic graph mining, multiple graph kernel learning deep graph difficulty kernels to seizure structural and contextual info

6.6. Bio-Inspired Anti-Malware

By using bio-inspired like biological immune system, biological evolution, swarm intelligence and genetic algorithms) methods, it may be possible to overcome some of the limitations of conventional anti-malware programmes. These methods are lighter, more scalable, and less resource-constrained in comparison. Accuracy in the wild can be greatly improved by using adaptive bio-inspired algorithms for clever concealment-invariant feature extraction and categorization. A system under assault can be distinguished from a dysfunctional or failing system using bio-inspired methodologies that establish specific objective functions. One of the more interesting directions hasn't been investigated as much in anti-malware programmes, but it involves combining deep neural networks and bioinspired algorithms.

6.7. Defence-in-Depth Anti-Malware

Defence-in-Depth (DiD) is an anti-malware method that uses many defensive levels or lines in place of a single line of defence. As it doesn't rely on a single method of defence and is not compromised if one is one would think that a powerful defensive mechanism will be more resilient. Each machine or cyber-system architecture can be broken down into different stages of depth; for instance, in a power grid scheme, metres, communication outlines and smaller mechanisms might be considered at the lowest, middle, and highest levels, respectively. Active or adaptive malware defence is another option. Due to its intrinsic complexity, active defence hasn't gotten much attention. The developer anticipates attack situations at various levels and creates malware countermeasures appropriately. In adaptive defence, the system is dynamically changed in response to changing situations or persistently updated by retraining/adding fresh features. In adaptive defence, the system is dynamically changed in response to changing situations or persistently updated by retraining/adding fresh features. Adaptive defences might make advantage of unsupervised learning and concept drift and would need to be quick, automated, and computationally efficient.

6.8. Attacks on Internet of Things (IoT)

IoT are used more and more in a variety of fields, from smart capitals to military grids. Even with the best security measures in place, IoT devices and systems are susceptible to creative cyber-attacks. IoT equipment is continually connected to a network, making security increasingly important. Due to heterogeneous systems with multiple sources of information and different types of nodes. Cybersecurity using IoT is comparatively new investigation area and rather difficult to understand. Several approaches (such as block chain and predictive analytics) may be successful in achieving this. Predictive safety is obtaining cyber resiliency through building copies that forecast forthcoming threats and avoid in advance. Predictive models should take into account social sciences, computer networking, descriptive theory, uncertain behaviour model, and psychology after attackers', users', and administrators' perceptions at various granularity stages because there is durable association between safety lapses and social errors.

6.9. Deception and Moving Target Anti-Malware Techniques

By luring enemies to attack and misleading them with false information, malware is detected and prevented via deception techniques (such as honeypots). Client and server honeypots are the two different types of honeypots. Using honeypots can lessen false positives and stop DDoS attacks. Sophisticated assaults and tools (such polymorphic malware, for example) are becoming more prevalent, either to locate honeypots or to change the behaviour of the honeypots themselves. Moreover, attackers can use honeypots to compromise other delicate components of frameworks. As a compromised honeypot puts the security of the entire organisation in peril, more complex honeypot and honey net (a group of honeypots) schemes (such as shadow honeypots) should be developed. Dynamically randomising system components using moving target methods (also known as dynamic platform approaches or DPMs) reduces the risk of successful attacks and expedites.

6.10. Decentralized Anti-Malware

Current antimalware innovation is hampered by data sharing and trust management; however, decentralised malware detectors utilising block chain technology can address these issues. Yet up until today, it hasn't gotten much notice. Future directions for the intersection of antimalware and block chain technology include investigating overhead handling traffic, high-quality and signatures of sparse malware, construction of accurate dynamic usual traffics, dropping a lot of untrue alarms, cost and energy, block chain inactivity, case-by-case situation investigation and further proof of idea applications.

6.11. Privacy Preservation

Sensitive information-stealing malware has drawn a lot of attention. Yet, protecting privacy of user with malware analysis (particularly at third or cloud party servers) and data sharing malware is still an unresolved issue. After user's privacy or data has been compromised, it will be difficult to restore it and to rebuild faith in commercial antimalware software. The majority of previous anti-malware programmes ignore user, data, and network privacy and security. In order to respect public and legal perspectives relatively framework is done to develop privacy protection. To balance security, effectiveness, privacy, and battery consumption, it is important to take great care while designing light-weight detection and privacy protection systems that can be used on mobile devices. Several experts have emphasised the need for more cutting-edge privacy preservation techniques in malware analysis.

6.12. Malware Analysis Visualization Systems

Malware analysts must devote a lot of effort to the current methods of malware analysis. Extremely dynamic visual analysis would make it easier for researchers and professionals to compare, summarise, and classify malware. The majority of previous methods have extremely few interactivity, temporal mapping, scalability and illustration space options. Malware visualisation system development is a crucial and developing topic that covers a wide range of malware types and situations. In the coming years, encyclopaedic visualisation tools will help analysts and researchers identify brand-new study domains.

6.13. Hardware Based Solutions

Recently, hardware-based malware detectors have gained popularity as countermeasure. Some detection systems make use of low-level architectural features that can be achieved by changing the microarchitecture of processors in computer, such as CPU's with specific records that provide software and hardware anomaly actions. Nonetheless, there is still more work to be done in this area of research and trustworthy systems are naturally reliable and secure beside human mistake and hostile parties that have a long way to go. Also, there are few research on the effectiveness of anti-malware programmes that combine hardware- and software based methodologies because they have a great potential to find more complex malware. Moreover, data from smart device sensors, such as GPS and ambient light sensors, may be utilised to characterise malware.

6.14. Malware Adversarial Learning

Recently, effective malware defences have been achieved using machine learning (ML), however these defences are not intended for circumstances in which an adversary is actively attempting to influence outcomes. Deep learning-based defences against hostile examples in particular lack robustness. Attackers also inject harming samples in (adaptive /online) training record with the purpose to dramatically decrease malware countermeasures with ML accuracy during testing stage. Designing ML anti-malware that is resilient in an adversarial situation is still a challenging task. Researchers should investigate malware adversarial ML in order to pinpoint potential countermeasure weaknesses during both the development and testing phases, design analogous attacks and analyse their effects, and create methods to improve the resilience of based anti-malwares based on ML.

6.15. Malware Education

Mostly malware is successful because it views people as its weakest link. Also, there is a rising need for cybersecurity talent, thus spreading awareness of malware safety is crucial. Malware investigation and associated courses would be trained in academic institutions both graduate and undergraduate levels. However, only a small number of schools and universities provide malware courses. This may be due to lack of fundamental topical agreement among institutions a lack of training and book providers, and the ethical difficulty of educating or producing white-hats. In addition, the majority of academic courses are practitioner concerned with rather than science or research oriented, they deeply rely on outdated textbooks. Companies and groups occasionally host training camps and workshops open to the general public, but they are incredibly expensive. The availability of online, open-access training courses will undoubtedly reduce virus harm.

7. MALWARE AVAILABLE TOOL

Network administrators have a variety of options for dealing with issues of malware: here explored some of them:

- Implementing antivirus and anti-malware software to combat threats; educating network users about technology to stop theft and data leaks, whether deliberate or not; and
- Putting regulations into place and implementing them guaranteeing the physical security of hardware strategies
- Often patching and updating the application software and operating system

A strong defence strategy must be put in place in the event of an impending danger based on real-time behavioural data analysis from your network.

7.1. Malware Detection Tools

To combat persistent network threats, a variety of detection and analysis of malware software clarifications have emerged. Millions of networks all over the world are constantly in danger from a wide variety of threats and sources. In reality, there are hundreds of attacks happening right now one every single second.

It would take proactive analysis of prior attacks and threat projection to successfully defend against such a bombardment. Administrators will only be able to fend off attackers with the support of a proactive strategy that makes use of the data that the network has already stored. A system that tracks notifies us something that goes wrong would be an efficient defence strategy.

7.1.1. Solar Winds Security Event Manager

It is a pioneer in threat mitigation and intrusion detection technologies. Its Log & Event Manager (LEM) was its previous name, and its main characteristics were:

On-premises package; Log collection and consolidation; Centralized threat hunting; Response orchestration

It is a tool with all the features needed to protect a network. With the use of a SEM, network administration and security workers are better able to identify malware or other questionable activity react to it report.

7.1.2. LogRhythm NextGen

It is a SIEM Platform Comprehensive defensive system that handles threats in a single, integrated architecture from beginning to end. It combines log management, endpoint monitoring and security analytics making an effective tool for spotting threats to preventing breaches. These are the Important Features: Online assistance; Analytics of user and object behaviour; Zero-day detection.

LogRhythm SIEM stands out from the competition thanks to a special feature called Threat Lifecycle Management. This organisation has developed a distinctive strategy for handling task with end-to-end threat treating abilities in order to sort effective in stopping and detecting threats.

7.1.3. Splunk Enterprise Security

Another SIEM solution with excellent reviews is this one. You can check out a free version to see just how fantastic a solution is. Splunk ES has won plaudits, despite the fact that you can only index 500 MBs each day. These are the Important Features: Effective analytical tool; SIEM add-on; Beneficial in hybrid environments

7.1.4. CrowdStrike Falcon

CrowdStrike Falcon is a platform for Endpoint Security (EPP). Instead of using network event data to operate it gathers event data from specific endpoints that sends to analysis engine over the network. This is a SIEM tool as a result. Each protected endpoint has an agent that acts as the activity monitor. The CrowdStrike server's analysis engine is located in the cloud. This is an on-site/cloud hybrid system. These are the Important Features: Provides a response platform; Shares endpoint event data; Protects endpoints; Cloud-based coordination; Anomaly detection.

7.1.5. Security McAfee Enterprise

Enterprise Security Manager (SEM) with McAfee comes from a numerical variety that is well-known and has been at the forefront of antivirus and anti-malware technology. There is one thing that sceptics need to take into account: The Essential

Features are: Integration challenges and issues with normalisation of information from networks, systems, databases and presentations are alleviated by using only McAfee's extensive toolkit as sources of data. Compiles McAfee Endpoint Security event data; Forecasting; Service desk integration

In addition to providing its individual implements and solutions, McAfee also facilitates normalisation of information from goods produced a large number of its business partners.

7.1.6. Micro Focus ArcSight ESM Real-Time Correlation

An initiative security manager called Micro Focus ArcSight ESM has been around for approximately 20 years. It has continued to expand and change over those years to become the absolutely incredible malware analysis and detection tool. Important characteristics: Quick processing; well-tested by prolonged use; suitable for MSSPs.

This programme can currently analyse 100,000 events per second making it one of the greatest SIEM products available. It can scale to meet any scalability requirements.

8. FEATURE RESEARCH PROSPECTS

With the increasing sophistication of cyberattacks, safeguarding physical operations requires a reliable and secure mechanism. The safe, continuous, dependable and secure industrial operations of Cyber physician system (CPS) (Yaacoub et al., 2020) require next-generation defence systems to leverage the usage of methodologies inspired by nature to achieve high accuracy and durability with low false positives (Wang et al., 2021). If Critical Infrastructure service providers adopt this method, to detect malware threats to their network in real time, automatically, and with the use of actionable intelligence. In the next stage, the researchers can try to answer:

- Researchers have not had access to benign and malicious databases. Even when available, the process used to generate these data sets is not disclosed, making replication impossible.
- There is a dearth of CPS-related malware analysis studies. In order to categorise traits that differentiate general and CPS malware, we want to analyse malware that has penetrated. If this works, could become much more stable and secure. Our research thus far also reveals that there are only a small number of publicly available CPS bound malware executables/binaries (and variants thereof). This is a more difficult task since it would result in a smaller dataset from analyses performed on fewer samples.

- Limited efforts to reduce the false positives unique to CPS, which are directly related to the risk of fatality and may be seen as counterproductive to bringing trust-level for the consumers.
- Limited or almost non-existent use of available nature-inspired metaheuristic algorithms that can be leveraged to bring optimisation in malware-detection processes.

9. CONCLUSION

The majority of the current security issues, including those involving smart and mobile devices, which become additional sophisticated and prevalent over the past few years on the internet, are being caused by malware, which has quickly grown to be a significant security threat for the computing community. Although though malware detection and analysis have received a lot of research attention, it is still a difficult task. In addition, some older solutions have poor applicability to unidentified malwares and scalability problems due to the fact that malware makers regularly hide the info in attacks or modify attacks of cyber to get around newer protection tactics. This chapter has explained the about malwares, types of malware, how it affecting the users, static malware limitations analysis, dynamic malware tools analysis that used for analyzing malicious software. Further focused on issues, challenges that facing in malware analysis and available online malware analysis tools that work on cloud.

REFERENCES

Adelstein, F., Stillerman, M., & Kozen, D. (2002). Malicious code detection for open firmware. *18th Annual Computer Security Applications Conference Proceedings*. IEEE.

Beaucamps, P. (2007). Advanced polymorphic techniques. *International Journal of Computational Science*, 2(3), 194–205.

Bergeron, J. (2001). Static detection of malicious code in executable programs. *Int. J. of Req. Eng, 79*.

Christodorescu, M., & Jha, S. (2006). *Static analysis of executables to detect malicious patterns*. Wisconsin Univ-Madison Dept of Computer Sciences. doi:10.21236/ADA449067

Elhadi, A., Maarof, M., & Osman, A. (2012). Malware detection based on hybrid signature behaviour application programming interface call graph. *American Journal of Applied Sciences 9*(3), 283.

Idika, N. & Mathur, A. (2007). *A survey of malware detection techniques*. Purdue University.

Jacob, G., Debar, H., & Filiol, E. (2008). Behavioral detection of malware: From a survey towards an established taxonomy. Journal in computer *Virology, 4*(3), 251–266.

Konstantinou, E., & Wolthusen, S. (2008). Metamorphic Virus: Analysis and Detection Technical Report. University of London.

Landage, J., & Wankhade, M. P. (2013). Malware and malware detection techniques: A survey. *International Journal of Engineering Research & Technology (Ahmedabad), 2*(12), 2278–0181.

Li, J., & Stafford, S. (2014). Detecting smart, self-propagating Internet worms. *Communications and Network Security (CNS), 2014 IEEE Conference*. IEEE.

Spafford, E. (1989). The internet worm incident. *Lecture Notes in Computer Science, 89*, 446–468. doi:10.1007/3-540-51635-2_54

Szor, P. (2005). *The art of computer virus research and defense*. Pearson Education.

Wang, Z., Xie, W., Wang, B., Tao, J., & Wang, E. (2021). A Survey on Recent Advanced Research of CPS Security. *Applied Sciences (Basel, Switzerland), 11*(9), 3751. doi:10.3390/app11093751

William, S. (2008). *Computer Security: Principles and Practice*. Pearson Education India.

Yaacoub, J.-P. A., Salman, O., Noura, H. N., Kaaniche, N., Chehab, A., & Malli, M. (2020). Cyber-physical systems security: Limitations, issues and future trends. *Microprocessors and Microsystems, 77*, 103201. doi:10.1016/j.micpro.2020.103201 PMID:32834204

Yin, H. (2007). Panorama: capturing system-wide information flow for malware detection and analysis. *Proceedings of the 14th ACM conference on Computer and communications security*. ACM. 10.1145/1315245.1315261

You, I., & Yim, K. (2010). Malware obfuscation techniques: A brief survey. *Broadband, Wireless Computing, Communication and Applications (BWCCA), 2010 International Conference on*. IEEE.

Chapter 12
Malware Analysis and Its Mitigation Tools

D. R. Janardhana
iD https://orcid.org/0000-0002-1652-4322
Nitte Meenakshi Institute of Technology, Bengaluru, India & Visvesvaraya Technological University, Belagavi, India

A. P. Manu
PES Institute of Technology and Management, Shivamogga, India & Visvesvaraya Technological University, Belagavi, India

K. Shivanna
iD https://orcid.org/0000-0001-8127-4545
Malnad College of Engineering, India

K. C. Suhas
Channabasaveshwara Institute of Technology, India

ABSTRACT

In the present digital era, most of our communication and personal sensitive information are transmitted through smart devices and stored on them. Therefore, it becomes imperative to secure both the device and the data from various security and privacy threats. These threats aim to gain unauthorized access to the data, or worse, destroy it. This chapter presents an overview of malware analysis and its mitigation tools. Malware has become a serious threat to computer systems and networks, and it is important to understand how to analyze and mitigate the risks associated with it. Here, the authors discuss malware and its classification, as well as various techniques used in malware analysis, including static and dynamic analysis. The chapter also presents an overview of the mitigation tools available to prevent and detect malware, including antivirus software, firewalls, intrusion detection systems, and sandboxes. Furthermore, the chapter highlights some of the limitations of these tools and provides insights into the future direction of malware analysis and mitigation.

DOI: 10.4018/978-1-6684-8666-5.ch012

INTRODUCTION

Malware attacks are becoming more frequent, and new, advanced varieties are being created daily. These assaults have the potential to do a great deal of harm, including data theft and destruction, monetary losses, and reputational harm. Malware analysis tools are useful for analysing the structure and behaviour of malware attacks to detect and mitigate them (Aboaoja et al., 2022). Malware analysis tools are sophisticated programmes that can look through and evaluate malware to ascertain its features and activity. In this paper, we examine the capabilities of various malware analysis tools.

Tools for Malware Analysis: These programmes' main purpose is to locate and examine malware. Static, dynamic, and hybrid analysis tools are three categories into which these tools can be divided.

- **Static Analysis Tools:** Without running the malicious code, static analysis tools analyse it. These tools analyse the structure of the malware to look for patterns and signatures that can be used to identify it. They can also identify the routines and API calls the infection employs, which can provide insight into its behaviour. Examples of static analysis tools are IDA Pro, Ghidra, and Radare2.
- **Dynamic Analysis Tools:** To investigate malware, it is launched in a sandbox or virtual system, which is a controlled environment. These tools can follow the behaviour of the infection and expose its network activities, system calls, and file modifications. Dynamic analysis approaches might provide a more complete picture of the behaviour of the malware than static analysis techniques. For example, dynamic analysis tools like FireEye, VMRay Analyzer, and Cuckoo Sandbox.
- **Hybrid Analysis Tools:** These tools integrate the capabilities of static and dynamic analysis tools. These tools could analyse the malware code and execute it in a controlled environment to provide a full understanding of the infection's activities. Hybrid analysis methods can provide a more detailed investigation of the malware than static or dynamic analysis tools alone. Examples of hybrid analytic tools are Reversing Labs Titanium Platform, Symantec Advanced Threat Protection, and McAfee Advanced Threat Defence.
- **Evaluation Standards:** Functionality, usability, and efficacy are three factors that are considered when evaluating the malware analysis programme. Functionality describes a tool's capacities, including the types of analyses it can conduct and the volume of data it can handle. Usability is the ability of a tool to be used effectively and to integrate with other tools and systems.

Effectiveness refers to the tool's capacity to identify and analyse malware as well as the reliability of its conclusions.

BACKGROUND

Malware analysis is the process of looking at malicious software, also referred to as malware, to understand its nature, function, and potential effects. Malware (Komatwar R. & Kokare, M. 2021), which can include viruses (Vermisoglou E. et al., 2020), worms, trojan horses, spyware, and ransomware, is designed to damage, steal, or seize control of the victim's computer system or data.

To identify and lessen the risks that are posed by dangerous software, malware analysis is performed. Malware analysis can be carried out using a variety of methods, including static analysis, dynamic analysis, hybrid analysis, machine learning-based methods (Akhtar, M. S. & Feng, T. 2023) (Qiu J et al., 2020), deep learning methods (Yadav, C. S. et al., 2022), vinayakumar R et al., 2019, and other approaches (Chakkaravarthy et al. These methods entail analysing malware's code and activity to determine its functioning, traits, and potential effects (Gaurav et al., 2022). Mitigation tools (Barsha, F. L., and Shahriar, H. 2023) aim to stop or reduce the harm that malware can do. Some of these tools include firewalls, antivirus programmes, intrusion detection and prevention systems, and sandboxing tools. Antivirus software finds and deletes known infections, whereas intrusion detection and prevention systems monitor network traffic for unusual activity and block or alert administrators of potential attacks. Sandboxing techniques isolate potentially malicious software to prevent it from doing harm, and firewalls prevent unauthorised users from accessing a system or network.

For many years, malware has been developed along with tools to counteract it. The threat posed by malware has increased with the proliferation of the internet and computer technology (Alzaylaee et al., 2020), which has sparked the creation of more complicated and advanced malware (Kara, I., & Aydos, M. 2022) and mitigation solutions. The effectiveness of malware analysis and mitigation systems is always being worked on by researchers and developers to lessen the risks that malicious software poses (Venkatasubramanian M. et al., 2023).

Static Malware Analysis Tools

There are various static malware analysis tools available. Some of these tools are listed below:

- **IDA ProA:** IDA Pro is the name of a popular disassembler and decompiler tool used in reverse engineering. Software engineers, malware analysts, and security researchers frequently utilise it to examine and comprehend how computer systems and software programmes operate. Code from a variety of systems and architectures, such as x86, ARM, PowerPC, MIPS, and others, can be disassembled and decompiled using IDA Pro. Users can browse and examine code that has been disassembled, find functions and subroutines, and explore data structures and constants.

However, because of its complicated user interface and the technical nature of reverse engineering, IDA Pro can be difficult for beginners to use. Additionally, a licence is needed to utilise the software, which can be costly for individual users or small businesses.

- **Ghidra:** The National Security Agency (NSA) created Ghidra, a potent and cost-free reverse engineering tool, and made it available to the public in 2019. It is a software decompiler and disassembler that can be used to examine software programmes and computer systems, uncover security holes, and do forensic analysis (Kumar, M. 2022). Ghidra's potential for collaborative analysis, which enables numerous users to work on a single project, is a standout feature. When several analysts are working together on the same project in a team setting, this might be helpful.

Ghidra has the advantage of being open source and free, making it available to anyone who wants to use it. Comparatively speaking, alternative reverse engineering tools might need a licence or be prohibitively expensive for small businesses or individual users.

- **Radare2:** The powerful and open-source Radare2 reverse engineering framework, which is available for free, offers a number of tools for evaluating and comprehending software programmes and computer systems. It functions as a disassembler, debugger, and hex editor and may be used to reverse engineer software, find security flaws, do forensic analysis, and more. The capacity of Radare2 to analyse code from a variety of platforms and architectures, including as x86, ARM, MIPS, PowerPC, and others, is well recognised. Both static and dynamic analyses are carried out using Radare2. In other words, it can assess software programmes both before and during execution, enabling users to spot any security flaws.
- **OllyDbg:** OllyDbg is a popular and free open-source debugger for the Windows platform. Security researchers, malware analysts, and software

developers frequently utilise it since it is largely used for reverse engineering and evaluating software applications. OllyDbg analyses software programmes both statically and dynamically.

Debugging capabilities including breakpoint management, register and memory dump analysis, and disassembly and decomplication tools are also included in OllyDbg. These instruments can be used to inspect and update software applications as well as identify security flaws.

- **Hopper Disassembler:** For the macOS and Linux operating systems, there is a commercial disassembler and decompiler called Hopper Disassembler. Reverse engineering and software application analysis are its main uses. A variety of debugging tools are also included with Hopper Disassembler, including breakpoints, stack and register analysis, and memory dump analysis. These instruments can be used to assess and fix software programmes as well as look for security flaws.

Hopper Disassembler is a paid tool, which may prevent certain individuals or small businesses from using it. Its Linux platform support is also less comprehensive than its support for the macOS platform.

- **Binary Ninja:** x86, ARM, MIPS, PowerPC, and other architectures and file formats are supported by the commercial disassembler and reverse engineering platform known as Binary Ninja. Cross-referencing, data-flow analysis, and control-flow graph visualisation are just a few of Binary Ninja's well-known advanced analytic features. These tools make it simpler to comprehend how software applications function by quickly identifying and analysing the code and data structures that make up the programme. A selection of debugging tools, including as breakpoints, stack and register analysis, and memory dump analysis, are also included with Binary Ninja.
- **PEiD:** The free and well-known PEiD (Portable Executable Identifier) programme is used to find compilers, packers, and other code obfuscation methods in Windows executables. To determine whether an executable file has been packed or protected, it consults a database of well-known packers and signatures.

Being able to tell whether an executable file has been altered or if it contains malicious code makes PEiD a valuable tool for malware analysis and reverse engineering. It is also possible to utilise it to determine the packer that was used to compress the executable, which may then be used to select the appropriate tools and techniques to use while attempting to analyse or reverse engineer the file. An executable file can be swiftly scanned, and information on packing and protection can be provided.

- **ExeinfoPE:** A free and compact programme called ExeinfoPE is used to find and examine executable files on Windows computers. The type of file, file header information, and whether or not the file is compressed or encrypted are just a few of the many characteristics of executable files that it can recognise.

One of ExeinfoPE's main advantages is its ability to recognise various packers, crypters, and other code obfuscation techniques. It is a helpful tool for malware research and reverse engineering since it uses a combination of signature scanning and heuristic analysis to discover these strategies.

- **VirusTotal:** The free web service VirusTotal allows users to analyse files and URLs for potential malware infestations using a variety of antivirus engines and other analytical tools. Security experts, researchers, and others who want to guarantee the security of their files and websites frequently utilise it because it is owned by Google.

To use VirusTotal, users merely need to upload a file or enter a URL into the website's scanning interface. The service will then check the file or URL using more than 70 antivirus engines as well as other methods like machine learning algorithms, behavioural analysis, and signature-based detection. Users can immediately determine if a file or URL is safe or not thanks to Virus Total's analysis results being given in a simple and easy-to-understand style. If a file is found to contain malware, VirusTotal will alert the user of the sort of malware found and provide links to resources for its removal.

Table 1 provides the summary of the static analysis tools and its advantages and disadvantages.

Dynamic Malware Analysis Tools

There is various dynamic malware analysis (Or-Meir O et al., 2019) tools available. Some of these tools are listed below.

- **Cuckoo Sandbox:** To automatically assess unknown files and operations, Cuckoo Sandbox is an open-source malware analysis tool. It enables malware behaviour studies by security researchers and analysts in a safe and controlled environment.

Table 1. Static Malware analysis tools and its description

Tool	Summary	Pros	Cons
IDA ProA	A potent debugger and disassembler for binary code analysis.	- Powerful analytical ability -Supports a variety of file types and architectures - An ecosystem of plugins for extensibility	cost-prohibitive commercial licence
Ghidra	NSA-developed package of open-source tools for reverse engineering software.	- Supports a variety of architectures and file types; free and open-source - Teamwork-enhancing features in collaborative mode	The learning curve is steeper than some commercially available tools.
Radare2	A command-line interface-based disassembler and debugger that is free and open-source.	-Free and open-source - Support for multiple platforms - Capable in writing a potent scripting	CLI is not user friendly
OllyDbg	It is used for revers engineering applications and analysis purpose using a window debugger	- An intuitive interface - Features for dynamic debugging - Excellent support for Windows executables	There are no updates for the new versions of windows.
Hopper Disassembler	A tool for decompiling and disassembling executables that is used in reverse engineering.	- Supports a variety of file types and architectures. - Offers decompilation as well as disassembly. - An intuitive interface	Accuracy will vary according to the code complexity
Binary Ninja	A business-oriented reverse engineering tool with a binary analysis focus.	- Features for advanced analysis - Handles a different kind of files and architectures - An ecosystem of extensions for extensibility	Cost effective
PEiD	A device for identifying compilers, packers, and cryptors in Windows executables.	- Simple to use interface. specialised for detecting packers and compilers. - Adepts multiple signature databases	Beyond the signature-based detection support is limited
ExeinfoPE	A tool for identifying compilers, packers, and cryptors in Windows executables.	- Lists different packers and compilers - An easy-to-use interface - Offers more details regarding the executable	Beyond the signature-based detection capabilities are limited
VirusTotal	A cloud-based tool that performs static analysis, checks files and URLs for viruses, and scans them with a variety of antivirus engines	- Makes use of several antivirus engines - Quick and simple method of scanning files for malware - A quick and simple method of detecting malware in files - Offers more details about the file, such as behavioural analysis	Depends mainly on signature based detection and not able to detect Zero-day malware.

Cuckoo Sandbox handles the suspicious file or URL in a simulated environment to track and evaluate its activity. The utility then generates a detailed report of the malware's activities, including any network traffic generated, any newly created or edited files, and any system modifications made. The Cuckoo Sandbox can be expanded and altered. It can be coupled with a wide range of virtualization platforms, network analysis tools, and virus analysis tools, to name a few. Users can therefore alter the tool to meet their unique needs and preferences.

The community-driven development of Cuckoo Sandbox is another advantage, and it benefits from contributions from a global community of developers and security experts who work to continuously enhance its features and functionalities because it is an open-source application. A web-based interface is also a part of Cuckoo Sandbox, which enables users to easily prepare, launch, and administer malware analyses as well as see and manage analysis data. Users may easily discover the most important details regarding the behaviours and effects of the infection using a variety of visualisation tools that are included in the interface.

- **Wireshark:** The widely used open-source Wireshark network protocol analyzer tool allows users to record and evaluate network data in real-time. It can be used to assess network security, address network issues, and investigate incidents by involving networks. Wireshark records network traffic and provides it in an understandable format so that users can inspect and explain the data (Liu K et al., 2020; Qiu J et al., 2020). The programme can gather traffic from a variety of sources, including Ethernet, Wi-Fi, and Bluetooth, and it supports a number of protocols, including TCP/IP, HTTP, DNS, and FTP.

Users may swiftly isolate and evaluate particular packets or network flows thanks to its robust filtering and search capability. A number of sophisticated capabilities are also included in Wireshark, such as the ability to examine VoIP and multimedia data as well as support for collecting and decrypting encrypted traffic.

- **Process Monitor:** Users can monitor system processes, as well as follow file and registry activity in real-time, thanks to a powerful Windows utility tool called Process Monitor. Performance, security, and application compatibility issues can be fixed using it.

Process Monitor operates by keeping track of system operations and logging activities involving files and registries (Omer, M. 2021). It records specific information about each event, such as the process that caused it, the location of the file or registry entry, and the nature of the operation. This information can be utilised to diagnose issues with file and registry access as well as performance and compatibility issues with applications. Other Windows programmes and utilities can be integrated with it. It can be combined with additional system diagnostic and troubleshooting tools, such Process Explorer, and the Windows Performance Toolkit, to give a thorough overview of system activity and performance.

- **Fiddler:** The web debugging proxy tool Fiddler may record, analyse, and change an HTTP and HTTPS conversation between a client and server. Problems with services, APIs, and web applications can be identified using it.

When a client and server exchange web traffic, Fiddler intercepts it and records it. It records every request and return in detail, including headers, cookies, and query strings. A web-based interface for studying and altering requests and responses is one of the many tools included for inspecting and editing the gathered data.

- **ApateDNS:** ApateDNS is a free, community-driven, and open-source tool that allows users to mimic various DNS-related attacks for the purposes of testing and verifying. It can be used to assess the effectiveness of security measures as well as detect and fix DNS-related security issues.

By intercepting and rerouting DNS requests, ApateDNS simulates many types of DNS attacks, including DNS spoofing, DNS cache poisoning, and DNS tunnelling. It also offers tools for logging and analysing DNS data, as well as a range of adjustable options for tailoring how the simulated assaults are carried out.

It may be used on any platform that supports Python and is easily integrated with other security testing tools and scripts. Additionally, it has instruments for assessing the effectiveness of DNS-based security measures like DNSSEC and DNS filtering.

- **VMRay Analyzer:** A malware analysis software called VMRay Analyzer was created to offer consumers a quick and precise examination of malware. It provides a thorough report on malware behaviours and its effects on a system using a combination of virtual machine technologies and behavioural analysis methodologies.

VMRay Analyzer builds a virtual environment to execute the malware in a safe and secure setting. Then, it monitors the actions of the malware, such as file system changes, network activities, and system modifications, to provide a full analysis report. The platform uses several behavioural analysis techniques, including as machine learning and memory analysis, to pinpoint malware activity and produce an accurate report.

VMRay Analyzer also has features like precise reporting and quick malware analysis. Additionally, it could recognise even the most sophisticated malware and provide details about the virus's activity that may be used to strengthen a company's security measures. The VMRay Analyzer is both flexible and scalable.

- **Sysinternals Suite:** The Sysinternals Suite is a collection of innovative, cost-free system utilities and diagnostic tools for Microsoft Windows operating systems. It was initially developed by Mark Russinovich and Bryce Cogswell, and Microsoft later bought it.

Numerous utilities and tools are included in the Sysinternals Suite, which is meant to assist users in managing and troubleshooting Windows systems. Process Explorer, which offers thorough details on active processes and system efficiency, and Autoruns, which enables users to control startup programmes and services, are two of the suite's more well-known utilities. Other tools in the package include TCPView, which offers a thorough examination of TCP and UDP connections, Regmon, which monitors registry activity, and Filemon, which continuously keeps track of file system activities. Additionally, there are tools for diagnosing system crashes, such as Bluescreen View, and tools for tracking down and assessing system performance, such as Process Monitor.

- **Burp Suite:** Burp Suite is an all-inclusive tool for controlling vulnerabilities and evaluating the security of web applications. Security professionals, penetration testers, and developers regularly use this tool to find and patch vulnerabilities in web applications.

Among the tools in the package are a proxy server, a web crawler, a scanner, and several modules for intercepting, altering, and analysing web traffic. The proxy server enables users to intercept and alter requests and replies between the client and the server, whereas the spider can be used to scan a web application and learn about its operation and structure. The various modules give additional functions like session management, brute-force testing, and encoding and decoding. The scanner can be used to discover gaps and weak spots in the online application.

- **FireEye:** Modern cyberthreats can be found, stopped, and countered using a number of technologies provided by the cybersecurity firm FireEye. It is well known for its expertise in threat intelligence, incident response, and malware analysis.

Table 2. Dynamic malware analysis tools and its description

Tool	Summary	Pros	Cons
Cuckoo Sandbox	An automated malware analysis tool that is open source, runs files in a safe environment, and keeps track of how they behave.	- Offers malware behavioural analysis - Enables dynamic malware behaviour analysis - Integrates with various tools and systems	More tedious task for configuration and its setup process
Wireshark	It Analyses the network traffic by capturing the traffic patterns	- Strong network packet analysis tool - Supports a variety of protocols - Offers thorough explanations of network communication	For beginners, Learning curve is steeper.
Process Monitor	It monitors the system activity, including file system, registry, and process/thread operations, using a Windows application.	- Aids in spotting malware activity and system modifications by recording in-depth information about system occurrences - Capabilities for real-time monitoring and filtering	It collects large amount of data and analysis process makes more complex
Fiddler	A proxy tool for web debugging that records and examines the HTTP/HTTPS traffic between a client and server.	-aids in the analysis and troubleshooting of web traffic provide thorough details about requests, replies, and headers, supports extensions and unique scripts	Analysis is limited to HTTP/HTTPS
ApateDNS	A DNS server emulator that can divert DNS requests to a regulated setting enables the investigation of malware sample network activity.	- Facilitates study of malware's DNS-related operations - Offers a restricted environment for DNS analysis - Simple to set up and use	Analysis is restricted only to DNS related
VMRay Analyzer	Static and dynamic analysis methods are combined by an automated malware analysis platform to find and evaluate risks.	- Advanced threat detection and analysis is available. - Provides detailed insights into the traits and behaviour of malware - Works in conjunction with other security systems and technologies	Business licence is required
Sysinternals Suite	Microsoft created a set of Windows applications to help monitor and troubleshoot Windows systems.	- provides a variety of tools for system analysis, monitoring, and troubleshooting that assist in spotting malicious activity and system changes. - Highly regarded and widely applied in the sector	Compatibility issue with newer versions of windows
Burp Suite	Various modules for scanning, intercepting, and modifying HTTP/HTTPS requests and responses are included in this web application security testing tool.	- Full-featured web application security testing tool - Provides strong functionality for locating vulnerabilities and evaluating security measures - Offers in-depth studies and vulnerability assessments	For beginners, Learning curve is steeper.
FireEye	Comprehensive security suite including detection, analysis, and mitigation tools.	- Offers sophisticated threat detection and analysis abilities - Provides a variety of security-related goods and services. - Complements existing security systems and technologies with threat intelligence	Alternatives available on the market, with costs

One of FireEye's highlight offerings is its advanced threat intelligence platform, which uses machine learning and artificial intelligence to assess and identify emerging threats in real time. This technology can help with proactive security against cyberattacks by providing organisations with early warning of potential hazards.

Among FireEye's other products and services are network security solutions, endpoint security solutions, and cloud security solutions. Some of its network security solutions include next-generation firewalls, intrusion detection and prevention systems, and email security gateways. Some of its endpoint security offerings include advanced endpoint protection, threat hunting, and incident response services.

Table 2 provides the summary of Dynamic analysis tools and its advantages and disadvantages.

Hybrid Malware Analysis Tools

Here are a few tools mentioned below that perform both static and dynamic analysis (Venkatraman S. et al., 2019).

- **Sandboxie:** A computer's virtual "sandbox," created by the software package Sandboxie, allows users to execute programmes and access the internet without impacting the operating system that is underneath. Users can test out new software or browse potentially dangerous websites without worrying about their system being harmed because the sandbox is meant to isolate any modifications made to the system by the programmes operating within it.

The ability of Sandboxie to give an additional layer of security against malware and other harmful software is one of its main advantages. When programmes are contained within a sandbox, any modifications they make will only impact the sandbox rather than the underlying system. This can provide a secure environment for running programmes with unknown sources and can also assist to stop malware from propagating to other areas of the system.

- **ThreatAnalyzer:** Sophisticated tool called ThreatAnalyzer is used to analyse and find harmful activity in computer systems. Investigators and security experts are the main users of it to recognise and comprehend dangers to computer networks and systems.

Analysis of malware and other possibly dangerous files is one of ThreatAnalyzer's primary features. From executable files, the software can recognise and extract the code, which it may then examine for any unusual behaviour. This may entail keeping an eye out for behaviours that are frequently linked to malware, such as efforts to change system files or create network connections to distant services.

ThreatAnalyzer can be used to find vulnerabilities in computer systems in addition to studying malware. The software is able to examine system setups and spot any vulnerabilities that an attacker might use. This might involve flaws in operating systems, programmes, and other software parts.

- **Falcon Sandbox:** A cloud-based malware analysis platform called Falcon Sandbox is made to identify and analyse malware in real-time. It is an excellent tool used by security experts and researchers to quickly discover and address risks related to malware.

Falcon Sandbox's capability to analyse files and URLs for malware is one of its primary capabilities. The programme employs several cutting-edge methods, such as static and dynamic analysis, behavioural analysis, and machine learning algorithms, to spot suspicious activities. As a result, it can recognise even the trickiest and highly complex malware attacks.

Falcon Sandbox is also very scalable, enabling users to assess many files and URLs swiftly and effectively. The time needed to analyse vast amounts of data is decreased by the software's ability to conduct numerous analysis operations concurrently.

- **Deep Discovery Analyzer:** A network security tool called Deep Discovery Analyzer is made to identify and evaluate sophisticated threats in real-time. It is an effective technique for immediately identifying and neutralising emerging risks. The Deep Discovery Analyzer was capable of real-time network traffic analysis. Advanced machine learning techniques are used by the programme to spot suspicious activity, such as efforts to exfiltrate data or create unauthorised network connections. This enables us to identify even the most complex and elusive threats, such as sophisticated persistent hazards and zero-day attacks.

Table 3 describes the hybrid malware analysis tools and its advantages and disadvantages.

Table 3. Hybrid malware analysis tools and its description

Tools	Summary	Pros	Cons
Sandboxie	Sandboxing is a method of isolation that keeps apps from permanently altering the system by putting them in a controlled environment.	- Malware is prevented from infecting the host system by providing a secure environment for the execution of potentially harmful files. - It is also simple to use and setup.	- Only permitted to use the sandbox to run programmes
Threat Analyzer	Static and dynamic analysis methods are combined by an automated malware analysis platform to find and evaluate risks.	- Provides sophisticated threat detection and analysis abilities - Integrates with various security products and systems and offers detailed insights into malware behaviour	Business licence is required
Falcon Sandbox	Automatic cloud-based malware analysis tool that runs files in a sandbox to observe their behaviour.	- Allows for dynamic malware examination in a safe, isolated environment - Offers behavioural analysis and detects malicious activity - Scalable and capable of handling high volume of malware samples.	For analysis network connection is essential.
Deep Discovery Analyzer	Platform for advanced threat detection and analysis that uses a number of methods to recognise and address targeted assaults.	- Enables complete threat evaluation and identification capabilities - Provides network-wide visibility and sophisticated threat detection - Works with various security tools and systems	Business licence is required

Malware Mitigation Tools

There are some potential malware mitigation tools listed below to prevent malware from spreading across computing devices and networks.

- **Antivirus software:** Computers and other electronic devices are protected from viruses and other security hazards by using antivirus software's. It will depend on a number of factors, including capability, usability, and cost, to determine the best antivirus programme to use. Here are a few well-known instances of antivirus software:
  - **Norton Antivirus:** The organisation that created the well-known antivirus programme Norton Antivirus is called Norton LifeLock. It offers continuing protection against viruses, spyware, malware, and

other internet dangers. Norton Antivirus offers defence against spam, phishing, and online identity theft among its many features.

- **McAfee Antivirus:** Created by McAfee LLC, McAfee Antivirus is antivirus software. Malware, spyware, and other security dangers are all supplied with real-time defence. McAfee Antivirus has a number of features, including email protection, a firewall, and online security.

- **Kaspersky Antivirus:** Kaspersky Lab created the well-known antivirus application Kaspersky Antivirus. It provides protection from malware, spyware, and other internet threats. Kaspersky Antivirus offers features like network protection, parental settings, and real-time scanning.

- **Avast Antivirus:** The antivirus application Avast Antivirus was created by Avast Software. It offers continuing protection against viruses, spyware, malware, and other internet dangers. A firewall, internet security, and email protection are among the features provided by Avast Antivirus.

- **Bitdefender Antivirus:** Bitdefender is a producer of antivirus programmes. It provides protection from viruses, spyware, malware, and other internet threats. Bitdefender Antivirus offers a wide range of features, including ransomware defence, anti-phishing, and internet security.

- **AVG Antivirus:** AVG Technologies created antivirus software. It offers constant protection against spyware, malware, and other security threats. Among its many features, AVG Antivirus offers a firewall, online security, and email protection.

- **Firewall:** A firewall is a network security tool that monitors and controls both incoming and outgoing network traffic based on previously specified security rules. Firewalls are essential for preventing unauthorised access and security hazards on networks. The following features, as well as ease of use and affordability, should be found in the finest firewall software. A few well-known examples of firewall software are provided below:

  - **Cisco ASA:** Cisco Systems created the well-known firewall programme known as Cisco ASA (Adaptive Security Appliance). Content filtering, VPNs, and intrusion prevention are among the security features it provides.

  - **PfSense:** The open-source firewall programme PfSense can be installed on a physical or virtual system. It contains features like traffic shaping, VPN, and numerous WAN ports.

  - **Fortinet FortiGate:** A firewall programme with several features, such as Fortinet FortiGate, can perform antivirus, anti-spam, and web filtering functions. It also provides safe remote access and application control.

- ○ **Check Point Firewall:** A well-known firewall programme with features like VPN, application control, and intrusion prevention is Check Point Firewall. Furthermore, it offers sophisticated threat protection capabilities, such as Sandblast technology.
- ○ **SonicWall Firewall:** SonicWall Inc. created the firewall application called as SonicWall Firewall. Content filtering, a VPN, and intrusion detection are among the functions it provides. Along with comprehensive threat security measures, it also offers application control.
- ○ **Windows Firewall:** Windows Firewall is a firewall application that comes with Microsoft Windows. It provides basic protection against both incoming and outgoing traffic, and it can be configured to enable application connectivity.

- **IPS, or intrusion prevention system:** An intrusion prevention system (IPS), a type of network security device, monitors network traffic to spot and thwart prospective security threats. For real-time detection and prevention of intrusion attempts, IPS monitors network data and compares it to known attack patterns. Some well-known IPS examples are provided below:
  - ○ **Snort:** Cisco Systems created the well-known open-source IPS application Snort. When identifying unknown dangers, it uses anomaly-based detection, and when identifying known threats, it uses signature-based detection.
  - ○ **Suricata:** Suricata is a state-of-the-art intrusion prevention system (IPS) that is open-source. It utilises multi-threaded packet processing to evaluate network traffic and offers support for a number of protocols, including HTTP, SMTP, and DNS.
  - ○ **Cisco Firepower:** An all-encompassing intrusion prevention system (IPS), Cisco Firepower offers cutting-edge threat detection tools like network sandboxing and machine learning-based detection. It also offers VPN and application control capabilities.
  - ○ **Palo Alto Networks IPS:** A business named Palo Alto Networks developed this programme. It offers powerful threat detection tools like machine learning-based detection and behavioural analysis. It also enables integration with other Palo Alto Networks security products.
  - ○ **Fortinet IPS:** Fortinet created the IPS programme known as Fortinet IPS. Among the sophisticated threat detection technologies it provides are sandboxing and machine learning-based threat detection. Integration with additional Fortinet security solutions is additionally offered.
  - ○ **McAfee Network Security Platform:** The IPS programme known as the McAfee Network Security Platform was made by McAfee. There are sophisticated threat detection methods available, including signature-

based and behavior-based detection. Another aspect is the compatibility with other McAfee security products.

- ○ **Application control:** This security measure prevents unauthorised programmes from being run on a computer system. It can prevent malware from executing on a computer system by limiting the types of software that can be executed.

- Patch management is the discipline of putting new software into place to fix vulnerabilities and improve a computer system's safety. Software updates can prevent malware from exploiting vulnerabilities.

  - ○ **Device management:** Device control software, among other things, is used to govern the operation of USB drives and other external devices. It can halt the spread of infection via removable storage devices.

  - ○ **Encryption:** Encryption is the process of converting data into a format that can only be read with a decryption key. Encryption helps to protect sensitive data from unauthorised access and intentional data theft.

  - ○ **Backup and disaster recovery:** Backup and disaster recovery solutions are used to create backups of data and systems in the case of a virus infestation or other disaster. Data can be recovered using routine backups in the case of a malware attack.

Table 4 provides the details about the new and existing tools to analyse malwares and its various applications with efficacy.

FUTURE RESEARCH DIRECTIONS

Future research around malware analysis and mitigation technologies will take a number of different paths. A few of these are:

- **Advanced malware analysis methods:** As malware becomes more complex, it will require new and advanced methods of analysis. Researchers can investigate novel approaches to malware analysis that can handle sophisticated evasion strategies, code obfuscation, and polymorphism.

- **Machine learning-based approaches:** Malware identification and classification have shown to offer a lot of potential for machine learning-based techniques. In the future, malware analysis and mitigation may make use of deep learning and other cutting-edge machine learning techniques.

- **Malware analysis in the IoT:** As IoT devices proliferate, it is necessary to develop malware analysis and mitigation methods specifically for these gadgets. The development of specialist tools and approaches for IoT devices,

Table 4. New and existing tools to analyse malware and its efficacy

Tool	Description	Applications	Efficacy
Xori	Automates the extraction and analysis of macros, embedded objects, and VBA code from dangerous Excel documents.	Excel-based malware analysis	High
MASTIFF	A framework for static analysis that may be used to examine numerous file types, such as executables, documents, and multimedia files.	Static file analysis to find typical malware indicators	High
ViperMonkey	A Python toolbox with de-obfuscation and detection features for examining dangerous macros in Office documents.	Office macros' embedded code is examined and extracted	High
YARA	A tool that matches patterns to identify and categorise malware according to predetermined rules.	Detection and classification of known malware using signatures	High
Binee	A platform for automated malware analysis that uses both static and dynamic analysis methods to find and describe malware.	Advanced malware threats are identified through behavioural analysis.	High
Radare2	A debugger and disassembler for binary code analysis that is open-source and supports a variety of file formats and architectures.	Binary reverse engineering and low-level analysis	High
DRAKVUF Sandbox	A dynamic malware analysis tool that executes malware in a regulated setting while recording and examining system-level actions.	Behavioural analysis, keeping an eye on how malware behaves, and looking for evasion methods	High
CuckooDroid	A Cuckoo Sandbox add-on made especially for examining Android malware.	Investigating specific malware artefacts and analysing general malware to spot harmful activity on the Android platform.	High
Remnux	Automates the extraction and analysis of macros, embedded objects, and VBA code from dangerous Excel documents.	Quick file scanning, malware detection, and threat intelligence driven by the community	High
VirusTotal	A framework for static analysis that may be used to examine numerous file types, such as executables, documents, and multimedia files.	Excel-based malware analysis	Moderate to High

which can have constrained resources and computing capacity, can be the subject of future study.

- **Real-time malware analysis:** With the emergence of sophisticated malware, it is crucial to analyse malware in real-time to stop it from doing harm.

Future studies can look on real-time malware analysis methods that can catch malware as it's happening and react to it.

- **Collaborative analysis:** Attackers can change malware to evade detection by conventional malware analysis approaches. Malware frequently targets several computers. Future studies may look towards the usage of collaborative analysis, in which several systems study malware together and share data to enhance detection and mitigation.

- **Zero-day attack mitigation strategies:** Attacks that are referred to as "zero-day" take use of vulnerabilities that have not yet been found or fixed. Future research can focus on developing mitigation techniques that can protect systems from zero-day attacks by identifying and neutralising them prior to any damage being done.

Overall, since malware is continually evolving and becoming more complex, future research should concentrate on creating novel and cutting-edge tools and methods to increase the efficiency of malware analysis and mitigation.

CONCLUSION

Malware analysis is a crucial step in identifying and reducing the threats that malicious software poses. To ascertain the function and potential consequences of malware, its behaviour and traits must be analysed. Numerous methods, including static and dynamic analysis, hybrid approaches, and machine learning-based approaches, can be used to analyse malware. Code obfuscation, polymorphism, and evasion strategies are just a few of the difficulties in malware analysis that can make it challenging to identify and analyse malware. To get around these issues and boost the efficiency of malware analysis and mitigation, researchers are constantly creating new tools and methods. Mitigation tools are intended to stop or reduce the harm that malware can do. Among these tools are firewalls, intrusion detection and prevention systems, antivirus software, and sandboxing tools. Although mitigation techniques are helpful in defending systems from malware, they are not impenetrable, and there is always a chance that brand-new, undiscovered malware will get past these defences.

In general, malware mitigation and analysis are essential to safeguarding computer systems from the potential harm that malicious software can do. Along with continued research and education, the creation of new tools and methods can enhance the efficiency of these procedures and lessen the dangers that malware poses.

REFERENCES

Aboaoja, F. A., Zainal, A., Ghaleb, F. A., Al-rimy, B. A. S., Eisa, T. A. E., & Elnour, A. A. H. (2022). Malware detection issues, challenges, and future directions: A survey. *Applied Sciences (Basel, Switzerland), 12*(17), 8482. doi:10.3390/app12178482

Akhtar, M. S., & Feng, T. (2023). Evaluation of Machine Learning Algorithms for Malware Detection. *Sensors (Basel), 23*(2), 946. doi:10.339023020946 PMID:36679741

Alzaylaee, M. K., Yerima, S. Y., & Sezer, S. (2020). DL-Droid: Deep learning based android malware detection using real devices. *Computers & Security, 89*, 101663. doi:10.1016/j.cose.2019.101663

Barsha, F. L., & Shahriar, H. (2023). Mitigation of Malware Using Artificial Intelligence Techniques: A Literature Review. *Security Engineering for Embedded and Cyber-Physical Systems*, 221–234.

Chakkaravarthy, S. S., Sangeetha, D., & Vaidehi, V. (2019). A survey on malware analysis and mitigation techniques. *Computer Science Review, 32*, 1–23. doi:10.1016/j.cosrev.2019.01.002

Gaurav, A., Gupta, B. B., & Panigrahi, P. K. (2022). A comprehensive survey on machine learning approaches for malware detection in IoT-based enterprise information system. *Enterprise Information Systems*, 1–25.

Kara, I., & Aydos, M. (2022). The rise of ransomware: Forensic analysis for windows-based ransomware attacks. *Expert Systems with Applications, 190*, 116198. doi:10.1016/j.eswa.2021.116198

Komatwar, R., & Kokare, M. (2021). A Survey on Malware Detection and Classification. *Journal of Applied Security Research, 16*(3), 390–420. doi:10.1080/19361610.2020.1796162

Kumar, M. (2022). Scalable malware detection system using big data and distributed machine learning approach. *Soft Computing, 26*(8), 3987–4003. doi:10.100700500-021-06492-9

Liu, K., Xu, S., Xu, G., Zhang, M., Sun, D., & Liu, H. (2020). A review of android malware detection approaches based on machine learning. *IEEE Access : Practical Innovations, Open Solutions, 8*, 124579–124607. doi:10.1109/ACCESS.2020.3006143

Omer, M. A., Zeebaree, S. R. M., Sadeeq, M. A. M., Salim, B. W., Rashid, Z. N., & Haji, L. M. (2021). Efficiency of malware detection in android system: A survey. *Asian Journal of Research in Computer Science*, *7*(4), 59–69. doi:10.9734/ajrcos/2021/v7i430189

Or-Meir, O., Nissim, N., Elovici, Y., & Rokach, L. (2019). Dynamic malware analysis in the modern era—A state of the art survey. *ACM Computing Surveys*, *52*(5), 1–48. doi:10.1145/3329786

Qiu, J., Zhang, J., Luo, W., Pan, L., Nepal, S., & Xiang, Y. (2020). A survey of android malware detection with deep neural models. *ACM Computing Surveys*, *53*(6), 1–36. doi:10.1145/3417978

Qiu, J., Zhang, J., Luo, W., Pan, L., Nepal, S., & Xiang, Y. (2020). A survey of android malware detection with deep neural models. *ACM Computing Surveys*, *53*(6), 1–36. doi:10.1145/3417978

Ucci, D., Aniello, L., & Baldoni, R. (2019). Survey of machine learning techniques for malware analysis. *Computers & Security*, *81*, 123–147. doi:10.1016/j.cose.2018.11.001

Venkatasubramanian, M., Lashkari, A. H., & Hakak, S. (2023). IoT Malware Analysis using Federated Learning: A Comprehensive Survey. *IEEE Access : Practical Innovations, Open Solutions*, *11*, 5004–5018. doi:10.1109/ACCESS.2023.3235389

Venkatraman, S., Alazab, M., & Vinayakumar, R. (2019). A hybrid deep learning image-based analysis for effective malware detection. *Journal of Information Security and Applications*, *47*, 377–389. doi:10.1016/j.jisa.2019.06.006

Vermisoglou, E., Panáček, D., Jayaramulu, K., Pykal, M., Frébort, I., Kolář, M., & Otyepka, M. (2020). Human virus detection with graphene-based materials. *Biosensors & Bioelectronics*, *166*, 112436. doi:10.1016/j.bios.2020.112436 PMID:32750677

Vinayakumar, R., Alazab, M., Soman, K. P., Poornachandran, P., & Venkatraman, S. (2019). Robust intelligent malware detection using deep learning. *IEEE Access : Practical Innovations, Open Solutions*, *7*, 46717–46738. doi:10.1109/ACCESS.2019.2906934

Wang, D., Chen, T., Zhang, Z., & Zhang, N. (2023). A Survey of Android Malware Detection Based on Deep Learning. *International Conference on Machine Learning for Cyber Security*, (pp. 228–242). Springer. 10.1007/978-3-031-20096-0_18

Yadav, C. S., Singh, J., Yadav, A., Pattanayak, H. S., Kumar, R., Khan, A. A., Haq, M. A., Alhussen, A., & Alharby, S. (2022). Malware Analysis in IoT & Android Systems with Defensive Mechanism. *Electronics (Basel)*, *11*(15), 2354. doi:10.3390/electronics11152354

Chapter 13
Malware Forensics:
An Application of Scientific Knowledge to Cyber Attacks

C. V. Suresh Babu
iD https://orcid.org/0000-0002-8474-2882
Hindustan Institute of Technolgy and Science, India

G. Suruthi
Hindustan Institute of Technology and Science, India

C. Indhumathi
Hindustan Institute of Technology and Science, India

ABSTRACT

Malware continues to plague all organizations causing data loss and reputational damage. Malware forensics helps protect companies from such attacks. The data is going to be organized in a manner that covers the multiple malware attacks, the methods for detecting them, and then makes a suggestion for a tool that is comparable but also equivalent to reach the attacker. Considering that the concept signifies that malware forensics will be performed using a variety of tools and techniques, a procedure will be followed in order to get the desired outcome. This chapter discusses these issues in detail with an intensive literature review and feasible recommendations and suggestions.

DOI: 10.4018/978-1-6684-8666-5.ch013

1. INTRODUCTION

Malware forensics is the practice of investigating malware incidents by examining the evidence left behind. It involves detecting malware through system logs or antivirus software, isolating and containing it to prevent further spread, and then acquiring information about the incident using various tools like hard drive imaging, memory dump analysis, and network traffic capture. The collected evidence is carefully examined to determine the type and extent of the malware attack, including analyzing the malware's code, network behavior, and reverse engineering. The goal is to understand the motives, identify the attackers, and assess the damage caused. Finally, a comprehensive report is generated, summarizing the analysis results, methodologies used, and providing recommendations for future security improvements. Malware forensics is crucial for organizations to learn from past attacks, take appropriate actions, and prevent future incidents.

1.1. Existing Systems

- Memory Forensics: One limitation is the loss of network connections and running processes when malware is running in memory, hindering comprehensive analysis.
- Machine Learning-based Malware Detection: Hackers develop sophisticated malware to confuse algorithms, requiring collaborative approaches and additional technologies for improved efficiency
- Binary Content Comparison for Malware Analysis: Static analysis cannot detect unknown malware types and uses excessive memory resources.
- Dynamic Malware Analysis: Existing systems consume significant memory and battery, impacting performance and scalability.

2. TYPES OF MALWARES

2.1. Ransomware

Ransomware, a malicious software program used by cybercriminals, has become a significant threat in the digital realm. It encrypts valuable data, rendering it inaccessible to victims who must then pay a ransom to obtain the decryption key necessary for recovery. Organizations are the primary targets of ransomware attacks. Attackers demand payment in cryptocurrency, typically Bitcoin, through a process involving instructions and a link to purchase the required funds. However, there is no guarantee that paying the ransom will result in the release of the decryption key. Ransomware attacks have seen a substantial increase in frequency since the emergence of the AIDS Trojan in 1989, with 623 million incidents reported in 2021. Small businesses, with weaker security measures, often find themselves compelled to comply with ransom demands. The economic impact of such attacks is severe, threatening countries by extorting exorbitant ransom amounts while holding critical data hostage. Heightened awareness and effective countermeasures are essential for organizations, especially small businesses, to mitigate the impact of ransomware attacks and protect sensitive data (Kaspersky,)[2].

2.2. Adware

Adware is the form of malware where unwanted advertisements are displayed on user's screen and collects sensitive user information after user download the application bundled with malicious code.

In adware attack, the ads are delivered as pop- up windows on victim's device or the bars the appear on the program's user interface, these ads or either displayed or downloaded when an application is running (Dell Technologies, 2021).

Mostly the adware attack is targeted on PC's but that doesn't mean mobile devices are free from adware attacks. Mobile devices are also attacked but the percentage is less compared to attack happening on PC's.

There are two types of adware attacks:

Legitimate adware

The user's download the application with full consent where the user is gaining some benefit in return. For example: a user getting a paid application for discount with ads or user can go for paid version to experience ad-free working. This legitimate adware intentionally creates vulnerabilities and the victims emerges in these ways.

Malicious adware

Malicious adware is harmful and a forceful adware where it forces the user into receiving something without their consent (Kaspersky, n.d.).

Example: In some websites, if a user wants view data and the irrelevant advertisement pop-ups are shown to users where the user in order to view the data, they will see all these ads without willingness. Some people may be triggered and attracted to the ads and they may click the link in a curiosity and temptation. Once after the clicking the link, malicious software is installed on victim's device (Crowdstrike, 2023).

2.3. Spyware

Spyware, a form of adware, poses a significant threat as it targets victims through pop-up ads or malicious links in emails. The primary objective of spyware attacks is to infiltrate and steal sensitive information, including passwords and credentials. Even if the attacker fails to extract such data, the targeted device's performance is often compromised. Spyware thrives in unsecure free sources, with Wi-Fi connections serving as prime targets for successful attacks. One notable example is Pegasus, developed by NSO Group in 2011, which has infected mobile devices worldwide, regardless of their operating system (iOS or Android) (Crowdstrike, 2023).

2.4. Trojan

A Trojan is a malicious code that disguises itself as trustworthy software. Once installed, it carries out a range of harmful activities, including file deletion, modification, data theft, vulnerability exploitation, and creating backdoors for future attacks (Dell Technologies, 2021). Unlike worms, Trojans do not self-replicate and require a means to enter a device or network. They are often packaged with game or app downloads, making them a form of social engineering attack, similar to phishing and spoofing. Initially, Trojans remain undetected, lying dormant for weeks before initiating actions such as changes in settings and file deletion. To identify Trojans, utilizing specialized tools like Trojan scanners and malware removal software is essential (Kaspersky, n.d.). Stay vigilant and protect your devices from these deceptive threats.

Types of Trojans (Crowdstrike, 2023):

- Distributed Denial of Service (DDoS) Trojan
- Downloader Trojan
- Exploit Trojan
- Fake Antivirus Trojan
- Backdoor Trojan
- Game Thief Trojan
- Banker Trojan
- Rootkit Trojan
- Ransom Trojan
- Spy Trojan

Trojan can also affect mobile devices like smartphones, tablets, etc. For example: If a Trojan is created to look for sensitive information and to modify it. It waits and stay still until the victim access this information of his own on the device. Trojan can spread from a computer to computer (Fortinet, n.d.).

Examples of Trojan Virus attack:

- Zesus
- WannaCry
- I Love You

2.5. Worms

Worms are malicious code that have the ability to self-replicate and spread autonomously from one device to another. Unlike other malware, worms do not require human intervention or the attachment to specific files or applications to infect a device. They exploit vulnerabilities in networks and propagate through various means such as social networking sites, portable drives, USB devices, network packets, text messages, and email attachments. Worms consume significant memory resources, resulting in performance degradation of the infected device. Their objectives include stealing sensitive information, corrupting files, slowing down device performance, and establishing backdoors for future attacks (Dell Technologies, 2021; TechTarget Security, 2022). It is crucial to implement robust security measures and regularly update software to protect against worm infections and their detrimental effects.

Types of Worms:
- Internet Relay Chat Worm
- Instant Messenger Worm
- P2P Worm
- Net Worm

Activities of Worms:
- Loss and modification of files.
- Lack of speed and performance.
- Less Hardware Space.

2.6. Fileless Malware

Fileless malware is a deceptive form of malicious code that infiltrates systems by posing as legitimate software. Unlike traditional malware, it operates without user interaction, making it challenging to detect. Rather than leaving traceable files, fileless malware manipulates native system tools, complicating its identification and increasing the difficulty of detection. Defending against fileless malware requires advanced security measures equipped to recognize and counter these stealthy threats (Crowdstrike, 2022).

Types of Fileless Malware techniques:

- Hijacked Native Tools
- Exploit Kits
- Memory-Only Malware
- Fileless Ransomware
- Stole Credentials
- Registry Resident malware (Crowdstrike, 2023)

2.7. Virus

Viruses are malicious code intentionally created to alter the operations and functionality of computer devices. They propagate by replicating files, enabling them to spread from one computer to another. Viruses can impact the programming and functioning of systems, leading to disruptions and vulnerabilities. Common means of virus transmission include accessing untrusted web sources, engaging in file sharing through peer-to-peer networks, and utilizing virus-infected USB devices (Kaspersky, n.d.).

Types of Viruses:

- File Virus
- Source code Virus
- Boot Sector Virus
- Macro Virus
- Tunneling Virus
- Encrypted Virus
- Multipartie Virus
- Memory Resident
- Browser Hijacker
- Armored Virus
- Polymorphic Virus
- Stealth Virus (Crowdstrike, 2023).

2.8. Rootkits

Rootkits are malicious software designed to covertly conceal their presence and provide unauthorized access to restricted areas of a system. Detecting rootkits can be challenging due to their ability to remain hidden. Once installed, rootkits can carry out malicious activities, such as stealing sensitive data including financial and personal information. While they primarily affect operating systems and software, certain types of rootkits are specifically crafted to target hardware and firmware, further enhancing their impact (Crowdstrike, 2023).

2.9. Keyloggers

Keyloggers is a type of spyware, monitor and record the keystrokes and movements made by users on their input devices, particularly keyboards. This allows them to gather valuable information, including passwords, logins, and other sensitive credentials. The collected keylogs are subsequently exploited to steal records and confidential data (Crowdstrike, 2023).

2.10. Botnets

Bots are malicious scripts designed to gain unauthorized access to user accounts and scan devices to obtain contact information, often engaging in activities such as sending spam. These bots can be interconnected to form botnets, which are utilized for various cyberattacks. One common use of botnets is Distributed Denial of Service (DDoS) attacks. The individual who controls the hijacked bots is known as the "Bot Herder" (Crowdstrike, 2023).

3. MALWARE INFLUENCE OVER VARIOUS DOMAINS

3.1. Healthcare

Healthcare businesses are frequently targeted by ransomware attacks due to their heavy reliance on data access, particularly patient information, to ensure smooth operations. Even minor delays in accessing documents can have harmful consequences for patients. During the pandemic, ransomware offenders have expedited their attacks on healthcare networks, seeking higher payoffs with minimal effort. Exploiting the often-lax security measures in healthcare institutions, such as insufficient network scanning, virus protection, and two-factor authentication, cybercriminals have caused significant disruptions. Reports indicate that ransomware attacks have resulted in treatment delays and disruptions, with a rise in medical treatment problems reported by respondents. Disruptions in patient care, particularly with medical procedures, have had a profound impact, leading to an increased likelihood of care diversion. Additionally, the lack of HIPAA compliance in many cloud-based solutions makes healthcare systems an easy target for attackers (Crowdstrike, 2023).

3.2. Cloud

Malware delivery over the cloud has witnessed a significant increase of 68% in early 2021, exposing cloud environments to various cyberattacks. While on premise infrastructure may be considered less resilient to cyber threats, cloud environments are equally vulnerable. Malware can infiltrate the cloud through file uploads, leading to data theft or destruction, resulting in data loss for organizations. By infecting servers, software, and other components of the cloud infrastructure, malware can disrupt services, causing downtime, reduced productivity, and financial losses. Furthermore, malware attacks can render cloud systems noncompliant with regulations and industry standards, undermining client confidence and tarnishing the provider's brand. The aftermath of a malware attack in a cloud environment can be costly, requiring additional security measures and remediation efforts to prevent future attacks. Robust security measures such as firewalls, antivirus software, and intrusion detection systems are essential, complemented by regular security audits and assessments to identify vulnerabilities and prevent malware assaults. Prioritizing employee malware defense training and establishing a reporting procedure for staff can significantly contribute to safeguarding the cloud environment against attackers (Sugumaran et al., 2022).

3.3. Mobile Device

Mobile malware has become a significant concern as an increasing number of mobile devices fall prey to malicious software. In 2020 alone, there were over 15.3 billion malware detections on mobile devices, indicating a 54% surge compared to the previous year. Mobile malware poses serious threats as it can steal sensitive data, manipulate services to incur unauthorized charges, lock devices or data for ransom, and hinder device performance while draining battery life. Certain malware types target specific mobile operating systems and technologies. Notably, the Joker malware has emerged in various Google Play Store apps, collecting personal data and surreptitiously enrolling users in premium services. Another example is the Emotet malware, which compromises mobile phones to extract private information from individuals and businesses. To mitigate the risk of mobile malware infestations, adhering to recommended security practices is essential. This includes regular hardware and software updates, installation of robust antivirus programs, and avoiding suspicious links and downloads. By taking these precautions, individuals and organizations can safeguard their devices and protect their valuable information from harm (Qamar et al., 2019).

3.4. Internet of Things

The IoT is vulnerable to malware attacks due to inherent security challenges, with attackers exploiting IoT devices to gain unauthorized financial benefits. The constantly connected nature of IoT devices, coupled with their lack of robust security measures, creates a conducive environment for malware infiltration (Suresh Babu, 2023). A notable example is the Mirai malware attack in September 2016, targeting French host OVH and leveraging default user credentials on vulnerable IoT devices. In specific applications like agriculture and environmental monitoring, battery-operated IoT devices deployed in remote areas necessitate efficient malware detection techniques to optimize battery life. Traditional antivirus software serves as the initial defense against known viruses, but it falls short in providing decentralized and robust security for the IoT. Transferring conventional security approaches to the IoT is limited by device constraints and computational capacity. Therefore, an effective defense strategy for the IoT should embrace a distributed, reactive, adaptable, and self-monitoring approach, aligning with the unique characteristics and design of IoT systems. Implementing a well-defined plan prioritizing fundamental security principles is crucial to effectively protect IoT devices (Humayun et al., 2020; Swarnalatha et al., 2023).

3.5. Industry

Malware poses significant risks to the industrial sector, impacting supply chain operations, intellectual property theft, and disrupting production processes. Manufacturing systems such as HMIs, SCADA systems, and PLCs are susceptible to malware infections, resulting in downtime and decreased productivity. The WannaCry ransomware attack in 2017 targeted manufacturing companies, causing production disruptions. Another notable incident is the Triton malware attack on a Saudi Arabian petrochemical plant, leading to facility shutdown and substantial financial losses. Malware can also infiltrate supply chain activities, infecting distributors and suppliers and causing manufacturing and delivery delays, as well as reputation damage. Implementing strong security measures, including access controls, data encryption, and regular security assessments, is crucial. Employee education and awareness programs play a vital role in preventing malware infections by enabling staff to recognize and avoid suspicious emails and websites. By adopting these precautions, organizations can protect themselves from the detrimental effects of malware and maintain the trust of stakeholders and customers (Aljaidi et al., 2022).

3.6. Digital

Malware poses a significant threat to digital platforms like Google, impacting user trust and the platform's overall functionality. Google's systems, including the Google Play Store and Google AdWords, are vulnerable to malware infections that can result in the theft of sensitive user data and reputational damage. The Google Play Store can be a source of malicious applications that take control of devices, collect user data, and display intrusive advertisements. Similarly, Google AdWords can be exploited to distribute malware, redirecting users to dangerous websites that can infect their devices. The Gooligan malware, which compromised over 1 million Google accounts in 2016, exemplifies the targeting of Google's services. This malware spread through malicious applications on the Google Play Store, aiming to gather private user information and authentication credentials. Such malware not only undermines user trust but also has a negative impact on the reputation of digital platforms like Google, potentially leading to decreased customer engagement and revenue. Implementing robust security measures, including regular security evaluations, automated malware detection and removal tools, and user awareness and training initiatives, is crucial to mitigate the risks associated with malware on digital platforms. By taking these precautions, digital platforms like Google can protect their users from malware, maintain their reputation, and foster user confidence (Zhang et al., 2021).

4. MALWARE FORENSICS TOOLS

4.1. Wireshark

Wireshark is an open-source and free protocol analyzer used for real-time recording and analysis of network data. It is widely utilized by system administrators, security experts, and IT professionals to address network problems, assess performance, and identify security vulnerabilities. With Wireshark, users can capture packets, analyze them comprehensively, and gain insights into network behavior. Real-time traffic monitoring, examination of past packets, and data packet filtering based on specific criteria are possible. Wireshark supports decoding of numerous network protocols, presenting results in a user-friendly format for easy troubleshooting and problem-solving. Overall, Wireshark is a powerful tool that provides in-depth visibility into network activity, enabling efficient identification and resolution of network issues (Mabsali et al., 2023).

4.2. Pestudio Tool

PeStudio is a powerful program designed for analyzing Windows executables to identify security vulnerabilities, unusual behaviors, or unwanted features. It is extensively used by security experts, malware analysts, software developers, and IT administrators to assess the risks associated with executing executable files. PeStudio provides a comprehensive overview of the executable program, presenting details about its resource management, imported and exported functions, segments, and other structural elements. The program's ability to detect malware and malicious behaviors is a key feature, as it examines the file for suspicious code, known malware signatures, or hidden data. PeStudio also examines the file's imports and exports to identify any signs of malicious code injection. Additionally, it offers insights into the file's digital certificate, enabling users to verify its authenticity and integrity. PeStudio is capable of recognizing anti-debugging and anti-analysis techniques commonly employed by malware developers, providing valuable information for developing effective defenses. The program also includes plugins that enhance its capabilities, such as the strings plugin for searching specific strings within the file and the entropy plugin for assessing file compression or encryption. Overall, PeStudio is an indispensable tool for analyzing Windows executables, offering a comprehensive understanding of their structure, behavior, and potential security risks. Its ability to identify malware, detect anti-debugging tactics, and inspect digital signatures makes it essential for software development and IT management (Lee & Cho, 2012).

4.3. Cuckoo Sandbox Tool

Cuckoo Sandbox is a free and open-source automatic malware analysis system widely used by cybersecurity professionals and malware analysts to identify and classify malicious software. It creates a secure virtual environment to execute suspicious files and monitors their behavior to gather information about their intentions. The system provides a user-friendly online interface where users can submit files for analysis and view the results. Cuckoo Sandbox supports a variety of analytic plugins and modules, including signature-based detection, behavioral analysis, and memory analysis, enhancing its capabilities. Its automation feature enables security experts to process a large number of malicious files efficiently, generating detailed reports on their behavior. Additionally, Cuckoo Sandbox integrates with various security technologies and tools, such as antivirus software, advanced threat platforms, and

SIEM systems, further enhancing its functionality. Overall, Cuckoo Sandbox offers a systematic and scalable approach to malware analysis, making it a valuable tool for security professionals seeking to enhance their advanced analytics capabilities (Jamalpur et al., 2018).

4.4. Radare2 Tool

Radare2/Cutter is a powerful and flexible free and open-source reverse engineering system that provides a comprehensive set of tools and libraries for analyzing binary files. It offers a command-line interface (CLI) tool with features like disassembling, diagnostics, analysis, and exploitation. The system is designed to be highly expandable and modular, allowing developers to create their own custom analysis tools and workflows. Radare2/Cutter utilizes the Radare2 engine, which is known for its robust dismantling and debugging capabilities across various data formats and architectures. Cutter, the graphical user interface (GUI), enhances the user experience with interactive visualization plugins and tools for in-depth examination of binary files. With built-in scripting support for languages like Python and Lua, Radare2/Cutter enables the creation of specialized analytic tools. It supports various analytic methods, including static and dynamic analysis as well as symbolic execution, making it suitable for flaw detection, reverse engineering, and understanding the operations of malicious software. Overall, Radare2/Cutter is a valuable resource for programmers, security experts, and reverse engineers seeking to study and analyze binary files due to its adaptable framework and support for customized plugins and scripts (Pang et al., 2021).

4.5. Ghidra Tool

Ghidra is an open-source software tool developed by the National Security Agency (NSA) for reverse engineering purposes. It is designed to aid security researchers, programmers, and experts in analyzing and understanding the inner workings of software applications, including malware. Ghidra offers features such as binary code decompilation and disassembly, support for multiple CPU architectures, script writing capabilities, code analysis, and debugging functionalities. Its graphical user interface facilitates easier navigation and visualization of complex code structures. Additionally, Ghidra stands out for its ability to handle large and intricate software projects with multiple modules and dependencies. It also provides collaboration tools that allow multiple individuals to work on the same project simultaneously. With its versatility, Ghidra serves as a powerful tool for various software analytics and reverse engineering tasks, including malware analysis, vulnerability discovery, and software development (Park et al., 2023).

4.6. ProcMon

Process Monitor, also known as ProcMon, is a commercial Windows system analysis tool developed by Microsoft. It provides detailed information about system activities, including file and registry access, process and thread activities, and network-based actions. With ProcMon, users can monitor real-time system activity, allowing them to identify running programs and their operations. This tool is useful for troubleshooting performance issues, detecting application failures, and resolving system problems. One of ProcMon's notable features is its ability to record and present comprehensive data about system activity, including the process or application responsible for the action, the type of activity (such as file access or registry modification), and the location of the accessed file or registry key. This level of detail aids in thorough system analysis and diagnosis (Al-Sofyani et al., 2023).

5. REVIEW OF LITERATURE

5.1. NetMD: Network Traffic Analysis and Malware Detection

This chapter emphasizes the significance of data networks and the necessity of digital investigation. Data networks play a vital role in connecting individuals across vast distances and facilitating communication. Ensuring the security and privacy of data is crucial in today's environment. Protecting networks and data from malware attacks is paramount. It is also important to maintain the integrity and proper delivery of data to prevent data loss and breaches during transmission. To enhance the security of data network communication, machine learning algorithms have been implemented using datasets such as CICIDS2017, NetML, and non-vpn2016 for malware detection. The results of this analysis have surpassed expectations, yielding exceptional outcomes in network traffic analysis, particularly with Nettle network traffic analysis, CICIDS2017, and non-vpn2016 datasets. This research has contributed significant advancements in this field (Katherasala et al., 2022).

5.2. Internet of Things for Digital Forensics Application in Saudi Arabia

This research focuses on the digital forensics of an Internet of Things (IoT) system, specifically targeting the Facebook (FB) platform. The increasing prevalence of IoT technology necessitates the development of forensic frameworks for investigating IoT settings. The study examines an IoT-based smart apartment controlled by the owner's smartwatch, which automates decision-making processes and offers useful functionalities. The communication among various IoT devices is facilitated through a MySQL server. These devices include door sensors, cameras, gas detectors, motion sensors, humidity sensors, glass break sensors, water leakage detectors, temperature sensors, alarms, fans, shower switches, and more. The system also incorporates health monitoring capabilities for patients with cardiovascular and epilepsy conditions, all controllable through a smartwatch (Swarnalatha et al., 2023). The FB system architecture comprises three agents: security, convenience, and communication agents, along with databases and the user's smartwatch. By utilizing IoT technology in households, the flexibility and quality of life for residents can be significantly enhanced. The research incorporates critical elements such as storing server and network logs, ensuring portability by enabling control of the entire FB system through a single smartwatch, and providing an efficient monitoring and tracking system for users (Bindrwish et al., 2023).

5.3. We Are Meeting on Microsoft Teams: Forensic Analysis in Windows, Android, and iOS Operating Systems

This chapter focuses on the digital forensics of Microsoft Teams, a platform that gained significant popularity during the COVID-19 pandemic for online education and organizational purposes. As Microsoft Teams is a relatively new platform, there is a lack of forensic research on it. The study addresses this gap by conducting forensic analysis to examine traces of data left by Microsoft Teams on Windows 10, Android, and Apple iOS mobile operating systems. The analysis was performed in an isolated environment using tools such as Cellebrite UFED Physical Analyzer and Magnet AXIOM. The devices used for analysis were either jailbroken or rooted and wiped to obtain more comprehensive results. The analysis revealed that approximately 77.6% of artifacts were partially or completely recovered, with forensic tools yielding only around 13.8% of artifact recovery. Recovered artifacts included account information, messages, files, calls, shared files, and calendar data. The manual approach proved to be more effective in recovering a significant amount of data and providing reliable output (Bowling et al., 2023).

5.4. Artificial Intelligence and the Internet of Things Forensics in a National Security Context

In this chapter, the significance of digital forensics in the context of IoT devices is highlighted. With the increasing prevalence of data and security attacks, both public and private sectors are at risk. IoT forensics plays a crucial role in investigating crimes, identifying attack patterns, and extracting digital evidence from IoT devices. The vulnerability of IoT devices, which can be compromised within minutes of being connected, has led to widespread attacks across various sectors. Data breaches are particularly concerning, and IoT forensics can provide insights into the extent of compromised data. This chapter delves into the application of machine learning and natural language processing techniques in IoT forensics, specifically focusing on anomaly and steganography detection (Swarnalatha et al., 2023). Moreover, it addresses the challenges associated with algorithmic bias and transparency in military AI applications. The chapter concludes by offering policy recommendations to enhance transparency and reduce bias in AI algorithms (Montasari, 2023).

5.5. Cloud Forensics and Digital Ledger Investigation: A New Era of Forensics Investigation

In this chapter, the focus is on the importance of cloud computing and its widespread adoption by organizations. Cloud computing offers numerous benefits such as data protection and automatic updates, making it a preferred choice for many. However, with its popularity, criminal activities targeting the cloud have also increased. This has led to a significant demand for cloud forensics and digital ledger investigations. The research explores the technical challenges involved in digital forensics and presents a cloud investigation architecture. The most common attacks encountered in cloud forensics are data breaches and Denial of Service (DoS) attacks, which compromise sensitive information and disrupt server operations, respectively. Challenges in cloud forensics include the remote location of cloud services, lack of jurisdiction support, instability of cloud services, data decentralization, and data erasure. The chapter also covers topics such as forensics on edge computing and fog computing, as well as the relevant legal aspects. This research provides valuable insights into the complexities and considerations of conducting forensics in cloud computing environments (Khan et al., 2023).

5.6. Digital Forensic Investigation Framework for the Metaverse

This chapter explores the concept of the metaverse, a combination of augmented reality and virtual reality technology, and its impact on the real world. The metaverse is structured around a seven-layered architecture, enabling immersive experiences, information exchange, user-generated content, spatial computing, decentralization, human interaction, and improved infrastructure. However, the emergence of the metaverse also brings new challenges and potential crimes, necessitating digital forensics investigation. The research delves into crimes like virtual theft and money laundering in the metaverse and presents a metaverse forensics architecture with four phases: data gathering, evidence collection, analysis, and reporting. The chapter emphasizes the positive and negative impacts of the metaverse, highlighting the need for privacy, anti-forensics measures, and data ownership considerations in metaverse digital forensics. Overall, this research contributes to understanding the potential and challenges of the metaverse, providing insights into responsible use and risk mitigation in this emerging technology (Seo et al., 2023).

5.7. Digital Forensic Analysis of Discord on Google Chrome

This chapter focuses on the contribution of social media, particularly Google Chrome's Discord platform, in facilitating criminal activities, using digital forensics as the investigative approach. Discord, a popular Voice over Internet Protocol (VoIP) platform, enables users to exchange information in various forms, including audio, files, videos, and text. While Discord can be a useful communication tool, it also poses risks, especially when interacting with unknown individuals and sharing personal details. The investigation adopted an attacker's perspective to uncover potential information that could be retrieved from Google Chrome's Discord platform. Surprisingly, the investigation successfully revealed sensitive data such as payment details, conversations, shared files, and account settings. Discord was chosen for investigation due to its association with illicit activities and its use as an information-gathering tool for criminal exploits. The investigation process involved three steps: pretest, where data stored in Google Chrome was extracted and evaluated; treatment, where common user behaviors were utilized to extract artifacts from Google Chrome; and posttest, which compared the extracted data from the treatment phase with the pretest data to identify anomalies (Gupta et al., 2023).

5.8. Addressing Insider Attacks via Forensic-Ready Risk Management

In this chapter, the focus is on insider attacks and the proposal of a forensic-ready risk management strategy to mitigate the risks associated with such attacks. Insider threats, which originate from trusted individuals within an organization, are recognized as highly detrimental and challenging to detect. The chapter argues that traditional security measures like firewalls and access control lists are insufficient in preventing insider attacks, emphasizing the need for a proactive and comprehensive approach. The suggested forensic-ready risk management strategy comprises several crucial steps: identification of critical resources and potential insider threats, analysis of risks associated with insider threats, implementation of technical and procedural controls to mitigate risks, establishment of incident response plans and preservation of forensic evidence in advance, and continuous monitoring and evaluation of control effectiveness. By adopting this strategy, organizations can better prepare for and respond to insider attacks while collecting the necessary evidence to hold offenders accountable. The chapter emphasizes the importance of tailoring the strategy to each organization's specific needs and regularly reassessing and adapting it to address emerging threats and advancements in technology. Overall, the chapter provides a valuable framework for effectively addressing the complex issue of insider attacks and underscores the significance of a proactive and comprehensive risk management approach (Daubner et al., 2023).

5.9. Multi-Pronged Approach for Ransomware Analysis

In this chapter, the focus is on the increasing danger posed by ransomware attacks and the need for robust detection and mitigation measures. The study presents a comprehensive strategy for ransomware analysis, combining static and dynamic analysis methods. The authors emphasize the importance of understanding the characteristics of specific ransomware families, such as WannaCry, in order to develop effective detection and prevention measures. The chapter targets researchers and professionals in the cybersecurity field who are interested in devising strategies to detect and mitigate ransomware attacks. The study proposes a multifaceted analysis approach, utilizing static analysis techniques to examine the ransomware's file structure, disassemble its code, and identify encryption algorithms and targeted file types. Dynamic analysis techniques are employed to observe the ransomware's behavior and detect malicious activities, using sandbox environments and virtual machines. The authors highlight the significance of understanding the unique traits of each ransomware group when designing effective detection and mitigation solutions. This chapter provides valuable insights and guidance for addressing the challenges posed by ransomware attacks in the field of cybersecurity (Malik & Agrawal, 2021).

5.10. Enhancing Cloud Forensic Investigation System in Distributed Cloud Computing Using Dk-Cp-ECC Algorithm and Ek-Anfis

This chapter focuses on the challenges faced in digital forensics (DF) investigations, particularly when dealing with decentralized Cloud Servers (CS) and the use of cloud sources, which can complicate the gathering, preservation, and submission of evidence. While DF methodologies have been applied, there are still persistent issues in combating cybercrime. To address these challenges, a robust distributed cloud computing (CC)-based cloud forensic investigation system is proposed, consisting of three phases. The Group Key Generation (GKG) phase enables authorized users to securely upload and download evidence, ensuring its credibility. The Secure Data Transfer (SDT) phase employs the Distributed Key Cypher Policy with Elliptic Curve Cryptography (DK-CP-ECC) algorithm, ensuring confidentiality and privacy of the evidence. The CS selection process is performed using a genetic algorithm developed for deer hunting and the Exponential Membership Function Adaptive Neuro-Fuzzy Interference System (EK-ANFIS). This minimizes reporting issues and ensures secure evidence storage. The proposed system achieves a high Security Level (SL) of 97%, aligning closely with existing frameworks. This chapter offers valuable insights and presents a comprehensive approach to address the complexities of conducting digital forensics investigations in decentralized cloud environments (Nasreen & Mir, 2023).

5.11. Digital Forensics as Advanced Ransomware Pre-Attack Detection Algorithm for Endpoint Data Protection

This chapter focuses on the utilization of the K-Nearest Neighbor (KNN) technique in digital forensics investigations, specifically in the context of Windows computers. The authors highlight the importance of gathering a comprehensive dataset containing relevant system data, such as audit trails, network activity, file descriptions, and registry entries. The paper explores various applications of KNN in digital forensics, including malware detection and the identification of suspicious or malicious activity. By subjecting the dataset to the KNN algorithm, new data points can be categorized based on their similarity to pre-classified data. The study emphasizes the speed and effectiveness of KNN in analyzing large datasets. The methodology involves creating a substantial dataset, applying the KNN algorithm, and evaluating the results. The authors also address the limitations of KNN and emphasize the significance of proper dataset curation and algorithm optimization to ensure accurate findings in digital forensic investigations. This chapter provides valuable insights into the application of the KNN algorithm in digital forensics research, highlighting the importance of meticulous dataset management and algorithm refinement to obtain reliable outcomes (Du et al., 2022).

5.12. Digital Forensic Case Studies for In-Vehicle Infotainment Systems Using Android Auto and Apple Carplay

This chapter presents two case studies focusing on digital forensics of in-vehicle infotainment systems, specifically examining the Android Auto and Apple CarPlay platforms. The first case study involves analyzing a 2017 Hyundai Ioniq and a Samsung Galaxy S8 smartphone connected to an Android Auto system. The authors investigate data from the smartphone, car head unit, and USB cable, collecting evidence such as phone logs, messages, and location data. The second case study examines an iPhone 7 and a 2017 Volkswagen Golf connected to an Apple CarPlay system, following a similar analysis approach to gather phone logs, messages, and GPS data. The study highlights the challenges posed by the lack of system uniformity and complexity in the digital forensic process of in-vehicle infotainment systems. It demonstrates that significant amounts of personal data can be stored in these systems and can be retrieved using digital forensic techniques. The authors emphasize the importance of including in-car infotainment systems in digital forensic investigations, as they may contain crucial information for legal proceedings in civil or criminal cases (Shin et al., 2022).

5.13. Understanding the Digital Forensics Framework of Cloud Computing-Cloud Forensics

This chapter provides a comprehensive overview of cloud forensics, focusing on the challenges and framework for conducting digital investigations in cloud computing environments. The study explores various types of cloud-based cybercrimes, such as data theft, insider attacks, and illegal access, emphasizing the impact of cloud service models (SaaS, PaaS, and IaaS) and deployment strategies (public, private, and hybrid cloud) on the digital forensics process. As cloud computing continues to gain popularity, the article highlights the importance of incorporating cloud forensics as a critical component of cybersecurity. It underscores the need for proactive planning in incident response and digital forensics within the cloud, as well as the development of standardized processes and tools for effective cloud forensics. Collaboration among cloud service providers, law enforcement agencies, and forensic experts is also emphasized to effectively assess and prevent cloud-based cybercrimes (Shaji, 2020).

6. MALWARE FORENSICS CASE STUDIES

6.1. Attack on Scientology (2008)

This chapter examines a significant cyber attack that occurred in 2008 on the website Scientology.org, which resulted in a substantial impact on both the users and the website owners. Scientology.org is a religious website dedicated to self-knowledge and spiritual fulfillment. The attack, known as a Distributed Denial of Service (DDoS) attack, targeted the website following an interview with Tom Cruise. The attackers initially posted a warning message on YouTube, signaling their intent to target Scientology. The DDoS attack involved flooding the website's server with an overwhelming amount of data, causing it to become inaccessible and offline for several days. The attack generated approximately 220 Mbps of traffic, lasting an average of 30 minutes and utilizing up to 163 Mbps of bandwidth. The FBI later identified the perpetrators, including a New Jersey teenager named Dmitriy Guzner from Verona, who was associated with a hacker group involved in the attack. It was discovered that Google bomb and YouTube were used as tools by the hackers. Guzner, considered the main individual behind the attack, was sentenced to 10 years in prison, a fine of $250,000, and was required to pay $37,500 to the owners of the Scientology website (CNET, 2008).

6.2. Attack on Cosmos Bank Pune

This case study focuses on a significant malware attack that targeted Cosmos Bank on August 11, 2018, resulting in a loss of Rs. 94 crores. The attack lasted for approximately seven hours and affected not only Cosmos Bank but also impacted 28 other countries. The attackers were able to breach the path to the main server and gain access to the main server, allowing them to clone the debit cards of Cosmos Bank customers. Using these cloned debit cards, the attackers carried out transactions from thousands of ATM accounts, totaling Rs. 78 crores from Indian account holders and Rs. 2.5 crores from account holders in other countries. Subsequently, the attackers transferred Rs. 13.92 crores to a Hong Kong account. Sambhaji Kadam, who was involved in the investigation, suspected the attackers to be foreigners and was able to locate their whereabouts. Following this, a red corner notice was issued, and 18 individuals were arrested. By December 2018, the Special Investigation Team (SIT) filed a 1700-page charge sheet against nine accused individuals. While some money was recovered, there are still four individuals, including Kunal Shukla, Abdul Bhai, and Sumer Shaikh, who are wanted in connection with the case and are believed to be in Dubai. The collaboration between Pune City police and Cosmos Bank played a crucial role in the recovery of approximately Rs. 5.72 crores (The Indian Express, 2020).

6.3. Attack on Google Chrome

The attack on Google Chrome had a significant impact on users, with approximately 2 billion people falling victim to a high-level security flaw (CVE-2022-3656) affecting Google Chrome and Chromium-based browsers. The vulnerability, discovered during a pen testing process by Imperva Red, resulted in the theft of cryptocurrency wallets, sensitive files, and login credentials. Exploiting the flaw, attackers created fake cryptocurrency wallets and tricked users into downloading a zip file for recovery keys, granting access to their accounts. This was made possible through the manipulation of symlinks, which redirected victims to folders where sensitive information was stored. Google Chrome promptly addressed the vulnerability and urged users to update to Chrome-108, mitigating the risk and protecting users from further exploitation (HT Tech., 2023).

6.4. Attack on SolarWinds

In 2020, SolarWinds fell victim to a group of attackers suspected to be Russian hackers who launched a backdoor attack. These attackers gained unauthorized access to SolarWind's systems, specifically targeting Orion, a widely used software employed by numerous IT firms for IT resource management. A malicious code was injected into the software, impacting approximately 33,000 users. SolarWinds, like many other companies, released updates without conducting comprehensive vulnerability testing, leading to around 18,000 customers unknowingly installing the compromised updates. Exploiting this vulnerability, the attackers further injected additional malware into the victims' systems, utilizing them for surveillance purposes. It was only later that SolarWinds became aware of this vulnerability and identified the 18,000 customers who had installed the compromised updates, resulting in a significant impact on more than 500 high-profile companies, including Microsoft, Cisco, and Intel. The attack remained undetected for several months until unusual activities were noticed at the Treasury Department, such as unauthorized access to email accounts and networks. Cybersecurity experts and federal investigators initially suspected Russian hackers due to their history of similar attacks, although the Russian government denied involvement, and Chinese hackers were also considered as potential culprits for the security breach. Microsoft President Brad Smith later expressed his belief that Russian hackers were responsible for the breach, although the true identity of the hackers remains undisclosed (TechTarget, 2022).

6.5. Attack on Facebook

In July 2017, a vulnerability was discovered on Facebook, but the company remained unaware of it. It wasn't until September 16, 2018, when abnormal activities were detected, that Facebook became aware of an ongoing attack. The exact duration of the attack was uncertain due to long-standing vulnerabilities. As a result of this security breach, approximately 50 million user accounts were exposed to the hackers. Facebook swiftly took action to protect the 40 million unaffected accounts. Fortunately, no credit card or credential information was compromised. The breach was attributed to three vulnerabilities in the video uploader feature, specifically related to the "view as" functionality. Facebook promptly addressed the issue and fixed the access token vulnerability on September 27 (Techcrunch & Techcrunch, 2018).

7. LIMITATIONS

As technology advances, current forensic tools may become outdated, and new attacks may emerge. It is crucial to recognize the limitations of existing tools and prepare for future challenges in cybersecurity.

1. Anti-forensic techniques: Malware authors possess knowledge of forensic analysis methods and actively employ countermeasures to hinder investigations. They use tactics like data wiping, file deletion, and tampering with system logs to conceal their actions and erase traces. Gathering the necessary information for a thorough examination becomes challenging due to these anti-forensic procedures.
2. Resource-intensive analysis: Malware analysis requires significant computational power and expertise. Specialized tools and procedures are necessary to analyze infections, along with the establishment of isolated environments to limit further damage. In the case of complex malware samples, extensive analysis can consume considerable time and resources.
3. Zero-day exploits: Zero-day exploits refer to software vulnerabilities unknown to manufacturers, lacking fixes or protections. These exploits enable malware to bypass standard security measures and persist undetected for extended periods. Investigating and analyzing such malware is difficult due to limited accessible information and the potential incompatibility of current tools and procedures.

8. SCOPE OF THE WORK

The primary objective of this chapter is to provide an overview of the best tools and technologies available in the current landscape. By exploring these tools, readers can gain insights into the various types of malware attacks perpetrated by attackers. Malware is classified based on its impact, ranging from low to high. Understanding these variations is crucial for individuals to comprehend the potential risks associated with malware attacks. The case studies presented in this research highlight significant attacks targeting well-known platforms. This serves as an awareness mechanism, educating users about the risks associated with the platforms they use and empowering them with fundamental knowledge to prevent falling victim to such attacks. Furthermore, the case studies not only describe the attacks but also demonstrate the evolution of malware from past to present. Understanding the importance of malware prevention becomes apparent when considering the detrimental effects on data confidentiality, integrity, and availability. By emphasizing prevention measures, this research aims to mitigate the potential loss and damage caused by malware attacks.

9. FUTURE SCOPE

This research chapter highlights the growing scope of malware forensics tools in response to advancing technologies. It sets the stage for future research by discussing the addition of new tools and providing a comparative analysis of the tools presented. A survey will be conducted to assess the success rate of these tools, offering valuable insights. Real-world case studies of malware attacks will be thoroughly examined, shedding light on attack methods, mitigation duration, and resulting damages. Additionally, superior mitigation techniques will be explored, surpassing current approaches. The chapter concludes with a comprehensive discussion on various mitigation strategies tailored to counter specific types of malware attacks. This research aims to captivate readers with its crisp and engaging approach, emphasizing the importance of malware prevention and effective forensic analysis in today's technological landscape.

10.SUGGESTIONS

This research chapter establishes a foundation by discussing various tools and case studies related to malware attacks. It emphasizes the importance of analyzing past incidents and leveraging the best tools and technologies for future prevention and detection. Multilevel security measures should be implemented, tailored to the specific types of malware discussed, in order to effectively combat the evolving threat landscape. By understanding different forms of malware and their prevention techniques, organizations can enhance their cybersecurity posture and mitigate potential risks.

10. RECOMMENDATIONS

Malware attacks continue to be a significant threat in today's digital landscape, necessitating the implementation of effective prevention and detection measures. This research chapter highlights the best tools currently available for combating malware attacks. To ensure comprehensive protection, it is recommended to adopt a layered approach that combines static and dynamic analysis methodologies. This approach enables a thorough understanding of malware traits, behavior, and impact. Additionally, leveraging reputable and up-to-date analysis tools enhances the recognition, examination, and extraction of information from malware samples, streamlining the analysis process. Staying informed about emerging threats is crucial, as malware tactics and vulnerabilities constantly evolve. Regular updates on the latest trends and techniques enable proactive adjustments to analytical methods and detection capabilities. Furthermore, maintaining a comprehensive knowledge base that includes malware analysis methods, indicators of compromise (IOCs), forensic evidence, and best practices is essential. This knowledge base should be regularly updated and shared across the organization or security community. By adhering to these recommendations, malware forensics experts can enhance their analysis skills, ensure the integrity of evidence, and facilitate effective incident response and mitigation strategies. This research provides valuable insights into building a robust defense against malware attacks, contributing to a safer digital environment.

11. CONCLUSION

Malware attack these days are the most threatening and widely implemented attack which used for small breach to big attacks. All the sectors and every individual can be victims of this attack. Awareness about what happening around is very important factor for being secure. In order to secure or use tool for prevention and detection one must know the attacks that can occur, understanding and working of attack and also the loses that can be created because of the attacks must be known. The increasing technology is a bliss for people as it ensure sophistication but too much anything is dangerous so wise usage and implementation of the technology is needed to adapt and receive the benefits that an technology can provide to the user.

12. REFERENCES

Al-Sofyani, S., Alelayani, A., Al-zahrani, F., & Monshi, R. (2023). A Survey off Malware Forensics Analysis Techniques And Tools. In *2023 1st International Conference on Advanced Innovations in Smart Cities (ICAISC)* (pp. 1-6). Jeddah, Saudi Arabia. 10.1109/ICAISC56366.2023.10085474

Aljaidi, M., Alkhalidi, Y., Al-dmour, H., Al-Howaide, A., & Al-Tarawneh, M. (2022). *NHS WannaCry Ransomware Attack: Technical Explanation of The Vulnerability, Exploitation, and Countermeasures.* In *2022 International Engineering Conference on Electrical, Energy, and Artificial Intelligence.* Zarqa, Jordan. 10.1109/ EICEEAI56378.2022.10050485

Bindrwish, F., Ali, A., Ghabban, W., Alrowwad, A., Fallatah, N., Ameerbakhsh, O., & Alfadli, I. (2023). Internet of Things for Digital Forensics Application in Saudi Arabia. *Advances in Internet of Things*, *13*(1), 1–11. doi:10.4236/ait.2023.131001

Bowling, H., Seigfried-Spellar, K., Karabiyik, U., & Rogers, M. (2023). We are meeting on Microsoft Teams: Forensic analysis in Windows, Android, and iOS operating systems. *Journal of Forensic Sciences*, *68*(2), 434–460. doi:10.1111/1556-4029.15208 PMID:36734289

CNET. (2008). Anonymous hackers take on the Church of Scientology, Cosmos Bank malware attack: Interpol issues red corner notice against prime suspect traced in foreign country. *Cities News, The Indian Express.*

Crowdstrike. (2022). *Fileless Malware Explained, What is Fileless Malware?* CrowdStrike.

Crowdstrike. (2023). *12 Types of Malware + Examples That You Should Know.* Crowdstrike.

Daubner, L., Macak, M., Matulevičius, R., Buhnova, B., Maksović, S., & Pitner, T. (2023). Addressing insider attacks via forensic-ready risk management. *Journal of Information Security and Applications*, *73*, 103433. doi:10.1016/j.jisa.2023.103433

Dell Technologies. (2021). *What are the different types of Viruses, Spyware and Malware that can infect my computer?* Dell India

Deochakke, A., & Tyagi, A. K. (2022). Analysis of Ransomware Security on Cloud Storage Systems. In V. Sugumaran, D. Upadhyay, & S. Sharma (Eds.), *Advancements in Interdisciplinary Research. AIR 2022. Communications in Computer and Information Science* (Vol. 1738, pp. 45–54). Springer. doi:10.1007/978-3-031-23724-9_5

Du, J., Raza, S. H., Ahmad, M., Alam, I., Dar, S. H., & Habib, M. A. (2022). Digital forensics as advanced ransomware pre-attack detection algorithm for endpoint data protection. *Security and Communication Networks*, *2022*, 1–16. doi:10.1155/2022/1424638

Fortinet. (n.d.) *What Is a Trojan Horse? Trojan Virus and Malware Explained.* Fortinet.

Gupta, K., Varol, C., & Zhou, B. (2023). Digital forensic analysis of discord on google chrome. *Forensic Science International: Digital Investigation, 44*. Science Direct. doi:10.1016/j.fsidi.2022.301479

HT Tech. (2023). 2 BILLION Google Chrome users hit by browser security flaw! *Tech News, Hindustan Times.*

Humayun, M., Jhanjhi, N. Z., Alsayat, A., & Ponnusamy, V. (2020). Internet of things and ransomware: Evolution, mitigation and prevention. *Electronic International Journal of Time Series Economics*, *11*(2), 21–36. doi:10.1016/j.eij.2020.05.003

Iorliam, A. (2019). Cybersecurity and Mobile Device Forensic. In *Cybersecurity in Nigeria. SpringerBriefs in Cybersecurity*. Springer. doi:10.1007/978-3-030-15210-9_4

Jamalpur, S., Navya, Y. S., Raja, P., Tagore, G., & Rao, G. R. K. (2018). Dynamic Malware Analysis Using Cuckoo Sandbox. In *2018 Second International Conference on Inventive Communication and Computational Technologies (ICICCT)* (pp. 1056-1060). IEEE. 10.1109/ICICCT.2018.8473346

Kaspersky. (n.d.-a). *What are the different types of malware?* Kasper sky.

Kaspersky. (n.d.-b). *What is a Botnet?* Kasper Sky.

Kaspersky. (n.d.-c). *What is Adware?* Tech Target.

Katherasala, S. K., Sri Manvith, V., Therala, A., & Murala, M. (2022). *NetMD-Network Traffic Analysis and Malware Detection.* 2022 International Conference on Artificial Intelligence in Information and Communication (ICAIIC), Jeju Island, Korea. 10.1109/ICAIIC54071.2022.9722691

Khan, A. A., Shaikh, A. A., Laghari, A. A., & Malook Rind, M. (2023). Cloud forensics and digital ledger investigation: A new era of forensics investigation. *International Journal of Electronic Security and Digital Forensics*, *15*(1), 1–23. doi:10.1504/IJESDF.2023.127745

Lee, M.-C., & Cho, S.-B. (2012). Interactive differential evolution for image enhancement application in smartphone. In *IEEE Congress on Evolutionary Computation* (pp. 1-6). Brisbane, QLD, Australia: IEEE. 10.1109/CEC.2012.6256653

Mabsali, N. A. L., Jassim, H., & Mani, J. (2023). Effectiveness of Wireshark Tool for Detecting Attacks and Vulnerabilities in Network Traffic. In *Proceedings of the 3rd International Conference on Computer Science, Electronics and Communication Engineering (CSECE 2023)* (pp. 113-122). IEEE. 10.2991/978-94-6463-110-4_10

MalikS.AgrawalA. K. (2021). Multi pronged approach for ransomware analysis, SSRN. doi:10.2139/ssrn.4017025

Montasari, R. (2023). Artificial Intelligence and the Internet of Things Forensics in a National Security Context. In *Countering Cyberterrorism. Advances in Information Security* (Vol. 101). Springer. doi:10.1007/978-3-031-21920-7_4

MUO. (2021) AIDS Trojan: The Story Behind the First Ever Ransomware Attack. Make Use Of.

Nasreen, S., & Mir, A. H. (2023). Enhancing cloud forensic investigation system in distributed cloud computing using DK-CP-ECC algorithm and EK-ANFIS. *Journal of Mobile Multimedia*, *19*(03), 679–706. doi:10.13052/jmm1550-4646.1933

Pang, C., Wang, X., Xu, S., Wang, C., Liu, P., & Liu, Y. (2021). SoK: All You Ever Wanted to Know About x86/x64 Binary Disassembly But Were Afraid to Ask. In *2021 IEEE Symposium on Security and Privacy (SP)*. San Francisco, CA, USA: IEEE, https://doi.org/10.1109/SP40001.2021.00012

Park, J., Lee, S., Hong, J., & Ryu, S. (2023). Static Analysis of JNI Programs Via Binary Decompilation. *IEEE Transactions on Software Engineering*, *49*(5), 3089–3105. doi:10.1109/TSE.2023.3241639

Qamar, A., Karim, A., & Chang, V. (2019). Mobile malware attacks: Review, taxonomy & future directions. *Future Generation Computer Systems*, *97*, 259–276. doi:10.1016/j.future.2019.03.007

Rahaman, M. (2022). Analysis of Attacks on Private Cloud Computing Services that Implicate Denial of Services (DOS). Cyber Security Insights Magazine, 4.

Seo, S., Seok, B., & Lee, C. (2023). Digital forensic investigation framework for the metaverse. *The Journal of Supercomputing*, *79*(9), 9467–9485. doi:10.100711227-023-05045-1

Shaji, P. S. (2020). Understanding the Digital Forensics Framework of Cloud Computing-Cloud Forensics. *International Journal of Legal Developments and Allied Issues, 6*(3).

Shin, Y., Kim, S., Jo, W., & Shon, T. (2022). *Digital forensic case studies for in-vehicle infotainment systems using Android Auto and Apple CarPlay*. MDPI. . doi:10.3390/s22197196

Suresh Babu, C. V. (2023a). *IoT and its Applications*. Anniyappa Publications.

Suresh Babu, C. V. (2023b). IoT-Based Smart Accident Detection and Alert System. In P. Swarnalatha, S. Prabu, & I. G. I. Global (Eds.), *Handbook of Research on Deep Learning Techniques for Cloud-Based Industrial IoT* (pp. 322–337)., doi:10.4018/978-1-6684-8098-4.ch019

Tamma, R., Skulkin, O., Mahalik, H., & Satish., B. (2020). *Forensically investigate and analyze iOS*. PACKT Publishing. https://books.google.co.in/books?id=TU_cDwAAQBAJ&lpg=PP1&dq=recent%20paperworks%20on%20malware%20forensics&lr&pg=PP2#v=twopage&q&f=false

Techcrunch (2018). Everything you need to know about Facebook's data breach affecting 50M users. Techcrunch.

TechTarget (2022). SolarWinds hack explained: Everything you need to know. *Tech Target*.

TechTarget Security. (2022). Computer worm. *Tech Target*.

The Conversation. (2021). The increase in ransomware attacks during the COVID-19 pandemic may lead to a new internet. *The Conversation*.

The Indian Express. (2020). Cosmos Bank malware attack: Interpol issues red corner notice against prime suspect traced in foreign country. *The Indian Express*.

Zhang, X., Breitinger, F., Luechinger, E., & O'Shaughnessy, S. (2021). Android application forensics: A survey of obfuscation, obfuscation detection and deobfuscation techniques and their impact on investigations. *Forensic Science International: Digital Investigation*, *37*, 301285. doi:10.1016/j.fsidi.2021.301285

Chapter 14
Malware Detection Using Yara Rules in SIEM

Priyam Subhash Patel
Rashtriya Raksha University, India

Rakesh Singh Kunwar
Rashtriya Raksha University, India

Akash Thakar
Rashtriya Raksha University, India

ABSTRACT

In this cyber world, working from the office to the home, security has never been more challenging. To detect attacks on the host computers and prevent further malicious activities, host intrusion detection systems (HIDS) are often used. Use of open-source SEIM tool Wazuh for monitoring and combines with YARA for file analysis. YARA rules are like those of a programming language that operates by specifying variables that indicate patterns identified in malware, depending on the rule. If any or all the conditions are satisfied, it can be used to effectively identify at least a portion of malware that defines variable parameters. YARA rules help SIEM operators analyse the file tag for malware detection before using it to its full potential. In this chapter, we are going to learn and implement malware analysis using Wazuh, and YARA rules before infecting the system fully. A flexible and effective method for detecting malware in system logs, network traffic, and other data sources is produced by combining WAZUH and YARA rules. By utilising the advantages of YARA rules and the sophisticated features of WAZUH, security teams can quickly identify malware attacks and respond to them. This lessens the effect on their business. A modern cybersecurity strategy must contain WAZUH SIEM and YARA rules. With YARA rules, security teams may spot malware attacks in WAZUH and take appropriate action to maintain the security and integrity of their organization's data and systems.

DOI: 10.4018/978-1-6684-8666-5.ch014

INTRODUCTION

The Internet has become a crucial component of many people's everyday lives. The number of services offered on the Internet is enormous and continues to increase daily. A rising number of individuals are using these services. Online banking and advertising are two examples of Internet business services. Just like in the real world, there are those on the Internet who have malevolent intentions and take advantage of innocent users if money is involved. Malware is malicious software that assists these persons in achieving their aims by allowing remote access or can causing a denial of service (DOS) in the system.

IDS are used to identify assaults and security breaches that can't be avoided by current security measures, according to the National Institute of Standards and Technology's (NIST) Special Publication on Intrusion Detection System. Abuse detection and anomaly detection are the two basic methods used to analyse detection (Bace & Mell, 2001). With a specified warning, the abuse detection may identify each instance of an assault. The character employed in the abuse detection process may be a sign of compromise (IoC). IoC may also be derived from the findings of malware analysis.

Detection of malware coming through the network is known as network monitoring and traffic analysis. These are divided into two: Active for live or real-time and Passive for captured network traffic analysis. Malicious files come to the system through these networks, extracting files from the real-time network traffic and analysing them for potential threats using YARA rules, then sending them to the SIEM.

MALWARE

Malicious software is referred to as "malware" informally. Without the owner's knowledge or approval, this kind of software is added to the system. Most of the time, untrusted third parties instal this harmful software to steal, corrupt, and harm the user's sensitive and personal data. The impact of malware is deteriorating daily; thus, the creators of malware must gain an advantage in disseminating their software, which includes Worms, Trojan, Horses, Spyware, Viruses, Rootkits, Ransomwares, Adware, and many more across the Internet's vast network.

WHAT IS MALWARE AND ITS TYPES

Malware is an alias for malicious software, which is meant to harm a computer system without the user's knowledge. Malwares can be categorised into the following categories:

- Virus: A malicious software that attaches itself to other programmes to infect them and perform some unwanted actions.
- Trojan: Trojan replicates itself and can be used for steals information. It is an application that attempts to infect other computers automatically by hiding itself behind other program, without the assistance of other forces, as other malware does.
- Worms: A worm is a self-replicating malicious computer programme that accesses computer and network resources without the authorization of an authenticated user. It is eating network bandwidth on the network.
- Spyware: It gets installed on other users' systems without the user's permission and to report on the user's behaviour.
- Rootkit: A rootkit is a malware programme that create a backdoor into the system for the hackers to access, alters files, and eliminates data files.

STATIC ANALYSIS OF MALWARE

When malware is analysed without being executed, it is called Static Analysis. In this case, the different properties of the PE file are analysed without running it. Similarly, in the case of a malicious document, exploring the document's properties without analysing it will be considered Static Analysis. Examples of static analysis include checking for strings in malware, checking the PE header for information related to different sections, or looking at the code using a disassemble. We will look at some of these techniques later in the room.

Malware often uses techniques to avoid static analysis. Some of these techniques use obfuscation, packing, or other means of hiding its properties. To circumvent these techniques, we often use dynamic analysis.

Information to Be Analysed

- File characteristics: Information about the file's kind, size, creation and modification dates, and other fundamental details might reveal where and why the infection came from.

- Strings and keywords: The malware's source code could include text strings, such URLs or file locations, that shed light on how it behaves.
- Code structure and functionality: The intended functionality of the malware, such as keylogging or data exfiltration, may be ascertained by looking at the code.
- System calls and API usage: To communicate with the operating system, the virus may employ certain system calls or APIs. You may use these to determine what the virus is attempting to do.
- Network communication: The malware's network traffic may be examined to determine the Command and Control (C&C) servers it uses, the information it spies on, and the domains it contacts.
- Obfuscated or packed code: Malware may be obfuscated or packed to avoid detection or complicate analysis. The code may be de-obfuscated and unpacked using tools.
- Signature and hash: A hash may be computed and compared to a database of known malware using MD5, SHA-1, or SHA-256.
- Sandbox analysis: Malware may also be used to study behaviour and find any extra functionality or network connections by running it in a controlled environment.

Popular Tools Used for Static Analysis

Table 1 List of software

· Disassembler
    o IDA disassembler
    o Debugger
    o IDA debugger
    o Immunity debugger
    o OllyDbg
    o Windbg
    o x64dbg
	· File viewers
	    o PE viewer
	    o PEiD
	    o CFF Explorer
	    o Bin Text
	    o Doc File
	    o ViewerEX

· Network analysis
    o Wireshark
    o Zeek
    o Fiddier
	· Others
	    o Volatility
	    o process hacker
	    o Sysinternals

Effects of Malware

- Malware can steal sensitive data, like login passwords, financial information, or personal information.

- Malware can harm or erase crucial system files, causing system corruption or malfunction and leaving a device or computer unusable.
- Malware can propagate to other computers on a network and create slowdowns or outages, which can disrupt the network.
- Malware can use system resources, slowing down or disrupting the operation of a computer or other device.
- Privacy invasion: Without the user's knowledge or consent, malware may follow and gather personal data, including browser history.
- Spread of further malware: Some viruses are made to infect other systems, which can cause the infection rate to increase exponentially.
- Crypto-jacking: Malware that uses a computer's computing power to mine cryptocurrencies is known as crypto-jacking. The impacted machine may become slower, crash, or overheat because of this.
- Ransomware encrypts the victim's files and demands payment to decrypt them.

WHAT IS SIEM

A SIEM tool gathers security-related information and events from variety of sources to monitor suspicious and malicious network activities and presents them via one system. If any anomaly detected in these slogs alert is generated which further been analysed.

WAZUH ELEMENTS

Wazuh is a combination of four different elements (Wazuh, 2023).

- Wazuh Indexer: A "extremely scalable, full-text search and analytics engine."
- Wazuh Server: "Analysing the data collected from the agents, the Wazuh Server triggers alarms when dangers or abnormalities are found," according to the company.
- Wazuh Dashboard: This "flexible and easy web user interface for analysing, mining and visualizing security events and alerts data" used for tracking security events and alerts.
- Wazuh Agent: The agent is responsible for system protection and offers a range of services, including threat detection, threat prevention, and response capabilities.

THINGS TO MONITOR

Escalation Paths

Determining the escalation channels for each client is one of the primary goals of the planning stage. Particularly, when and who the SOC can speak with in top management or the customer to escalate an incident. The client also must be aware of who to contact inside the SOC. Escalation routes are set forth for both internal departments and MSSP. To assist prevent confusion when an incident happens, these pre-specified messages are developed in advance.

Unwanted Download and Installation

Unwanted download and installation can occur when a user's device is infected with malware or when a user unknowingly visits a malicious website. This type of activity can lead to the installation of malware, unwanted software, or unwanted browser extensions on the user's device.

There are several methods that malware can be sent to a user's system, including through email attachments, software downloads, and compromised websites. Once on the user's device, the virus can carry out several undesirable tasks, such as downloading and installing further malware or unwanted programmes.

To Prevent Unwanted Download and Installation, It Is Important to Take Steps to Protect Your Device, Such As:

- Keeping the operating system and software updated with the latest security patches.
- Installing an anti-virus & anti-malware and regularly updating software
- Avoiding clicking on links or downloading attachments from unknown or suspicious sources
- Being cautious when visiting websites, especially those that offer free downloads or ask for personal information.
- Using a firewall and intrusion detection system, such as Wazuh

It's also important to be aware of the signs that your device may have been infected with malware, such as unexpected pop-ups, slow performance, and changes to your browser settings. If you suspect that your device has been infected, you should take immediate steps to remove the malware and protect your personal information.

Identifying the assets and their criticality for alarm prioritization:

Identifying assets and their criticality is an important step in alarm prioritization. Alarm prioritization is the process of sorting and organizing alarms based on their importance, so that the most critical alarms can be dealt with first.

To identify Assets and Their Criticality, You Can Use the Following Steps

- Identify the assets: These can be physical assets such as servers, workstations, and network devices, or they can be logical assets such as software systems, databases, and applications.
- Classify the assets: Once you have identified the assets, you need to classify them based on their criticality. This can be done by considering factors such as the asset's importance to the organization, the potential impact of an outage or security incident, and the likelihood of an incident occurring.
- Assign a priority level: Once you have classified the assets, you can assign a priority level to each one. This can be a numerical value, such as 1, 2, or 3, or a more descriptive value such as "critical", "high", and "medium".
- Map the assets to the alarms: Once you have assigned a priority level to each asset, you can map the assets to the alarms that are generated by the security tools. This will allow you to prioritize the alarms based on the criticality of the assets they relate to.
- Continuously update your asset inventory: The assets and the criticality of each can change over time, so it's important to regularly review and update the asset inventory.

By identifying the assets and their criticality, you can ensure that the most critical alarms are handled first, reducing the risk of an incident going unnoticed, and allowing for a more efficient incident response. Additionally, you can also use the asset's priority level to notify the right people and teams.

LAB SETUP

To set up a lab for using Wazuh, Ubuntu, YARA for file extraction and malware detection, you will need to perform the following steps:

- Install Ubuntu on a virtual machine or physical machine. Ubuntu is a popular Linux distribution that is widely supported and easy to use.
- Install and configure Wazuh. Wazuh can be installed on Ubuntu using apt-get package manager, or by downloading and installing the package from Wazuh'

s documentation. After installation, you can configure Wazuh to suit your needs by editing the configuration files.

- Install and configure YARA. YARA can be installed on Ubuntu using apt-get package manager. Once installed, you can create and edit YARA rules to suit your needs.
- Configure Wazuh to use YARA for malware detection. This can be done by adding YARA rules to the Wazuh configuration files and configuring Wazuh to use those rules.
- Test the lab setup by running Wazuh and capturing network traffic using then analysing the captured traffic using Wazuh and YARA. This will allow you to verify that the lab is working correctly and to test the detection capabilities of the system.

LAB NETWORK SETUP

In VMWare workstation 17 click on->Edit-> Virtual Network editor or. Select any network or create new network interface, set them to NAT network and enable DHCP, so any other guest so connects using that network it will get same IP address from the DHCP pool.

Figure 1. Wazuh network architecture (Gómez Vidal, 2019)

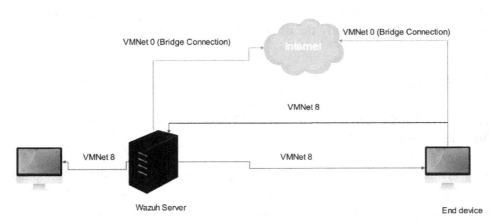

LAB NETWORK CONFIGURATIONS

Table 2. Network configuration

Figure 2. Wazuh network	Figure 3. Host machine
Figure 4. Wazuh server	Figure 5. Wazuh agent

INTRODUCTION OF WAZUH

Wazuh is an open-source log monitoring solution that provides a complete platform for detecting threats, responding to incidents, and complying with regulations. It is built on top of the Elastic Stack (formerly known as ELK stack), which provides the foundation for data indexing, search, and visualization.

Wazuh is designed to be a modular and scalable platform that can be used to monitor and protect different types of environments, including endpoint security, cloud security, and network security. To identify and address security risks, it offers a variety of functions, such as intrusion detection, vulnerability management, and log management.

One of the key features of Wazuh is its ability to detect and respond to security incidents in real-time. It has built-in support for intrusion detection and incident response and can be configured to alert on specific types of activity or to take automated action in response to an incident.

In addition to its security capabilities, Wazuh also provides a range of compliance features that can be used to ensure that an organization's security policies are being enforced. It can be configured to detect and alert on compliance violations and can provide detailed reports on compliance status.

Wazuh is also compatible with multiple platforms and environments, including Windows, Linux, macOS, and various cloud providers. It may be used to create a more complete security solution by being integrated with other security technologies and delivered both on-premises and in the cloud.

Wazuh is a powerful and flexible platform for security monitoring, threat detection and incident response, and compliance management. It can help organizations in detection and responding to security threats for quickly and effectively, and to ensure that their security policies are being enforced.

Wazuh Architecture

Figure 6. Wazuh architecture (Stanković et al., n.d.)

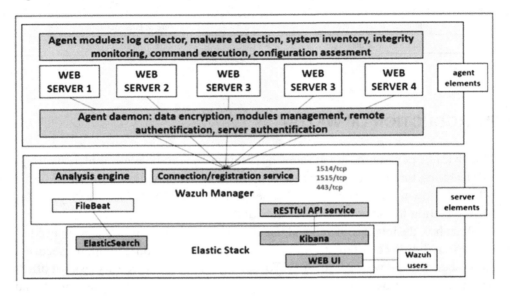

Script When Wazuh Dashboard Is Not Running

Figure 7. Error message

Figure 8. Wazuh login page

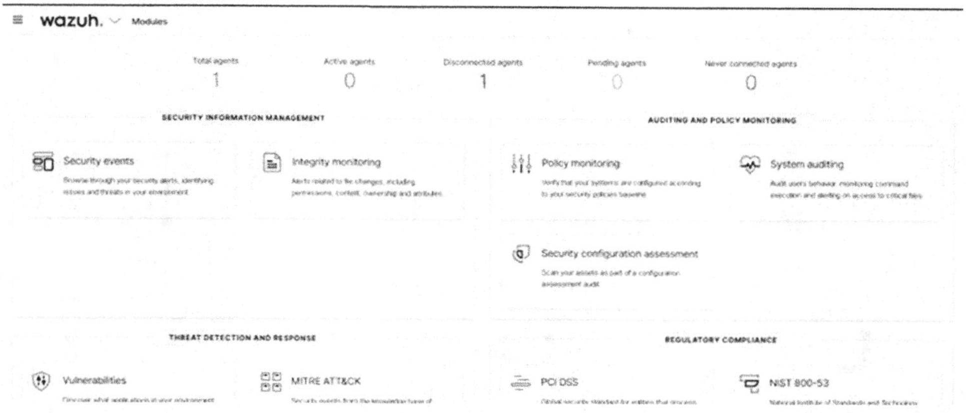

Figure 9. Wazuh dashboard

Run this script in Wazuh server with administrator privilege. Add this in Wazuh agent and restart it. This is the path which you want to monitor in the Wazuh agent for detection of any download file in the agent.

Add path of the directories <syscheck> block of the Wazuh agents of /ossec. conf file to monitor the directory.

Figure 10. Management configuration dashboard

Figure 11. Wazuh agent dashboard

SETUP WAZUH FOR DETECTION

Make Changes in Wazuh Server

- **/var/ossec/etc/decoders/local_decoder.xml, /ossec.conf**
- **/var/ossec/etc/rules/local_rules.xml**

Wazuh' s decoders are used to process and analyse log data. They help to extract useful information from raw logs and normalize it into a structured format that can be easily consumed and analysed by other security tools.

Decoders in Wazuh are used to:

- Parse log data: Decoders can extract relevant fields from raw logs, such as timestamps, IP addresses, and event details.

Figure 12. Local decoder

- Normalize log data: Decoders can standardize the format of log data, so that it can be easily understood and analysed by other tools.
- Enrich log data: Decoders can add additional context to log data, such as IP reputation, hostname, and geo-location.
- Identify log events: Decoders can match log data against a set of regular expressions or pattern to identify specific events, such as login failures or network connections.

Wazuh rules are used to detect specific security-related events on the system, such as:

- Attempts to access sensitive files or directories.
- Failed login attempts or changes to system users.
- Network connections to known malicious IP addresses.
- Modification to system files or configuration.
- Suspicious process execution or network activity.
- Misconfigurations in system settings or software.

Figure 13. Local rules

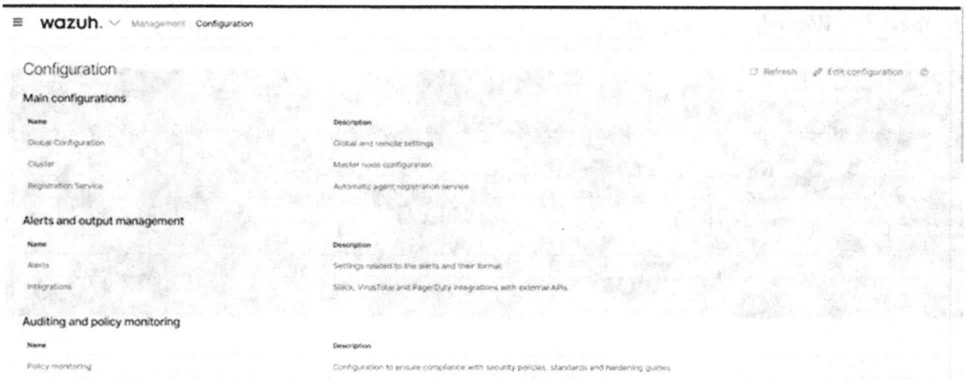

The configuration of Wazuh is used to customize and fine-tune the behaviour of the platform to meet the specific needs of an organization.

Some of the key uses of Wazuh configuration include:

- Setting up log collection: Wazuh can collect log data from variety of sources, such as syslog, event logs of windows, and Apache access logs. The configuration is used to specify which logs should be collected, where they are located, and how they should be processed.
- Configuring alerts and notifications: Wazuh can send alerts and notifications when specific security-related events are detected. The configuration is used to specify which events should trigger alerts, how they should be sent, and to whom they should be sent.
- Setting up decoders: Wazuh' s decoders are used to process and analyse log data. The configuration is used to specify which decoders should be applied to which log sources, and how they should be configured.
- Defining rules: Wazuh rules are used to detect specific security-related events on the system. The configuration is used to specify which rules should be applied and how they should be configured.
- Configuring scalability: Wazuh can be configured to scale horizontally, allowing to add more agents to the cluster and increasing the capacity to process large amounts of data.
- Setting up security: The Wazuh configuration can be used to configure security settings, such as encryption, authentication, and access control.
- Enabling integrations: Wazuh can integrate with other security tools and platforms, such as SIEM, to provide a more comprehensive security solution. The configuration is used to specify how these integrations should be configured.

Restart the Wazuh server to apply the changes.

Figure 14. Wazuh server config

```
# Mirai: https://en.wikipedia.org/wiki/Mirai_(malware)
Downloading malware sample...

Done!

# Xbash: https://unit42.paloaltonetworks.com/unit42-xbash-combines-botnet-ransomware-coinmining-worm-targets-linux-windows/
Downloading malware sample...
Done!

# VPNFilter: https://news.sophos.com/en-us/2018/05/24/vpnfilter-botnet-a-sophoslabs-analysis/
Downloading malware sample...
Done!

# WebShell: https://github.com/SecWiki/WebShell-2/blob/master/Php/Worse%20Linux%20Shell.php
Downloading malware sample...
Done!
```

Download malware in the specified folder which were added in the Wazuh server.

Figure 15. Downloading malware

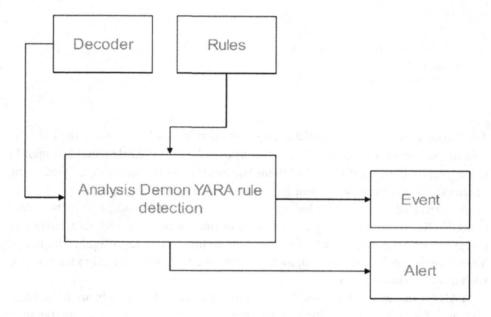

YARA

YARA is a tool used for identifying and classifying malware based on patterns in the code or other characteristics. It uses a set of rules, called YARA rules, to scan files and determine whether they match a specific pattern. YARA rules are written in a simple language and consist of a set of strings and conditions that specify what the tool should look for in a file. Each rule has a unique name and can be associated with multiple strings and conditions.

The Basic Structure of YARA Rules

```
rule <rule_name> {
strings:
        $string1 = "example"
        $string2 = "example2"
    condition:
        all of them
}
```

The "strings" section contains the strings that the rule should look for in the file. The "condition" section specifies the conditions under which the rule should trigger. In this example, the condition "all of them" means that all the strings specified in the "strings" section must be present in the file for the rule to trigger.

A variety of malware, including viruses, trojans, and rootkits, may be found using YARA rules. They may also be used to find malware and adware, two more categories of harmful software. To offer a more thorough defence against malware, YARA rules can be used in conjunction with other malware detection techniques, such as antivirus software.

YARA rules are widely used for analysing and identifying malware in incident response, forensic investigations, and hunting operations. It's also used in dynamic and static analysis tools, sandboxing, and other security tools. It's also important to note that YARA is not only limited to malware detection, it can be also used for detecting other types of files, such as documents and images, based on their characteristics.

MAKING OF IOC

Eight indicators that serve as a source for the creation of IoC on YARA were produced because of the analytical procedure (Akram & Ogi, 2020). The three positions meta, strings, and conditions are split among the eight indicators. These indications are used to create a rule for identifying malware. The constructed IoC reads, a "YARA rule's fundamental composition is as follows." The hash value of the sample, the compiler stamp, and information on the IoC manufacturer are all included in the meta. Special virus detection capabilities are built into strings. The condition specifies the prerequisites for malware detection. If all indications are recognised in IoC, then the following requirements must be satisfied (Akram & Ogi, 2020).

YARA Flow on SIEM

Figure 16. YARA flow (Gómez Vidal, 2019)

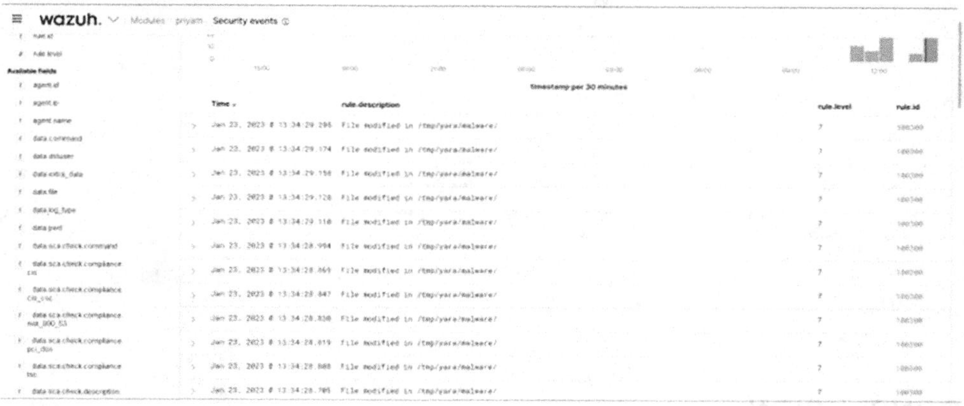

VALIDATION

Any modifications in the designated folder on the end device are shown in Figure 17. The YARA IoC validation procedure utilising the Wazuh dashboard is shown in Figure 18. On a directory containing samples, the IoC is running. any signs that YARA has picked up. Three signs were found in this validation by YARA. The IoC was deemed genuine since the three indications were found, proving that YARA had successfully found malware using the indicators listed in the directory.

Figure 17. Modification in the folder

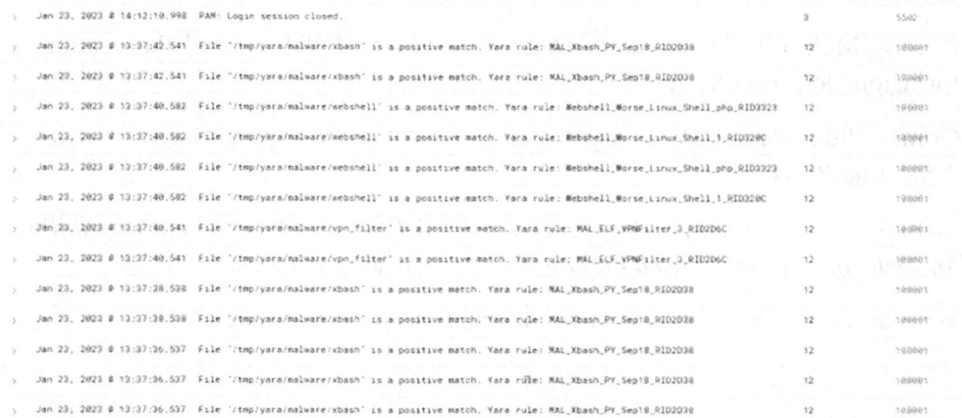

Figure 18. Malware detected

CONCLUSION

The IoC was created successfully utilising YARA rules and reverse engineering approaches, it can be said. The bytecode of a typical malware sample serves as the indication utilised in IoC. Other malware in the same directory is not found by IoC. This indicates that, in line with the predetermined objectives, the IoC has effectively discovered malware.

REFERENCES

Akram, B., & Ogi, D. (2020). The Making of Indicator of Compromise using Malware Reverse Engineering Techniques. *2020 International Conference on ICT for Smart Society (ICISS)*, 1-6. 10.1109/ICISS50791.2020.9307581

Bace & Mell. (2001). *Intrusion Detection Systems*. NIST Special Publication on Intrusion Detection Systems.

Gómez Vidal, A. S. (2019). *Improvements in IDS: adding functionality to Wazuh*. Academic Press.

Stanković, S., Gajin, S., & Petrović, R. (n.d.). *A Review of Wazuh Tool Capabilities for Detecting Attacks Based on Log Analysis*. Academic Press.

Wazuh. (2023). https://documentation.wazuh.com/current/index.html

Chapter 15
Malware Mitigation Tools

J. Jeyshri
https://orcid.org/0000-0002-9068-1545
SRM Institute of Science and Technology, India

R. Sasirekha
SRM Institute of Science and Technology, India

ABSTRACT

Over time, malware attacks have become more frequent and sophisticated, causing substantial harm to organisations and individuals. In response, malware mitigation technologies have been created by cybersecurity specialists in order to identify, stop, and correct such assaults. Network traffic is monitored by intrusion detection and prevention systems, which also notify security professionals of possible threats. By preventing unwanted access to a network, firewalls give an extra degree of security. Untrusted software is isolated and run in a secure environment using sandboxing technologies to look for suspected malware activities. Instead of relying on malware's signature, behavioural analysis techniques identify malware by its activity. Despite the availability of these technologies, malware assaults continue to pose a serious danger, necessitating ongoing improvement and updating of mitigation strategies. Future developments in malware mitigation solutions, such as the use of artificial intelligence and machine learning, will also be covered in this chapter.

INTRODUCTION

Because of our dependence on technology and the internet, malware assaults have become a major worry for both people and businesses. Malware assaults, which include viruses, worms, trojan horses, and ransomware, may seriously harm computer

DOI: 10.4018/978-1-6684-8666-5.ch015

systems, steal confidential data, and even take down whole networks. To identify, stop, and stop such assaults, cybersecurity specialists have created a variety of malware mitigation solutions.

Figure 1 statistics give the detail about the industries which are affected by malware attacks in common industries. An overview of the present status of malware mitigation technologies, including firewalls, sandboxing, intrusion detection and prevention systems, antivirus software, and behavioural analysis tools, will be given in this book chapter. The function of these tools, their advantages and disadvantages, and their efficiency in preventing malware assaults will all be covered in this chapter.

RELATED WORKS

Zahid Akhtar et al. (2021) The author offers a thorough analysis of malware mitigation methods and tools, including approaches based on behaviour analysis, machine learning, and signatures. The writers also go through the difficulties in identifying zero-day threats and the necessity to strike a balance between security and performance when it comes to malware mitigation. Ammar et al. (2020) Antivirus software, intrusion detection and prevention systems, and sandboxing methods are just a few of the several malware mitigation strategies included in this study. The authors also go through the difficulties in preventing malware, including the growing complexity of malware and the need for ongoing changes to mitigation solutions. Neda Sadat et al. (2020) This study examines methods for detecting malware as well as its mitigation, including signature-based, behavior-based, and machine learning-based methods. The limits of signature-based techniques and the need for real-time network traffic analysis are only two of the difficulties that the writers mention while discussing malware detection and mitigation. Zeinab Khosravi, et al. (2021) This paper gives a general overview of malware mitigation strategies, including sandboxing, intrusion detection, and prevention systems. The authors also cover the difficulties in preventing malware, including the need for improved zero-day attack detection and prevention. Seyedeh et al. (2021) This study focuses on deep learning, reinforcement learning, and transfer learning as machine learning approaches for malware detection and mitigation. The difficulties of employing machine learning for malware detection and mitigation are also covered by the authors, including the need for a significant quantity of training data and the possibility of adversarial assaults.

Background on the Threat of Malware

Software that is intended to damage computer systems, networks, or other devices is referred to as malware, short for malicious software. Malware may appear as viruses, worms, trojan horses, spyware, ransomware, and adware, among other things. Cybercriminals often employ malware to steal confidential data, disrupt operations, demand money, or gain illegal access to networks.

Malware is a serious problem that worries both people and organisations as well as governments. Malware assaults have the potential to do a great deal of harm, including monetary losses, damage to one's reputation, and legal responsibilities. Since cybercriminals and nation-states may employ malware to perform espionage or launch assaults on vital infrastructure, malware attacks can potentially be a danger to national security. Malware assaults may happen in a variety of methods, such as through phishing schemes, social engineering techniques, taking advantage of software flaws, or by utilising harmful code that is embedded in trustworthy software. Malware may also infect several systems or devices by spreading across networks.

Ransomware, which encrypts data or locks users out of their computers until a ransom is paid, is one of the most prevalent forms of malware. Attacks using ransomware have increased in frequency over the last several years, with well-publicized assaults hitting institutions including hospitals, companies, and governmental organisations. These assaults have the potential to injure patients and clients as well as cause considerable financial losses and business interruptions.

Cryptojacking is another kind of malware that has become well-known in recent years. Without the device owner's knowledge or agreement, cryptojacking entails utilising the processing power of infected devices to mine cryptocurrencies. Cryptojacking may make equipment function poorly by draining its battery and slowing it down.

Internet of Things (IoT) devices, including smart household appliances, medical equipment, and industrial control systems, are also susceptible to malware assaults. These gadgets often have poor security measures, which fraudsters may simply employ to access networks or damage people.

Nation-states, organised criminal groups, or lone hackers often launch malware assaults. These attackers may use a variety of strategies and methods, such as encryption, obfuscation, or zero-day vulnerabilities, to avoid detection and do damage.

Malware has been a growing concern in recent years, with attackers using more complex methods and equipment. With conventional malware mitigation technologies, it may be challenging to find fileless malware, which runs fully in memory and leaves no traces on disc. Attackers may even deceive workers into disclosing private information or making money transfers by using social engineering techniques like spear phishing or CEO fraud.

Overall, cybersecurity experts and companies throughout the globe continue to have serious concerns about the danger posed by malware. Traditional malware mitigation methods and tactics may not be sufficient to keep up with the evolving threat environment due to the rapid development of malware and the growing expertise of attackers. In order to keep one step ahead of attackers and guard against these constantly changing dangers, malware mitigation solutions need to be continuously improved and innovated.

OVERVIEW OF MALWARE MITIGATION TOOLS AND TECHNIQUES

The term "malware mitigation" describes the methods and equipment used to stop or lessen the effects of malware infections. Successful malware mitigation calls for a multi-layered strategy that combines both conventional and cutting-edge tools and procedures.

Antivirus Software: A classic malware mitigation technology, antivirus software checks files and programmes for known malware signatures. This programme has the ability to recognise and eliminate a wide variety of malware, including viruses, worms, and trojans.

Intrusion Detection and Prevention Systems (IDPS): An IDPS is a piece of hardware or software that keeps an eye on system logs and network traffic for indications of malware activity. A real-time malware detection and blocking system like IDPS may help stop assaults before they can do any harm.

Firewalls: Another common malware mitigation technique, firewalls regulate the movement of data between networks and devices. Firewalls may stop malware from connecting with command-and-control servers and can block incoming traffic from known dangerous sources.

Running untrusted programmes or data in a virtual environment that is separate from the rest of the system is known as sandboxing. This enables analysis of the virus without contaminating the host system and may reveal malware that was previously unidentified.

Tools for Behavioral Analysis: These programmes keep track of how programmes and files behave, searching for any unusual behaviour that could point to the existence of malware. These techniques are capable of detecting malware that conventional signature-based tools have not yet been able to detect.

Zero-trust Security: This kind of security works on the premise that all users and devices are at risk of being infiltrated. This implies that rather than a user's position on the network, access to resources is limited based on the user's identification and the security posture of their device.

Cloud-based Security Solutions: As businesses shift their data and apps to the cloud, cloud-based security solutions are growing in popularity. Sandboxing and machine learning are only a few of the sophisticated malware detection and mitigation features that these systems may provide.

Threat hunting is actively looking for indications of malware or other security threats in the networks and systems of a company. This may include doing vulnerability assessments, examining logs and network traffic, and spotting unusual activities.

Deception Technology: Using decoys like phoney servers or files, deception technology entices attackers into disclosing their existence. Attackers may be located, isolated, and kept from moving laterally via the network with the use of deception technologies.

With artificial intelligence and machine learning, it is possible to examine vast volumes of data and spot trends that could be related to the activities of malware. These technologies may aid in the detection of previously unidentified malware and can instantly adapt to new dangers.

TRADITIONAL MALWARE MITIGATION TOOLS

This has been around for a while and is still used often to battle malware. These programmes operate by locating and eliminating known malware signatures using a continuously updated database of virus definitions. Traditional malware mitigation methods that are often used include:

Antivirus Software: Malicious software may be found and eliminated from a computer or other device using antivirus software. Antivirus software searches through files, applications, and other data for patterns that resemble malware and other infections. If malware is discovered, the antivirus programme may either quarantine it or delete it to stop it from doing any damage.

Computer networks are protected by firewalls against unwanted access and harmful activities. Firewalls stop outgoing communication to known harmful destinations and block incoming traffic from unauthorised sources. In order to stop malware from propagating to other networked devices and from contacting command-and-control sites, firewalls may be deployed.

Email filters are used to stop viruses from entering a network of a company through email attachments or links. To recognise and prevent emails containing malware, email filters combine reputation-based filtering with content-based filtering.

Backup and recovery tools are used to save data safely so that it may be recovered to a prior, malware-free state in the event that a device becomes infected. Frequent backups may lessen the harm that malware assaults do.

Operating System Updates and Patches: Operating System updates and patches are made to close holes in the operating system that malware may exploit. Malware assaults may be avoided by frequently upgrading operating systems, software, and apps.

Traditional malware mitigation technologies still have a place, but they have certain drawbacks. These instruments are reactive, which means they can only find and get rid of known malware. They are also susceptible to zero-day attacks, which take advantage of flaws that had not yet been discovered. Organizations are thus increasingly using more sophisticated malware mitigation solutions.

Antivirus Programme

Maybe the most well-known malware mitigation technology is antivirus software. It operates by checking computer system files for recognised malware signatures and preventing any malware discovered. In order to find and stop previously unidentified malware, antivirus software has developed throughout time to incorporate cutting-edge technologies like heuristic analysis and machine learning. In contrast to machine learning, which use algorithms to learn from prior malware samples and identify new variations, heuristic analysis focuses on searching for unusual behaviour that may be an indication of the existence of malware.

Antivirus software has limits even if it is good at finding and preventing known infections. Malware authors may readily change their code to avoid detection by antivirus software, and zero-day assaults (in which criminals take use of previously undiscovered flaws) can completely avoid antivirus security. Hence, antivirus software is just one weapon among a bigger collection of malware mitigation strategies.

Systems for Detecting and Preventing Intrusions

Another weapon in the arsenal for preventing malware is intrusion detection and prevention systems (IDPS). Network traffic is monitored by IDPS, which notifies security professionals of possible risks. They may be host-based or network-based. Whereas host-based IDPS monitors traffic on individual computers, network-based IDPS keeps an eye on activity at the network's edge.

Network traffic is compared to known patterns of harmful behaviour by IDPS in order to function. For instance, an IDPS may spot a brute-force assault on a system that requires a password and notify security professionals of the possible danger. Certain IDPS systems have the ability to block communication that seems malicious, stopping an attack in its tracks.

While certain forms of attacks may be detected and prevented using IDPS, they are not without flaws. Attacks that employ encrypted or unconventional protocols could go undetected by IDPS. Moreover, IDPS may produce a huge number of false positives, which can cause alert fatigue and cause real threats to go unnoticed.

Firewalls

Another essential element of the malware mitigation toolset is the firewall. A firewall is a kind of network security system that keeps track of and regulates incoming and outgoing network traffic in accordance with pre-established security rules. Hardware- or software-based firewalls are also options.

Each packet of network traffic that passes through a firewall is examined and compared to a set of predetermined rules. The firewall may prevent a packet from accessing the network if it disobeys a rule or notify security teams of possible dangers. Moreover, firewalls may be set up to reject traffic from certain IP addresses, ports, or protocols.

Firewalls have some limits even if they may be successful at preventing known threats. Firewalls are unable to identify all forms of malware, and attackers may get around them by employing encrypted communication or taking advantage of flaws in the firewall software.

Sandboxing

In order to identify suspected malware activity, sandboxing is a malware mitigation strategy that includes executing untrusted software in a secure setting. Security teams may analyse the behaviour of the programme and identify any malicious activity by using sandboxing technology, which separates untrusted software and runs it in a controlled environment.

Before they are permitted into a network, suspected files, emails, or websites may be tested via sandboxing. Moreover, sandboxing may be utilised to examine the actions of malware that has already

While sandboxing is a useful technique for locating malware, it has certain drawbacks. Sandboxing may use a lot of resources and might not be suitable for usage on all systems. Attackers may also create malware that recognises when it is operating in a sandbox and modifies its behaviour to escape detection.

Tools for Behavioural Analysis

Another kind of malware mitigation solution that identifies malware based on its behaviour rather than its signature is behavioural analysis software. Tools that analyse system behaviour, such as file updates, network connections, and system changes, look for indications of malicious activity.

Malware that has eluded other mitigation strategies, such as antivirus software, may be found using behavioural analysis methods. Moreover, zero-day attacks and other unknown risks may be found using behavioural analysis technologies.

While behavioural analysis techniques are good at finding malware, they have several drawbacks. Tools for behavioural analysis may provide false positives, causing alert fatigue and the possibility of overlooking real threats. Moreover, using behavioural analysis techniques on all systems may not be feasible due to their resource-intensive nature.

While cybercriminals continuously develop new strategies and tools to avoid detection and wreak damage, malware assaults continue to constitute a serious danger to people and companies. As a result, there has never been a greater pressing demand for efficient malware mitigation tools and approaches.

The increased usage of artificial intelligence (AI) and machine learning (ML) technology is one current trend in malware mitigation. With the use of these technologies, enormous data sets may be analysed to find patterns and abnormalities that can point to hostile activities. AI and ML may also aid in automating certain malware detection and response processes, enabling cybersecurity experts to react swiftly to attacks.

The usage of containerization and microsegmentation is a new trend in malware mitigation. Encapsulating apps and services in separate contexts via containerization gives users more protection and control. Networks are divided into smaller pieces called microsegments, and each segment is subject to tougher access restrictions and monitoring. Combining these methods may assist to lessen the attack surface and stop malware from spreading.

The growing use of threat intelligence is another new trend in malware mitigation. To better comprehend the strategies, methods, and motives of known threats and attackers, threat intelligence entails gathering and evaluating data about them. After that, this information may be utilised to enhance threat detection and response times as well as malware mitigation measures.

Together with these changes, there is an increasing need for enhanced interoperability and integration across various malware mitigation techniques and solutions. Malware assaults sometimes entail numerous phases and strategies, and no one solution can guarantee total security. The visibility and coordination of various mitigation measures may be improved with better integration and interoperability, which can also increase the overall efficacy of malware mitigation techniques.

Last but not least, it is critical to understand that malware assaults are both a technological and a human issue. Human mistake, such as weak passwords, phishing schemes, or social engineering techniques, often results in malware assaults being successful. Many assaults may be stopped in their tracks by informing staff members about the dangers of malware attacks and increasing awareness of these threats.

EMERGING TRENDS IN MALWARE MITIGATION

Artificial Intelligence and Machine Learning

The use of artificial intelligence (AI) and machine learning (ML) to the detection and remediation of malware is one of the most exciting new developments in malware mitigation. Instead than depending on existing fingerprints, AI and ML may be used to identify and classify malware based on behaviour. This method, known as behavioural analysis, may be used to find malware and zero-day assaults that were previously undetected. In order to lighten the strain on security professionals and enable quicker reaction times, AI and ML may also be utilised to automate malware detection and response.

Containerization and Micro Segmentation

By separating workloads and applications from one another, containerization and microsegmentation are two strategies that may assist to increase security. Applications may be packaged and operated inside of containers, which are small, mobile software units that can be utilised in a safe, isolated setting. Microsegmentation is a method for controlling access across various areas of a network by using network virtualization to create tiny, isolated network segments. Organizations may decrease the attack surface and lessen the effect of malware if it does manage to get past their defences by employing containerization and microsegmentation.

Threat intelligence

Information on cyberthreats and the people who are behind them is gathered and analysed as part of threat intelligence. This data may be utilised to spot emerging risks, foresee assaults, and build prepared defences. Threat intelligence may be used to increase the precision and efficacy of conventional malware mitigation technologies by informing the creation of malware signatures and behavioural models. Moreover, it may be used to prioritise security spending and find weak points in an organization's defences.

Integration and Interoperability

The integration and interoperability of security technologies and systems is a new trend in malware mitigation. This strategy acknowledges the necessity for a layered defence since no one tool or system can provide total protection against malware. Organizations may develop a security posture that is more complete and well-coordinated by combining various technologies and systems. Via fewer false positives and quicker reaction times, this strategy may also serve to increase the effectiveness of security operations. The ecosystem's overall security may be increased by facilitating the exchange of threat information across various enterprises and security systems via interoperability.

HUMAN FACTORS IN MALWARE MITIGATION

Employee Training and Awareness

Employee education and awareness is one of the most crucial human variables in the mitigation of malware. Attacks by malware often depend on user actions, such as opening a corrupted attachment or clicking on a malicious link. Organizations may lower the probability of successful attacks by teaching staff about the dangers of malware and how to prevent it. A wide variety of subjects should be included in employee training and awareness, such as:

Social engineering and phishing: Workers should get training on how to spot phishing emails and other social engineering scams. These assaults often involve social engineering strategies to persuade workers into disclosing private data or installing malware.

Malware Detection and Prevention: Workers should get training on how to spot malware infestations, which might manifest as sluggish performance or unforeseen pop-up windows. Also, they should learn about virus prevention techniques including avoiding dubious websites and updating software.

Workers should get incident response training on how to handle malware attacks, including who to call and what to do to stop the infection from spreading.

Reporting: It should be emphasised to staff members that they should notify the IT department of any unusual activities or possible malware infestations.

To keep staff members abreast of the most recent hazards and mitigation strategies, training should be continuous and often updated. Simulated malware and phishing assaults may also be used to enhance employee awareness since they can show workers where they are vulnerable and teach them how to defend against future attacks.

Social Engineering and Phishing Scams

These frauds, which mainly depend on human factors, pose a serious danger to enterprises. Social engineering is the practise of using psychological deception to persuade others to divulge private information or do acts that are not in their best interests. The use of phoney emails or websites to deceive people into disclosing personal information is characteristic of phishing schemes, a sort of social engineering assault. Organizations should put the following procedures into practise to lessen the dangers of social engineering and phishing scams:

Employee Training and Awareness: As was said before, combating social engineering and phishing schemes requires staff training and awareness. Workers should be educated to spot the symptoms of social engineering assaults, such as strange emails or phone calls, and to avoid disclosing sensitive information until they are assured of the legality of the request.

Anti-Phishing Software: Anti-Phishing software may be used to detect and stop phishing emails and websites. These solutions combine many methods, including reputation score and content analysis, to find and remove dangerous information.

Two-Factor Authentication: By requiring a second authentication factor, such as a code texted to a mobile device in addition to a password, two-factor authentication may assist to thwart social engineering attacks. Even if a password is hacked, this may aid in preventing illegal access.

Companies should have incident response procedures in place to deal with phishing and social engineering assaults. The measures to be done in the case of an attack, including who to call and what procedures to take to limit and minimise the damage, should be included in these plans.

D. Password Policy and Management: Passwords are an important part of any security plan, and effective management of them is necessary to reduce malware. Passwords that are weak, obvious, or frequently used might make it simple for attackers to access systems and data. Organizations should put the following methods into practise to increase password security:

Strong Password Policies: Businesses should have rules in place requiring staff members to create strong passwords and to update them often. Moreover, password regulations have to prohibit the use of passwords that are simple to guess, such "password" or "123456."

Multi-Factor Authentication: By requiring an extra authentication element, such as a code texted to a mobile device in addition to a password, multi-factor authentication may assist to increase password security.

Tools for Managing Passwords: These tools may assist in increasing the security of passwords.

OVERVIEW OF MALWARE DETECTION TECHNIQUES

Nowadays, it is crucial to keep data secure from attackers. Attackers try to steal data from individuals using malware. It is essential to keep data safe from malware.

Figure 1. Widely used malware detection methodologies

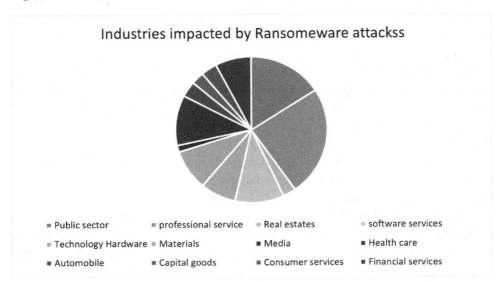

Several malware detection techniques are used, but the detection is shallow. In this section, highly used malware detection techniques (Akhtar et al., 2021) are discussed. Malware such as viruses, worms, botnets, and ransomware.

Every day a new arrival of malware releasing through online. The safety measures should concentrate on unethical activities of unknown individuals who try to inject a malicious virus to hack the data.

Heuristics-based detection seeks malware by scrutinizing documents for fishy factors without a precise signature contest. An event identified an antimalware tool strength look for wrong instructions or junk in the taken document. Computer viruses and different digital fishy often get more cagey. In this section, a brief study on virus detection has been carried out.

It is not a new case, but these conditions' trickery with the harshness has only aggravated over the years as more recent methodologies are being made open to the public. Widely known detection methods for virus attacks include **signature-based**, **behavioural**, and **cloud-based**.

Signature-Based Detection

The familiar method for detecting fishy or viruses is known as **signature-based protection**. It consists separate database. Once the virus is identified using its signature at every moment, that virus information is added to the online threat database continuously based on the identified signature. But this tool can't predict or add unknown threats. These type of detection technique can be implemented in the cybercrime (Ahmad & Rahman, 2020) to identify the threats easily.

Behavioural- Based Detection

Behavioural detection is a dynamic method in that it often supervises the activities of the installed applications for any fishy behaviors. Some of those behaviours include pushing the offending application to begin with, the computer, and injuring security characteristics. Behavioural detection (Safavi et al., 2020) is the predominant approach, with a more increased detection rate than signature-based detection. Since attackers are always modifying the signatures to inject malware, overlooking the installed applications for exhaustive moves is more beneficial than endeavoring to oppose the signatures.

Cloud-Based Detection

This detection methodology is needed to secure the data shared over the cloud network. It is not easy to decrypt the data for the authenticated user (Khosravi et al., 2021). There is a lot of possibilities for hacking data over the cloud, and unknown individual can inject malicious threats over the cloud. It is very difficult to find that kind of malicious threat. This cloud-based methodology can be used to identify the threats created over the cloud and ensure the encryption and decryption of data happen between authorized users.

Overview of Malware Removal Techniques

Malware protection is essential to keep data secure. Every day there is a new arrival of malware, and many techniques are implemented based on the nature of the malware. In this section, a detailed study on malware protection has been carried out.

The malware protection (Rafiei & Rahmani, 2021) mechanism is implemented based on the type of threat identified in the context. The widely used detection mechanisms have been taken to detect the threat, and based on the identified threats, the protection mechanism is studied deeply.

Protection Mechanisms Used for the Malware Through Email

Most of the detection mechanism can found the threats by means of comparing that with the online threat database. In this section, the protection mechanism used to identify and prevent the malware injected in the email. An Individual can inject malicious threat through email links. When user click on that links then the data can

Figure 2. Email-malware protection mechanism

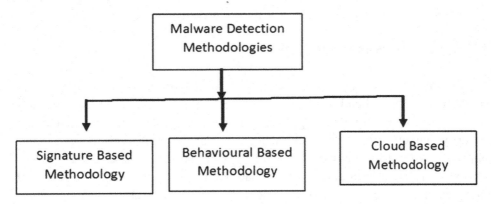

be steeled by the unkown attacker. These type of threats can be handled by using Random forest (Kim et al., 2019) approach the legitimate and the malicious emails can be identified and the mechanism used to protect the legitimate information from the threats.

Protection Mechanisms Used for the Cloud Environment

Identifying threats while transferring data from server to client is more complicated. The protection mechanism starts with identifying the nature of the threat and comparing that threat with the existing threats. Protection has been given to the data shared in the cloud network (Agrawal & Saini, 2016).

Figure 3. Cloud storage protection

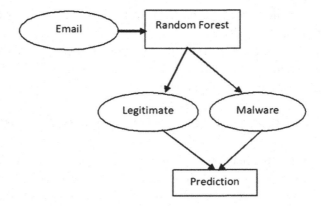

The data file from the cloud storage can be divided into several sub-files, and these sub-files will be considered to check the presence of malware. Machine learning algorithms are used to identify the threat in the files. The legitimate files are compared with the files containing malware.

FUTURE TRENDS

Despite the availability of these technologies, malware assaults continue to pose a serious danger, necessitating ongoing improvement and updating of mitigation strategies. The use of machine learning and artificial intelligence (AI) is a trend in malware mitigation solutions. To evaluate vast volumes of data and find patterns that can point to the existence of malware, AI and machine learning can be employed.

The use of blockchain technology is another trend in malware reduction. A decentralized, impenetrable log of network activity may be created using blockchain, making it more difficult for attackers to hide their traces.

CONCLUSION

In conclusion, malware assaults provide a serious risk to both people and businesses. Cybersecurity specialists have created a variety of malware mitigation solutions, including as antivirus software, intrusion detection and prevention systems, firewalls, sandboxing, and behavioural analysis tools, to reduce the danger of malware assaults. These technologies have limits even if they are good at spotting and stopping certain threats. Upcoming advances in malware mitigation include using blockchain technology, AI, and machine learning. To remain one step ahead of attackers, it is crucial to keep malware mitigation strategies up to date and improved as the malware threat evolves.

REFERENCES

Agrawal, S., & Saini, S. (2016). A Review of Malware Detection Techniques. In *Proceedings of the International Conference on Computing and Communication Systems (I3CS 2016),* (pp. 261-265). IEEE. doi: 10.1109/I3CS.2016.7823468

Ahmad, A., & Rahman, A. A. (2020). A Literature Survey on Malware Mitigation Approaches and Challenges. *International Journal of Computer Science and Network Security, 20*(5), 46–54.

Akhtar, Z., Khan, S. A., & Minhas, A. A. (2021). A Survey on Malware Mitigation Techniques and Tools. *Journal of Cybersecurity*, 7(1).

Al-Asli, M., & Ghaleb, T. A. (2019). Review of Signature-based Techniques in Antivirus Products. *2019 International Conference on Computer and Information Sciences (ICCIS)*, Sakaka, Saudi Arabia. 10.1109/ICCISci.2019.8716381

Arshad, M., Muhammad, A. R., & Alhakami, R. (2022, May). Malware detection using machine learning: A comprehensive review. *Security and Communication Networks*, *2020*, 1–18.

Hu, Y., & Li, J. (2020). A Deep Learning-Based Malware Detection Approach Using a Hybrid Feature Selection Method. *IEEE Access : Practical Innovations, Open Solutions*, *8*, 151983–151992. doi:10.1109/ACCESS.2020.3017017

Jadhav, P. N., & Pore, P. D. (2016). Comparative Analysis of Various Malware Detection Techniques. *Proceedings of the International Conference on Computing, Communication and Automation (ICCCA 2016)*, (pp. 104-10). IEEE. 10.1109/CCAA.2016.7813841

Khosravi, Z., Hosseini-Asl, E., & Yaghmaee, M. H. (2021). A Review of Malware Mitigation Techniques: State of the Art and Future Directions. *Journal of Cybersecurity*, 7(1).

Kim, T. H., Park, J., & Cho, H. (2019). A Dynamic Malware Analysis Method Using Reverse Engineering. *IEEE Access : Practical Innovations, Open Solutions*, *7*, 43315–43324. doi:10.1109/ACCESS.2019.2907512

Maggi, F., Matteucci, M., & Zanero, S. (2010, October-December). Detecting Intrusions through System Call Sequence and Argument Analysis. *IEEE Transactions on Dependable and Secure Computing*, *7*(4), 381–395. doi:10.1109/TDSC.2008.69

Memon, R. A., & Mallah, R. A. (2020, July). Malware detection using machine learning techniques: A comprehensive survey. *Journal of Ambient Intelligence and Humanized Computing*, *11*(7), 2811–2835. doi:10.100712652-020-02145-w

Menezes, N. J., Rocha, L. M., & Junior, R. M. C. (2019, December). Malware detection using static analysis techniques: A survey. *Journal of Computer Virology and Hacking Techniques*, *15*(4), 241–262. doi:10.100711416-019-00320-x

Mira, F. (2021). A Systematic Literature Review on Malware Analysis. *2021 IEEE International IOT, Electronics and Mechatronics Conference (IEMTRONICS)*, (pp. 1-5). IEEE. 10.1109/IEMTRONICS52119.2021.9422537

Qaisar, Z. H., Almotiri, S. H., Al Ghamdi, M. A., Nagra, A. A., & Ali, G. (2021). A Scalable and Efficient Multi-Agent Architecture for Malware Protection in Data Sharing Over Mobile Cloud. *IEEE Access : Practical Innovations, Open Solutions*, *9*, 76248–76259. doi:10.1109/ACCESS.2021.3067284

Rafiei, S. Y., & Rahmani, A. M. (2021). A Survey on Machine Learning Techniques for Malware Detection and Mitigation. *Journal of Cybersecurity*, *7*(1).

Safavi, N. S., Hosseini-Asl, E., & Yaghmaee, M. H. (2020). A Survey on Malware Detection and Mitigation Techniques. *Journal of Cybersecurity*, *6*(1).

Sharma, D. D., Tripathi, D. D., & Gaur, M. K. (2016). Anomaly Based Malware Detection Using Machine Learning. *Proceedings of the 5th International Conference on Advances in Computing, Communications and Informatics (ICACCI 2016)*, (pp. 2655-2660). IEEE. 10.1109/ICACCI.2016.7732399

Tripathi, D. D., & Sharma, D. D. (2014). Malware Mitigation through Machine Learning Algorithms. *Proceedings of the 6th International Conference on Computational Intelligence and Communication Networks (CICN 2014)*, (pp. 543-547). IEEE. 10.1109/CICN.2014.134

Yang, S., Zhou, H., & Zhao, C. (2020, December). A malware detection system based on dynamic analysis and deep learning. *Journal of Intelligent & Fuzzy Systems*, *38*(6), 6701–6711. doi:10.3233/JIFS-191769

Zeng, Y. G. (2017). Identifying email threats using predictive analysis. *2017 International Conference on Cyber Security And Protection Of Digital Services (Cyber Security)*, (pp. 1-2). IEEE. 10.1109/CyberSecPODS.2017.8074848

Chapter 16
The Future of Cyber Security Starts Today, Not Tomorrow

C. V. Suresh Babu

(iD) https://orcid.org/0000-0002-8474-2882
Hindustan Institute of Technolgy and Science, India

P. Andrew Simon
Hindustan Institute of Technology and Science, India

S. Barath Kumar
Hindustan Institute of Technology and Science, India

ABSTRACT

This study dives into the field of cybersecurity, analyzing current trends and laying out a conceptual framework for spotting new issues with societal bearing that call for more study in the area. The research eventually seeks to better society's general cybersecurity posture by effectively spotting trends and new risks by using text mining to examine cybersecurity material distributed between 2008 and 2018 in both scholarly and media sources. There is a significant time-based connection between the resources, as shown by the study's discovery of both convergences and divergences between the two cybersecurity corpora. Overall, the study's methodology shows how well automatic methods can be used to offer insightful information on socially significant and new cybersecurity subjects. The framework directs future academic study in this area with the intention of strengthening society's overall cybersecurity stance.

DOI: 10.4018/978-1-6684-8666-5.ch016

1. INTRODUCTION

Implementing procedures, safeguards, and technologies in the area of cybersecurity entails protecting information, software, networks, and systems from possible cyberattacks (Dey & Dasgupta, 2019). In order to counter attacks that target network systems and apps in an organization's internal or exterior environment, a variety of tools and technologies related to cybersecurity are used. According to statistical data, the average expense of a data leak is $3.86 million globally and $8.64 million in the USA. These expenses cover the immediate effects of the breach, the inquiry that follows to determine its origin, related reactions, income loss, downtime, and reputational brand harm (Mylrea et al., 2018).

The majority of organizations have implemented cybersecurity strategies based on best practices to avoid such costs and losses. To fight against cyberattacks and maintain the secrecy, integrity, and availability of cyber assets, an effective cybersecurity strategy usually uses tiered defense. It seeks to stop instances of financial extortion that interfere with regular company operations. A cybersecurity structure was created by the National Institute of Standards and Technology (NIST) to assist organizations in safeguarding their computer networks, systems, and other assets that support governmental, public health, and safety, as well as national security, activities (Hussain et al., 2020). International Organization for Standardization (ISO) has also developed the series of ISO27000 information security standards to address comparable requirements.

Even with the most robust defenses, attackers can still discover security framework flaws despite the presence of such approaches and standards. Due to weaknesses in remote access tools, cloud services, and other tools used for remote working, cybersecurity risks developed during the epidemic as work standards changed from in-office to work-from-home. Malware, ransomware, phishing, insider threats, distributed denial-of-service (DDOS) threats, advanced persistent threats (APTs), man-in-the-middle assaults, and other threats are among the ever-evolving dangers. The primary goal of this chapter is to describe how cyber security will be a component of everything we use on a daily basis and what obstacles we will encounter in the future (Upadhyay & Yadav, 2018).

2. THREATS AND VULNERABILITY

Cybersecurity threats and vulnerabilities are constantly shifting, creating a challenging and dynamic environment for businesses and people to operate in. The following are some of the most important dangers and weaknesses to be mindful of, both now and in the future:

PRESENT:

1. **Phishing attacks** are a type of hack that use social engineering strategies to trick people into disclosing private data, like login passwords or banking information. These assaults frequently take the form of phoney emails, messages, or webpages that seem to be from a reliable source but are actually made to trick the receiver into disclosing their private or confidential information. Once the perpetrator has this information, they can use it for illegal activities like financial scams, identity theft, and other nefarious schemes. It's crucial to use security precautions like two-factor authentication and anti-phishing software, as well as to be watchful and wary when opening links in emails or clicking on unsolicited messages in order to defend against phishing assaults.

2. **Malware:** Without the user's awareness or permission, malware, such as viruses and Trojan horses, can be installed on a system, giving attackers access to data or causing the system harm (Perarasi et al., 2020).

3. **Insider threats:** People who have access to confidential data may unintentionally or deliberately reveal it to unapproved parties (Sun et al., 2022).

4. **DoS (denial-of-service) assaults** Cyberattacks known as denial-of-service (DoS) attacks overload a system with data, making it inaccessible to users. A solitary attacker or a collection of attackers using a can initiate these assaults. a range of methods, including overloading the system's resources, delivering a system a ton of data, and exploiting system weaknesses. A DoS assault aims to obstruct regular operations and deny authorized users access to the system or its services. DoS assaults can seriously harm companies and organizations by interfering with their daily operations, resulting in financial losses, and harming their image. Organizations can put firewalls, intrusion detection systems, load balancers, and a thorough incident response strategy in place to defend against DoS assaults.

5. **Ransomware:** This type of malware encrypts data belonging to an organization and requests a ransom in return for the access key (Dyke Parunak, 2022).

FUTURE:

1. **Attacks on the Internet of Things (IoT):** As more and more devices are linked to the internet, the danger of IoT attacks that take advantage of flaws in these devices to access other systems is rising. (Suresh Babu, 2023)

2. **Assaults powered by artificial intelligence (AI):** AI can be used to automate assaults, making them more complex and challenging to discover.

3. **Quantum computing** has the ability to defeat many of the data security encryption methods presently in use.
4. **Supply chain attacks** are becoming more likely as businesses depend more on outside vendors for software and other services. These attacks aim to compromise these vendors' systems so that they can access those of their clients.
5. **Cyberwarfare:** A new period of cyberwarfare has emerged as a result of nation-states' growing use of cyberattacks as a sabotage and espionage weapon.

Organizations and people must maintain vigilance, keep their software and systems up to date, and put strong security practices such as two-factor authentication, encryption, and routine backups into place to reduce these dangers and weaknesses.

For example, Take for instance that you get an email that seems to be from your bank. The subject line of the email reads, "Urgent Action Required: Your Account Security Compromised!" The email's content includes the bank's logo, an official-looking layout, and a statement that your account has been the subject of suspicious activity.

The email requests that you click on a specified link right away to safeguard your account. It warns that doing otherwise might lead to your account being suspended or to money being stolen. The urgency of the email makes you feel worried about the security of your account and apprehensive. Unbeknownst to you, the email's link does not, in fact, take you to your bank's website. It takes you to a bogus website that is skillfully made to resemble the login page for your bank. Your username, password, and other personal details are requested on the page, which claims that doing so is necessary to safeguard your account and confirm your identity. The attackers will have successfully acquired your login information if you fall for the phishing scam and submit your information on the false page. They can then use this information to carry out fraudulent activities, sell your credentials on the dark web, or even get unauthorized access to your actual bank account. It's crucial to exercise caution and scepticism when opening unexpected emails, particularly those that demand personal information and convey a feeling of urgency. Always check the sender's credibility, look for telltale phishing indications in the email (such as bad language, misspelt words, or generic greetings), and stay away from clicking on dubious links if you want to defend yourself from phishing attempts. When in doubt, get in touch with the company directly using their official contact details to verify the email's legitimacy. Likewise there are lot of example for others also.

3. REVIEW OF LITERATURE

Positive Effects of future of cyber security:

1. Internet Of Thing And Artificial Intelligence: The Internet of Things (IoT) can be protected from online dangers and weaknesses, and safety in this area has a bright future. And Artificial intelligence's (Al) potential for defense is complicated and multifaceted. Al has the potential to transform cybersecurity by making attack discovery, reaction, and prevention more rapid and effective. It also poses important difficulties, such as the possibility of Al algorithms being controlled or used by hackers (Banafa, 2018; Oblaender, 2019; Suresh Babu, 2023).

2. Aviation And Financial: Future developments in technology, a changing danger environment, and governmental regulations will all have an impact on aircraft cybersecurity. Companies that provide financial services are adopting the use of cutting-edge technologies, such as Blockchain and artificial intelligence (AI) which helps to make them more secure and fast (Perarasi & Vidhya, 2020).

3. Healthcare and Education: In order to combat the evolving cyber threats, cybersecurity in flight will require a proactive and coordinated strategy. Cybercriminals are increasingly targeting healthcare organizations that invest in sophisticated MME. because to the significant information—including sensitive health information, financial data, and intellectual property—that it includes. Future developments in technology, commercial demand, and altering societal and cultural values are anticipated to have a significant influence on cybersecurity education. Therefore, a number of fresh trends and resources are expected to have an impact on how cybersecurity education develops in the future (National Institute of Standards and Technology, 2020).

Negative Effects of future of cyber security:

1. Internet of Thing and Artificial Intelligence: Due to the pervasive use of these devices, which are frequently linked to the internet and may have vulnerabilities that can be exploited by cybercriminals, IoT security is becoming an increasing worry. Even if AI is being utilised more and more in cybersecurity, hackers may still use it to launch increasingly sophisticated assaults. AI may be used to circumvent security measures or create highly customised phishing attacks (Dey, 2019; Mohamed, 2020).

2. Aviation and Financial: The aviation industry has grown more digitised with the introduction of extensive computerised systems for managing everything from air traffic control to passenger check-in. Automation has numerous benefits,

but there are also new cybersecurity concerns that the aircraft sector has to address. Financial institutions are finding it more difficult to fight against cyberattacks as hackers' methods and techniques develop. In ransomware attacks, hackers are increasingly encrypting user data and demanding money to unlock it (Hussain, 2019; Razali, 2020).

3. Healthcare and Education: Healthcare is increasingly going digital. The challenges listed below are some that healthcare organisations may likely face in the future. increasing complexity of cyber threats As hacker tactics and plans develop, healthcare organisations are finding it harder to defend against cyberattacks. As educational institutions employ digital tools and platforms for teaching and learning more and more, cybersecurity concerns are becoming a growing concern (Upadhyay, 2018).

Methodological Limitations and Gaps in the Literature:

1. Lack of Real-World Data: The scarcity of real-world data is a serious obstacle to cybersecurity research. The complexity and diversity of real cyber threats and assaults may not be fully reflected by the many research that use simulated or synthetic datasets. The creation and assessment of efficient cybersecurity solutions may be hampered by a lack of access to extensive and high-quality datasets.

2. Limited Generalizability: Cybersecurity is a fast developing topic, and security measures' efficacy can change between various systems, businesses, and situations. Numerous studies concentrate on particular situations or circumstances, which may restrict the applicability of their conclusions. Future study should aim to encompass a wide variety of real-world contexts and assess the efficacy of cybersecurity measures across many areas in order to overcome this restriction.

3. Ethical and Legal Restraints: Dealing with sensitive data and potentially destructive acts is a common part of doing cybersecurity research. Concerns around data privacy, permission, and compliance with laws and regulations provide ethical and legal challenges for researchers. These limitations may restrict the kinds of research that may be done and may affect the reliability and relevance of the results.

4. Lack of Longitudinal Studies: Longitudinal studies that track changes in security postures over time are necessary due to the dynamic nature of cyber threats and the developing nature of cybersecurity solutions. However, there aren't many longitudinal studies in the cybersecurity literature, which makes it difficult for us to grasp how security measures will affect society over the long run.

Conclusion: According to the material studied here, cyber security will likely have both beneficial and negative implications in the future. The IOT, AI, aviation, financial, healthcare, and educational sectors may all use it to assist and aid in the expansion of these industries. Future study should adopt more reliable methodology, include a variety of demographics, and investigate probable processes behind these impacts in order to establish a complete cyber security. To further promote a good future scope of cyber security practises while minimising their negative effects, tailored initiatives and guidance are required.

4. CYBER SECURITY FUTURE

A number of new patterns and technologies are expected to have an impact on the direction of cybersecurity. Here are some possible changes that could affect safety in the future:

4.1. Cyber Security Future in IoT

The Internet of Things (IoT) can be protected from online dangers and weaknesses, and safety in this area has a bright future.

The enormous number and diversity of IoT devices that need to be secured, from basic sensors to sophisticated industrial machinery, is one of the major obstacles in doing so. Because many IoT devices are frequently constructed with outdated and vulnerable software or with limited security features, this intricacy poses serious security risks. This makes them desirable targets for cybercriminals who attempt to access confidential data or initiate attacks on other systems or networks by taking advantage of their flaws (Banafa, 2018).

New technologies and approaches are being created to handle these issues and enhance IoT security devices. To protect interactions between IoT devices and the cloud, for instance, new encryption protocols like Transport Layer Security (TLS) and Datagram Transport Layer Security (DTLS) are being created. In order to recognize and react to cyber dangers in real-time, machine learning algorithms and artificial intelligence methods are also being used (Swarnalatha et al., 2023).

Using Blockchain technology, which can offer a tamper-proof and secure record of all transactions and interactions between devices, is another strategy for protecting IoT devices. This can make it more difficult for cyber attackers to meddle with or alter IoT data and help to guarantee its integrity and validity.

Overall, the Internet of Things' future of safety is both bright and complex. These linked gadgets can be secured and protected from cyberattacks with the appropriate technologies and strategies. The sheer quantity and variety of IO T devices present one of the greatest obstacles in terms of security. Small monitors to big industrial machines—all various sizes and types of IOT devices—each with their own powers and security needs. Consequently, it is crucial to adopt, The security of the complete IOT ecosystem, including the networks and cloud services that serve these devices, can be expected to receive more attention in future advancements. This might entail putting in place security measures like zero trust, in which every device and person is verified and given permission before being allowed access to resources. Artificial intelligence (AI) and machine learning (ML) will be crucial in the future of IOT protection for real-time attack detection and response. AI and ML can analyze enormous quantities of data to find anomalies and trends that could be signs of attacks or security lapses. Additionally, Blockchain technology may be used to provide decentralized and private communication, enhancing the resistance of IOT devices to assaults. By guaranteeing the availability, stability, and secrecy of interconnected systems and devices, these technologies will be essential to the development of IOT cybersecurity in the future (Banafa, 2018).

Case Study on IoT

IoT cybersecurity was highlighted by the Mirai botnet assault in 2016, which showed how important it is. Unsecured devices were taken over and used to initiate DDoS attacks on websites, highlighting the importance of putting security measures in place to protect IoT devices. This assault, which had an effect on several well-known websites, was among the biggest and longest DDoS attacks ever documented. The Mirai botnet assault made it clear how crucial it is to put security precautions like encryption, authorization, and access control in place to protect IoT devices. Many IoT devices come pre-configured with weak preset passwords, leaving them open to intrusion. Therefore, manufacturers must make sure that gadgets arrive with distinctive, secure passwords that the user can alter. Adopting software upgrades is a crucial additional safeguard for Internet of Things (IoT) devices. Numerous gadgets might have security flaws that an attacker could abuse because they weren't built with security in mind. Regular firmware upgrades can fix these flaws and guarantee that the device is protected from the most recent dangers.

4.2. Cyber Security Future in AI

Artificial intelligence's (AI) potential for defense is complicated and multifaceted. AI has the potential to transform cybersecurity by making attack discovery, reaction, and prevention more rapid and effective. It also poses important difficulties, such as the possibility of AI algorithms being controlled or used by hackers. AI's capacity to analyze more data and identify trends in cyberattacks is among its most important advantages in cybersecurity (Chan et al., 2019). Algorithms that use machine learning can also gain knowledge from earlier assaults and gradually increase their capacity for discovery. Organizations' capacity to react can be aided by this. This could facilitate organizations quicker and more efficient responses to dangers (Kamoun et al., 2020). Al, however, also offers fresh assault methods that demand attention. Attackers, for instance, might use Al algorithms to create more complex and focused assaults, or they might take advantage of flaws in Al systems themselves. Additionally, because these algorithms handle and analyse significant quantities of sensitive data, their use in cybersecurity may raise privacy issues (Kuppa & Le-Khac, 2021). In order to overcome these difficulties, organizations must be open and honest about how they gather and use data. Machine learning algorithms can enhance their detection skills over time by learning from previous attacks, which can help organizations react more swiftly and effectively to new threats. In order to safeguard our digital systems and infrastructure, the future of cybersecurity in Al will necessitate a mix of cutting-edge technologies, strong security frameworks, and successful business, government, and academic collaboration (Nikolskaia & Naumov, 2021).

Case Study on AI

AI Cybersecurity Solution from Darktrace

Machine learning is used by the UK-based surveillance company Darktrace, which uses AI to detect and stop intrusions. The Enterprise Immune System, the company's flagship offering, replicates the way the immune system of the body reacts to threats in real time. The system makes use of AI methods to learn about the network and typical behavioral patterns of an organization. After that, it employs this knowledge to spot irregular behavior that might point to a hack. The system is capable of detecting a variety of cyber threats, including phishing assaults, ransomware, and insider threats .The ability of Darktrace's AI cybersecurity system to identify new dangers is one of its main advantages. The systems used in conventional cybersecurity solutions are rule-based and can only identify recognized risks. However, based on their behavioral trends, AI algorithms can identify fresh and undiscovered dangers. Given the increase in sophisticated and focused cyberattacks that are made to bypass conventional security measures, this is especially crucial.

4.3. Cyber Security Future in Aviation

Future developments in technology, a changing danger environment, and governmental regulations will all have an impact on aircraft cybersecurity. The following are some major patterns that will probably influence aircraft cybersecurity in the future:

1. Increased use of linked systems: As connected systems in aircraft, like the Internet of Things (loT), are used more frequently, there is an increased danger of cyberattacks. Therefore, aircraft businesses will need to make sure that their systems are safe and secure from online dangers (, , 2020).

2. Increased emphasis on data security: As the aircraft business collects and shares more data, data security will receive more attention. Businesses will need to make sure that their info is secure and protected.

3. More complex attacks: Aviation businesses will need to keep up with these changing dangers as cyberattacks become more sophisticated and targeted. To discover the issues that are occurring in real-time, this will necessitate spending in cutting-edge cybersecurity solutions like artificial intelligence (Al) and machine learning (ML) (Upadhyay & Yadav, 2018).

4. Regulatory requirements: As governments and regulatory agencies concentrate more on aircraft cybersecurity, they are enacting laws to make sure that businesses are taking the necessary precautions to safeguard their systems and data. These rules must be followed by businesses or they risk sanctions and fines (The White House, 2020).

5. Greater collaboration: Collaboration between aircraft businesses, cybersecurity specialists, and government organizations will be crucial in tackling cyber dangers in the aviation sector. To strengthen their cybersecurity stance, businesses will need to collaborate and exchange threat information, best practices, and resources (Oberlaender, 2019).

Figure 1.

A Review on Cybersecurity: Challenges & Emerging Threats

Case Study on Aviation

Boeing's 787 Dreamliner Cybersecurity Incident 787 Dreamliner Cybersecurity Incident by Boeing

A portion of Boeing's 787 Dreamliner airplane was found to be susceptible to cyberattacks in 2018. The flight management system of the aircraft was vulnerable due to a flaw in its software, which allowed for possible hacker entry and manipulation. Researchers at the cybercrime consulting company IO Active made the finding while evaluating the components of the 787's security. They discovered a number of security flaws in the software, including hardcoded passwords and out-of-date encryption methods. These flaws could possibly give an attacker access to the system without authorization, allowing them to alter it to change the plane's height or course, among other things. Boeing issued a software update that fixed the security flaws in response to the results. Additionally, the business collaborated with the FAA to guarantee that the upgrade was thoroughly examined and approved before being made available.

Lessons Learned

The cybersecurity mishap involving the Boeing 787 Dreamliner emphasizes how crucial cybersecurity is to the aircraft sector. Aircraft are more susceptible to cyberattacks as they become more technologically linked and dependent. Manufacturers and carriers must take action to safeguard their systems and defend against dangers.

Some of the lessons learned from this incident include:

- Regular security evaluations of airplane components should be carried out to spot possible weaknesses, according to some of the lessons gained from this event.
- Firmware and other software used in aviation systems shouldn't contain hardcoded passwords or other security flaws.
- Before being installed in crucial systems, software upgrades and fixes should undergo thorough testing and certification.
- To ensure the security of aircraft systems, cooperation between industry stakeholders is crucial, including manufacturers, airlines, and regulatory organisations.

4.4. Cyber Security Future in Health Care

Overall, the future of cybersecurity in flight will demand a proactive and collaborative strategy to handle the changing cyber threats. Healthcare companies that make investments in sophisticated MME are increasingly becoming a target for cybercriminals. due to the important data it contains, including intellectual property, financial information, and confidential health information. The future of cybersecurity in the healthcare sector will be influenced by a number of variables, including technological developments, governmental regulations, and new security dangers. The following are some major patterns that will probably influence hospital cybersecurity in the future:

1. Adoption of advanced technologies: Telemedicine, electronic health records (EHRs), and wearable technology are just a few examples of the advanced technologies that healthcare organizations are progressively embracing. Although these technologies have many advantages, they also introduce new weaknesses that cybercriminals can take advantage of. Therefore, in order to safeguard their data and networks, healthcare organizations will need to implement cutting-edge cybersecurity steps (Oberlaender, 2019).
2. Legal requirements: Healthcare organizations must abide by a number of legal requirements, such as the General Data Protection Regulation (GDPR) and the Health Insurance Portability and Accountability Act (HIPAA). (GDPR). Healthcare organizations will continue to place a high emphasis on adhering to these laws because failure to do so may result in harsh fines and other legal repercussions.
3. Greater awareness: Healthcare organizations are spending more money on staff education and training programs as they become more conscious of the value of cybersecurity. It is crucial for employees to be aware of cybersecurity best practices because they are frequently the first line of defense against cyber-attacks (The White House, 2020).
4. Collaboration and information sharing: In order to combat the changing cyber threats, collaboration between healthcare groups, cybersecurity professionals, and government entities will be essential. To strengthen their cybersecurity stance, healthcare organizations will need to exchange threat information, best practices, and resources.
5. The future of cybersecurity in healthcare will require a multifaceted approach that combines cutting-edge technologies, regulatory compliance, employee education, collaboration, and information sharing. AI and ML technologies have the potential to significantly enhance the cybersecurity posture of healthcare organizations, making it easier for them to identify and respond to threats

Figure 2.

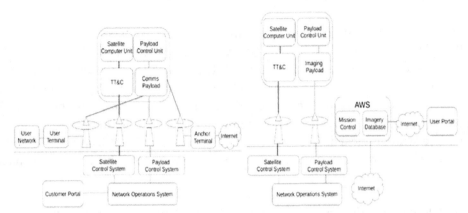

(a) Ground segment for communications satellites.   **(b)** Ground segment architecture for web-based access e.g. Planet [75].

Ground segment architectures. Red lines represent satellite TT&C communications, green lines represent payload control communications, and blue lines represent the link between two users of the communication service. Black lines represent terrestrial networking links

while also maintaining regulatory compliance. Healthcare organizations will be better able to defend their data and systems against cyber-attacks if they priorities cybersecurity and engage in cutting-edge cybersecurity solutions (Upadhyay & Yadav, 2018).

Case Study on Health Care

The growing danger of cyber-attacks is one important problem facing the healthcare sector today. Cybercriminals who want to take private patient information or interfere with vital medical services may target hospitals, healthcare providers, and other medical institutions. In this case study, a recent cyber-attack on a healthcare provider is examined along with the measures that were taken to lessen its effects.

Background

A major healthcare organization was the victim of a ransomware assault in 2021 that exposed patient data and interfered with medical services. For the data to be released and services to be restored, the cybercriminals requested a sizeable amount of money. The healthcare company called cybersecurity specialists right away to look into the breach and minimize harm.

The healthcare company responded to the cyberattack in a number of ways, including:

Using Cybersecurity Professionals: The healthcare provider called a cybersecurity company to evaluate the harm and pinpoint the flaws that allowed the hack to happen. The healthcare supplier and the cybersecurity professionals collaborated to create a strategy for service restoration and assault prevention.

These consisted of improving security procedures, enhancing staff training, and carrying out frequent security assessments.

Restoring Services: The healthcare provider worked with the cybersecurity firm to restore essential services, such as electronic medical records and communication systems. The process was time-consuming and challenging, but the healthcare provider made restoring services a top priority.

Enhancing Security Measures: After the attack, the healthcare provider implemented additional security measures to prevent future attacks. These included upgrading security protocols, increasing staff training, and conducting regular security audits.

Outcome: The healthcare provider was able to restore essential services and protect patient data from being compromised. The cybercriminals did not receive the ransom they demanded, and law enforcement authorities were notified of the attack. The healthcare provider's response to the attack demonstrated the importance of having robust cybersecurity measures in place to protect against cyber-attacks.

Lessons Learned

The experience of the healthcare supplier offers several takeaways for other healthcare organizations. To begin with, in order to defend against cyberattacks, a thorough cybersecurity strategy must be in place. Organizations must conduct routine security assessments, educate staff, and implement the most recent security procedures if they want to improve hacking in the healthcare industry. Swift action should be taken in the event of a cyber-attack, such as isolating the impacted systems and hiring cybersecurity professionals to lessen the harm. In the event of a cyberattack, it is vital to have a backup strategy in place for critical services like manual record-keeping and contact tools.

4.5. Cyber Security Future in Financial Schemes and Services

Companies that provide financial services are adopting the use of cutting-edge technologies, such as Blockchain, artificial intelligence (AI), cloud processing, and new threats. Shaped in cybersecurity is a crucial phrase to some upcoming financial services:

1. Adoption of advanced technologies: Financial services firms are embracing cutting-edge technologies like bitcoin, quantum computing, and big data. While these technologies offer many advantages, they also create new weaknesses that cyber thieves can abuse. Therefore, in order to safeguard their data and networks, financial services firms will need to make investments in cutting-edge cybersecurity methods (Alagheband et al., 2020).

2. Increased emphasis on data security: Financial services organizations will need to give data protection top priority and make sure they are in line with rules like GDPR and PCI DSS. In order to combat the growing cyber dangers, cooperation and information exchange between businesses, cybersecurity professionals, and governmental organizations will be essential. Sharing tools, best practices, and danger information can enhance cybersecurity preparedness.

3. Collaboration and information sharing: In order to combat the changing cyber threats, collaboration between financial services firms, cybersecurity professionals, and government organizations will be crucial. To strengthen their cybersecurity stance, businesses will need to exchange threat information, best practices, and resources.

4. Financial organizations also have a cyber-attack. Procedures for locating and stopping the assault, assessing the level of harm, and restoring compromised systems and data should all be part of the incident reaction strategy. Additionally, to ensure the efficacy of their crisis reaction strategy, financial institutions should evaluate and revise it frequently.

5. Emergence of new threats: Because cybercriminals are constantly changing their strategies, financial services businesses must keep up with new threats and implement cutting-edge technology to combat them. In conclusion, a multifaceted strategy that includes cutting-edge technologies, regulation compliance, cooperation, and information exchange will be needed to address cybercrime in financial services in the future. Companies providing financial services will be better able to safeguard their data and systems from cyber threats if they prioritize cybersecurity and engage in cutting-edge cybersecurity solutions (Alagheband et al., 2020).

Case Study on Finance

As a result of the confidential information they manage and the potential financial rewards from successful assaults, financial organizations are frequently top targets for hackers. In this case study, a recent cyberattack on a financial organization is examined along with the measures that were taken to lessen its effects.

Background

A significant financial organization was the target of a sophisticated cyberattack in 2022 that jeopardized the security of client data and put the stability of the financial system in jeopardy. To access the financial institution's networks and take private information, the cybercriminals combined sophisticated hacking methods with social engineering.

The banking organization responded to the cyberattack in a number of ways, including:

Engaging Cybersecurity Experts: To evaluate the harm and determine the weaknesses that resulted in the hack, the financial institution quickly called cybersecurity experts. The financial organization and the cybersecurity professionals collaborated to create a strategy for service restoration and attack prevention.

Customers were informed of the intrusion and the actions being taken to lessen its effects through communication from the financial organization. Customers who were impacted by the breach were given free credit tracking services by the financial organization, and they were also urged to change their passwords and keep an eye on their accounts for any unusual behavior.

Isolating the Network: To stop the assault from spreading, the financial organization isolated the impacted network. The harm was contained by the isolation, which also helped keep other networks secure.

Increasing Security Measures: To stop future attacks, the banking organization increased security measures. These included enhancing staff training, updating security procedures, and performing frequent security assessments.

Results: The financial organization was able to restore services while preventing the compromise of client data. Law enforcement agencies were informed of the assault, and the hackers did not profit financially from it. The way the financial organization handled the attack showed how crucial it is to have effective cybersecurity means in place to defend against cyberattacks.

Lessons Acquired: Other financial institutions can learn a number of things from the financial institution's experience. To begin with, in order to defend against cyberattacks, a thorough cybersecurity strategy must be in place. The measures to be taken in the event of a cyberattack must be outlined in a comprehensive incident reaction strategy that is in place for financial institutions. Procedures for locating and stopping the assault, assessing the level of harm, and restoring compromised systems and data should all be part of the incident reaction strategy. Additionally, to ensure the efficacy of their crisis reaction strategy, financial institutions should evaluate and revise it frequently. In the event of a cyberattack, it is vital to effectively interact with clients, offering prompt information and assistance to lessen the impact of the assault.

4.6. CYBER SECURITY FUTURE IN EDUCATION

A number of new trends and tools are likely to influence the direction of cybersecurity education in the future. The following possible changes could have an impact on how hacking is taught in the future:

1. Greater Focus on Practical Experience It's crucial for students to have hands-on practice defending against cyber threats as they advance in sophistication. Future cybersecurity education may place a greater emphasis on actual instruction, with students working in virtual settings to gain useful skills.
2. AI and ML: Machine learning (ML) and artificial intelligence (AI) are both important instruments for cybersecurity workers. The integration of these technologies into cybersecurity education is likely to increase as they develop, with pupils learning how to identify and react to cyber threats using AI and machine learning (Alagheband et al., 2020).
3. Greater Industry Collaboration: More companies and organizations are likely to get engaged in cybersecurity education as the need for cybersecurity workers increases. This could result in more joint programs that invite business professionals to teach and guide pupils in the classroom.
4. More Diversity and Inclusion: Although traditionally dominated by men, there is a rising movement for more diversity and inclusion in the cybersecurity business. Future cybersecurity education might put more of an emphasis on fostering an atmosphere that is accepting and inclusive of students from all backgrounds.
5. Put More Emphasis on Soft Skills: Cybersecurity experts need to have strong technological skills, but they also need to be able to work well in teams, handle challenging tasks, and communicate clearly. Future cybersecurity schooling may place a focus on developing these soft skills may place an emphasis on developing these soft skills (Alagheband et al., 2020).

Overall, technical advancements, business demand, and shifting societal and cultural norms are likely to have a major impact on the future of cybersecurity education. It will be crucial for educators to remain current on these developments and modify their curricula to better prepare students for the challenges of the future as online threats continue to develop.

Case Study on Education

Due to the vast amounts of private data that educational institutions store, including student records, financial information, and personal information, they have become appealing targets for hackers. The following is a case study of a recent cyberattack on a university and the measures done to mitigate the damage.

Background

A significant institution was the target of a cyberattack in 2021 that exposed the academic and confidential information of students and employees. The hackers gained access to the university's computer through a phishing assault and stole sensitive data.

The institution responded to the cyberattack in a number of ways, including:

Engaging Cybersecurity Experts: To evaluate the harm and determine the weaknesses that resulted in the hack, the institution quickly called a cybersecurity company. The institution and the cybersecurity professionals collaborated to create a strategy for resuming services and stopping further assaults.

Students and employees were informed of the breach and the actions being taken to lessen its effects through communication from the institution. Affected people were given access to free credit monitoring services from the institution, and they were urged to change their passwords and keep an eye on their accounts for any unusual behavior.

Network Isolation: To stop the assault from spreading, the institution isolated the impacted network. The harm was contained by the isolation, which also helped keep other networks secure.

Enhancing Security Measures: To stop future assaults, the institution added more safeguards. These included enhancing staff training, updating security procedures, and performing frequent security assessments.

The institution was successful in restoring services and preventing the compromise of student and confidential information. Law enforcement agencies were informed of the assault, and the hackers did not profit financially from it. The way the institution handled the attack showed how crucial it is to have effective cybersecurity means in place to defend against cyberattacks.

Lessons Discovered: Other educational organizations can learn a number of things from the university's experience. To begin with, in order to defend against cyberattacks, a thorough cybersecurity strategy must be in place. This includes implementing the most recent security procedures, staff training, and routine security assessments. In order to stop cyberattacks, educational institutions must move quickly. This includes isolating the impacted systems and hiring cybersecurity professionals to minimize the harm. In the event of a cyberattack, it is vital to speak clearly with students and employees, offering timely information and assistance to lessen the impact of the attack.

5. CHALLENGES IN CYBER SECURITY

Future hacking problems are anticipated to increase in complexity and difficulty. Challenges that may be faced include the following:

APTs, or advanced persistent threats: APTs are persistent, ongoing, stealthy assaults that target businesses over time. These assaults, which frequently combine various tactics like social engineering, malware, and network exploitation (, , 2020), can be difficult to identify and neutralize.

Internet of Things (IoT) Security: Due to the pervasive use of these devices, which are frequently linked to the internet and may have vulnerabilities that can be exploited by cybercriminals, IoT security is becoming an increasing worry. Insecure medical devices have the potential to harm patients, and insecure IoT devices can be taken over by botnets and used to initiate DDoS assaults. Encryption, authentication, access control, and routine security upgrades and patches to fix known flaws are all necessary components of a multi-layered strategy to ensure the security of IoT devices (Dey & Dasgupta, 2019).

Attacks utilizing artificial intelligence (AI): Although AI is being used more and more in cybersecurity, it can also be used by hackers to initiate more advanced attacks. AI can be used, for instance, to design highly tailored phishing assaults or to get around security precautions.

Supply Chain assaults: These assaults, which are on the rise, target a target organization's vendors or suppliers in an effort to enter their network. These assaults may be challenging to identify and may have negative effects across a wide area.

Lack of Cybersecurity Professionals: Organizations find it challenging to fight against cyberattacks due to the severe dearth of cybersecurity experts. Future predictions indicate that this scarcity will persist, making it even harder for organizations to defend themselves against online dangers.

Cybersecurity laws: Organizations may find it difficult to keep up with the evolving requirements as cybersecurity laws become more complicated and strict. For lesser organizations with fewer resources, compliance with these laws can be difficult (Upadhyay & Yadav, 2018).

Overall, the difficulties associated with cybersecurity are predicted to increase in complexity and difficulty in the future, necessitating the development of strong cybersecurity strategies by organizations as a means of defense against online dangers.

5.1. Challenges in IoT on Cyber Security

The Internet of Things (IoT) has shaped contemporary living by connecting objects and systems in previously unthinkable ways. But as IoT devices proliferate, the risk of breaches has grown as well, creating a number of issues with IoT safety that must be resolved in the future (Banafa, 2018). Future IoT safety problems include some of the following, among others:

System Security: Many IoT devices are susceptible to attacks because they lack fundamental security precautions like encryption and safe authentication. This is particularly concerning because IoT devices are a prime target for hackers because they frequently gather sensitive personal data.

Interoperability: It can be challenging to adopt uniform security measures across all IoT devices because they frequently come from different makers and use different operating systems. As a result, there may be openings for cyberattacks.

Scalability: Managing and securing all IoT devices becomes more difficult as their number rises. IoT device data generation is so massive that it can be challenging to spot dangers and take the necessary precautions.

Privacy: IoT devices gather a tone of personal data, including details about your position, health, and finances. The privacy and security of this data present a major problem for IoT cybersecurity.

Lack of Standards: Since there are currently no standardized security procedures for IoT devices, putting them into place can be challenging. It is also more difficult to regulate the sector and ensure adherence to security standards because of the absence of standardization. Many Internet of Things (IoT) devices lack the ability to upgrade their firmware, making them susceptible to new kinds of assaults as they develop over time.

Collaboration between producers, lawmakers, and cybersecurity professionals will be necessary to address these issues. To guarantee that IoT devices are safe and private by design, industry standardization and legislation will also be required (Perarasi et al., 2020).

5.2. Challenges on AI in Cyber Security

Threat identification, vulnerability analysis, and incident reaction are just a few of the cybersecurity-related areas where artificial intelligence (AI) has the potential to revolutionize the industry. As with any technology, AI poses a number of safety issues that will need to be resolved in the future. Future obstacles for AI and cybersecurity include the following: adversative assaults Adversarial attacks seek to deceive an AI system by feeding it inputs that have been carefully constructed to make it create the incorrect result. The danger of adversarial assaults will rise as AI becomes more common in cybersecurity, necessitating the development of stronger defences against such attacks (Chan et al., 2019).

Fairness and bias: Depending on the data that they are educated on, AI programs may be unfair. Results from this may be unfair or discriminatory, especially in situations where employment or financing choices are involved. For the purpose of increasing confidence in AI-powered cybersecurity solutions, prejudice in AI must be addressed and justice must be ensured.

Explain ability and transparency: AI programs have the potential to be opaque, making it challenging to comprehend how they make choices. It may be difficult to identify the underlying cause of cybersecurity events or to verify the veracity of threat data produced by AI as a result of this absence of transparency (Kamoun et al., 2020). AI in defense and cybercrime: As AI becomes more common, cybercriminals are likely to use AI in their assaults. Attacks might become more complex, difficult to discover, and damaging as a result. Creating efficient defenses against AI-based assaults will be essential for protecting the digital world. Data security: It's critical to safeguard the anonymity of data used by AI-powered protection solutions. The data must be collected and kept securely, and organizations must put stringent access controls and data security mechanisms in place. Additionally, businesses must be open and honest about how they gather client data and how that data is used. Losing the confidence of customers, facing legal repercussions, and harming a company's image can all result from failing to safeguard data privacy. Collaboration between AI academics, cybersecurity professionals, lawmakers, and business stakeholders will be necessary to overcome these obstacles. Prioritizing cybersecurity in AI research and development will be crucial, as will creating guidelines and best practices for the ethical application of AI in cybersecurity.

5.3. Challenges in Aviation on Cyber Security

Since the advent of broad computerized systems for managing everything from air traffic control to passenger check-in, the aircraft sector has become more and more digitized. While there are many advantages to automation, there are also new cybersecurity issues that need to be handled in the aircraft industry. The following are some difficulties in aircraft hacking that we can anticipate in the future:

System vulnerabilities in aero planes In order to manage everything from engine efficiency to navigation, modern aero planes significantly depend on computerized systems. These systems are susceptible to hacking, which could cause the aero plane or other safety-critical systems to lose control (Dyke Parunak, 2022).

Threats to air traffic control: Cyberattacks on air traffic control networks have the potential to delay flights.

Insider threats: A significant number of workers, including pilots, air traffic controllers, and ground personnel, are necessary for the aircraft sector. These staff members could be dangerous if they participate in malicious behavior because they have access to confidential data and networks. Risks to third parties Many airports and planes depend on outside suppliers to provide services like catering, security checking, and baggage management. These suppliers could lack the same degree of cybersecurity precautions as the airports and planes they provide services to, which would make them a possible weak link in the network of aviation cybersecurity (Upadhyay & Yadav, 2018).

International cooperation: Because the aircraft sector is international, cyberattacks could come from any location in the globe. For the air transportation system to remain safe and secure, it will be crucial to ensure international collaboration and planning on aircraft hacking.

Collaboration between carriers, airports, air traffic control groups, states, and cybersecurity specialists will be necessary to overcome these obstacles. Prioritizing cybersecurity in the aviation sector will be crucial. Standards and best practices for the ethical use of digital technologies in flight will also need to be developed. (Aboti, 2020)

5.4. Challenges in Healthcare on Cyber Security in Future

Healthcare is becoming more and more digitalized. The following are some difficulties that healthcare organizations will probably experience in the future: rising cyber threat sophistication Healthcare organizations are finding it more challenging to fight against cyberattacks as hackers' strategies and techniques advance. Attacks known as ransomware, in which hackers encode private data and demand money to decrypt it, have grown more prevalent (Kuppa & Le-Khac, 2021). Systems that are interconnected: As healthcare organizations use these systems more and more to exchange information and work together, the risk of a hack that targets multiple systems rises. A agreement has been reached regarding the use of medical equipment in the field of cybersecurity.

Healthcare organizations need to be on guard not only against exterior dangers but also against internal hazards. Personnel or freelancers with access to confidential data may jeopardize security either knowingly or unknowingly. Compliance with laws: In order to safeguard patient information and preserve their image, healthcare organizations must comply with regulations. Non-compliance can result in severe financial fines, judicial action, and reputational harm to the company.

Scarce goods: It can be challenging to put effective security measures into place for healthcare organizations because they frequently have restricted resources to dedicate to cyber security.

In order to safeguard patient data and guarantee the security of their networks, healthcare organizations will generally need to continue to prioritize cyber security. Technical solutions, staff education, and adherence to rules will all be necessary (Dyke Parunak, 2022).

5.5. Challenges in Finance on Cyber Security in Future

Cybersecurity threats are rising in importance as the financial services industry continues to accept digital change. The following are some difficulties that banking institutions will probably experience in the future: rising cyber threat sophistication financial institutions are having a tougher time defending against cyberattacks as hackers' strategies and techniques advance. Hackers now more frequently encrypt private data and demand payment to decrypt it in ransomware assaults.

Systems that are interconnected: As financial organizations use these systems more and more to exchange information and work together, the risk of a hack that targets multiple systems rises. When crucial systems, such as those in charge of managing trading or handling payments, are compromised, this can be particularly troublesome.

Financial institutions need to be cautious not only against exterior dangers but also against internal threats. Personnel or freelancers with access to confidential data may jeopardize security either knowingly or unknowingly. Regulation compliance: For financial organizations to keep their cybersecurity stance, managing third-party partnerships and remaining up to date on the newest cybercrime risks and trends are important. Companies must make sure that third-party suppliers have sufficient security measures in place to safeguard confidential data because they can also pose security threats. Financial organizations can foresee and quickly react to new risks by keeping up with the latest cybersecurity threats and patterns (Alagheband et al., 2020).

Limited resources: Financial institutions frequently lack the funding necessary to invest in cyber security, which can make it challenging to put in place practical security measures.

Risk associated with third parties: Financial institutions frequently use third parties to provide services like cloud computing and payment handling. If they don't have robust security steps in place, these vendors may be a security concern. Overall, to safeguard client data and guarantee the security of their systems, banking organizations will need to continue to give cyber security top priority. Technical methods, employee instruction, and adherence to rules will all be necessary for this.

5.6. Challenges in Education on Cyber Security in Future

Cybersecurity risks are a rising worry as educational establishments use digital tools and platforms for teaching and learning more and more. The following are some difficulties that educational organizations will probably encounter in the future: scarce goods It can be challenging to put in place effective security measures in educational organizations because they frequently have limited resources to dedicate to cyber security. Smaller institutions that might not have a devoted IT team or strong security procedures in place may find this to be particularly problematic (Alagheband et al., 2020). Insider dangers: Institutions of higher learning must be watchful not only against exterior dangers but also against internal threats. Access to confidential information by students, teachers, and staff members opens the door to intentional or unintentional security breaches. Compliance with regulations: Compliance with FERPA and COPPA regulations is crucial for education institutions to protect student data privacy and avoid any legal consequences.

Cyberbullying: A rising issue in education, cyberbullying can have negative effects on students' emotional health and wellbeing. Institutions of higher learning must have procedures and rules in place to deal with and avoid cyberbullying.

Assaults using social engineering to trick people into disclosing private information, such as login passwords or banking information, are known as phishing assaults. These assaults frequently take the form of emails, messages, or webpages that seem to be from a reliable source but are actually made to trick the receiver into disclosing their private or confidential information. Once the perpetrator has this information, they can use it for illegal activities like financial scams, identity theft, and other nefarious schemes. It's crucial to use security precautions like two-factor authentication and anti-phishing software, as well as to be watchful and wary when opening links in emails or clicking on unsolicited messages in order to defend against phishing assaults.

Protection of student data: Educational schools are required to safeguard student information, such as grades, attendance logs, and private data. Hackers are frequently drawn to this info, which they can sell on the black web. In order to safeguard pupil information and guarantee the security of their networks, educational institutions will need to continue to give cyber security top priority. In the education sector, phishing attacks, where hackers use social engineering techniques to trick users into sharing sensitive information or downloading malware, are on the rise. This will require a combination of technical measures, employee and student training, and adherence to regulations. Educational institutions must place a high priority on instructing students, teachers, and employees on how to recognize and avoid these types of attacks in order to reduce this danger.

For example: we consider your ordering some product in online now a delivery person is coming to deliver it we can say that your customer details is only with that person, But in future if a drone is delivering your product your customer details is not in it but it is added to the computer controlling the drone but if anyone hacks the computer your customer details can be stolen this becomes a major threat so the cybersecurity professionals as to take some proper security measures .

6. FUTURE SCOPE

IOT as slowly becoming are part of day to day life, As we speak about IOT has been implemented in almost all the area right from agriculture to big companies. The same goes to AI also as it is making our life easier, But it is very hard to protect the data it stores we all moving to an environment where everything is done by internet, it is a good thing as it make our life and jobs easier but the data we create by using it is very huge so it is going to be a challenging task to protect these data .Now the world is like we don't need to now coding we just need some knowledge about it as everything become plug and play that's is already the code is available we just need to copy and apply it these type of attackers called cyber kiddeis they will not do any coding instead of it they will just copy the code from some expert hackers and apply it in future they are going to be a big threat to cyber security experts but however as these type of attacks are emerging new techniques and technologies to stop it also emerging, So we don't need to worry about it .

7. SUGGESTION

1. A novel challenge in the area of cybersecurity is presented every day. The following are a few obstacles we can anticipate in the future:
2. Cyberattack Using Machine Learning: One of the finest tools for processing data is machine learning. It can, however, also be utilized to initiate cyberattacks.
3. Ransomware: A form of malware that locks a victim's data is known as ransomware. After that, the perpetrator requests a ransom payment to unlock the data.
4. Attacks via IoT: The Internet of Things (IoT) is a network of linked objects. These gadgets are hackable and can be used to initiate online assaults.
5. Crypto jacking and Blockchain hacking: Cryptocurrencies are secured using Blockchain technology. But it can also be compromised.
6. Two-factor authentication and weak passwords: Weak passwords continue to be a significant vulnerability issue. Two-factor verification may be able to lessen this issue.
7. Hacking of Physical Infrastructure: Cyberattacks on physical infrastructure, such as water treatment facilities and electricity networks, can have catastrophic results.
8. AI-based hacking: Advanced cyberattacks can be carried out using artificial intelligence (AI).

9. Email phishing and Mailsploit: An email phishing assault is a form of social engineering that employs email to persuade victims into disclosing personal information.
10. These are merely a few of the difficulties that lie ahead. But cybersecurity experts are continuously working to remain ahead of these threats and protect our info.

8. LIMITATION

1. A network of online-connected objects is known as the Internet of Things (IoT). IoT offers numerous advantages, but it also presents significant safety challenges.12. The following are a few examples of safety in IoT limitations:
2. Lack of Standardization: Different makers frequently create IoT devices using various standards. It is challenging to create a common security structure because of this.(Aboti, 2020)
3. Feeble Authentication: A lot of Internet of Things (IoT) gadgets have feeble authentication processes, which leaves them open to online assaults.
4. IoT gadgets gather a lot of information about consumers. If this info ends up in the wrong hands, it might be used maliciously.
5. IoT-based services provide customers, crew members, and other staff with a smooth and effortless experience, but reduction of cybersecurity risks in aviation.(Aboti, 2020)

9. CONCLUSION

In summary, the future of cybersecurity appears to be both difficult and thrilling. The strategies and tactics employed by cybercriminals to initiate assaults change along with technology (Hussain et al., 2020). In order to safeguard sensitive data and systems, cybersecurity experts must continuously be on the lookout for threats and take preventative measures. The need to secure an ever-growing number of devices and endpoints, the increasing sophistication of cyberattacks, the widening skills gap in the cybersecurity sector, and the requirement for improved collaboration and information sharing between organizations and governments are just a few of the challenges that cybersecurity professionals must deal with (Banafa, 2018).

Organizations must prioritize cybersecurity and make the required investments in people, training, and technology if they want to remain ahead of these problems. To remain ahead of new dangers, cybersecurity workers must also be flexible and keep up with skill updates (Oberlaender, 2019). Overall, there is cause for hope even though the defense business faces substantial obstacles. Organizations and people can better defend themselves against breaches and safeguard their data and systems for the long term with the proper expenditures and tactics (Alagheband et al., 2020).

REFERENCES

Aboti, C. (2020). Studies of Challenges to Mitigating Cyber Risks in IoT-Based Commercial Aviation. *International Journal for Scientific Research & Development\, 7*(11).

Alagheband, M., Mashatan, A., & Zihayat, M. (2020). Time-based Gap Analysis of Cybersecurity Trends in Academic and Digital Media. ACM.

Banafa, A. (2018). *C*ybersecurity Challenges and Solutions for the Internet of Things (loT). *IEEE Consumer Electronics Magazine, 7*(2).

Chan, L., Morgan, I., Simon, H., Alshabanat, F., Ober, D., Gentry, J., Min, D., & Cao, R. (2019). Survey of ai in cybersecurity for information technology management. In 2019 IEEE technology & engineering management conference (TEMSCON). IEEE.

Dey, A., Dasgupta, K. (2019). Challenges and Opportunities in Cybersecurity. *Journal of Cybersecurity and Information Management, 2*(1).

Dyke Parunak, H. V. (2022). A grammar-based behavioral distance measure between ransomware variants. *IEEE Transactions on Computational Social Systems*, *9*(1), 8–17. doi:10.1109/TCSS.2021.3060972

Hussain, A., Mohamed, A., Razali, S. (2020). *A Review on Cybersecurity: Challenges & Emerging Threats*. ACM.

Islam, R. (2020). Cybersecurity Challenges in Critical Infrastructure Protection: A Review. *Journal of Cybersecurity and Information Management*, *3*(1).

Kamoun, F., Iqbal, F., Esseghir, M. A., & Baker, T. (2020). Ai and machine learning: A mixed blessing for cybersecurity. *2020 International Symposium on Networks, Computers and Communications (ISNCC)*. IEEE. 10.1109/ISNCC49221.2020.9297323

Kuppa, A., & Le-Khac, N.-A. (2021). Adversarial ai methods in cybersecurity. *IEEE Transactions on Information Forensics and Security*, *16*, 4924–4938. doi:10.1109/TIFS.2021.3117075

Mylrea, M., Gourisetti, S. N. G., Larimer, C., & Noonan, C. (2018, May). Insider threat cybersecurity framework webtool & methodology: Defending against complex cyber-physical threats. In *2018 IEEE Security and Privacy Workshops (SPW)* (pp. 207--216). IEEE

Nikolskaia, K. Y., & Naumov, V. B. (2021). The relationship between cybersecurity and artificial intelligence. In *2021 International Conference on Quality Management, Transport and Information Security, Information Technologies (IT&QM&IS)*. IEEE. 10.1109/ITQMIS53292.2021.9642782

Oberlaender, M. (2019). The Future of Cybersecurity: Emerging Threats and Trends. *International Journal of Cybersecurity Intelligence & Cybercrime, 2*(1).

Perarasi, T., Vidhya, S., & Ramya, P.. (2020). Malicious vehicles identifying and trust management algorithm for enhance the security in 5g-vanet. *2020 Second International Conference on Inventive Research in Computing Applications (ICIRCA)*. IEEE. 10.1109/ICIRCA48905.2020.9183184

Pienta, D., Tams, S., & Thatcher, J. (2020). Can trust be trusted in cybersecurity? *Proceedings of the 53rd Hawaii International Conference on System Sciences*. Scholar Space. . 10.24251/HICSS.2020.522

Sun, R., Botacin, M., Sapountzis, N., Yuan, X., Bishop, M., Porter, D. E., Li, X., Gregio, A., & Oliveira, D. (2022). A praise for defensive programming: Leveraging uncertainty for effective malware mitigation. *IEEE Transactions on Dependable and Secure Computing, 19*(1), 353–369. doi:10.1109/TDSC.2020.2986112

Suresh Babu, C. V. (2023a). *IoT and its Applications*. Anniyappa publications.

Suresh Babu, C. V. (2023b). IoT-Based Smart Accident Detection and Alert System. In P. Swarnalatha, S. Prabu, & I. G. I. Global (Eds.), *Handbook of Research on Deep Learning Techniques for Cloud-Based Industrial IoT* (pp. 322–337). doi:10.4018/978-1-6684-8098-4.ch019

The White House. (2020). The Future of Cybersecurity: A Strategic Roadmap. National Institute of Standards and Technology.

Upadhyay, V. & Yadav, S. (2018). Study of Cyber Security Challenges Its Emerging Trends: Current Technologies. *International Journal of Engineering Research and Management 5*(7).

Compilation of References

Abd Elminaam, D. S., Abdual-Kader, H. M., & Hadhoud, M. M. (2010). Evaluating The Performance of Symmetric Encryption Algorithms. *International Journal of Network Security*, *10*(3), 216–222.

Aboaoja, F. A., Zainal, A., Ghaleb, F. A., Al-rimy, B. A. S., Eisa, T. A. E., & Elnour, A. A. H. (2022). Malware detection issues, challenges, and future directions: A survey. *Applied Sciences (Basel, Switzerland)*, *12*(17), 8482. doi:10.3390/app12178482

Aboti, C. (2020). Studies of Challenges to Mitigating Cyber Risks in IoT-Based Commercial Aviation. *International Journal for Scientific Research & Development\, 7*(11).

Abu Al-Haija, Q., & Ishtaiwi, A. (2021). Machine learning-based model to identify firewall decisions to improve Cyber-Defense. *International Journal on Advanced Science, Engineering and Information Technology*, *11*(4), 1688. doi:10.18517/ijaseit.11.4.14608

Academy. (n.d.). https://academy.binance.com/en/articles/what-is-multichain-multi

Acharya, M. (2020). *Proof of Document using Multichain and Ethereum, (vol. 07)*. IOP Publishing. www.irjet.net doi:10.1007/s12243-021-00868-6

Adelstein, F., Stillerman, M., & Kozen, D. (2002). Malicious code detection for open firmware. *18th Annual Computer Security Applications Conference Proceedings*. IEEE.

Agana, M. A., & Inyiama, H. C. (2015). Cyber Crime Detection and Control Using the Cyber User Identification Model. *IRACST – International Journal of Computer Science and Information Technology & Security(IJCSITS)*, *5*(5).

Agrawal, S., & Saini, S. (2016). A Review of Malware Detection Techniques. In *Proceedings of the International Conference on Computing and Communication Systems (I3CS 2016)*, (pp. 261-265). IEEE. doi: 10.1109/I3CS.2016.7823468

Ahmad, A., & Rahman, A. A. (2020). A Literature Survey on Malware Mitigation Approaches and Challenges. *International Journal of Computer Science and Network Security*, *20*(5), 46–54.

Aitzhan, N. Z., & Svetinovic, D. (2016). Security and privacy in decentralized energy trading through multi-signatures, blockchain and anonymous messaging streams. *IEEE Transactions on Dependable and Secure Computing*, *15*(5), 840–852. doi:10.1109/TDSC.2016.2616861

Akhtar, M. S., & Feng, T. (2023). Evaluation of Machine Learning Algorithms for Malware Detection. *Sensors (Basel)*, *23*(2), 946. doi:10.339023020946 PMID:36679741

Akhtar, Z., Khan, S. A., & Minhas, A. A. (2021). A Survey on Malware Mitigation Techniques and Tools. *Journal of Cybersecurity*, *7*(1).

Akram, B., & Ogi, D. (2020). The Making of Indicator of Compromise using Malware Reverse Engineering Techniques. *2020 International Conference on ICT for Smart Society (ICISS)*, 1-6. 10.1109/ICISS50791.2020.9307581

Alagheband, M., Mashatan, A., & Zihayat, M. (2020). Time-based Gap Analysis of Cybersecurity Trends in Academic and Digital Media. ACM.

Al-Asli, M., & Ghaleb, T. A. (2019). Review of Signature-based Techniques in Antivirus Products. *2019 International Conference on Computer and Information Sciences (ICCIS)*, Sakaka, Saudi Arabia. 10.1109/ICCISci.2019.8716381

Al-Behadili, H. N. K. (2021). Decision Tree for Multi-class Classification of Firewall Access. *International Journal of Intelligent Engineering and Systems*, *14*(3), 294–302. doi:10.22266/ijies2021.0630.25

Ali, A., Warren, D., & Mathiassen, L. (2017). Cloud-based business services innovation: A risk management model. *International Journal of Information Management*, *37*(6), 639–649. doi:10.1016/j.ijinfomgt.2017.05.008

Ali, W. (2017). Phishing Website Detection based on Supervised Machine Learning with Wrapper Features Selection. *International Journal of Advanced Computer Science and Applications*, *8*(9). doi:10.14569/IJACSA.2017.080910

Aljabri, M., Alahmadi, A. A., Mohammad, R. M., Aboulnour, M., Alomari, D. M., & Almotiri, S. H. (2022). Classification of firewall log data using multi-class machine learning models. *Electronics (Basel)*, *11*(12), 1851. doi:10.3390/electronics11121851

Aljaidi, M., Alkhalidi, Y., Al-dmour, H., Al-Howaide, A., & Al-Tarawneh, M. (2022). *NHS WannaCry Ransomware Attack: Technical Explanation of The Vulnerability, Exploitation, and Countermeasures*. In *2022 International Engineering Conference on Electrical, Energy, and Artificial Intelligence*. Zarqa, Jordan. 10.1109/EICEEAI56378.2022.10050485

Alkhalil, Z., Hewage, C. T. E. R., Nawaf, L., & Khan, I. (2021). Phishing Attacks: A Recent Comprehensive Study and a New Anatomy. *Frontiers of Computer Science*, *3*, 563060. Advance online publication. doi:10.3389/fcomp.2021.563060

Allagi, S., & Rachh, R. R. (2019). Analysis of Network log data using Machine Learning. *International Conference for Convergence for Technology*. IEEE. 10.1109/I2CT45611.2019.9033737

Allix, K., Bissyande, T. F. D. A., Klein, J., & Le Traon, Y. (2014). *Machine learning-based malware detection for Android applications: History matters!*. University of Luxembourg, SnT.

Allodi, L., & Massacci, F. (2014). Comparing vulnerability severity and exploits using case-control studies. [TISSEC]. *ACM Transactions on Information and System Security*, *17*(1), 1–20. doi:10.1145/2630069

Almomani, A., Alauthman, M., Shatnawi, M. T., Alweshah, M., Alrosan, A., Alomoush, W., Gupta, B. B., Gupta, B. B., & Gupta, B. B. (2022). Phishing website detection with semantic features based on machine learning classifiers. *International Journal on Semantic Web and Information Systems*, *18*(1), 1–24. doi:10.4018/IJSWIS.297032

Almseidin, M., Zuraiq, A. A., Alkasassbeh, M., & Alnidami, N. (2019). Phishing Detection Based on Machine Learning and Feature Selection Methods. *International Journal of Interactive Mobile Technologies*, *13*(12), 171. doi:10.3991/ijim.v13i12.11411

Alnafrani, R., & Wijesekera, D. (2022). An automated framework for generating attack graphs using known security threats. In *2022 10th International Symposium on Digital Forensics and Security (ISDFS)*, pages 1–6. 10.1109/ISDFS55398.2022.9800833

Alneyadi, S., Sithirasenan, E., & Muthukkumarasamy, V. (2016, February). A survey on data leakage prevention system. *Journal of Network and Computer Applications*, *62*, 137–152. doi:10.1016/j.jnca.2016.01.008

Alperin, K. B., Wollaber, A. B., & Gomez, S. R. (2020). Improving interpretability for cyber vulnerability assessment using focus and context visualizations. In *2020 IEEE Symposium on Visualization for Cyber Security (VizSec)*, (pp. 30–39). IEEE. 10.1109/VizSec51108.2020.00011

Al-Sofyani, S., Alelayani, A., Al-zahrani, F., & Monshi, R. (2023). A Survey off Malware Forensics Analysis Techniques And Tools. In *2023 1st International Conference on Advanced Innovations in Smart Cities (ICAISC)* (pp. 1-6). Jeddah, Saudi Arabia. 10.1109/ICAISC56366.2023.10085474

Alzaylaee, M. K., Yerima, S. Y., & Sezer, S. (2020). DL-Droid: Deep learning based android malware detection using real devices. *Computers & Security*, *89*, 101663. doi:10.1016/j.cose.2019.101663

Amer, E., & El-Sappagh, S. (2022). Robust deep learning early alarm prediction model based on the behavioural smell for android malware. *Computers & Security*, *116*, 102670. doi:10.1016/j.cose.2022.102670

Angelini, M., Blasilli, G., Catarci, T., Lenti, S., & Santucci, G. (2019). Vulnus: Visual vulnerability analysis for network security. *IEEE Transactions on Visualization and Computer Graphics*, *25*(1), 183–192. doi:10.1109/TVCG.2018.2865028 PMID:30136974

APWG. (2019). *APWG trend Report*. APWG. https://docs.apwg.org/reports/apwg_trends_report_q3_2019.pdfAccessed from 20 July 2020.

Arden, O., George, M. D., Liu, J., Vikram, K., Askarov, A., & Myers, A. C. (2012). Sharing Mobile Code Securely With Information Flow Control. In *Proceedings of the IEEE Symposium on Security and Privacy*. IEEE. 10.1109/SP.2012.22

Arshad, M., Muhammad, A. R., & Alhakami, R. (2022, May). Malware detection using machine learning: A comprehensive review. *Security and Communication Networks*, *2020*, 1–18.

Aslan, Ö., & Samet, R. (2017, October). Investigation of possibilities to detect malware using existing tools. In *2017 IEEE/ACS 14th International Conference on Computer Systems and Applications (AICCSA)* (pp. 1277-1284). IEEE. 10.1109/AICCSA.2017.24

Aslan, Ö., & Yilmaz, A. A. (2021). A new malware classification framework based on deep learning algorithms. *IEEE Access : Practical Innovations, Open Solutions*, 9, 87936–87951. doi:10.1109/ACCESS.2021.3089586

As-Suhabni, H. E. Q., & Khamitkar, S. D. Dr. (2020a, February 25). Discovering anomalous rules in firewall logs using data mining and machine learning classifiers. *International Journal of Scientific & Technology Research*. https://www.ijstr.org/paper-references.php?ref=IJSTR-0120-29748.

As-Suhbani, H. E., & Khamitkar, S. (2019). Classification of Firewall Logs Using Supervised Machine Learning Algorithms. *International Journal on Computer Science and Engineering*, 7(8), 301–304. doi:10.26438/ijcse/v7i8.301304

Avira Press Center. (2007). *Avira warns: targeted malware attacks increasingly also threatening German companies*. Avira. http://www.avira.com/en/security news/targeted attacks threatening companies.html.

Bace & Mell. (2001). *Intrusion Detection Systems*. NIST Special Publication on Intrusion Detection Systems.

Bakour, K., & Ünver, H. M. (2021). DeepVisDroid: Android malware detection by hybridizing image-based features with deep learning techniques. *Neural Computing & Applications*, 33(18), 11499–11516. doi:10.100700521-021-05816-y

Baldangombo, U., Jambaljav, N., & Horng, S. J. (2013). A static malware detection system using data mining methods. arXiv preprint arXiv:1308.2831.

Banafa, A. (2018). Cybersecurity Challenges and Solutions for the Internet of Things (IoT). *IEEE Consumer Electronics Magazine, 7*(2).

Barsha, F. L., & Shahriar, H. (2023). Mitigation of Malware Using Artificial Intelligence Techniques: A Literature Review. *Security Engineering for Embedded and Cyber-Physical Systems*, 221–234.

Basit, A., Zafar, M., Liu, X., Javed, A. R., Jalil, Z., & Kifayat, K. (2021b). A comprehensive survey of AI-enabled phishing attacks detection techniques. *Telecommunication Systems, 76*(1), 139–154. doi:10.100711235-020-00733-2 PMID:33110340

Beaucamps, P. (2007). Advanced polymorphic techniques. *International Journal of Computational Science, 2*(3), 194–205.

Bergeron, J. (2001). Static detection of malicious code in executable programs. *Int. J. of Req. Eng, 79*.

Biener, C., Eling, M., & Wirfs, J. H. (2015). Insurability of cyber risk: An empirical analysis. *The Geneva Papers on Risk and Insurance. Issues and Practice, 40*(1), 131–158. doi:10.1057/gpp.2014.19

Bindrwish, F., Ali, A., Ghabban, W., Alrowwad, A., Fallatah, N., Ameerbakhsh, O., & Alfadli, I. (2023). Internet of Things for Digital Forensics Application in Saudi Arabia. *Advances in Internet of Things*, *13*(1), 1–11. doi:10.4236/ait.2023.131001

Black, P. E. (2018). A software assurance reference dataset: Thousands of programs with known bugs. *Journal of Research of the National Institute of Standards and Technology*, *123*, 1. doi:10.6028/jres.123.005 PMID:34877127

Blanc, W., Hashem, L. G., Elish, K. O., & Hussain Almohri, M. J. (2019). Identifying Android Malware Families Using Android-Oriented Metrics. 2019 IEEE International Conference on Big Data (Big Data), (pp. 4708-4713). IEEE. 10.1109/BigData47090.2019.9005669

Blockchain Healthcare Today. (n.d.). https://blockchainhealthcaretoday.com/index.php/journal/article/view/34

Bodin, L., Gordon, L. A., & Loeb, M. P. (2008). Information security and risk management. *Communications of the ACM*, *51*(4), 64–68. doi:10.1145/1330311.1330325

Booth, H., Rike, D., & Witte, G. A. (2013). *The national vulnerability database (nvd)*. Overview.

Bordoloi, S., & Kalita, B. (2013). E-R Model to an Abstract Mathematical Model for Database Schema Using Reference Graph. *International Journal of Engineering Research and Development*, *6*(4).

Boue, M. (2011). Inspire Ontology Handler: automatically building and managing a knowledge base for Critical Information Infrastructure Protection. 12th IFIP/IEEE 1M, Poster Session. IEEE.

Boulahia-Cuppens, N., Cuppens, F., Gabillon, A., & Yazdanian, K. (1992). MultiView model for object-oriented database. *Proceedings of 9th Annual Computer Security Applications Conference*. Springer.

Bowling, H., Seigfried-Spellar, K., Karabiyik, U., & Rogers, M. (2023). We are meeting on Microsoft Teams: Forensic analysis in Windows, Android, and iOS operating systems. *Journal of Forensic Sciences*, *68*(2), 434–460. doi:10.1111/1556-4029.15208 PMID:36734289

Buczak, A. L., & Guven, E. (2015). A survey of data mining and machine learning methods for cyber security intrusion detection. *IEEE Communications Surveys and Tutorials*, *18*(2), 1153–1176. doi:10.1109/COMST.2015.2494502

Burton, J., & Christou, G. (2021). Bridging the gap between cyberwar and cyberpeace. *International Affairs*, *97*(6), 1727–1747. doi:10.1093/ia/iiab172

Cabaj, K., Domingos, D., Kotulski, Z., & Respício, A. (2018). Cybersecurity education: Evolution of the discipline and analysis of master programs. *Computers & Security*, *75*, 24–35. doi:10.1016/j.cose.2018.01.015

Cakir, B., & Dogdu, E. (2018, March). Malware classification using deep learning methods. In *Proceedings of the ACMSE 2018 Conference* (pp. 1-5). ACMSE.

Calleja, J. T., & Caballero, J. (2019, December). The MalSource Dataset: Quantifying Complexity and Code Reuse in Malware Development. *IEEE Transactions on Information Forensics and Security*, *14*(12), 3175–3190. doi:10.1109/TIFS.2018.2885512

Cardon, O. (2018). *Classification of cyber-physical production systems applications: Proposition of an analysis framework*. Science Direct.

Catak, F. O., Yazı, A. F., Elezaj, O., & Ahmed, J. (2020). Deep learning based Sequential model for malware analysis using Windows exe API Calls. *PeerJ. Computer Science*, *6*, e285. doi:10.7717/peerj-cs.285 PMID:33816936

Ch, R., Gadekallu, T., Abidi M., & Al-Ahmari, A. (2020). *Computational System to classify Cyber Crime Offences using Machine Learning*. MPDI.

Chakkaravarthy, S. S., Sangeetha, D., & Vaidehi, V. (2019). A survey on malware analysis and mitigation techniques. *Computer Science Review*, *32*, 1–23. doi:10.1016/j.cosrev.2019.01.002

Chakraborty, S., Krishna, R., Ding, Y., & Ray, B. (2021). Deep learning based vulnerability detection: Are we there yet. *IEEE Transactions on Software Engineering*.

Chan, L., Morgan, I., Simon, H., Alshabanat, F., Ober, D., Gentry, J., Min, D., & Cao, R. (2019). Survey of ai in cybersecurity for information technology management. In 2019 IEEE technology & engineering management conference (TEMSCON). IEEE.

Chandrashekar, G., & Sahin, F. (2014). A survey on feature selection methods. *Computers & Electrical Engineering*, *40*(1), 16–28. doi:10.1016/j.compeleceng.2013.11.024

Chen, L., Ye, Y., & Bourlai, T. (2017, September). Adversarial machine learning in malware detection: Arms race between evasion attack and defense. In *2017 European intelligence and security informatics conference (EISIC)* (pp. 99-106). IEEE.

Chhillar, K., & Shrivastava, S. (2021). Vulnerability scanning and management of university computer network. In *2021 10th International Conference on Internet of Everything, Microwave Engineering, Communication and Networks (IEMECON)*, (pp. 01–06). IEEE. 10.1109/IEMECON53809.2021.9689207

Choi, D.-L., Kim, B.-W., Lee, Y.-J., Um, Y., & Chung, M. (2011). Design and Creation of Dysarthric Speech Database for Development of QoLT Software Technology. *2011 International Conference on Speech Database and Assessments (Oriental COCOSDA)*. IEEE. 10.1109/ICSDA.2011.6085978

Chowdhury, M., Rahman, A., & Islam, R. (2018). Malware analysis and detection using data mining and machine learning classification. In *International conference on applications and techniques in cyber security and intelligence: applications and techniques in cyber security and intelligence* (pp. 266-274). Springer International Publishing. 10.1007/978-3-319-67071-3_33

Christodorescu, M., & Jha, S. (2006). *Static analysis of executables to detect malicious patterns*. Wisconsin Univ-Madison Dept of Computer Sciences. doi:10.21236/ADA449067

Chu, Y., Yue, X., Wang, Q., & Wang, Z. (2020). Secureas: A vulnerability assessment system for deep neural network based on adversarial examples. *IEEE Access : Practical Innovations, Open Solutions*, 8, 109156–109167. doi:10.1109/ACCESS.2020.3001730

CNET. (2008). Anonymous hackers take on the Church of Scientology, Cosmos Bank malware attack: Interpol issues red corner notice against prime suspect traced in foreign country. *Cities News, The Indian Express*.

Conway, M. (2006). Terrorism and the Internet: New media—New threat? *Parliamentary Affairs*, 59(2), 283–298. doi:10.1093/pa/gsl009

Crowdstrike. (2022). *Fileless Malware Explained, What is Fileless Malware?* CrowdStrike.

Crowdstrike. (2023). *12 Types of Malware + Examples That You Should Know*. Crowdstrike.

Cui, Z., Xue, F., Cai, X., Cao, Y., Wang, G., & Chen, J. (2018, July). Detection of Malicious Code Variants Based on Deep Learning. *IEEE Transactions on Industrial Informatics*, 14(7), 3187–3196. doi:10.1109/TII.2018.2822680

Dahl, G. E., Stokes, J. W., Deng, L., & Yu, D. (2013). Large-scale malware classification using random projections and neural networks. *2013 IEEE International Conference on Acoustics, Speech and Signal Processing*, Vancouver, BC, Canada. 10.1109/ICASSP.2013.6638293

Dandurand, O. (2013). *5th International Conference on Cyber Conflict*. NATO CCD COE Publications, Tallinn.

Das, A., Pramod, & S, S. B. (2022). An efficient feature selection approach for Intrusion Detection System using decision tree. *International Journal of Advanced Computer Science and Applications*, 13(2). doi:10.14569/IJACSA.2022.0130276

Daubner, L., Macak, M., Matulevičius, R., Buhnova, B., Maksović, S., & Pitner, T. (2023). Addressing insider attacks via forensic-ready risk management. *Journal of Information Security and Applications*, 73, 103433. doi:10.1016/j.jisa.2023.103433

De la Hoz, E., Cochrane, G., Moreira-Lemus, J. M., Paez-Reyes, R., Marsa-Maestre, I., & Alarcos, B. (2014, June). Detecting and defeating advanced man-in-the-middle attacks against TLS. In *2014 6th International Conference On Cyber Conflict (CyCon 2014)* (pp. 209-221). IEEE. 10.1109/CYCON.2014.6916404

Dekel, O., & Shamir, O. (2008, July). Learning to classify with missing and corrupted features. In *Proceedings of the 25th international conference on Machine learning* (pp. 216-223). ACM. 10.1145/1390156.1390184

Dell Technologies. (2021). *What are the different types of Viruses, Spyware and Malware that can infect my computer?* Dell India

Deochakke, A., & Tyagi, A. K. (2022). Analysis of Ransomware Security on Cloud Storage Systems. In V. Sugumaran, D. Upadhyay, & S. Sharma (Eds.), *Advancements in Interdisciplinary Research. AIR 2022. Communications in Computer and Information Science* (Vol. 1738, pp. 45–54). Springer. doi:10.1007/978-3-031-23724-9_5

Dey, A., Dasgupta, K. (2019). Challenges and Opportunities in Cybersecurity. *Journal of Cybersecurity and Information Management, 2*(1).

Drew, J., Moore, T., & Hahsler, M. (2016, May). Polymorphic malware detection using sequence classification methods. In 2016 IEEE Security and Privacy Workshops (SPW) (pp. 81-87). IEEE. doi:10.1109/SPW.2016.30

Du, J., Raza, S. H., Ahmad, M., Alam, I., Dar, S. H., & Habib, M. A. (2022). Digital forensics as advanced ransomware pre-attack detection algorithm for endpoint data protection. *Security and Communication Networks, 2022*, 1–16. doi:10.1155/2022/1424638

Dyke Parunak, H. V. (2022). A grammar-based behavioral distance measure between ransomware variants. *IEEE Transactions on Computational Social Systems, 9*(1), 8–17. doi:10.1109/TCSS.2021.3060972

Elhadi, A., Maarof, M., & Osman, A. (2012). Malware detection based on hybrid signature behaviour application programming interface call graph. *American Journal of Applied Sciences 9*(3), 283.

Elmasri, R., & Navathe, S. B. (2019). *Fundamentals of Database Systems* (7th ed.). Pearson.

Enck, W., Octeau, D., McDaniel, P. D., & Chaudhuri, S. (2011, August). A study of android application security. In USENIX security symposium (Vol. 2). William Enck.

Ertam, F., & Kaya, M. (2018). Classification of firewall log files with multi-class support vector machine. *2018 6th International Symposium on Digital Forensic and Security (ISDFS)*. IEEE. 10.1109/ISDFS.2018.8355382

Fadheel, W., Abusharkh, M., & Abdel-Qader, I. (2017). *On Feature Selection for the Prediction of Phishing Websites*. Dependable Autonomic and Secure Computing., doi:10.1109/DASC-PICom-DataCom-CyberSciTec.2017.146

Fasano, F., Martinelli, F., Mercaldo, F., & Santone, A. (2019). Cascade Learning for Mobile Malware Families Detection through Quality and Android Metrics. *2019 International Joint Conference on Neural Networks (IJCNN)*, Budapest, Hungary. 10.1109/IJCNN.2019.8852268

FBI Warns of Dramatic Increase in Business E-Mail Compromise (BEC) Schemes. (2018b, June 27). FBI. https://www.fbi.gov/contact-us/field-offices/memphis/news/press-releases/fbi-warns-of-dramatic-increase-in-business-e-mail-compromise-bec-schemes

Feng, R., Sen Chen, X. X., Meng, G., Lin, S.-W., & Liu, Y. (2020, September). A performance-sensitive malware detection system using deep learning on mobile devices. *IEEE Transactions on Information Forensics and Security, 16*, 1563–1578. doi:10.1109/TIFS.2020.3025436

Firdausi, I., Erwin, A., & Nugroho, A. S. (2010, December). Analysis of machine learning techniques used in behavior-based malware detection. In *2010 second international conference on advances in computing, control, and telecommunication technologies* (pp. 201-203). IEEE. 10.1109/ACT.2010.33

Fortinet. (n.d.) *What Is a Trojan Horse? Trojan Virus and Malware Explained*. Fortinet.

Gajda, J., Kwiecien, J., & Chmiel, W. (2022). Machine learning methods for anomaly detection in computer networks. *2022 26th International Conference on Methods and Models in Automation and Robotics (MMAR)*. IEEE. 10.1109/MMAR55195.2022.9874341

Galvan. (n.d.-a). https://www.galvan.health/nodes

Galvan. (n.d.-b). *A New Kind of Node*. Galavan Nodes. https://www.galvan.health/nodes

Gaurav, A., Gupta, B. B., & Panigrahi, P. K. (2022). A comprehensive survey on machine learning approaches for malware detection in IoT-based enterprise information system. *Enterprise Information Systems*, 1–25.

Ghaleb Al-Mekhlafi, Z., Abdulkarem Mohammed, B., Al-Sarem, M., Saeed, F., Al-Hadhrami, T., & Alshammari, T., M., Alreshidi, A., & Sarheed Alshammari, T. (. (2022). Phishing websites detection by using optimized stacking ensemble model. *Computer Systems Science and Engineering*, *41*(1), 109–125. doi:10.32604/csse.2022.020414

Github. (n.d.). [Data set]. https://raw.githubusercontent.com/PacktPublishing/Mastering-Machine-Learning-for-Penetration-Testing/master/Chapter03/Chapter3-Practice/dataset.csv

Gómez Vidal, A. S. (2019). *Improvements in IDS: adding functionality to Wazuh*. Academic Press.

Gong, L., Lin, H., Li, Z., Qian, F., Li, Y., Ma, X., & Liu, Y. (2020). Systematically landing machine learning onto market-scale mobile malware detection. *IEEE Transactions on Parallel and Distributed Systems*, *32*(7), 1615–1628. doi:10.1109/TPDS.2020.3046092

Gong, L., Li, Z., Qian, F., Zhang, Z., Chen, Q. A., Qian, Z., & Liu, Y. (2020, April). Experiences of landing machine learning onto market-scale mobile malware detection. In *Proceedings of the Fifteenth European Conference on Computer Systems* (pp. 1-14). ACM. 10.1145/3342195.3387530

Greenspan, G. (2019). *Ten Enterprise Blockchains that Actually Work*. Multichain. https://www.multichain.com/blog/2019/06/ten-enterprise-blockchains/

Griffin, M. P., & Mitchell, R. J. (1992). Regenerating Database Techniques for Real-time Creation and Maintenance of Very Large Scale Databases. *IEEE Colloquium on Using Virtual Worlds*. IEEE.

Guendouz, M., & Amine, A. (2022). A new wrapper-based feature selection technique with fireworks algorithm for Android Malware detection. *International Journal of Software Science and Computational Intelligence*, *14*(1), 1–19. doi:10.4018/IJSSCI.312554

Compilation of References

Gupta, K., Varol, C., & Zhou, B. (2023). Digital forensic analysis of discord on google chrome. *Forensic Science International: Digital Investigation, 44.* Science Direct. doi:10.1016/j.fsidi.2022.301479

Habib, M. K. (2018). *CPS: Role, Characteristics, Architectures and Future Potentials.* Science Direct.

Hadnagy, C., & Fincher, M. (2015). *Phishing dark waters: The offensive and defensive sides of malicious Emails.* John Wiley & Sons. doi:10.1002/9781119183624

Han, K. S., Lim, J. H., Kang, B., & Im, E. G. (2015). Malware analysis using visualized images and entropy graphs. *International Journal of Information Security, 14*(1), 1–14. doi:10.100710207-014-0242-0

Hansman, S., & Hunt, R. (2005). A taxonomy of network and computer attacks. *Computers & Security, 24*(1), 31–43. doi:10.1016/j.cose.2004.06.011

Hardy, W., Chen, L., Hou, S., Ye, Y., & Li, X. (2016). DL4MD: A deep learning framework for intelligent malware detection. In *Proceedings of the International Conference on Data Science (ICDATA)* (p. 61). The Steering Committee of The World Congress in Computer Science, Computer Engineering and Applied Computing (WorldComp).

Hashizume, K., Rosado, D. G., Fernández-Medina, E., & Fernandez, E. B. (2013). An analysis of security issues for cloud computing. *Journal of Internet Services and Applications, 4*(1), 1–13. doi:10.1186/1869-0238-4-5

Hasselgren, A., Kralevska, K., Gligoroski, D., & Pedersen, S. A. (2020). Blockchain in healthcare and health sciences—A scoping review. *International Journal of Medical Informatics, 134.* doi:10.1016/j.ijmedinf.2019.104040

He, W., Li, H., & Li, J. (2019). Unknown vulnerability risk assessment based on directed graph models: A survey. *IEEE Access : Practical Innovations, Open Solutions, 7,* 168201–168225. doi:10.1109/ACCESS.2019.2954092

Hommes, S., State, R., & Engel, T. (2012). A distance-based method to detect anomalous attributes in log files. *Network Operations and Management Symposium.* IEEE. 10.1109/NOMS.2012.6211940

Hosseini, S., Nezhad, A. E., & Seilani, H. (2021). Android malware classification using convolutional neural network and LSTM. *Journal of Computer Virology and Hacking Techniques, 17*(4), 307–318. doi:10.100711416-021-00385-z

Hsiao, S.-W., Sun, Y. S., & Chen, M. C. (2016). *Behavior grouping of Android malware family. 2016 IEEE International Conference on Communications (ICC),* Kuala Lumpur, Malaysia. 10.1109/ICC.2016.7511424

HT Tech. (2023). 2 BILLION Google Chrome users hit by browser security flaw! *Tech News, Hindustan Times.*

Huang, F., Xie, G., & Xiao, R. (2009). Research on Ensemble Learning. *International Conference on Artificial Intelligence and Computational Intelligence*. IEEE. 10.1109/AICI.2009.235

Humayun, M., Jhanjhi, N. Z., Alsayat, A., & Ponnusamy, V. (2020). Internet of things and ransomware: Evolution, mitigation and prevention. *Electronic International Journal of Time Series Economics*, *11*(2), 21–36. doi:10.1016/j.eij.2020.05.003

Hussain, A., Mohamed, A., Razali, S. (2020). *A Review on Cybersecurity: Challenges & Emerging Threats*. ACM.

Hu, Y., & Li, J. (2020). A Deep Learning-Based Malware Detection Approach Using a Hybrid Feature Selection Method. *IEEE Access: Practical Innovations, Open Solutions*, *8*, 151983–151992. doi:10.1109/ACCESS.2020.3017017

Hyeisum, S. L., Kim, B., & Lee, T. (2016). The Data Indexing for Cyber Threat Resources. *IEEE Eighth International Conference on Ubiquitous and Future Networks (ICUFN)*. IEEE. 10.1109/ICUFN.2016.7536960

Idika, N. & Mathur, A. (2007). *A survey of malware detection techniques*. Purdue University.

Imtiaz, S. I., Rehman, S., Javed, A. R., Jalil, Z., Liu, X., & Alnumay, W. S. (2021). DeepAMD: Detection and identification of Android malware using high-efficient Deep Artificial Neural Network. *Future Generation Computer Systems*, *115*, 844–856. doi:10.1016/j.future.2020.10.008

Internet firewall data. UCI Machine Learning Repository. (n.d.). https://archive.ics.uci.edu/ml/datasets/Internet+Firewall+Data. Last accessed: July 11, 2023

Iorliam, A. (2019). Cybersecurity and Mobile Device Forensic. In *Cybersecurity in Nigeria. SpringerBriefs in Cybersecurity*. Springer. doi:10.1007/978-3-030-15210-9_4

Islam, R. (2020). Cybersecurity Challenges in Critical Infrastructure Protection: A Review. *Journal of Cybersecurity and Information Management*, *3*(1).

Islam, R., Tian, R., Batten, L., & Versteeg, S. (2010, July). Classification of malware based on string and function feature selection. In *2010 Second Cybercrime and Trustworthy Computing Workshop* (pp. 9-17). IEEE. 10.1109/CTC.2010.11

Jacob, G., Debar, H., & Filiol, E. (2008). Behavioral detection of malware: From a survey towards an established taxonomy. Journal in computer *Virology*, *4*(3), 251–266.

Jacobs, J., Romanosky, S., Adjerid, I., & Baker, W. (2020). Improving vulnerability remediation through better exploit prediction. *Journal of Cybersecurity*, *6*(1), tyaa015. doi:10.1093/cybsec/tyaa015

Jadhav, P. N., & Pore, P. D. (2016). Comparative Analysis of Various Malware Detection Techniques. *Proceedings of the International Conference on Computing, Communication and Automation (ICCCA 2016)*, (pp. 104-10). IEEE. 10.1109/CCAA.2016.7813841

Jagatic, T. N., Johnson, N. A., Jakobsson, M., & Menczer, F. (2007). Social phishing. *Communications of the ACM*, *50*(10), 94–100. doi:10.1145/1290958.1290968

Jamalpur, S., Navya, Y. S., Raja, P., Tagore, G., & Rao, G. R. K. (2018). Dynamic Malware Analysis Using Cuckoo Sandbox. In *2018 Second International Conference on Inventive Communication and Computational Technologies (ICICCT)* (pp. 1056-1060). IEEE. 10.1109/ICICCT.2018.8473346

Jiang, J. (2019). Android Malware Family Classification Based on Sensitive Opcode Sequence. *2019 IEEE Symposium on Computers and Communications (ISCC)*, Barcelona, Spain. 10.1109/ISCC47284.2019.8969656

Jing, S., Liu, X., Cheng, C., Shang, X. Q., & Xiong, G. (2014). Study on a Process Safety Management System Design of a Chemical Accident Database. *IEEE International Conference on Service Operations and Logistics, and Informatics*. IEEE. 10.1109/SOLI.2014.6960736

Jovic, A., Brkić, K., & Bogunović, N. (2015). A review of feature selection methods with applications. *International Convention on Information and Communication Technology, Electronics and Microelectronics*. IEEE. 10.1109/MIPRO.2015.7160458

Kadivar, M. (2015). *Entity Relationship Diagram Approach to Defining Cyber Attacks* [Thesis, Carleton University].

Kafle K, Moran K, Manandhar S, Nadkarni A and Poshyvanyk D. (2020). Security in Centralized Data Store-based Home Automation Platforms. *ACM Transactions on Cyber-Physical Systems*, (pp. 1-27). ACM.

Kamiya, K., Aoki, K., Nakata, K., Sato, T., Kurakami, H., & Tanikawa, M. (2015). The method of detecting malware-infected hosts is analyzing firewall and proxy logs. *Asia-Pacific Symposium on Information and Telecommunication Technologies*. IEEE. 10.1109/APSITT.2015.7217113

Kamoun, F., Iqbal, F., Esseghir, M. A., & Baker, T. (2020). Ai and machine learning: A mixed blessing for cybersecurity. *2020 International Symposium on Networks, Computers and Communications (ISNCC)*. IEEE. 10.1109/ISNCC49221.2020.9297323

Kao-ming, B., & Geng-guo, C. (2009). Design the Database of Laboratory Management System. *IEEE First International Conference on Information Science and Engineering*. IEEE.

Kara, I., & Aydos, M. (2022). The rise of ransomware: Forensic analysis for windows-based ransomware attacks. *Expert Systems with Applications*, *190*, 116198. doi:10.1016/j.eswa.2021.116198

Kaspersky Lab Machine-Learning. (2018). *Machine Learning for Malware Detection*. (Whitepaper).

Kaspersky. (n.d.-a). *What are the different types of malware?* Kasper sky.

Kaspersky. (n.d.-b). *What is a Botnet?* Kasper Sky.

Kaspersky. (n.d.-c). *What is Adware?* Tech Target.

Katherasala, S. K., Sri Manvith, V., Therala, A., & Murala, M. (2022). *NetMD- Network Traffic Analysis and Malware Detection.* 2022 International Conference on Artificial Intelligence in Information and Communication (ICAIIC), Jeju Island, Korea. 10.1109/ICAIIC54071.2022.9722691

Kazim, M., & Doreswamy. (2019). Machine Learning Based Network Anomaly Detection. *International Journal of Recent Technology and Engineering (IJRTE), 8*(4), 542–548. doi:10.35940/ijrte.D7271.118419

Kellette M. & Bernier, M. (2016). Cyber Threat Data Model high level model and use cases. *Defence Research and Development Canada, Reference Document.* Defense Canada.

Khan, A. A., Shaikh, A. A., Laghari, A. A., & Malook Rind, M. (2023). Cloud forensics and digital ledger investigation: A new era of forensics investigation. *International Journal of Electronic Security and Digital Forensics, 15*(1), 1–23. doi:10.1504/IJESDF.2023.127745

Khatun, M., Mozumder, M. A., Polash, M., Hasan, M. R., Ahammad, K., & Shaiham, M. D. S. (2022). An approach to detect phishing websites with features selection method and Ensemble Learning. *International Journal of Advanced Computer Science and Applications, 13*(8). doi:10.14569/IJACSA.2022.0130888

Khezr, S., Moniruzzaman, M., Yassine, A., & Benlamri, R. (2019). Blockchain Technology in Healthcare: A Comprehensive Review and Directions for Future Research. *Applied Sciences 9*(9), 1736. doi:10.3390/app9091736

Khosravi, Z., Hosseini-Asl, E., & Yaghmaee, M. H. (2021). A Review of Malware Mitigation Techniques: State of the Art and Future Directions. *Journal of Cybersecurity, 7*(1).

Kim, N., Kim, B., Lee, S., Cho, H., & Park, J. (2017). Design of a Cyber Threat Intelligence Framework. *International Journal of Innovation Research in Technology & Science (IJIRTS), 5*(6).

Kim, J., Ban, Y., Ko, E., Cho, H., & Yi, J. H. (2022). MAPAS: A practical deep learningbased android malware detection system. *International Journal of Information Security*, 1–14. doi:10.100710207-020-00537-0

Kim, T. H., Park, J., & Cho, H. (2019). A Dynamic Malware Analysis Method Using Reverse Engineering. *IEEE Access : Practical Innovations, Open Solutions, 7*, 43315–43324. doi:10.1109/ACCESS.2019.2907512

Komarkova, J., Lastovicka, M., Husak, M., & Tovarnak, D. (2018). CRUSOE: Data Model for Cyber Situational Awareness. *International Conference on Availability, Reliability, and Security.* ACM.

Komashinskiy, D., & Kotenko, I. (2010, February). Malware detection by data mining techniques based on positionally dependent features. In *2010 18th Euromicro Conference on Parallel, Distributed and Network-based Processing* (pp. 617-623). IEEE. 10.1109/PDP.2010.30

Komatwar, R., & Kokare, M. (2021). A Survey on Malware Detection and Classification. *Journal of Applied Security Research, 16*(3), 390–420. doi:10.1080/19361610.2020.1796162

Konstantinou, E., & Wolthusen, S. (2008). Metamorphic Virus: Analysis and Detection Technical Report. University of London.

Kowalski, K., & Geinitz, H. (2006). Analysis of Log Files Intersections for Security Enhancement. *International Conference on Information Technology: New Generations.* IEEE. 10.1109/ ITNG.2006.32

Kshirsagar, M., Patil, A., Deshmukh, S., Vaidya, G., Rahangdale, M., Kulkarni, C., & Kshirsagar, V. (2020). *Mutichain Enabled EHR Management System and Predictive Analytics.* Springer. ,. doi:10.1007/978-981-15-0077-0_19

Kshirsagar, V. K., Tidke, S. M., & Vishnu, S. (2012). Intrusion detection system using genetic algorithm and data mining: An overview. [PRINT]. *International Journal of Computer Science and Informatics ISSN, 2231*(5292), 118–122. doi:10.47893/IJCSI.2012.1076

Kumar, A., & Goyal, S. (2016). Advance Dynamic Malware Analysis Using Api Hooking. *International Journal of Engineering and Computer Science, 5*(3). Advance online publication. doi:10.18535/ijecs/v5i3.32

Kumar, A., Kuppusamy, K. S., & Aghila, G. (2019). A learning model to detect maliciousness of portable executable using integrated feature set. *Journal of King Saud University-Computer and Information Sciences, 31*(2), 252–265. doi:10.1016/j.jksuci.2017.01.003

Kumar, M. (2022). Scalable malware detection system using big data and distributed machine learning approach. *Soft Computing, 26*(8), 3987–4003. doi:10.100700500-021-06492-9

Kunal Sinha, K. K. (2022). *Creation of Novel Database for Knowledge Repository on Cyber Security.* In: First International Conference on Cyber Warfare, Security and Space Research. Thapar University.

Kuppa, A., & Le-Khac, N.-A. (2021). Adversarial ai methods in cybersecurity. *IEEE Transactions on Information Forensics and Security, 16*, 4924–4938. doi:10.1109/TIFS.2021.3117075

Kuresan, H., Samiappan, D., & Masunda, S. (2019). Fusion of wpt and mfcc feature extraction in parkinsons disease diagnosis. *Technology and Health Care, 27*(4), 363–372. doi:10.3233/ THC-181306 PMID:30664511

Landage, J., & Wankhade, M. P. (2013). Malware and malware detection techniques: A survey. *International Journal of Engineering Research & Technology (Ahmedabad), 2*(12), 2278–0181.

Lee, M.-C., & Cho, S.-B. (2012). Interactive differential evolution for image enhancement application in smartphone. In *IEEE Congress on Evolutionary Computation* (pp. 1-6). Brisbane, QLD, Australia: IEEE. 10.1109/CEC.2012.6256653

Li, J., & Stafford, S. (2014). Detecting smart, self-propagating Internet worms. *Communications and Network Security (CNS), 2014 IEEE Conference.* IEEE.

Li, D., Li, Q., Ye, Y., & Xu, S. (2021). A framework for enhancing deep neural networks against adversarial malware. *IEEE Transactions on Network Science and Engineering*, *8*(1), 736–750. doi:10.1109/TNSE.2021.3051354

Lin, G., Wen, S., Han, Q.-L., Zhang, J., & Xiang, Y. (2020a). Software vulnerability detection using deep neural networks: A survey. *Proceedings of the IEEE*, *108*(10), 1825–1848. doi:10.1109/JPROC.2020.2993293

Lin, G., Zhang, J., Luo, W., Pan, L., De Vel, O., Montague, P., & Xiang, Y. (2021). Software vulnerability discovery via learning multi-domain knowledge bases. *IEEE Transactions on Dependable and Secure Computing*, *18*(5), 2469–2485. doi:10.1109/TDSC.2019.2954088

Liu, K., Xu, S., Xu, G., Zhang, M., Sun, D., & Liu, H. (2020). A review of android malware detection approaches based on machine learning. *IEEE Access : Practical Innovations, Open Solutions*, *8*, 124579–124607. doi:10.1109/ACCESS.2020.3006143

Liu, S., Dibaei, M., Tai, Y., Chen, C., Zhang, J., & Xiang, Y. (2020). Cyber vulnerability intelligence for internet of things binary. *IEEE Transactions on Industrial Informatics*, *16*(3), 2154–2163. doi:10.1109/TII.2019.2942800

Li, Z., Rios, A. L., Xu, G., & Trajkovic, L. (2019). Machine learning techniques for classifying network anomalies and intrusions. *2019 IEEE International Symposium on Circuits and Systems (ISCAS)*. IEEE. 10.1109/ISCAS.2019.8702583

Li, Z., Zou, D., Tang, J., Zhang, Z., Sun, M., & Jin, H. (2019). A comparative study of deep learning-based vulnerability detection system. *IEEE Access : Practical Innovations, Open Solutions*, *7*, 103184–103197. doi:10.1109/ACCESS.2019.2930578

Lu, N., Li, D., Shi, W., Vijayakumar, P., Piccialli, F., & Chang, V. (2021). An efficient combined deep neural network based malware detection framework in 5G environment. *Computer Networks*, *189*, 107932. doi:10.1016/j.comnet.2021.107932

Lyon, G. (2014). Nmap security scanner. *l'ınea] URL:* http://nmap. org/*[Consulta: 8 de junio de 2012].*

Mabsali, N. A. L., Jassim, H., & Mani, J. (2023). Effectiveness of Wireshark Tool for Detecting Attacks and Vulnerabilities in Network Traffic. In *Proceedings of the 3rd International Conference on Computer Science, Electronics and Communication Engineering (CSECE 2023)* (pp. 113-122). IEEE. 10.2991/978-94-6463-110-4_10

Machine Learning-Driven Firewall. (n.d.). KDnuggets.https://www.kdnuggets.com/2017/02/machine-learning-driven-firewall.html.

Maggi, F., Matteucci, M., & Zanero, S. (2010, October-December). Detecting Intrusions through System Call Sequence and Argument Analysis. *IEEE Transactions on Dependable and Secure Computing*, *7*(4), 381–395. doi:10.1109/TDSC.2008.69

Mahmoud, B. S., & Garko, A. B. (2022). A Machine Learning Model for Malware Detection Using Recursive Feature Elimination (RFE) For Feature Selection and Ensemble Technique. IOS Journals.

MalikS.AgrawalA. K. (2021). Multi pronged approach for ransomware analysis, SSRN. doi:10.2139/ssrn.4017025

Malzahn, D., Birnbaum, Z., & Wright-Hamor, C. (2020). Automated vulnerability testing via executable attack graphs. In *2020 International Conference on Cyber Security and Protection of Digital Services (Cyber Security)*, (pp. 1–10). IEEE. 10.1109/CyberSecurity49315.2020.9138852

Martinez, L. F. M. (2021, August 19). How data science could make cybersecurity troubleshooting easier: Firewall logs analysis. *Medium*. https://towardsdatascience.com/how-data-science-could-make-cybersecurity-troubleshooting-easier-firewall-logs-analysis-591e4832f7e6.

McGhin, T., Choo, K.-K. R., Liu, C. Z., & He, D. (2019). Blockchain in healthcare applications: Research challenges and opportunities. *Journal of Network and Computer Applications, 135*, 62-75. doi:10.1016/j.jnca.2019.02.027

Mell, P., Scarfone, K., & Romanosky, S. (2006). Common vulnerability scoring system. *IEEE Security and Privacy, 4*(6), 85–89. doi:10.1109/MSP.2006.145

Memon, R. A., & Mallah, R. A. (2020, July). Malware detection using machine learning techniques: A comprehensive survey. *Journal of Ambient Intelligence and Humanized Computing, 11*(7), 2811–2835. doi:10.100712652-020-02145-w

Mendsaikhan, O., Shimada, H., Hasegawa, H., Yamaguchi, Y., & Shimada, H. (2020, September 28). Quantifying the Significance and Relevance of Cyber-Security Text Through Textual Similarity and Cyber-Security Knowledge Graph. *IEEE Access : Practical Innovations, Open Solutions, 8*, 177041–177052. doi:10.1109/ACCESS.2020.3027321

Menezes, N. J., Rocha, L. M., & Junior, R. M. C. (2019, December). Malware detection using static analysis techniques: A survey. *Journal of Computer Virology and Hacking Techniques, 15*(4), 241–262. doi:10.100711416-019-00320-x

Milosevic, N., Dehghantanha, A., & Choo, K. K. R. (2017). Machine learning aided Android malware classification. *Computers & Electrical Engineering, 61*, 266–274. doi:10.1016/j.compeleceng.2017.02.013

Mira, F. (2021). A Systematic Literature Review on Malware Analysis. *2021 IEEE International IOT, Electronics and Mechatronics Conference (IEMTRONICS)*, (pp. 1-5). IEEE. 10.1109/IEMTRONICS52119.2021.9422537

Mirkovic, J., & Reiher, P. (2004). A taxonomy of DDoS attack and DDoS defense mechanisms. *Computer Communication Review, 34*(2), 39–53. doi:10.1145/997150.997156

Mirtskhulava, L., Iavich, M., Razmadze, M., & Gulua, N. (2021). Securing Medical Data in 5G and 6G via MultichainBlockchain Technology using Post-Quantum Signatures. *2021 IEEE International Conference on Information and Telecommunication Technologies and Radio Electronics (UkrMiCo)*, (pp. 72-75). IEEE. 10.1109/UkrMiCo52950.2021.9716595

Moedjahedy, J., Setyanto, A., Alarfaj, F. K., & Alreshoodi, M. (2022). CCrFS: Combine correlation features selection for detecting phishing websites using machine learning. *Future Internet*, *14*(8), 229. doi:10.3390/fi14080229

Mohanta, A., & Saldanha, A. (2020). Malware Packers. In Apress. Doi:10.1007/978-1-4842-6193-4_7

Mohanty, S., Sahoo, M., & Acharya, A. A. (2022). Predicting phishing URL using filter based univariate feature selection technique. *2022 Second International Conference on Computer Science, Engineering and Applications (ICCSEA)*. IEEE. 10.1109/ICCSEA54677.2022.9936298

Montasari, R. (2023). Artificial Intelligence and the Internet of Things Forensics in a National Security Context. In *Countering Cyberterrorism. Advances in Information Security* (Vol. 101). Springer. doi:10.1007/978-3-031-21920-7_4

Moser, C. K., & Kirda, E. (2007). Limits of Static Analysis for Malware Detection. *Twenty-Third Annual Computer Security Applications Conference (ACSAC 2007)*, Miami Beach, FL, USA. pp. 421-430. 10.1109/ACSAC.2007.21

Moubarak, J., & Feghali, T. (2020). Comparing Machine Learning Techniques for Malware Detection. *ICISSP*, *10*, 0009373708440851. doi:10.5220/0009373708440851

Multichain. (n.d.). https://docs.multichain.org/getting-started/introduction

MUO. (2021) AIDS Trojan: The Story Behind the First Ever Ransomware Attack. Make Use Of.

Mylrea, M., Gourisetti, S. N. G., Larimer, C., & Noonan, C. (2018, May). Insider threat cybersecurity framework webtool & methodology: Defending against complex cyber-physical threats. In *2018 IEEE Security and Privacy Workshops (SPW)* (pp. 207--216). IEEE

Nadkarni, A., & Enck, W. (2013). Preventing accidental data disclosure in modern operating system. *Proceedings of 2013 ACM SIGSAC Conference on Computer & Communication Security*. ACM. 10.1145/2508859.2516677

Nalayini, C. M. & Katiravan, J. (2023). A New IDS for Detecting DDoS Attacks in Wireless Networks using Spotted Hyena Optimization and Fuzzy Temporal CNN. *Journal of Internet Technology, 1*(24).

Nalayini, C. M., & Katiravan, J. (2018). Block Link Flooding Algorithm for TCP SYN Flooding Attack. *International Conference on Computer Networks and Communication Technologies. Lecture Notes on Data Engineering and Communications Technologies*. Springer. 10.1007/978-981-10-8681-6_83

Nalayini, C. M., Katiravan, J., & Prasad, A. (2017). Flooding Attack on MANET – A Survey. *International Journal of Trend in Research and Development (IJTRD)*.

Nalayini, C. MKatiravan, J. (2022). Detection of DDoS Attack using Machine Learning Algorithms. *Journal of Emerging Technologies and Innovative Research, 9*(7).

Nalayini, C. M., & Gayathri, T. (2022). A Comparative Analysis of Standard Classifiers with CHDTC to Detect Credit Card Fraudulent Transactions. In A. Sivasubramanian (Ed.), *Shastry, in Electrical Engineering* (Vol. 792). Springer. doi:10.1007/978-981-16-4625-6_99

Nalayini, C. M., & Katiravan, JImogen, PSahana, J. M. (2023). *A Study on Digital Signature in Blockchain Technology*. IEEE Explore. doi:10.1109/ICAIS56108.2023.10073680

Nalayini, C. M., Katiravan, J., Sathyabama, A. R., Rajasuganya, P. V., & Abirami, K. (2023). Identification and Detection of Credit Card Frauds Using CNN. In M. Mishra, N. Kesswani, & I. Brigui (Eds.), *Applications of Computational Intelligence in Management & Mathematics. ICCM 2022. Springer Proceedings in Mathematics & Statistics* (Vol. 417). Springer. doi:10.1007/978-3-031-25194-8_22

Naryanto, R. F., & Delimayanti, M. K. (2022). Machine learning technique for classification of internet firewall data using rapid miner. *2022 6th International Conference on Electrical, Telecommunication and Computer Engineering (ELTICOM)*. IEEE. 10.1109/ELTICOM57747.2022.10037798

Nasreen, S., & Mir, A. H. (2023). Enhancing cloud forensic investigation system in distributed cloud computing using DK-CP-ECC algorithm and EK-ANFIS. *Journal of Mobile Multimedia, 19*(03), 679–706. doi:10.13052/jmm1550-4646.1933

Nataraj, L., Karthikeyan, S., Jacob, G., & Manjunath, B. S. (2011, July). Malware images: visualization and automatic classification. In *Proceedings of the 8th international symposium on visualization for cyber security* (pp. 1-7). ACM.

Naway, A., & Li, Y. (2019). Using deep neural network for Android malware detection. arXiv preprint arXiv:1904.00736.

Nawir, M., Amir, A., Yaakob, N., & Bi Lynn, O. (2019). Effective and efficient network anomaly detection system using machine learning algorithm. *Bulletin of Electrical Engineering and Informatics, 8*(1), 46–51. doi:10.11591/eei.v8i1.1387

Ndichu, S., McOyowo, S., Okoyo, H., & Wekesa, C. (2023). Detecting Remote Access Network attacks using supervised machine learning methods. *International Journal of Computer Network and Information Security, 15*(2), 48–61. doi:10.5815/ijcnis.2023.02.04

Newman, M. (2023, May 9). *Firewall logging & monitoring*. HOBSoft. https://www.loganalysis.org/firewall-logging/.

Nikolskaia, K. Y., & Naumov, V. B. (2021). The relationship between cybersecurity and artificial intelligence. In *2021 International Conference on Quality Management, Transport and Information Security, Information Technologies (IT&QM&IS)*. IEEE. 10.1109/ITQMIS53292.2021.9642782

Nimbalkar, P., Mulwad, V., Puranik, N., Joshi, A., & Finin, T. (2016). Semantic Interpretation of Structured Log Files. *2016 IEEE 17th International Conference on Information Reuse and Integration (IRI)*. IEEE. 10.1109/IRI.2016.81

Ni, S., Qian, Q., & Zhang, R. (2018). Malware identification using visualization images and deep learning. *Computers & Security*, *77*, 871–885. doi:10.1016/j.cose.2018.04.005

Nugraha, A. F., Tama, D. A., Istiqomah, D. A., Ramadhani, S. T., Kusuma, B. N., & Windarni, V. A. (2022). Feature selection technique for improving classification performance in the web-phishing detection process. *Conference Series*, *4*, 25–31. doi:10.34306/conferenceseries.v4i1.667

O'Kane, P., Sezer, S., & Carlin, D. (2018). Evolution of ransomware. *IET Networks*, *7*(5), 321–327. doi:10.1049/iet-net.2017.0207

Oberlaender, M. (2019). The Future of Cybersecurity: Emerging Threats and Trends. *International Journal of Cybersecurity Intelligence & Cybercrime, 2*(1).

Okun, V., Delaitre, A., & Black, P. E. (2013). Report on the static analysis tool exposition (sate) iv. *NIST Special Publication*, *500*, 297. doi:10.6028/NIST.SP.500-297

Omar, M. (2022). *Static Analysis of Malware*. Springer International Publishing. doi:10.1007/978-3-031-11626-1_2

Omer, M. A., Zeebaree, S. R. M., Sadeeq, M. A. M., Salim, B. W., Rashid, Z. N., & Haji, L. M. (2021). Efficiency of malware detection in android system: A survey. *Asian Journal of Research in Computer Science*, *7*(4), 59–69. doi:10.9734/ajrcos/2021/v7i430189

Or-Meir, O., Nissim, N., Elovici, Y., & Rokach, L. (2019). Dynamic malware analysis in the modern era—A state of the art survey. *ACM Computing Surveys*, *52*(5), 1–48. doi:10.1145/3329786

Pang, C., Wang, X., Xu, S., Wang, C., Liu, P., & Liu, Y. (2021). SoK: All You Ever Wanted to Know About x86/x64 Binary Disassembly But Were Afraid to Ask. In *2021 IEEE Symposium on Security and Privacy (SP)*. San Francisco, CA, USA: IEEE, https://doi.org/10.1109/SP40001.2021.00012

Park, J., Lee, S., Hong, J., & Ryu, S. (2023). Static Analysis of JNI Programs Via Binary Decompilation. *IEEE Transactions on Software Engineering*, *49*(5), 3089–3105. doi:10.1109/TSE.2023.3241639

Parsons, K., McCormac, A., Butavicius, M., Pattinson, M., & Jerram, C. (2014). Determining employee awareness using the human aspects of information security questionnaire (HAIS-Q). *Computers & Security*, *42*, 165–176. doi:10.1016/j.cose.2013.12.003

Patil, S. (2021a, June 29). Routing network traffic based on firewall logs using machine learning. *Medium*. https://medium.com/mlearning-ai/routing-network-traffic-based-on-firewall-logs-using-machine-learning-dc5e5c8c6bb3.

Pavlychev, A. V., Soldatov, K. S., & Skazin, V. A. (2021). Network anomaly detection in the Microsoft Windows system logs using machine learning methods. *Proceedings of Tomsk State University of Control Systems and Radio Electronics, 24*(4), 27–32. doi:10.21293/1818-0442-2021-24-4-27-32

Pawar, S. L., & Hiwarkar, T. (2022). Analysis of various machine learning approaches to detect anomalies from Network Traffic. *International Journal of Computer Science and Mobile Computing, 11*(6), 137–151. doi:10.47760/ijcsmc.2022.v11i06.011

Perarasi, T., Vidhya, S., & Ramya, P.. (2020). Malicious vehicles identifying and trust management algorithm for enhance the security in 5g-vanet. *2020 Second International Conference on Inventive Research in Computing Applications (ICIRCA)*. IEEE. 10.1109/ICIRCA48905.2020.9183184

Perlroth, N. (2021). *This is how they tell me the world ends: The cyberweapons arms race*. Bloomsbury Publishing USA.

Peterson, K., Deeduvanu, R., Kanjamala, P., Boles, K., & Mayo Clinic. (2016). *A Blockchain-Based Approach to Health Information Exchange Networks*. Mayo Clinic.

Pienta, D., Tams, S., & Thatcher, J. (2020). Can trust be trusted in cybersecurity? *Proceedings of the 53rd Hawaii International Conference on System Sciences*. Scholar Space. . 10.24251/HICSS.2020.522

Podins, K., Stinissen, J., & Maybaum, M. (2013). Towards Improved Cyber Security Information Sharing. *L Requirements for a Cyber Security Data Exchange and Collaboration Infrastructure*. (CDXI)uc.

Pollman, E., & Barry, J. M. (2016). Regulatory entrepreneurship. *S. Cal. L. Rev., 90*, 383.

Ponniah, P. (2019). *Data Warehousing Fundamentals for IT Professionals*. Wiley.

Porgo, T. V., Norris, S. L., Salanti, G., Johnson, L. F., Simpson, J. A., Low, N., Egger, M., & Althaus, C. L. (2018). *The Use of Mathematical Modeling Studies for Evidence Synthesis and Guideline Development: A Glossary*. Research Synthesis Methods, Published by John Wiley & Sons Ltd.

Probst, C. W., Hunker, J., Bishop, M., & Gollmann, D. (Eds.). (2010). *Insider threats in cyber security* (Vol. 49). Springer Science & Business Media. doi:10.1007/978-1-4419-7133-3_1

Prokofieva, M., & Miah, S. (2019). Blockchain in healthcare. *AJIS. Australasian Journal of Information Systems, 23*. Advance online publication. doi:10.3127/ajis.v23i0.2203

Qaisar, Z. H., Almotiri, S. H., Al Ghamdi, M. A., Nagra, A. A., & Ali, G. (2021). A Scalable and Efficient Multi-Agent Architecture for Malware Protection in Data Sharing Over Mobile Cloud. *IEEE Access : Practical Innovations, Open Solutions, 9*, 76248–76259. doi:10.1109/ACCESS.2021.3067284

Qamar, A., Karim, A., & Chang, V. (2019). Mobile malware attacks: Review, taxonomy & future directions. *Future Generation Computer Systems, 97*, 259–276. doi:10.1016/j.future.2019.03.007

Qiu, J., Zhang, J., Luo, W., Pan, L., Nepal, S., & Xiang, Y. (2020). A survey of android malware detection with deep neural models. *ACM Computing Surveys*, *53*(6), 1–36. doi:10.1145/3417978

Rafiei, S. Y., & Rahmani, A. M. (2021). A Survey on Machine Learning Techniques for Malware Detection and Mitigation. *Journal of Cybersecurity*, *7*(1).

Rafique, M. F., Ali, M., Qureshi, A. S., Khan, A., & Mirza, A. M. (2019). Malware classification using deep learning-based feature extraction and wrapper-based feature selection technique. arXiv preprint arXiv:1910.10958.

Rahaman, M. (2022). Analysis of Attacks on Private Cloud Computing Services that Implicate Denial of Services (DOS). Cyber Security Insights Magazine, 4.

Rai, B. K., Fatima, S., & Satyarth, K. (2022). Patient-Centric Multichain Healthcare Record. *International Journal of E-Health and Medical Communications*, *13*(4), 1–14. doi:10.4018/IJEHMC.309439

Rapidqube. (n.d.). https://www.rapidqube.com/

Romanosky, S. (2016). Examining the costs and causes of cyber incidents. *Journal of Cybersecurity*, *2*(2), 121-135.

Russell, R., Kim, L., Hamilton, L., Lazovich, T., Harer, J., Ozdemir, O., Ellingwood, P., & McConley, M. (2018). Automated vulnerability detection in source code using deep representation learning. In *2018 17th IEEE international conference on machine learning and applications (ICMLA)*, pages 757–762. IEEE. 10.1109/ICMLA.2018.00120

Safavi, N. S., Hosseini-Asl, E., & Yaghmaee, M. H. (2020). A Survey on Malware Detection and Mitigation Techniques. *Journal of Cybersecurity*, *6*(1).

Saxe, J., & Berlin, K. (2015). *Deep neural network based malware detection using two dimensional binary program features*. 2015 10th International Conference on Malicious and Unwanted Software (MALWARE), Fajardo, PR. 10.1109/MALWARE.2015.7413680

Scarfone, K., & Mell, P. (2007). Guide to intrusion detection and prevention systems (idps). *NIST special publication, 800*(2007), 94.

Security Magazine. (n.d.). https://www.securitymagazine.com/articles/92157-coronavirus-related-spear-phishing-attacks-see-667-increase-in-march-2020

Senthil Kumar, N., Saravanakumar, K., & Deepa, K. (2015).On Privacy and Security in Social Media – A Comprehensive Study. *International Conference on Information Security & Privacy (ICISP2015)*. Elsevier

Seo, S., Seok, B., & Lee, C. (2023). Digital forensic investigation framework for the metaverse. *The Journal of Supercomputing*, *79*(9), 9467–9485. doi:10.100711227-023-05045-1

Sethi, K., Kumar, R., Sethi, L., Bera, P., & Patra, P. K. (2019). *A Novel Machine Learning Based Malware Detection and Classification Framework.* 2019 International Conference on Cyber Security and Protection of Digital Services (Cyber Security), Oxford, UK. 10.1109/CyberSecPODS.2019.8885196

Setiawan, H., Erlangga, L. E., & Baskoro, I. (2020). Vulnerability analysis using the interactive application security testing (iast) approach for government x website applications. In *2020 3rd International Conference on Information and Communications Technology (ICOIACT)*, (pp. 471–475). IEEE.

Shaheed, A., & Kurdy, M. H. D. B. (2022). Web Application Firewall Using Machine Learning and Features Engineering. *Security and Communication Networks, 2022*, 1–14. doi:10.1155/2022/5280158

Shaji, P. S. (2020). Understanding the Digital Forensics Framework of Cloud Computing-Cloud Forensics. *International Journal of Legal Developments and Allied Issues, 6*(3).

Shakarian, P., Shakarian, J., & Ruef, A. (2013). *Introduction to cyber-warfare: A multidisciplinary approach.* Newnes.

Shang, S., Zheng, N., Xu, J., Xu, M., & Zhang, H. (2010, October). Detecting malware variants via function-call graph similarity. In *2010 5th International Conference on Malicious and Unwanted Software* (pp. 113-120). IEEE. 10.1109/MALWARE.2010.5665787

Sharafaldin, I., Lashkari, A., Hakak, S., & Ghorbani, A. (2019). Developing Realistic Distributed Denial of Service (DDoS) Attack Dataset and Taxonomy. *IEEE 53rd International Carnahan Conference on Security Technology.* IEEE.

Sharma, D. D., Tripathi, D. D., & Gaur, M. K. (2016). Anomaly Based Malware Detection Using Machine Learning. *Proceedings of the 5th International Conference on Advances in Computing, Communications and Informatics (ICACCI 2016)*, (pp. 2655-2660). IEEE. 10.1109/ICACCI.2016.7732399

Sharma, D., Wason, V., & Johri, P. (2021). Optimized Classification of Firewall Log Data using Heterogeneous Ensemble Techniques. *2021 International Conference on Advance Computing and Innovative Technologies in Engineering (ICACITE)*. IEEE. 10.1109/ICACITE51222.2021.9404732

Sharma, S. R., Parthasarathy, R., & Honnavalli, P. B. (2020). A Feature Selection Comparative Study for Web Phishing Datasets. *IEEE International Conference on Electronics, Computing and Communication Technologies.* IEEE. 10.1109/CONECCT50063.2020.9198349

Sheibani, R., Nikookar, E., & Alavi, S. (2019). An ensemble method for diagnosis of Parkinson's disease based on voice measurements. *Journal of Medical Signals and Sensors, 9*(4), 221. doi:10.4103/jmss.JMSS_57_18 PMID:31737550

Shi, F., Kai, S., Zheng, J., & Zhong, Y. (2022). Xlnet-based prediction model for cvss metric values. *Applied Sciences (Basel, Switzerland), 12*(18), 8983. doi:10.3390/app12188983

Shin, Y., Kim, S., Jo, W., & Shon, T. (2022). *Digital forensic case studies for in-vehicle infotainment systems using Android Auto and Apple CarPlay*. MDPI. . doi:10.3390/s22197196

Shu, X., Zhang, J. Danfeng, D., & Feng, W. C. (2016). Fast Detection of Transformed Data Leaks. IEEE Transactions on Information Forensics and Security. IEEE.

Sikorski, M., & Honig, A. (2012). *Practical malware analysis: the hands-on guide to dissecting malicious software*. No Starch Press.

Silberschatz, A., Forth, H. F., & Sudarshan, S. (2006). *Database System* (5th ed.). McGraw - Hill.

Singh, A., & Patel, N. D. (2023). Security Issues, Attacks and Countermeasures in Layered IoT Ecosystem. *International Journal of Next-Generation Computing*.

Singh, P., & Ranga, V. (2021). Attack and intrusion detection in cloud computing using an ensemble learning approach. *International Journal of Information Technology : an Official Journal of Bharati Vidyapeeth's Institute of Computer Applications and Management*, *13*(2), 565–571. doi:10.100741870-020-00583-w

Sinha, K. & Senapati, K. (2021). *Design and Development of Data Model for Cyber Threat*. Lambert Academic Publishing.

Skazin, V. A., Pavlychev, A. V., & Zotov, S. S. (2021). Detection of network anomalies in log files using machine learning methods. *IOP Conference Series. Materials Science and Engineering*, *1069*(1), 012021. doi:10.1088/1757-899X/1069/1/012021

SL, S. D., & Jaidhar, C. D. (2019). Windows malware detector using convolutional neural network based on visualization images. *IEEE Transactions on Emerging Topics in Computing*, *9*(2), 1057–1069.

Soares, L. F., Fernandes, D. A., Gomes, J. V., Freire, M. M., & Inácio, P. R. (2014). Cloud security: state of the art. *Security, Privacy and Trust in Cloud Systems*. Insiders.

SpacSec. (2021). *Communications in Computer and Information Science*, (vol 1599). Springer, Cham

Spafford, E. (1989). The internet worm incident. *Lecture Notes in Computer Science*, *89*, 446–468. doi:10.1007/3-540-51635-2_54

Sree Lakshmi, T., Govindarajan, M., & Sreenivasulu, A. (2022). *Malware visual resemblance analysis with minimum losses using Siamese neural networks. Theoretical Computer Science*. Elsevier BV., doi:10.1016/j.tcs.2022.07.018

Stanković, S., Gajin, S., & Petrović, R. (n.d.). *A Review of Wazuh Tool Capabilities for Detecting Attacks Based on Log Analysis*. Academic Press.

Stiffler, J. J. (1981). The vulnerability of computers: Malfunctions may be due to "illegal" operations, to hardware failures, or to combinations of hardware and software failures that simply elude pinpointing. *IEEE Spectrum*, *18*(10), 44–45. doi:10.1109/MSPEC.1981.6369634

Sun, R., Botacin, M., Sapountzis, N., Yuan, X., Bishop, M., Porter, D. E., Li, X., Gregio, A., & Oliveira, D. (2022). A praise for defensive programming: Leveraging uncertainty for effective malware mitigation. *IEEE Transactions on Dependable and Secure Computing*, *19*(1), 353–369. doi:10.1109/TDSC.2020.2986112

Suresh Babu, C. V. (2023a). *IoT and its Applications*. Anniyappa Publications.

Suresh Babu, C. V. (2023b). IoT-Based Smart Accident Detection and Alert System. In P. Swarnalatha, S. Prabu, & I. G. I. Global (Eds.), *Handbook of Research on Deep Learning Techniques for Cloud-Based Industrial IoT* (pp. 322–337)., doi:10.4018/978-1-6684-8098-4.ch019

Surwade, A. P. (2020). Phishing e-mail is an increasing menace. *International Journal of Information Technology : an Official Journal of Bharati Vidyapeeth's Institute of Computer Applications and Management*, *12*(2), 611–617. doi:10.100741870-019-00407-6

Syafiq, M. & Soewitob, B. (2022). A Blockchain For Secure Data Storing With Multi Chain On Smart Healthcare System. *Journal of Theoretical and Applied Information Technology, 100*(13).

Szor, P. (2005). *The art of computer virus research and defense*. Pearson Education.

Sztaho, D., Valalik, I., & Vicsi, K. (2019). Parkinson's disease severity estimation on hungarian speech using various speech tasks. In: *10th Int. Conf. Speech Technol. Human-Computer Dialogue*. SpeD. 10.1109/SPED.2019.8906277

Taher, K. A., Mohammed Yasin Jisan, B., & Rahman, Md. M. (2019). Network intrusion detection using supervised machine learning technique with feature selection. *2019 International Conference on Robotics, Electrical and Signal Processing Techniques (ICREST)*. IEEE. 10.1109/ICREST.2019.8644161

Tahir, M., Asghar, S., Zafar, A., & Gillani, S. (2016). A Hybrid Model to Detect Phishing-Sites Using Supervised Learning Algorithms. *International Conference on Computational Science*. IEEE. 10.1109/CSCI.2016.0214

Tamma, R., Skulkin, O., Mahalik, H., & Satish., B. (2020). *Forensically investigate and analyze iOS*. PACKT Publishing. https://books.google.co.in/books?id=TU_cDwAAQBAJ&lpg=PP1&dq=recent%20paperworks%20on%20malware%20forensics&lr&pg=PP2#v=twopage&q&f=false

TanC. S. (2018, March 24). *Phishing Dataset for Machine Learning: Feature Evaluation*. doi:10.17632/h3cgnj8hft.1

Tang, M., Alazab, M., & Luo, Y. (2019). Big data for cybersecurity: Vulnerability disclosure trends and depen- dencies. *IEEE Transactions on Big Data*, *5*(3), 317–329. doi:10.1109/TBDATA.2017.2723570

Techcrunch (2018). Everything you need to know about Facebook's data breach affecting 50M users. Techcrunch.

TechTarget (2022). SolarWinds hack explained: Everything you need to know. *Tech Target*.

TechTarget Security. (2022). Computer worm. *Tech Target.*

Telecom Review. (2022). *Cyber-Physical Systems: The Integrated Form of ICT.* Telecom Review.

Telnarova, Z. (2010). Relational Database as a Source of Ontology Creation. *Proceedings of the International Multiconference on Computer Science and Information Technology.* UDEMY. www.google.co.in www.udemy.com www.geeksforgeeks.com www.tutorialspoints.com

The Conversation. (2021). The increase in ransomware attacks during the COVID-19 pandemic may lead to a new internet. *The Conversation.*

The Indian Express. (2020). Cosmos Bank malware attack: Interpol issues red corner notice against prime suspect traced in foreign country. *The Indian Express.*

The significance and role of firewall logs. (2023, June 9). Exabeam. https://www.exabeam.com/siem-guide/siem-concepts/firewall-logs.

The White House. (2020). The Future of Cybersecurity: A Strategic Roadmap. National Institute of Standards and Technology.

Tobiyama, S., Yamaguchi, Y., Shimada, H., Ikuse, T., & Yagi, T. (2016). Malware Detection with Deep Neural Network Using Process Behavior *2016 IEEE 40th Annual Computer Software and Applications Conference (COMPSAC),* (pp. 577-582). IEEE. 10.1109/COMPSAC.2016.151

Tracy, J. M., Özkanca, Y., Atkins, D. C., & Hosseini Ghomi, R. (2020). Investigating voice as a biomarker: Deep phenotyping methods for early detection of Parkinson's disease. *Journal of Biomedical Informatics, 104,* 103362. doi:10.1016/j.jbi.2019.103362 PMID:31866434

Tripathi, D. D., & Sharma, D. D. (2014). Malware Mitigation through Machine Learning Algorithms. *Proceedings of the 6th International Conference on Computational Intelligence and Communication Networks (CICN 2014),* (pp. 543-547). IEEE. 10.1109/CICN.2014.134

Tubis, A., Werbińska-Wojciechowska, S., Góralczyk, M., Wróblewski, A., & Ziętek, B. (2020). Cyber-Attacks Risk Analysis Method for Different Levels of Automation of Mining Processes in Mines Based on Fuzzy Theory Use. *Sensors (Basel), 20*(24), 7210. doi:10.339020247210 PMID:33339301

Ucci, D., Aniello, L., & Baldoni, R. (2019). Survey of machine learning techniques for malware analysis. *Computers & Security, 81,* 123–147. doi:10.1016/j.cose.2018.11.001

Udayakumar, N. (2019). *Malware Classification Using Machine Learning Algorithms.* Research Gate.

Upadhyay, V. & Yadav, S. (2018). Study of Cyber Security Challenges Its Emerging Trends: Current Technologies. *International Journal of Engineering Research and Management 5*(7).

Urmila, T. S. (2022). Machine learning-based malware detection on Android devices using behavioral features. *Materials Today: Proceedings, 62,* 4659–4664. doi:10.1016/j.matpr.2022.03.121

Vaishanav, L. (2017). Behavioural Analysis of Android Malware using Machine Learning. *International Journal of Engineering and Computer Science*, *6*(5). doi:10.18535/ijecs/v6i5.32

Venkatasubramanian, M., Lashkari, A. H., & Hakak, S. (2023). IoT Malware Analysis using Federated Learning: A Comprehensive Survey. *IEEE Access : Practical Innovations, Open Solutions*, *11*, 5004–5018. doi:10.1109/ACCESS.2023.3235389

Venkatraman, S., Alazab, M., & Vinayakumar, R. (2019). A hybrid deep learning image-based analysis for effective malware detection. *Journal of Information Security and Applications*, *47*, 377–389. doi:10.1016/j.jisa.2019.06.006

Vermisoglou, E., Panáček, D., Jayaramulu, K., Pykal, M., Frébort, I., Kolář, M., & Otyepka, M. (2020). Human virus detection with graphene-based materials. *Biosensors & Bioelectronics*, *166*, 112436. doi:10.1016/j.bios.2020.112436 PMID:32750677

Vinayakumar, R., Alazab, M., Soman, K. P., Poornachandran, P., & Venkatraman, S. (2019). Robust Intelligent Malware Detection Using Deep Learning. *IEEE Access : Practical Innovations, Open Solutions*, *7*, 46717–46738. doi:10.1109/ACCESS.2019.2906934

Voigt, P., & Von dem Bussche, A. (2017). The eu general data protection regulation (gdpr). A Practical Guide, 1st Ed., Cham: Springer International Publishing, 10(3152676), 10-5555.

Volkamer, M., Renaud, K., Reinheimer, B., & Kunz, A. (2017). User experiences of TORPEDO: TOoltip-poweRed Phishing E-mail DetectiOn. *Computers & Security*, *71*, 100–113. doi:10.1016/j.cose.2017.02.004

Von Solms, R., & Van Niekerk, J. (2013). From information security to cyber security. *Computers & Security, 38*, 97-102.

Wagh, K. S. (2018). A Survey: Data Leakge Detection Techniques. *International Journal of Electrical and Computer Engineering (IJECE), 8*(4).

Wang, D., Chen, T., Zhang, Z., & Zhang, N. (2023). A Survey of Android Malware Detection Based on Deep Learning. *International Conference on Machine Learning for Cyber Security*, (pp. 228–242). Springer. 10.1007/978-3-031-20096-0_18

Wang, H., Ye, G., Tang, Z., Tan, S. H., Huang, S., Fang, D., Feng, Y., Bian, L., & Wang, Z. (2021). Combining graph-based learning with automated data collection for code vulnerability detection. *IEEE Transactions on Information Forensics and Security*, *16*, 1943–1958. doi:10.1109/TIFS.2020.3044773

Wang, S., Balarezo, J. F., Kandeepan, S., Al-Hourani, A., Chavez, K. G., & Rubinstein, B. (2021). Machine learning in network anomaly detection: A survey. *IEEE Access : Practical Innovations, Open Solutions*, *9*, 152379–152396. doi:10.1109/ACCESS.2021.3126834

Wang, W., Dumont, F., Niu, N., & Horton, G. (2022). Detecting software security vulnerabilities via requirements dependency analysis. *IEEE Transactions on Software Engineering*, *48*(5), 1665–1675. doi:10.1109/TSE.2020.3030745

Wang, W., Shi, F., Zhang, M., Xu, C., & Zheng, J. (2020). A vulnerability risk assessment method based on heterogeneous information network. *IEEE Access : Practical Innovations, Open Solutions*, *8*, 148315–148330. doi:10.1109/ACCESS.2020.3015551

Wang, Z., Li, G., Zhuo, Z., Ren, X., Lin, Y., & Gu, J. (2022). A deep learning method for android application classification using semantic features. *Security and Communication Networks*, *2022*, 1–16. doi:10.1155/2022/1289175

Wang, Z., Xie, W., Wang, B., Tao, J., & Wang, E. (2021). A Survey on Recent Advanced Research of CPS Security. *Applied Sciences (Basel, Switzerland)*, *11*(9), 3751. doi:10.3390/app11093751

Wani, S., & Mohd, T. Sembok, T., & Wahiddin, M. (2022). Constructing a knowledge base for Al-Qur' an utilizing principles of human communication. Fourth International Conference on Information Retrieval and Knowledge Management. Springer.

Wazuh. (2023). https://documentation.wazuh.com/current/index.html

Weiser, M. (1984). Program slicing. *IEEE Transactions on Software Engineering*, *SE-10*(4), 352–357. doi:10.1109/TSE.1984.5010248

William, S. (2008). *Computer Security: Principles and Practice*. Pearson Education India.

Winding, R., Wright, T., & Chapple, M. (2006). System Anomaly Detection: Mining Firewall Logs. *2006 Securecomm and Workshops*. IEEE. doi:10.1109/SECCOMW.2006.359572

Wu, B., & Zou, F. (2022). Code vulnerability detection based on deep sequence and graph models: A survey. *Security and Communication Networks*, *2022*, 2022. doi:10.1155/2022/1176898

Xuan, C. D., Nguyen, H. L., & Nikolaevich, T. V. (2020). Malicious URL Detection based on Machine Learning. *International Journal of Advanced Computer Science and Applications*, *11*(1). Advance online publication. doi:10.14569/IJACSA.2020.0110119

Yaacoub, J.-P. A., Salman, O., Noura, H. N., Kaaniche, N., Chehab, A., & Malli, M. (2020). Cyber-physical systems security: Limitations, issues and future trends. *Microprocessors and Microsystems*, *77*, 103201. doi:10.1016/j.micpro.2020.103201 PMID:32834204

Yadav, C. S., Singh, J., Yadav, A., Pattanayak, H. S., Kumar, R., Khan, A. A., Haq, M. A., Alhussen, A., & Alharby, S. (2022). Malware Analysis in IoT & Android Systems with Defensive Mechanism. *Electronics (Basel)*, *11*(15), 2354. doi:10.3390/electronics11152354

Yaman, O., Ertam, F., & Tuncer, T. (2020). Automated Parkinson's disease recognition based on statistical pooling method using acoustic features. *Medical Hypotheses*, *135*, 109483. doi:10.1016/j.mehy.2019.109483 PMID:31954340

Yang, F., Wu, J., Tang, S., & Zhang, H. (2013). Dynamic Knowledge Repository-based Security Auxiliary System of User behavior. *IEEE International Conference on Green Computing and Communications and IEEE Internet of Things and IEEE Cyber, Physical and Social Computing*. IEEE. 10.1109/GreenCom-iThings-CPSCom.2013.390

Yang, S., Shi, Y., & Guo, F. (2019). Risk assessment of industrial internet system by using game-attack graphs. In *2019 IEEE 5th International Conference on Computer and Communications (ICCC)*, pages 1660–1663. IEEE. 10.1109/ICCC47050.2019.9064444

Yang, S., Zhou, H., & Zhao, C. (2020, December). A malware detection system based on dynamic analysis and deep learning. *Journal of Intelligent & Fuzzy Systems*, *38*(6), 6701–6711. doi:10.3233/JIFS-191769

Yin, H. (2007). Panorama: capturing system-wide information flow for malware detection and analysis. *Proceedings of the 14th ACM conference on Computer and communications security.* ACM. 10.1145/1315245.1315261

Yost, J. R. (2017). *Making IT Work: A History of the Computer Services Industry.* MIT Press. doi:10.7551/mitpress/9375.001.0001

You, I., & Yim, K. (2010). Malware obfuscation techniques: A brief survey. *Broadband, Wireless Computing, Communication and Applications (BWCCA), 2010 International Conference on.* IEEE.

Yu, H., Sun, H., Wu, D., & Kuo, T. T. (2019). Comparison of Smart Contract Blockchains for Healthcare Applications. *AMIA Symposium*, (pp.1266-1275). AMIA.

Yu, Z., Theisen, C., Williams, L., & Menzies, T. (2021). Improving vulnerability inspection efficiency using active learning. *IEEE Transactions on Software Engineering*, *47*(11), 2401–2420. doi:10.1109/TSE.2019.2949275

Zebpay. (n.d.). https://zebpay.com/blog/what-is-multichain

Zeng, Y. G. (2017). Identifying email threats using predictive analysis. *2017 International Conference on Cyber Security And Protection Of Digital Services (Cyber Security)*, (pp. 1-2). IEEE. 10.1109/CyberSecPODS.2017.8074848

Zeng, Z., Yang, Z., Huang, D., & Chung, C.-J. (2021). Licality–likelihood and criticality: Vulnerability risk prior- itization through logical reasoning and deep learning. *IEEE Transactions on Network and Service Management.*

Zhang, J., Gardner, R., & Vukotic, I. (2019). Anomaly detection in wide area network meshes using two machine learning algorithms. *Future Generation Computer Systems*, *93*, 418–426. doi:10.1016/j.future.2018.07.023

Zhang, M., de Carn'e de Carnavalet, X., Wang, L., & Ragab, A. (2019). Large-scale empirical study of important features indicative of discovered vulnerabilities to assess application security. *IEEE Transactions on Information Forensics and Security*, *14*(9), 2315–2330. doi:10.1109/TIFS.2019.2895963

Zhang, X., Breitinger, F., Luechinger, E., & O'Shaughnessy, S. (2021). Android application forensics: A survey of obfuscation, obfuscation detection and deobfuscation techniques and their impact on investigations. *Forensic Science International: Digital Investigation*, *37*, 301285. doi:10.1016/j.fsidi.2021.301285

Zhong, F., Chen, Z., Xu, M., Zhang, G., Yu, D., & Cheng, X. (2022). Malware-on-the-Brain: Illuminating Malware Byte Codes With Images for Malware Classification. *IEEE Transactions on Computers*. doi:10.1109/TC.2022.3160357

Zhou, Y., Liu, S., Siow, J., Du, X., & Liu, Y. (2019). Devign: Effective vulnerability identification by learning comprehensive program semantics via graph neural networks. *Advances in Neural Information Processing Systems*, 32.

Zhu, E., Chen, Y., Ye, C., Li, X., & Liu, F. (2019). OFS-NN: An Effective Phishing Websites Detection Model Based on Optimal Feature Selection and Neural Network. *IEEE Access : Practical Innovations, Open Solutions*, 7, 73271–73284. doi:10.1109/ACCESS.2019.2920655

Zuhair, H., Selmat, A., & Salleh, M. (2015). The Effect of Feature Selection on Phish Website Detection. *International Journal of Advanced Computer Science and Applications*, 6(10). doi:10.14569/IJACSA.2015.061031

About the Contributors

Manoj Kumar M V completed his Ph.D. from the department of computer science at National Institute of Technology Karnataka, Surathkal, Mangalore, India. He did his masters from Bapuji Institute of Engineering and Technology, Davanagere, India and is graduated from Vishweshwaraiah Technology University, Belgaum, India. His research interest is in data and process mining, mobile application, and statistical data analysis. R-programming is one of his key interest and building mobile apps is his hobby. He has been a resource person in various workshops on mobile application development and data analysis. He is currently working on a problem related to concept drift, in the context of process mining. He has a good number of publications in international journals and conferences. He has worked as a research scholar under Dr. Annappa, associate professor, NITK.

* * *

Roshni A is working as a Project Staff under Centre for Cyber Intelligence – DST – CURIE – AI in the Department of Computer Science, Avinashilingam Institute for Home Science and Higher Education for Women (Deemed to be University), Coimbatore, Tamil Nadu, India. She has published 7 conference papers, books and book chapters. She has conducted various training programmes, Workshops, Faculty Development Programmes and also served as a resource person. Her areas of interest include, Cyber Security, Machine Learning, Artificial Intelligence, Data Science and Data Analytics. She received Smt. Subha Gnana Durai Award in M.Sc Computer Science. She is an emerging researcher in Cyber Intelligence domain.

Manu A P, Professor in the Department of Computer Science and Engineering, having 20+ years of academic and industrial experience. Awarded Doctoral degree from IIIT, Allahabad. India. Has authored two books titled "A to Z Linux" and "ABC of Hadoop, Docker and Ansible". He is a Fellow of the Institution of Engineers (India), Members of CSI, and ISTE. His research area of interests are Cloud Computing, and Next Generation Networks. He is a reviewer of Elsevier, InderScience, Taylor and Francis journals.

Lalit Awasthi is serving as Director at National Institute of Technology Uttarakhand, India, Prof Awasthi has more than three and half decades of experience of teaching, research and institution building. He earlier served as Director of NIT Jalandhar, NIT Hamirpur India. He has also served as founder Director of Atal Bihari Vajpayee Govt. Institute of Engineering and Technology, Pragtinagar, India. He as published more than 250 research papers in reputed Journals and Conferences. He has filed 14 patents and designs. His research areas include Check-pointing, Mobile computing, Sensor Networks, P2P Networks, Cloud computing, Security.

C.V. Suresh Babu is a pioneer in content development. A true entrepreneur, he founded Anniyappa Publications, a company that is highly active in publishing books related to Computer Science and Management. Dr. C.V. Suresh Babu has also ventured into SB Institute, a center for knowledge transfer. He holds a Ph.D. in Engineering Education from the National Institute of Technical Teachers Training & Research in Chennai, along with seven master's degrees in various disciplines such as Engineering, Computer Applications, Management, Commerce, Economics, Psychology, Law, and Education. Additionally, he has UGC-NET/SET qualifications in the fields of Computer Science, Management, Commerce, and Education. Currently, Dr. C.V. Suresh Babu is a Professor in the Department of Information Technology at the School of Computing Science, Hindustan Institute of Technology and Science (Hindustan University) in Padur, Chennai, Tamil Nadu, India. For more information, you can visit his personal blog at .

Urvashi Bansal is Assistant Professor at Dr. BR Ambedkar NIT Jalandhar and her research area of interests are Security - Information Security, Cyber Warfare, Vulnerability Analysis and Management, Ransomware attacks, detection and mitigation, Biometric Authentication. Artificial Intelligence - Machine Learning, Adversarial ML, Deep Learning, Explainable AI.

C. M. Nalayini is working as Assistant Professor in the department of Information Technology at Velammal Engineering College, Chennai. She has completed B.Tech- Information Technology in Velammal Engineering College and secured First class with distinction, M.Tech-Computer Science and Engineering in Dr M.G.R. Educational and Research Institute and secured First class with honours, currently pursuing Ph.D in Anna University. She has 17.6 yrs of Teaching Experience. She has handled 17+ courses in her teaching experience. She has given many Computer Training programs to 11th and 12th standard students of many Government Higher Secondary Schools as social interest. She acted as coach For ACM ICPC Regional Contest sponsored by IBM. She handled CCNA classes for Non-IT students. She has handled Computer classes for Women Welfare SHG Group. She has delivered many Guest Lectures, workshops and Faculty Development Programs in various Engineering Colleges. She published papers in many International journals and Conferences. She has published many book chapters in Springer and IEEE explore. She authored books such as Computer Programming in C and Programming and Data Structures. She also posted her notes in vidyarthiplus plus for the benefit of the students. Recently she has received best paper award for her Blockchain paper. She has completed many certificate courses such as Cyber Security and Machine Learning.

Shanmugapriya D is an Assistant Professor and Head, Department of Information Technology, Avinashilingam Institute for Home Science and Higher Education for Women (Deemed to be University), Coimbatore, India since 2001. She has more than 20+ years of teaching experience and 10 years of research experience. Her areas of interest include, Cyber Security, Biometric security and Image Processing. She has executed funded projects sponsored by DRDO, DST and UGC. She is Supervising 4 scholars at Ph.D level. She has more than 25 publications in prestigious conferences and peer-reviewed journals. She is Reviewers for many Conferences and Journals. She is a content Writer of Virtual Currency, Block Chain Technology and Basics of Security Auditing for SWAYAM-MOOC course on Cyber Security.

Janardhana D R received his B.E in Electrical and Electronics Engineering from Jawaharlal Nehru National College of Engineering, Shivamogga, Karnataka, India in 2006, MTech degree in Computer Science and Engineering from Jawaharlal Nehru National College of Engineering, Shivamogga, Karnataka, India in 2009 and currently pursuing PhD degree from Visvesvaraya Technological University, Belagavi, India. He is an Assistant Professor in the Department of Computer Science and Engineering, Nitte Meenakshi Institute of Technology, Bengaluru, India. His research interests includes Network Security, Data Science, IoT, Machine learning and Deep Learning.

Padmavathi G is the Dean-School of Physical Sciences and Computational Sciences and Professor in the Department of Computer Science, Avinashilingam Institute for Home Science and Higher Education for Women (Deemed to be University), Coimbatore, India. She has more than 35 years of teaching experience and 25 years of research experience. Her areas of interest include, Cyber Security, Wireless Communication and Real Time Systems. She has executed funded projects worth 267.368 lakhs Sponsored by AICTE, UGC, DRDO and DST. She has supervised 22 scholars at Ph. D level. She has more than 200 publications in prestigious conferences and peer-reviewed journals. She is the life members of various professional bodies like CSI, ISTE, ISCA, WSEAS, AACE and AICW. She is reviewers for many IEEE

Conferences and Journals. She has visited many countries for technical deliberations. She is the Course Co-ordinator for SWAYAM-MOOC on Cyber Security. So far, more than 1,00,000 learners have enrolled for various sessions and benefitted.

Shivanna K, currently working as an Associate Professor, Dept. of CSE, Malnad College of Engineering, Hassan since from 12 September 2022. He have 14 years of teaching experience including research. He has completed BE in the year 2006, G M IT, Davanagere and M Tech in the year 2009, JNNCE, Shimoga. He has started his research work in the year 2013 with a Title "Techniques for Data Protection in Cloud Computing" under the Guidance of Dr. Prabhudeva S, Professor, JNNCE, Shimoga and He was received Ph. D degree from VTU in the year 2021. He has published 6 research papers on a reputed journals and presented a more than 6 papers on national and international conferences. He has received 2 best paper awards from national and international conferences during his Ph.D. He has organized number of workshop and served as a resource person in the workshop. He has received appreciation letters from the department and institution for enhancing the academic initiatives and also developing students in their personal and academic growth. He has submitted research proposal to VGST, KSCST and AICTE for seeking research funds. He has delivered a one week guest lecture on Cyber Forensics for M Tech students of Jain University, Bangalore. He has depth knowledge about new technologies like Eclipse IDE for Java programming, Net-Beans IDE for web application development, Network Simulator-2, Cloud Simulator, Amazon Web Services and Contiki for IoT applications. Finally his research interest includes Cryptography, Cloud Data Security, Internet of Things and Blockchain Technology.

Jeevaa Katiravan received his Ph.D degree from the Department of Information and Communication Engineering at Anna University. He is currently working as a Professor in the Department of Information Technology at Velammal Engineering College. His research interest includes Network Security, Wireless Networks.

Guneet Kaur BTECH in ECE from PTU in 2016 and M.E in ECE from Thapar University in 2018. Presently I am working as Junior Research Fellow at Dr. BR Ambedkar NIT Jalandhar under project entitled "An intelligent network analyzer cum patcher for advanced security hardening of the organizational network" sponsored by DST, India.

Abhishek Kumar is currently working with a major technology company as a Regulatory Compliance Lead. Abhishek comes from a rick background in cybersecurity and cybercrimes investigation. He has worked with premier national institutions such as the National Investigation Agency (NIA) and the National Police Academy.

He has also overseen cybersecurity investigations in organizations like UBER and the Bank of Newyork Mellon.

Rakesh Singh Kunwar has completed his Ph.D. in Cyber Security and his core domain is Malware Analysis from Rashtriya Raksha University (Formerly Raksha Shakti University), Lavad, Gandhinagar. He completed his M.Tech in Computer Network Engineering from Graphic Era University, Dehradun, Uttarakhand. He has more than 9 years of experience in Academics. He worked for 3 years as Assistant Professor in Bhutan through ITEC MEA under Colombo Plan Lecturers. He also worked as SSO in NICFS, New Delhi, MHA. Besides this, He delivered expert lectures on several occasions & has an interest in the field of Cyber Security.

Andrew Simon P is a student currently pursuing in Hindustan institute of technology and science.

Sasirekha R is currently doing her Full-time Ph.D. research work in the Department of Computer Science & Engineering at SRM Institute of Science & Technology, Kattankulathur, Chennai. Completed my B.E CSE at Anna University and M.E at Anna University, Chennai. Currently doing projects in Mixed Reality. Her main interests include Artificial Intelligence, Image processing,Deep learning.

Barath Kumar S is a college student pursuing a B.Tech in IT with a specialization in Cyber Security and iam a passionate about coding and computer security. In my free time, iam enjoys participating in online coding competitions and practicing ethical hacking. My ultimate goal is to become a cybersecurity expert and work for a top tech company.

Geethalakshmi S.N is the Professor and Head, Department of Computer Science, Avinashilingam Institute for Home Science and Higher Education for Women (Deemed to be University), Coimbatore, India. She has more than 32 years of teaching experience. Her area of specialization includes Software Project Management, Image Processing and Data Mining. She has published 85 articles in reputed journals and proceedings.

Kishore Kumar Senapati is an Assistant Professor in the Department of Computer Science and Engineering at Birla Institute of Technology, MESRA, Ranchi, INDIA. He completed his Master of Technology in Computer Science from UTKAL University ODISHA and PhD in Engineering from Birla Institute of Technology, MESRA. He has more than 20 years of teaching and research experience. He has guided more than 100 students as UG, 44 students as PG and 6 students as PhD scholar in the discipline of Computer Science domain and continue as guiding the students in the field of Algorithm design, Computer Vision, Image processing, Cyber Security and Machine learning. He as a Project Investigator and along with his team is carrying intensive research in many Govt. sponsored Research projects. He is also part of the National Mission Project on Inter disciplinary Cyber Physical system of Government of India. He has published more than 50 peer reviewed papers on various national and international journals of repute. Author of 6 book chapters and one book to his credit. In his Academic Career he has three patents to his credit, out of the three patents one is an International Patent. He has delivered invited talk at various national and international seminars, conference, symposium, and workshop. He is member of many national and international societies. He is also member in various program committees of many International conference and chaired the session. He is also editor of many International and National Journal of high repute. He is also conducted many workshops in his organization on various emerging areas such as Cyber Security, Deep Learning and High-Performance Computing.

Geeta Sikka is a Professor and HOD at NIT Delhi and her research area of interests are Data Mining, Data Warehousing, Databases, Data Science, Data Analytics, Big Data, Software Engineering, Security, Cloud computing.

Jairaj Singh is working as an OT Security Analyst at Dubai Electricity and Water Authority. He has pursued bachelors in Electrical & Electronics Engineering and Masters in Information Technology. Has over 4.5 years of experience in Cyber Security with applications in IT, IoT and OT infrastructures. Has high interest towards the field of cyber security and its integration with AI to protect organizations from cyber attacks.

Kunal Sinha is a M.Tech from Birla Institute of Technology and Science, Pilani, India. Kunal also holds more than a couple of certifications from different IIT's of India and did trainings on CCNA. He has more than thirteen years of experience in CS & IT research and development and is the founder of an organization Artificial Computing Machines (P) Ltd.

Akash Thakar is Certified Ethical Hacker, Computer Hacking Forensic Investigator and Certified EC-Council Instructor, having sound knowledge of Digital Forensics and VAPT. He has completed his PhD in Forensic Science, and masters in Forensic Science from Gujarat University. He has taught various subjects to the students of UG and PG courses like Computer Forensics, Network Forensics, Malware Analysis, Advance Digital Forensics, Memory Forensics etc. His research area is Digital Forensic Investigation Process and Memory Forensics.

V. Sathya is currently an Assistant Professor of Artificial Intelligence and Data Science at Panimalar Engineering College (Autonomous), Affiliated to Anna University. She did his Masters in Computer Science and Engineering at PRIST University. Her main research interests are Wireless Sensor Networks, Network Security, Sandboxing Technology, Block chain Technology, Wireless Communication. She has published more than 20 papers in IEEE digital xplore, SCOPUS, SCI journals, Springer and Elsiever publications. Also she has presented around 50 papers in international and national conferences and published in the proceedings. She is a reviewer in IET journal and IJCRT journal.

Harsh K Verma is a Professor and Dean Academics at Dr. BR Ambedkar NIT Jalandhar. His research area of interests are Software Systems, Numerical Computing, Computer Networks and Information Security.

Index

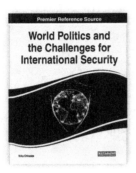

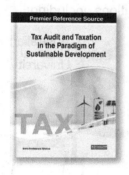

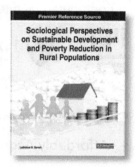

Printed in the United States
by Baker & Taylor Publisher Services